PARTICIPANTS IN MATHEMATICS TEACHER EDUCATION

The International Handbook of Mathematics Teacher Education

Series Editor:

Terry Wood
Purdue University
West Lafayette
USA

This *Handbook of Mathematics Teacher Education*, the first of its kind, addresses the learning of mathematics teachers at all levels of schooling to teach mathematics, and the provision of activity and programmes in which this learning can take place. It consists of four volumes.

VOLUME 1:
Knowledge and Beliefs in Mathematics Teaching and Teaching Development
Peter Sullivan, *Monash University, Clayton, Australia* and Terry Wood, *Purdue University, West Lafayette, USA* (eds.)
This volume addresses the "what" of mathematics teacher education, meaning knowledge for mathematics teaching and teaching development and consideration of associated beliefs. As well as synthesizing research and practice over various dimensions of these issues, it offers advice on best practice for teacher educators, university decision makers, and those involved in systemic policy development on teacher education.
paperback: 978-90-8790-541-5, hardback: 978-90-8790-542-2, ebook: 978-90-8790-543-9

VOLUME 2:
Tools and Processes in Mathematics Teacher Education
Dina Tirosh, *Tel Aviv University, Israel* and Terry Wood, *Purdue University, West Lafayette, USA* (eds.)
This volume focuses on the "how" of mathematics teacher education. Authors share with the readers their invaluable experience in employing different tools in mathematics teacher education. This accumulated experience will assist teacher educators, researchers in mathematics education and those involved in policy decisions on teacher education in making decisions about both the tools and the processes to be used for various purposes in mathematics teacher education.
paperback: 978-90-8790-544-6, hardback: 978-90-8790-545-3, ebook: 978-90-8790-546-0

VOLUME 3:
Participants in Mathematics Teacher Education: *Individuals, Teams, Communities and Networks*
Konrad Krainer, *University of Klagenfurt, Austria* and Terry Wood, *Purdue University, West Lafayette, USA* (eds.)
This volume addresses the "who" question of mathematics teacher education. The authors focus on the various kinds of participants in mathematics teacher education, professional development and reform initiatives. The chapters deal with prospective and practising teachers as well as with teacher educators as learners, and with schools, districts and nations as learning systems.
paperback: 978-90-8790-547-7, hardback: 978-90-8790-548-4, ebook: 978-90-8790-549-1

VOLUME 4:
The Mathematics Teacher Educator as a Developing Professional
Barbara Jaworski, *Loughborough University, UK* and Terry Wood, *Purdue University, West Lafayette, USA* (eds.)
This volume focuses on knowledge and roles of teacher educators working with teachers in teacher education processes and practices. In this respect it is unique. Chapter authors represent a community of teacher educators world wide who can speak from practical, professional and theoretical viewpoints about what it means to promote teacher education practice.
paperback: 978-90-8790-550-7, hardback: 978-90-8790-551-4, ebook: 978-90-8790-552-1

Participants in Mathematics Teacher Education

Individuals, Teams, Communities and Networks

Edited by

Konrad Krainer
University of Klagenfurt, Austria

and

Terry Wood
Purdue University, West Lafayette, USA

SENSE PUBLISHERS
ROTTERDAM / TAIPEI

A C.I.P. record for this book is available from the Library of Congress.

ISBN 978-90-8790-547-7 (paperback)
ISBN 978-90-8790-548-4 (hardback)
ISBN 978-90-8790-549-1 (e-book)

Published by: Sense Publishers,
P.O. Box 21858, 3001 AW Rotterdam, The Netherlands
http://www.sensepublishers.com

Cover picture:
Badell river, Tavernes de la Valldigna, Valencia, Spain
© Pepa and Ana Llinares 2007

One drop of water does not make a river, yet each drop bears in itself the full fluidity and power of water. A river is more than millions of drops, it is a large and vital system. It represents an astonishing journey from the source to its mouth at the sea, from the micro to the macro level. A river marks a steady coming together and growing but also finding different branches and maybe courses. It depends on and is influenced by external elements like rain and rocks, but also by pollution. It is formed by its environment, but is in turn a force upon its environment. A river is a journey of necessary collaboration in a joint process.
© Salvador Llinares and Konrad Krainer 2008

Printed on acid-free paper

TABLE OF CONTENTS

PREFACE

It is my honor to introduce the first *International Handbook of Mathematics Teacher Education* to the mathematics education community and to the field of teacher education in general. For those of us who over the years have worked to establish mathematics teacher education as an important and legitimate area of research and scholarship, the publication of this handbook provides a sense of success and a source of pride. Historically, this process began in 1987 when Barbara Jaworski initiated and maintained the first Working Group on mathematics teacher education at PME. After the Working Group meeting in 1994, Barbara, Sandy Dawson and I initiated the book, *Mathematics Teacher Education: Critical International Perspectives,* which was a compilation of the work accomplished by this Working Group. Following this, Peter de Liefde who, while at Kluwer Academic Publishers, proposed and advocated for the *Journal of Mathematics Teacher Education* and in 1998 the first issue of the journal was printed with Thomas Cooney as editor of the journal who set the tone for quality of manuscripts published. From these events, mathematics teacher education flourished and evolved as an important area for investigation as evidenced by the extension of JMTE from four to six issues per year in 2005 and the recent 15th ICMI Study, *The professional education and development of teachers of mathematics.* In preparing this handbook it was a great pleasure to work with the four volume editors, Peter Sullivan, Dina Tirosh, Konrad Krainer and Barbara Jaworski and all of the authors of the various chapters found throughout the handbook.

Volume 3, *Participants in mathematics teacher education: Individuals, teams, communities and networks,* edited by Konrad Krainer, focuses not only on individual prospective and practicing teachers as learners but also on teams, learning communities, networks of teachers, schools and on the teaching profession as a whole. In this volume, the emphasis is on describing and critically analysing participants' organizational contexts. This is the third volume of the handbook.

Terry Wood
West Lafayette, IN
USA

REFERENCES

Jaworski, B., Wood, T., & Dawson, S. (Eds.). (1999). *Mathematics teacher education: Critical international perspectives.* London: Falmer Press.

Krainer, K., & Wood, T. (Eds.). (2008). *International handbook of mathematics teacher education: Vol. 3. Participants in mathematics teacher education: Individuals, teams,* communities and networks. Rotterdam, the Netherlands: Sense Publishers.

Wood, T. (Series Ed.), Jaworski, B., Krainer, K., Sullivan, P., & Tirosh, D. (Vol. Eds.). (2008). *International handbook of mathematics teacher education.* Rotterdam, the Netherlands: Sense Publishers.

KONRAD KRAINER

INDIVIDUALS, TEAMS, COMMUNITIES AND NETWORKS: PARTICIPANTS AND WAYS OF PARTICIPATION IN MATHEMATICS TEACHER EDUCATION

An Introduction

This chapter outlines the main idea of the third volume of this handbook. The focus is to make transparent the large diversity of experiences evident in the field of mathematics teacher education and to describe and learn from these differences. This is achieved by focusing on the practices of various teacher education participants and the environments in which they work. Notions like individuals, teams, communities and networks are introduced. In addition, school development as well as regional and national teacher education initiatives are regarded. Each chapter considers differences within and among these distinctions.

THE MAIN IDEA OF THIS VOLUME

What is (mathematics) *teacher education* and who are its *participants*? The teacher educator can be regarded as the teacher of prospective or practising teachers. Although, traditionally, the latter are regarded mainly as the participants and learners, also the teacher educator is a part of the learning process and grows professionally from participating in the process. Therefore, it makes sense to regard student teachers, teachers and teacher educators as *teachers* and as (lifelong) *learners* at the same time (see also Llinares & Krainer, 2006). Teachers are active constructors of their knowledge, embedded in a variety of social environments. These environments influence and shape teachers' beliefs, knowledge and practice; similarly, teachers themselves influence and shape their environments. Therefore, teachers should be expected to continuously reflect in and on their practice and the environments in which they work; teachers should also be prepared to make changes where it is appropriate. Whereas teachers and students in a classroom (at a school or in a course for prospective teachers) mostly show considerable differences in age and experience, the relation in the context of professional development activities might be more diverse (e.g., having a young researcher working with experienced teachers).

   Teacher education is a goal-directed intervention in order to promote teachers' learning, including all formal kinds of teacher preparation and professional development as well as informal (self-organized) activities. *Mathematics teacher*

K. Krainer and T. Wood (eds.), Participants in Mathematics Teacher Education, 1–10.

education can aim at improving teachers' *beliefs*, their *knowledge* and their *practice*, at increasing their *motivation*, their *self-confidence* and their *identity* as mathematics teachers and, most importantly, at contributing to their *students' affective and cognitive growth.*

Although the education of prospective mathematics teachers is organized in a *wide variety of ways* in different countries and at different teacher education institutes, teacher education activities for practicing mathematics teachers are even more diverse. They include, for example: formal activities led by externals (e.g., by mathematics educators and mathematicians) *or* informal and self-organized ones (e.g., by a group of mathematics teachers themselves); single events *or* continuous and long-lasting programmes; small-group courses *or* nation-wide mathematics initiatives (eventually with hundreds of participants); heterogeneous groups of participants (e.g., mathematics and science teachers from all parts of a country) *or* a mathematics-focused school development programme at one single school; obligatory participation in courses *or* voluntary engagement in teacher networks; focus on specific contents (e.g., early algebra) *or* on more general issues (e.g., new modes of instruction); theory-driven seminars at universities *or* teaching experiments at schools; focus on primary *or* secondary schooling; teacher education accompanied by extensive research *or* confined to minimal evaluation; activities that aim at promoting teachers' (different kinds of) knowledge, *or* beliefs, *or* practice etc.

It is a challenge to find answers to the questions of where, under which conditions, how and why mathematics teachers learn and how important the domain-specific character of mathematics is. It is important to take into account that teachers' learning is a complex process and is to a large extent influenced by personal, social, organisational, cultural and political factors.

Discussions about "effective", "good", "successful" etc. mathematics teaching or teacher education indicate different aspects which need to be considered (see e.g., Sowder, 2007). However, in any case the dimensions *contents, communities* and *contexts* (see e.g., Lachance & Confrey, 2003; Krainer, 2006) are addressed at least implicitly:

- *Contents* are needed that are *relevant for all people* who are involved (e.g., contents that are interesting mathematical activities for the students, challenging experiments, observations and reflections for teachers, constructive initiatives and discussions for mathematics departments at schools);
- *Communities* (including small teams, communities of practice and loosely-coupled networks) are needed that allow *people to collaborate with each other* in order to learn autonomously but also to support others' and the whole system's content-related learning;
- *Contexts* (within a professional development program, at teachers' schools, in their school district, etc.) are needed that provide *conducive general conditions* (resources, structures, commitment, etc.).

The "community" aspect does not mean that initiatives by individual teachers are not essential. In contrast, the single teacher is of great importance, in particular at the classroom level. However, in order to bring about change at the level of a whole department, school, district or nation, thinking only in terms of individual teachers is not sufficient ("one swallow does not make a summer"). Research on "successful" schools shows that such schools are more likely to have teachers who have continual substantive interactions (Little, 1982) or that inter-staff relations are seen as an important dimension of school quality (Reynolds et al., 2002). The latter study illustrates, among others, examples of potentially useful practices, of which the first (illustrated by a US researcher who reflects on observations in other countries) relates to teacher collaboration and community building (p. 281):

> Seeing excellent instruction in an Asian context, one can appreciate the lesson, but also understand that the lesson did not arrive magically. It was planned, often in conjunction with an entire grade-level-team (or, for a first-year teacher, with a master teacher) in the teachers' shared office and work area. [Referring to observed schools in Norway, Taiwan and Hong Kong: ...] if one wants more thoughtful, more collaborative instruction, we need to structure our schools so that teachers have the time and a place to plan, share and think.

This example underlines the interconnectedness of the three dimensions content, community and context. Most research papers in mathematics teacher education put a major focus on the content dimension, much less attention is paid to the other two dimensions. In order to fill this gap, the major focus and specific feature of this volume is the emphasis on the "community" dimension. This dimension raises the *"who" question* and asks where and how teachers participate and collaborate in teacher education. It puts the *participants* and their *ways of participation* into the foreground.

How can a volume of a handbook that focuses on participants in teacher education deal with this diversity and offer a viable structure? One option is to pick one of the manifold differences (formal *versus* informal; single events *versus* continuous and sustained programmes etc., see above). A very relevant difference is the number of participants as, for example, shown (see Table 1) in the case of supporting practising teachers to improve their practice in mathematics classrooms and related research on their professional growth. Of course, entities like teams, communities, networks, schools, districts, regions and nations are only assigned provisionally to one of the levels. There might, for example, be teams with ten or more people or small schools (e.g., in rural primary schools) with less than ten people that teach mathematics (and also most other subjects).

Table 1. Levels of teacher education

	Number of M teachers	Relevant environments (in addition to mathematics teacher educators)	Major mathematics education research focus on [...]
Micro level	1s	Students, Parents, ...	Individual teachers, Teams
Meso level	10s	Colleagues, Leaders, ...	Communities, Networks, Schools
Macro level	100s	Superintendents, Policy makers, ...	Districts, Regions, Nations

However, in principle, it makes a difference whether we regard the professional growth of one or a few teachers in a mathematics department (micro level), or of tens of mathematics teachers at a larger school (meso level) or of hundreds or even thousands of mathematics teachers in a district or a whole nation (macro level).

Concerning the three levels, quite different people are interested in the impacts of teacher education initiatives: in the case of single classrooms, the students and their parents are the most concerned environments; in contrast, superintendents and (above all) policy makers are more interested to get a whole picture over all classrooms in a country. For example, PISA plays a major role for nations' system monitoring of mathematics teaching, but not so much for individual teachers and parents. They are more interested in the learning progress of their own students. Schools as organizations or networks of dedicated teachers lay somewhat in between. On the one hand, a school is important for teachers and parents since this organizational entity forms a crucial basis and environment for students' learning; for example, this includes important feelings of being accepted, autonomous, cognitively supported, a member of a community, safe, taken serious etc. On the other hand, reformers need to see schools as units of educational change since they cannot reach teachers and students directly. All in all, each of the three levels is important and the three should be regarded as closely interconnected.

However, our knowledge on teachers' learning is not equally distributed among these three levels. A survey by Adler, Ball, Krainer, Lin, and Novotná (2005) of recent research in mathematics teacher education culminated in three claims:

– *Claim 1: Small-scale qualitative research predominates.* Most studies investigate the beliefs, knowledge, or practice (and often also the professional growth) of individual or of a few teachers. So the focus is primarily laid on the micro (and partially on the meso) level, more emphasis is needed on the meso and the macro level.

– *Claim 2: Most teacher education research is conducted by teacher educators studying the teachers with whom they are working.* Also here, the focus is more on the micro (and partially on the meso) level since the context of the research is prospective or practising teachers' classrooms. Again, more research is needed on the meso and the macro level.

– *Claim 3: Research in countries where English is the national language dominates the literature.* Therefore, we do not know enough about research projects in countries where the dominant language is not English. It is more likely to get studies from individual researchers from these countries than reports about national reforms. There is a big need for comparison of cases of reform initiatives (in international publications).

Since the recent research focus in mathematics teacher education is still on the macro level – with a tendency to spread more and more also to the meso level, most chapters in this volume also deal with these two levels. This makes it necessary to offer a framework that allows us to differentiate between different kinds of groups in which teachers participate. A definition by Allee (2000), which distinguishes between the notions "teams", "communities" and "networks", is helpful here:

— *Teams* (and project groups) are regarded as mostly selected by the management, have pre-determined goals and therefore have rather tight and formal connections within the team.

— *Communities* are regarded as self-selecting, their members negotiating goals and tasks. People participate because they personally identify with the topic.

— *Networks* are loose and informal because there is no joint enterprise that holds them together. Their primary purpose is to collect and pass along information. Relationships are always shifting and changing as people have the need to connect.

I regard these distinctions (of course, others might be possible, too) as crucial since, for example, it makes a difference whether initiatives in teacher education are predominantly planned from top-down (e.g., by installing teams, task forces etc.) or whether they support bottom-up-approaches (e.g., by funding networks of teachers that establish their own plans and actions); and, of course, there are several approaches in between. The extent to which autonomy is given to participants is a crucial social aspect of the community dimension. Of great importance is also the extent to which participants feel that they are supported in their growth of a competent mathematics teacher and to which extent they belong to and might have an influence on a teacher education initiative. This is the kernel of the self-regulation theory of Deci and Ryan (2002) which proposes that perceived support of basic psychological needs (support of autonomy, support of competence and social relatedness) are associated with intrinsic motivation or self-determined forms of extrinsic motivation. Since I have become increasingly familiar with that approach, which seems to be particularly worthwhile for use in teacher education research, only in the last few months it was not possible for this volume to take this theory more into account when writing the chapters. However, the reader might focus on these ideas when reading the texts.

The differentiation between teams, communities and networks is used to structure this volume. In addition, where appropriate, different chapters focus on prospective or practising teachers specifically. In two cases, also a distinction is made whether teacher education is held (primarily) in face-to-face or in virtual settings. The idea behind working with these differences is that this format could facilitate the reader making comparisons between the various strands. Each of these chapters gives an overview of our recent knowledge on this particular issue and illustrates it through one or a few examples.

THE CHAPTERS OF THIS VOLUME

In the remainder of this chapter, each of the *six sections* and *sixteen chapters* will be introduced very briefly. Since both chapters of the critical respondents in Section 6 refer to all texts in the former five sections – and thus necessarily also provide descriptions and views on these chapters – I restrict myself here to sketch the main topic and to pick out a few issues that could focus readers' attention to potentially interesting commonalities and differences.

Section 1 is on *individual teachers* as learners. Whereas the chapter by *Hélia Oliveira and Markku S. Hannula* focuses on prospective mathematics teachers, *Marie-Jeanne Perrin-Glorian, Lucie DeBlois and Aline Robert* put practising mathematics teachers in the foreground. In both chapters, although focusing on individual teachers, not only the importance of the individual but also that of the social aspect of teacher learning is highlighted. Similarly, both chapters stress that teachers' beliefs, knowledge and practices cannot be separated (e.g., when aiming to understand teachers' practice or growth). This makes sense since the focus on the individual (and thus on the micro level of teacher education), in general, means closer proximity to teachers' practice than in the case of studies at the macro level; the nearness and the smaller sample provides the opportunity to go deeper with various qualitative methods and thus to see more commonalities and differences between teachers' beliefs, knowledge and practices. In contrast, at the meso and (in particular at) the macro level, in order to gather a larger data base, it is not easy to focus on teachers' beliefs, knowledge and practices within one study and also to combine them. In many cases (e.g., where quantitative approaches with larger numbers of questionnaires are taken and this is most easily done with regard to beliefs), teachers' beliefs (and sometimes also, or instead, their knowledge is tested) are measured.

Section 2 puts an emphasis on *teams of mathematics teachers* as learners. The chapter by *Roza Leikin* focuses on prospective mathematics teachers. In addition to that, *Susan D. Nickerson* deals with teams of practising teachers. The chapters on prospective teachers in Section 1 and Section 2 have in common that management skills and organizational issues are not given special attention. In contrast, both chapters on practising teachers deal intensively with issues to do with school context. There are a few reasons for this difference. For example, prospective teachers are only in schools for relatively short periods during their practicum and hence the full impact of school contextual issues might not be evident. Practising teachers are in a better position to both identify school contextual issues and to address these issues over an extended period. The four chapters in these two sections all have in common that the complexity of (mathematics) teaching is stressed in various ways. This leads to notions like (teaching) challenges, dilemmas, ethical questions, paradoxes, problems, tensions etc. I assume that this phenomenon (which cannot be found as much in the other sections) has to do with the specific focus of the micro dimension of teacher education. The chapters support the view that the complexity of teaching can be seen (at least) as a function of the diversity and richness of the mathematics (content), the varying relationship between the individual and the groups in which s/he is involved (community) and the resources and general conditions (context), which, however, play a bigger role in the case of practising teachers than prospective ones.

Section 3 puts an emphasis on *communities and networks of mathematics teachers* as learners. *Fou-Lai Lin and João Pedro da Ponte* focus on face-to-face learning communities of prospective mathematics teachers, whereas *Stephen*

Lerman and Stefan Zehetmeier do the same for *practising mathematics teachers*. In contrast to that, *Salvador Llinares and Federica Olivero* and *Marcelo C. Borba and George Gadanidis* deal with virtual communities and networks of prospective and practising mathematics teachers, respectively. Although the four chapters represent four different domains where communities (and partially also networks) can be initiated or emerge in a self-organized way, they have in common that each of them contains various communities representing a diversity of forms, goals and purposes. In all four cases, in particular in the face-to-face communities, the question of (internal and/or external) expertise or leadership (mathematical competent prospective teachers, teacher leaders, principals, qualified experts, more knowledgeable others, facilitators, steering group) is raised. This seems to highlight that the self-selective nature of communities and networks and the corresponding negotiation of goals and activities does not exclude issues of expertise or leadership, but in contrast, brings them to the fore. Although in all four cases – due to the issue of communities and networks – an important focus is on the social aspect, in particular the contents (and to some extent also the contexts) are in most cases well described and reflected. It is interesting that also in the chapters about virtual communities the integration of face-to-face periods (same room, same time) or at least synchronous periods of online-participation (same time, e.g., working interactively on the same mathematical problem using the same software) are suggested and realized. On the other hand, the flexibility concerning time and thus autonomy that asynchronous forms of online teacher education give to (in particular practising) teachers is so attractive that about 95% of continuing teacher education programmes of a particular university are organized online. One major difference between face-to-face and virtual learning environments seems to be generated by the tools: new technologies and tools seem to change the form of communication. Partially, the tools are not only regarded as mediators but also as co-actors in the communication process. The new technical options in the web allow a transformation from read-only to read-and-write communication (e.g., weblogs and wikis). Probably, it is not by chance that the chapters and many references on virtual forms of teacher education stem from countries with large distances to cover like Australia, Brazil, Canada, or Spain. It is worth noticing that beginning with Section 3 (and not in the sections before that which primarily belong to the micro level) the question of sustainability of teacher education is raised in several chapters.

Section 4 shows a shift of focus to the *development of schools, regions and nations* as a means of improving mathematics teaching and learning. *Elham Kazemi* puts an emphasis on school development and thus relates to the meso level most extensively. *Paul Cobb and Thomas Smith* deal with district development as a means of improving mathematics teaching and learning at scale, the same focus is taken by *John Pegg and Konrad Krainer* regarding regional and national reform initiatives. These two chapters put their primary focus on the macro level, the former one more extensively on the theoretical foundation and on planned activities, the latter more on reform initiatives (carried out or still continuing) reflecting and comparing cases from four countries concerning their genesis, goals, results of evaluation and research etc. Entering the meso and macro level, thus focusing on the improvement of a larger number of mathematics classrooms, the organizational aspects of change (development of schools, districts etc.), new relevant environments for mathematics teaching and learning like parents, principals, other kinds of leaders, but also organizations like universities and ministries come into play. They are regarded as crucial co-players of bringing about change, although the teachers and the students (and their interaction) are seen as the key for systemic change. Given the complexity of the different actors (from individuals, teams, communities, networks, organizations, media etc.), places, resources, goals to be defined or negotiated, reflection and evaluation, ways of communication and decision making, the content – at least at a first view – becomes less important. However, it is naïve to assume that bringing about change in mathematics teaching at a large scale can be reduced to defining central regulations, working out national mathematics standards, writing textbooks and research papers, golden rules about good teaching and to transfer it to individual teachers. Thinking that way, the autonomous culture established over years at schools, districts etc. are underestimated and not taken seriously. Systemic change needs to take into account the participants of initiatives at the micro, the meso and the macro level in order to avoid "system resistance" at one or more of these levels. The three chapters have in common that they deal with notions like (inter)national assessments and benchmarks, brokers, change agents, differences between designed and lived organizations, economic development, intervention strategies, key boundaries objects, leadership content knowledge, regional networks, stakeholders, support structures, systemic reform etc. which indicate that interconnections between different levels, social systems etc. need to be balanced. On the one hand, it is understandable that the three chapters deal to a large extent with practising teachers. On the other hand, the lack of putting an emphasis on prospective teachers might reveal the problem that schools and districts usually do not have strategies for integrating novice teachers in a way so that both sides can profit (or even do not have strategies for personal development at all). The journey from the micro to the macro level shows that not only the focus of attention is shifting from one class or a few to maybe thousands, but that also larger entities of teachers and their professional growth are investigated, using more qualitative studies at the micro and more quantitative studies at the macro level. Of course, the participants of teacher education and professional development initiatives (and not the students) form the focus of this volume, nevertheless, there is a tendency to look at students' growth (affective or cognitive) rather at the macro level, in particular with regard to (inter)national assessments that often are the starting point of national reform initiatives.

Section 5 focuses on teachers and teacher educators as key players in the further development of the mathematics teaching profession. *Gertraud Benke, Alena Hošpesová and Marie Tichá* analyse the use of action research in mathematics teacher education. *Barbara Jaworski* discusses a specific way of collaborating between teachers and didacticians. Finally, *Nanette Seago* reflects on the mathematics teaching profession in general. These three chapters form a kind of reflection on teacher education that does not go along the levels introduced in this volume, but along particular thematic issues relevant to the participants and organizers of teacher education. Often underestimated, however of particular importance, are forms of teacher education where prospective or practising teachers are investigating their own practice. Therefore, (critical) reflection is a key notion in the first of these chapters. It is interesting to follow the different ways action research is used and the issues educational researchers have to attend to when supporting teachers engaged in such projects. This is the bridge to the second chapter in this section where the focus is on the collaboration between teacher educators (didacticians) and practising teachers as partners and co-researchers in inquiry communities. Whereas the first chapter combines general considerations on characteristics and aspects of action research with examples from two countries, the second chapter explains the theoretical background of building and sustaining environments for co-learning inquiry and demonstrates this by giving an insight into a specific project, illuminating its issues and tensions. The third chapter addresses the professionalization of mathematics teaching, the specialized knowledge mathematics teachers need to have and design principles for professional development. This is illustrated by a specific mathematics teacher development programme that uses video-records of classroom practice. Like all other chapters, these three chapters aim at addressing general insights and research results as well as particular views on a few cases in order to make the general aspects more concrete and authentic.

Section 6 contains two chapters written by *Gilah C. Leder* and *Heinz Steinbring* who look in a kind of "critical response" to the whole volume from two specific perspectives. The first chapter follows the structure of this volume, refers to all sections, describes the chapters in the order they are published, sifts out interesting issues and indicates the complexity and diversity of the field and the variety of contributions, approaches, theoretical and practical stances in this volume. In contrast, the last chapter offers a theoretical perspective on fundamental problems in the context of investigating the communication issues raised in this volume. In particular, the theory-practice-problem within mathematics education and the importance of the subject (mathematics) and of teaching activity are raised. Doing that, links to all previous sections and chapters are made. These two chapters form a reflective closure of the whole volume.

ACKNOWLEDGEMENTS

Together with Terry Wood, I wish to gratefully thank all authors of this volume for their great efforts and efficient work on this challenging joint endeavour of putting the participants and community dimension into the foreground. We appreciate very much that Gilah C. Leder and Heinz Steinbring not only wrote the final chapters but also reviewed all chapters. In particular, we also want to highlight that the whole review process (each chapter was also peer-reviewed by a first author or a colleague of another chapter) was done in a critical but always constructive way. Furthermore, I thank Dagmar Zois for her helpful correction and layout work concerning all chapters. We hope that you, as the readers of this volume, will gain new and interesting insights into various aspects of mathematics teacher education that partially gorge new pathways; they are not paved, they are tentative in nature and work in progress. You are invited to collaborate and to be a participant in this joint process.

REFERENCES

Adler, J., Ball, D., Krainer, K., Lin, F.-L., & Novotná, J. (2005). Mirror images of an emerging field: Researching mathematics teacher education. *Educational Studies in Mathematics, 60*, 359–381.

Allee, V. (2000). Knowledge networks and communities of practice. *OD Practitioner, Journal of the Organization Development Network, 32*(4), 4–13.

Deci, E. L., & Ryan, R. M. (Eds.). (2002). *Handbook on self-determination research*. Rochester: University of Rochester Press.

Krainer, K. (2006). How can schools put mathematics in their centre? Improvement = content + community + context. In J. Novotná, H. Moraová, M. Krátká, & N. Stehlková (Eds.), *Proceedings of the 30th Conference of the International Group for the Psychology of Mathematics Education* (Vol. 1, pp. 84–89). Prague, Czech Republic: Charles University.

Lachance, A., & Confrey, J. (2003). Interconnecting content and community: A qualitative study of secondary mathematics teachers. *Journal of Mathematics Teacher Education, 6*, 107–137.

Little, J. W. (1982). Norms of collegiality and experimentation: Workplace conditions of school success. *American Education Research Journal, 19*, 325–340.

Llinares, S., & Krainer, K. (2006). Mathematics (student) teachers and teacher educators as learners. In A. Gutiérrez & P. Boero (Eds.), *Handbook of research on the psychology of mathematics education. Past, present and future* (pp. 429–459). Rotterdam, the Netherlands: Sense Publishers.

Reynolds, D., Creemers, B., Stringfield, S., Teddlie, C., & Schaffer, G. (Eds.). (2002). *World class schools. International perspectives on school effectiveness*. London: Routledge Falmer.

Sowder, J. (2007). The Mathematical Education and Development of Teachers. In F. Lester (Ed.), *Second handbook of research on mathematics teaching and learning* (pp. 157–223). Greenwich, CT: NCTM.

Konrad Krainer
Institut für Unterrichts- und Schulentwicklung
University of Klagenfurt
Austria

SECTION 1

INDIVIDUAL MATHEMATICS
TEACHERS AS LEARNERS

HÉLIA OLIVEIRA AND MARKKU S. HANNULA

1. INDIVIDUAL PROSPECTIVE MATHEMATICS TEACHERS

Studies on Their Professional Growth

There are two types of goals for those who learn to become mathematics teachers. Firstly, they need to learn mathematics, and secondly, they need to learn how to teach it. On the one hand, those who specialize in order to become secondary level subject teachers usually have a strong mathematical background but they may have weaker identities as teachers. Those who become elementary education teachers, on the other hand, often have problems with the mathematical content themselves, but they have stronger identities as teachers. In this chapter we will take three perspectives to mathematics teachers' learning during their teacher education: 1) the development of teachers' knowledge and beliefs during that period; 2) the development of necessary skills for the teaching profession, such as, observing and interpreting classroom incidents, and reflecting on them, as well as different modes of interaction with the class; and, 3) the adoption of a productive disposition and identity as a teacher who is a reflective and collaborative professional and is willing to engage in future professional development. The last one will be illustrated with a case study focusing on the development of the identity of beginning secondary mathematics teachers. We then discuss the challenges to initial teacher education of a perspective centred on the idea of the individual prospective teacher as learner.

INTRODUCTION

When we speak about becoming a (mathematics) teacher, we are talking about a learning experience that can be seen as an *individual* one, but also as a *social* one. Our focus in this chapter is on research on teacher education, mainly work published over the last ten years, which centres on the development of the individual prospective mathematics teacher and embraces both the uniformity and the diversity of individuals in this process. This would seem to be an easy task since for many years studies have centred on a small number of participants and focused on the individual. Adler, Ball, Krainer, Lin, and Novotná (2005) provided a detailed table which revealed that out of the 160 studies on teachers that were reported in the proceedings for the Psychology of Mathematics Education (PME), Journal of Mathematics Teacher Education (JMTE) and Journal of Research in Mathematics Education (JRME) over the years (1999–2003), 21 were reports on a single teacher, while only 10 had one hundred or more participants. In the review of research presented in PME about teacher education, from 1998 to 2003, the

K. Krainer and T. Wood (eds.), Participants in Mathematics Teacher Education, 13–34.

majority of studies also had less than 20 participants (Llinares & Krainer, 2006). Nevertheless, concentrating on the learning of the individual prospective teacher proved to be a very *complex task* because there are many studies but these quite often do not target the individual with great depth.

Since the launch of JMTE in 1998, this journal is the main forum for publishing studies on mathematics teacher education, and also in our review this journal has been a very important source. We also searched for papers in Educational Studies in Mathematics (ESM), JRME and PME conference proceedings, mainly between 1998 and 2007. We also included a few studies from other publications that seemed particularly relevant for the purposes of this chapter.

When we study prospective teachers' learning to become a teacher, we asked, what kind of learning are we expecting to see? To attain our goal, we have identified *three perspectives* on learning that we shall use to structure this chapter: 1) one view perceives *learning as acquiring knowledge or beliefs*, 2) another view perceives *learning as mastering a skill*, for example, the ability to observe and reflect, and 3) the third perspective perceives *learning as adoption of a certain disposition*, for example, an identity or an orientation.

COMPETENCE AS "MATTER": BELIEFS AND KNOWLEDGE

For the last two decades, research on prospective teachers' knowledge and beliefs has received enormous attention from the community of mathematics teacher educators. The recent work of Llinares and Krainer (2006), and Ponte and Chapman (in press) provide an extensive review of the literature on these areas and offer a good overview of the themes that are being addressed and of the knowledge that has been accumulated. In the present chapter we want to stress the *individual dimension of learning* to teach as the development of beliefs and knowledge.

Prospective Teachers' Beliefs

Research on teacher's beliefs (see also Leikin, this volume) has a long tradition in research on teacher education and has been "perhaps the predominant orientation in research on teachers and teacher education" (Lerman, 2001, p. 35). *Changes in beliefs are assumed to reflect development.* Experiences and reflection are two basic sources of influence that are considered to be important in the formation, development and change of beliefs. Llinares and Krainer (2006) highlight the importance of early experiences as a learner of mathematics in the formation of teachers' beliefs. Once beliefs have been formed, they are not easy to change. Liljedahl, Rolka, and Rösken (2007) have identified three different methods used to change elementary education teachers' mathematics-related beliefs. The first method is to challenge their beliefs. Many beliefs are held implicitly, but when they are challenged, they can become explicit and subject to reflection, creating the opportunity for change. The second method is to involve them as learners of mathematics, usually in a constructivist setting. A third method for producing changes in belief structures is to provide prospective teachers with experiences of mathematical discovery, which seems to have a profound, and immediate, transformative effect on their beliefs regarding the nature of mathematics, as well as the teaching and learning of mathematics (Liljedahl, 2005). Llinares and Krainer (2006) note that it is often assumed, not always correctly, that learning mathematics through inquiry will influence prospective teachers' beliefs and attitudes in a positive way, namely in regarding the implementation of those methodologies in their practice as in the case described by Langford and Huntley (1999).

In some cases it seems that the use of "reform-oriented" teaching material in teacher education has been useful in influencing prospective teachers' beliefs about the nature of mathematics. In Lloyd (2006, p. 77), one prospective teacher explained: "I am learning about how to look for reasons and explanations as opposed to simply believing 'the rules' that some really ancient dead guy came up with. I prefer being able to use my own mind in solving problems". However, according to Szydlik, Szydlik, and Benson (2003, p. 254), research has shown that prospective teachers tend to "see mathematics as an authoritarian discipline, and that they believe that doing mathematics means applying memorized formulas and procedures to textbook exercises".

One of the big issues in research on teachers' beliefs is the mismatch between teachers' personal theories of learning and their actual teaching practices that seem not to support the theory. This is a special case of a more general mismatch between espoused and enacted beliefs. It has been suggested that theory and practice can be connected if integrated in authentic contexts. Bobis and Aldridge (2002) have designed a continuum of authentic contexts for their master level elementary teacher education course. Their students experienced mathematics teaching and reflected on their experiences in typical student workshops and practice schools, but they also used university based clinics and school-based small group teaching. Somewhat paradoxically, they only were able to report changed beliefs of their students during the course, as they have not followed the students after they moved to their positions as teachers. The possibility of a dynamic interaction between coursework and fieldwork in the development of alternative perspectives on teaching and learning is illustrated by Ebby (2000). This research shows that the three prospective teachers learned from their teacher education coursework and fieldwork in quite different ways, influenced by their beliefs, dispositions, and individual experiences.

In many studies, the development of prospective elementary education teachers' *learning of content knowledge is intertwined with their changing beliefs* about the nature of mathematics (e.g., Amato, 2006; Nicol, Gooya, & Martin, 2002; Olsen, Colasanti, & Trujillo, 2006). One example of change in beliefs as a result of learning content is the case of the prospective elementary education teacher, Jennifer (in Davis & McGoven, 2001), in the context of a mathematics content course that was built around problem solving and included class discussions and reflective writing. Jennifer begun the course holding a typical belief that mathematics is about applying the right formula to get the right answer. She learned to see and value the mathematical connections between different tasks and her test performance improved from not satisfactory to excellent. One characteristic of Jennifer was her extensive and elaborated reflective writing. A similar bond between content knowledge and beliefs was identified by Kinach (2002), when she was challenging her prospective secondary mathematics teachers to provide instructional explanations for subtraction of negative numbers. She and her prospective teachers found themselves "to be in disagreement about what counted as an explanation, and even more fundamentally, about what counted as knowing, and therefore learning mathematics" (Kinach, 2002, p. 179). Hence, the problem of teaching mathematical content was essentially also a problem of changing the prospective teachers' beliefs about the nature of mathematics.

Prospective Teachers' Knowledge

The above indicated interdependence of knowledge and beliefs in learning to teach becomes more explicit from the growing body of empirical research dealing with both concepts (e.g., Llinares, 2003) and how theory is being built around them (Pehkonen & Pietilä, 2003). However, the analysis of the knowledge that prospective teachers should develop to teach is part of a long enterprise in research on teacher education (Ponte & Chapman, in press).

It is well recognized that research on teachers' knowledge is strongly influenced by the work of Shulman (1987), focusing mainly on the mathematical knowledge of teachers and on pedagogical content knowledge. Regarding the first aspect, studies have confirmed prospective teacher misconceptions (or lack of conceptual understanding) in different branches of subject matter knowledge (Llinares & Krainer, 2006; Ponte & Chapman, in press). This problem is more frequently addressed among prospective elementary education teachers, but also prospective secondary mathematics teachers at times struggle to attain a deep understanding of mathematics (Kinach, 2002). As one prospective teacher wrote in her journal: "Over the past semester, there have been a few times where I have stopped and realized that there are some math concepts that I thought I knew, but actually didn't" (Kinach, 2002, p. 176). This reflection about what one knows and how one is learning is fundamental in the process of becoming a mathematics teacher. In many countries, secondary mathematics teachers have a solid mathematic education, with three or more years of mathematics courses in several domains. However, the failure in some courses is very high, even for prospective teachers who see themselves as good at mathematics in secondary school. One of the reasons for this may be the way mathematics is taught to prospective teachers, and not only because of the content to which they are exposed.

One important question that arises concerning individual prospective teachers as learners is how they evaluate the mathematical knowledge they are developing in terms of the development of subject knowledge for teaching. For example, some of the beginning mathematics teachers studied by Oliveira (2004) did not see much relation between the mathematics they learnt in the mathematics courses they attended for three years and the way they are to teach. But they still considered that the study of "hard mathematics" enhanced their mathematical reasoning, giving them confidence to answer their students' questions and to solve mathematical problems. Curiously, the beginning teacher who scored the highest marks in the mathematics courses, and who deliberated between becoming a secondary mathematics or a mathematician, was the one who recognized that sometimes he had great difficulties in solving the mathematical problems given in methods courses. This made him question the "hard mathematics" he had been studying during that period in mathematics courses.

Certainly, prospective mathematics teachers also develop mathematical knowledge in different ways, as a consequence of their past experiences with school mathematics and in higher education. Sánchez and Llinares (2003, p. 21) describe four university graduates, prospective secondary mathematics teachers, who expressed different ways of knowing the function concept; this, according to the authors, "influenced what they considered important for the learner and affected their use of the modes of representation in teaching that were considered as teachers' tools to obtain his/her teaching goals". This raises another important question concerning prospective teachers' subject matter knowledge and its relationship with their emerging pedagogical content knowledge. Tirosh (2000, p. 329) argued that teacher education needs to take into account the prospective teachers' knowledge of students' common responses to given tasks, considering that "such knowledge is strongly related to prospective teachers' SMK [subject matter knowledge]". From a situated perspective on learning, the research developed by Llinares (2003, p. 205) showed that the case analysis that prospective teachers developed in interaction provided a context for them to attempt to understand the students' way of thinking and simultaneously "to think about the meanings of some elements of their subject matter knowledge and pedagogical content knowledge". With respect to the process of learning in a small group of four prospective primary teachers as learning in a community of practice, the author explained that they engaged differently in the task and assumed different responsibilities in exploring new domains. Despite their individual engagement, the interaction among them was very important for the reification of beliefs, something that Llinares contends could not be attained if reflection would stand merely at a discursive level.

Summary

The studies reviewed provide evidence, to a certain extent, of the attention paid to the individual prospective teacher. Collectively they show that there are *important differences* that can be relevant influences on how they are going to experience teacher education and develop as prospective teachers. Therefore, those *differences* should be taken into account, when designing and developing teacher education programmes. For teacher educators this means to further develop two competences: to *notice* such differences (see e.g., Krainer, 2005, referring to Willke, 1999, who writes about the *art of precise observation* being typical for experts in contrast to laymen); and to *produce* relevant differences (which Willke, 1999, in Krainer, 2005, defines as *interventions*). Such an intervention in teacher education could

17

be, for example, to make differences among prospective teachers' views fruitful for their joint reflection on these differences.

COMPETENCE AS SKILL: LEARNING IN AND FROM PRACTICE

The practicum experience is generally considered to be an integral part of teacher preparation. However, it has been argued that prospective teachers need to develop a critical stance towards their field experiences and a "certain distance" from the ongoing actions (Jaworski & Gellert, 2003) in order to reflect about the events of the classroom, otherwise "field experiences perpetuate apprenticeship and trial-and error views of teaching" (Mewborn, 1999, p. 318), and oversimplify its nature.

In this section, we are looking at the *role of practice* in learning to teach from three different – although in some cases complementary – approaches: 1) observing teachers and students engaged in mathematical activity, 2) prospective teachers' interaction with students, and 3) prospective teachers' reflection. In our opinion, these three ways of seeing how prospective teachers learn to teach entail different activities that are nuclear for the teaching profession (see Seago, this volume). There are additional important issues regarding the PCK prospective teachers are developing, namely when planning and selecting appropriate tasks and resources for students.

Observing Teachers and Students Engaged in Mathematical Activity

When prospective teachers come in contact with pedagogical situations in elementary and secondary schools, they have already spent many hours in classrooms as students. Therefore, the classroom environment and pedagogical situations may seem quite familiar for them. It is necessary for them to produce a shift of perspective from one of a prospective teacher to that of a teacher: "teaching is fundamentally about attention; producing shifts in the locus, focus, and structure of attention, and these can be enhanced for others by working on one's own awareness" (Mason, 1998, p. 244). It is not surprising that novice and expert teachers have different competencies in observing mathematics video taped teaching episodes. In a study that used eye-tracking technology, it was found that prospective elementary teachers attended more to mathematics content, while experienced teachers and mathematics educators focused more on the activities of the teacher and student (Philipp & Sowder, 2002). Some teacher education programmes prepare prospective teachers to conduct clinical interviews, considering that those are useful tools for learning to understand how students think mathematically and to "develop an increased awareness of the ways in which people learn mathematics" (Schorr, 2001, p. 159). Ambrose (2004) argues that by having prospective elementary teachers interviewing children, namely on specific difficult mathematical concepts, they realise that the mathematics they were supposed to teach was not so simply and required conceptual understanding.

Morris (2006) focused on the prospective teachers' ability to collect evidence about student learning to analyse the effects of instruction and to use the analysis to revise instruction. The results of this study suggested that prospective teachers possessed some initial diagnostic and revision skills, and that the quality of analysis was influenced by the instruction given prior to the task, namely that when a lesson was perceived as problematic it encouraged them to look more closely at students and to ask themselves questions about the situation.

In the case of a programme that used a multimedia resource, elementary and secondary prospective teachers investigated assessment and teaching strategies in a situated learning environment (Herrington, Herrington, Sparrow, & Oliver, 1998). They could observe video clips of teachers who were using different assessment and teaching strategies, and at the same time they had access to teachers' discussions about their approaches. Prospective teachers recognized the influence of this environment in the assessment strategies they adopted later in their teaching practice.

These initial experiences with the classroom reality and with students can have an impact on the development of certain attitudes and knowledge that are central for teaching, namely a disposition to listen to students and to try to understand how they think and reason mathematically. In all these studies, prospective teachers' practice is very limited in time and scope, but these experiences constitute also an opportunity for the prospective teacher to start feeling what it is like to be a teacher. Assuming that the teacher's role in classroom is much more complex than working with one student or a small group of students on a specific theme or concept, and that the teaching situations are so diverse, multimedia explorations can assist prospective teachers in grasping that reality.

Prospective Teachers' Interaction with Students

In spite of being, by definition, an interactive profession, teaching through meaningful interactions with students is one of the most demanding aspects of that practice. Research shows that prospective teachers often tend to focus their attention on issues concerning class management and pedagogy (Van Zoest & Bohl, 2002), considering subject matter learning less problematic.

Moyer and Milewicz's (2002) study on prospective teachers' questioning skills looked at the developing interaction skills of practicing teachers. They argued, that "when open-ended questioning is used and there are many right answers, the learning environment becomes complex and less predictable as teachers attempt to interpret and understand children's responses" (p. 296). In their research they gave prospective elementary teachers the task to interview individual students on mathematical concepts and later to reflect on the audio-recorded interview. They concluded that the prospective teachers did not yet have good questioning skills, but that the experience of interviewing "is a first step towards developing the questioning strategies that will be used in the multi-dimensional, simultaneous, unpredictable environment of the classroom" (p. 311).

The nature of discourse in the mathematics classroom is another way of looking at teachers' learning. Blanton (2002) describes the experiences of eleven secondary mathematics teachers in a course that attempted to challenge their notions about discourse as univocal or dialogical. Throughout the course, prospective teachers developed a positive stance toward dialogic discourse but they felt there were many obstacles to developing that kind of discourse in their practice. They recognized that their discourse was predominately univocal as, for example, they felt the need to structure and control the class. Blanton suggests that it is difficult for prospective teachers to develop a dialogic discourse due to aspects such as: sharing authority with students; focusing on students' thinking by acknowledging and incorporating their ideas; and in balancing the need for dialogic discourse with the time constraints of "covering the curriculum" (p. 149).

There is evidence from research that many prospective teachers begin their practice trying authentically to assume a new role as teacher, one that is attuned with *reform ideas* presented in university courses, but lack the skills to implement them. For example, Lloyd (2005) described the internship of one prospective secondary mathematics teacher who started his student teaching with an approach that was student-centred, relying on group work and the use of manipulatives and technology but that left unchanged the mathematical nature and content of students' activity. As a consequence of the students' complaint that they "were not being taught" (p. 457), he recognized that he had been emphasizing "how to solve problems rather than why certain ideas and methods are related" (p. 457). The prospective teacher was learning through interaction with students by attending to the students' feedback and then reflecting on his own actions as a teacher.

Questioning students, and communicational aspects, in a more general way, are central issues in learning to teach, but research shows that these are quite demanding for prospective teachers. Implementing reform ideas or changing approaches to mathematics teaching is challenging in many of the diverse classroom contexts (see also Leikin, this volume). The professional growth of prospective teachers depends on the opportunities to effectively experiment with teaching and in a context where they are stimulated to interact with students in meaningful ways, with the support of those responsible for their education as teachers.

Teachers' Reflection

Reflection has become a popular concept in teacher education and it is assumed to be a critical element in belief change in the process of becoming a teacher (Llinares & Krainer, 2006; Hannula, Liljedahl, Kaasila, & Rösken, 2007; Liljedahl, Rolka, & Rösken, 2007). Elements that have been found to support reflection are *collaboration* (Kaasila, Hannula, Laine, & Pehkonen, 2006) and *use of multimedia* (Masingila & Doerr, 2002; Goffree & Oonk, 2001).

Reflection is seen as an indispensable element in the process of learning from and in practice. Many teacher education programmes have implicitly addressed the idea of promoting reflection about prospective teachers' practice by creating moments for discussing their classroom lessons with tutors or/and mentors and helping them "to analyse in more detail their own teaching practices" (Jaworski &

Gellert, 2003, p. 843). This is done in different programmes in a more or less structured way.

In a study conducted by Artzt (1999), prospective secondary teachers were engaged in *structured reflection* on their teaching. The course built on prospective teachers' existing knowledge and beliefs and used both pre-lesson and post-lesson reflective activities. Prospective teachers were encouraged to think about the decisions they made in light of their goals for students. This research presents two contrasting cases. Mrs. Carol was revealed to be insecure about her teaching and mathematical abilities and about becoming a teacher. Through her writing assignment the supervisor could detect a low self-esteem. But these feelings constituted a motivation for her to be open-minded about learning new approaches and she started to plan and implement different lessons. By the end of the semester, she had understood the importance of reflecting about her underlying beliefs about students and how they learn. In contrast, the other prospective teacher, Mr. Wong, had strong beliefs about the "right" way to teach that left him inflexible and unmotivated to learn new instructional approaches. So the course did not cater equally for all prospective teachers.

Another study, about the teaching practicum, examines the role of reflection in prospective teachers' practice by looking at how they use their pedagogical content knowledge in solving problems identified from the classroom (McDuffie, 2004). The elementary prospective teachers approached teaching as a problem solving endeavour, since their internship included completing a classroom-based action research project on their own teaching (see also Benke, Hošpesová, & Tichá, this volume), and focused on facilitating their understanding and anticipating problems in teaching and learning.

As prospective teachers' observation skills are often limited, new technology has been introduced as *new means for reflection*. Multimedia allows the same episode to be watched several times and also to hear interviews of the people involved in the episode more than once. In the programme Multimedia Interactive Learning Environment (MILE), video clips of actual teaching situations are used, and elementary education students are invited into reflective discussions about the situations in order to enhance their practical knowledge (Goffree & Oonk, 2001). Nevertheless, the authors consider that it is still necessary to understand better "how to establish a link between the fieldwork of teacher education students and their investigation and discourses in MILE" (p. 143).

The connections established by prospective teachers between multimedia case studies and their practice was the focus of one study presented by Masingila and Doerr (2002), involving grade 7-12 prospective mathematics teachers. The cases were created in a way "that would reflect the complexities of classroom interactions, teacher decisions, and students' mathematical thinking" (p. 244), in order to promote investigation, analysis and reflection. Prospective teachers were asked to select a specific issue from their own practice that they saw addressed in the teacher's practice there and discuss it. They were able to discuss the case, taking into account their own practice, and focused on complex issues instead of the usual management concerns. However, the authors did not investigate if the prospective teachers subsequently changed their teaching practices.

Mewborn (1999), studying prospective teachers who participated in a field experience during a mathematics methods course, claimed that the ways they went about making sense of what they observed in a mathematics classroom "can be characterized as reflective thinking in the manner described by Dewey" (p. 324). This happened when the locus of authority was internal to the prospective teachers, and was promoted by the teacher educator and the classroom teacher who tried to remove themselves "from positions of authority" (p. 337). They tried not to answer directly to prospective teachers' questions, instead they "turn questions back to them and encouraged them to rely on their peers for evaluation of their ideas" (p. 337).

It is not surprising that reflection on teaching practice is such a difficult task for prospective teachers since learning in practice is so demanding for them. Even more challenging is to reflect about the events and to change rapidly the course of the lesson, adapting the plan that they made. Sometimes, they are supposed to reflect "on mathematical activity while participating in the discourse" (Lloyd, 2006, p. 462). This cannot be seen exclusively as a skill or disposition to reflect on the moment but as contingent action that relies on the (prospective) teacher's confidence and willingness to assume risks (Rowland, Huckstep, & Thwaites, 2005), in a situation where, at the same time, she or he is under the scrutiny of experts.

Summary

One of the classical problems of teacher education has been the bridging between *theory and practice*. Observing and practice teaching has been used as a general solution to this problem. Looking at the studies reported above it is possible to recognize the important role of university tutors and teacher mentors in helping prospective teachers to observe learning incidents in their complexity, to generate fruitful interaction with students, and to reflect upon them, even when that role is not specifically targeted. New multimedia learning environments hold a lot of promise to develop prospective teachers' understanding about the complexity of mathematics teaching, but educational environments that are supportive and flexible, taking into account their unicity and individuality, are also very important for their professional growth.

COMPETENCE AS DISPOSITION AND IDENTITY

Our last approach to prospective teachers' development through teacher education looks at their disposition as a teacher and at what they want to do as professionals (and as persons). Often the professional and personal aspects are intertwined and the development of a skill is necessary to promote the inclination to use it (Peretz, 2006). Learning to teach is also a "process of becoming" (Jaworski, 2006, p. 189), developing a new identity, one that integrates a professional side.

Disposition towards Mathematics and Its Learning

Disposition and identity issues have their specificities in the case of elementary teachers, considered as generalist teachers, and in the case of secondary teachers, usually regarded as specialized in mathematics. Especially among prospective elementary education teachers, there are several whose *attitude* towards mathematics is negative; sometimes they develop even a more serious condition – mathematics anxiety. As such, it is important that elementary teacher education programmes help students overcome this problem (e.g., Kaasila, 2006; Liljedahl et al., 2007; Pietilä, 2002; Uusimäki & Nason, 2004). These examples collectively use what is often referred to as a therapeutic approach (Hannula et al., 2007). One of the elements of a therapeutic approach is the effort to provide students with *positive experiences with mathematics*. This can be achieved within the context of elementary mathematics, where hands-on material is used to give prospective teachers an example of teaching in a constructivist way, whilst at the same time providing an opportunity for many of them to really understand mathematics for the first time in their life (Pietilä, 2002; Amato, 2006). In a supportive classroom climate, anxious prospective teachers may express their thoughts and feelings and ask for advice without fear of stigmatisation (Pietilä, 2002). However, experience alone is not sufficient for a major change in students' mathematical self-concept – it needs to be supported by *reflection* and *peer collaboration* (Hannula et al., 2007).

On the one hand, a negative view can seriously influence students' becoming good mathematics teachers (Uusimäki & Kidman, 2004), on the other hand, prospective teachers who have experienced only success in school mathematics may find it hard to understand students for whom learning is not so easy (Kaasila, 2000), and that happens quite often with secondary mathematics teachers. These teachers very often *identify themselves very strongly with the subject they teach*, but develop a stronger frame of reference to certain forms of teaching (Sowder, 2007), which constitutes a challenge to teacher education programmes. In fact, during their school years, prospective teachers begin to develop personal beliefs about teaching and perspectives about teacher's and student's roles, and the nature of the subject they are going to teach, through which they will interpret teacher education programmes.

Assuming Different Roles in Teacher Education

Another issue in research concerning the development of prospective teachers' professional identity is whether they identify themselves as learners of mathematics or if they already identify themselves as (prospective) teachers of mathematics. Although they are learning to become teachers, at the beginning of their studies they are primarily identifying themselves as students. This duality has been explicitly expressed, for example, in Bowers and Doerr (2001). Sometimes there is a multiplicity of roles to perform as documented in one case study presented by Stehlíková (2002). Molly, a prospective secondary mathematics teacher, over the course of her five-year education developed from "a role of a pupil [who] expected to be taught [...] into an independent problem solver, autonomous learner, 'mathematician' at times, teacher and teacher researcher" (p. 245). Although Molly was an exceptional case of an enthusiastic learner, she exemplifies the variety of different roles a prospective teacher is expected to unite into a coherent identity.

Teachers' Interactions with Students

Interactions with students constitute one of the main configurative elements in the process of *identity construction*. Quite often prospective teachers meet with students who do not match their expectations (Munby, Russell, & Martin, 2001). However, these interactions can promote a change in their perspectives. For example, Skott (2001) documented that learning to be a mathematics teacher involved more than "merely" teaching mathematics, and that it was important to (re)evaluate their priorities concerning teaching practice, namely the necessity to attend to students' problems. Oliveira (2004) also found that some secondary mathematics teachers started to realise, early in their career, that they had an important role as educators in spite of having to teach a socially "strong" subject.

Developing an Identity in Different Contexts

Sfard and Prusak (2005) define identities as collections of those narratives that are reifying, enforceable and significant. According to these authors, different identities may emerge in different situations and that might happen with prospective teachers as they emerge in different contexts. In a longitudinal study with four elementary prospective teachers, Steele (2001) illustrated "some of the problems and realities of the workplace that interfere with teachers sustaining a change in conceptions" (p. 168). Two of them remained attached to the conceptions developed in teacher education while the other two did not. One of these prospective teachers felt specially pressured by the school administration and implemented a "teacher-proof curriculum" (p. 169). This was also the prospective teacher who showed less change in her conceptions during the period of teacher education and simultaneously was more confident about mathematics. Steele conjectures that "perhaps her past experiences of learning mathematics were in the end more influential in her approach to teaching" (p. 168).

Opportunities for learning during teaching practice are shaped by the characteristics of the *contexts* in which teacher education occurs, in some instances by the strong evaluative flavour (Mewborn, 1999; Johnsen Høines & Lode, 2006) and they are also fused with "networks of power" (Walshaw, 2004). Using insights from the post-structural ideas of Foucault, Walshaw discusses what it means to engage in pedagogical work in the context of elementary mathematics classrooms. Teaching practice is regarded as a strategic and interested activity since the practice of prospective teachers "in schools always works through vested interests, both of their own and others' rhetoric of opinions and arguments" (Walshaw, 2004,

p. 78). In some cases, the institutional practices of the university course and of the school involve painful negotiations to produce individual subjectivity: "I wanted to introduce new ideas but did not have enough confidence. I just followed my associate's plans. I felt I could not try new things as my associate was set in the way things were done" (p. 78). Walshaw concluded that the best intentions of each prospective teacher can be prevented by "a history of response to local discursive classroom codes and wider educational discourse and practices" (p. 78).

Ensor (2001) analysed the case of Mary, a prospective teacher who expressed alignment with teacher educator's ideas, centred on the notion of innovation, but who begun to change her opinions during teaching practice in school. Mary started to identify herself with some classroom teachers and "to raise questions about the applicability of what she had learned in the mathematics method course" (p. 306), since some of them argued that their methods achieved results. Working for results is a central aim for many teachers and is part of a certain professional culture with which prospective teachers are acquainted.

In contrast to Ensor's observations, the case of a prospective teacher documented by Van Zoest and Bohl (2002) developed in a context of alignment between the university programme and the school internship site. The social context of the school was supportive of reform curricular materials and teachers indicated that they wanted to change their teaching practices. The prospective teacher had a profound conviction that the particular curriculum (CPMP) at this school contributed to the mathematical understanding of students. According to this, when she assumed a new position as teacher in a school with a traditional single-subject curriculum, she put a great effort in adapting it "so that students would do more of the types of thinking that she believed CPMP demanded" (p. 281). This shows the importance of *communication and negotiation* of philosophies between teacher education institutes and schools during the practicum.

Looking for Their Professional Development

One important aspect concerning the development of teachers' professional identity is how they *assume responsibility for their own professional development*. There are some studies which start to address this perspective. Olson, Colasanti, and Trujillo (2006) described two prospective teachers who accepted leadership roles when they began their teaching career. The researchers hypothesised that the transformative experiences (cognitive and affective ones) during university education promoted their self-efficacy and thus positioned them to assume leadership roles. The above mentioned study by Van Zoest and Bohl (2002) also described the first year in the career of a teacher who developed an important role as a reformer teacher at her new school, and it seems that "the fact that there was a social network of jointly-engaged educators working towards the same goals [...] had great impact" (p. 284).

Goos (2005) also presented evidence to illustrate how beginning teachers used their (technology-related) expertise "to act as catalysts for technology in schools"

(p. 56). The beginning teachers in the study showed initiative in trying to develop themselves as technology users. Particularly in the case of one of these, the author argued that he was "not simply reproducing the practices he observed nor yielding to environmental constraints, but instead re-interpreting these social conditions in the light of his professional goals and beliefs" (p. 55). Goos emphasized that this study shows it is possible that teachers implement innovative approaches from the very beginning of their careers.

Summary

The development of a professional identity as (mathematics) teachers is a process that is intrinsically connected with their participation in different communities. In some studies, attention is given to the activity of the prospective teachers as part of one or more communities as they practice teaching in the classroom. For example, reflection, as a central process in learning to teach, as presented in the studies above, does not exist in a social vacuum. Some of these studies illustrate conflicts between the perspectives of different communities involved in initial teacher education. For Lerman, "reflective practice takes place in communities of practice [...] and learning can be seen as increasing participation in that practice" (2001, p. 41), and that involves very strongly the development of a certain professional identity.

CASE STUDY: DEVELOPING PROFESSIONAL IDENTITY AS (MATHEMATICS) TEACHER

In a longitudinal study, Oliveira (2004) followed four secondary mathematics teachers, Cheila, Guilherme, Rita, and Susana, for three years after they finished their five year teacher education programme and she tried to characterize the development of their professional identity and the role of different contexts and processes. Adopting a psycho-sociological model of the person (Gohier, Anadón, Bouchard, Charbonneau, & Chevrier, 2001), professional identity is regarded as a process that starts from the time the first ideas of becoming a teacher appear. Assuming that professional identity develops through a complex and dynamic process that faces many constraints and threats with respect to continuity, congruence, self-esteem and personal and professional orientation (Oliveira, 2004), we choose to illustrate a tension that is pointed in this research as *continuity versus rupture*. The first significant rupture identified in the development of these beginning teachers' identities occurred during their teacher education programme. All of them recognized that the courses on the didactics of mathematics contributed strongly to a change in their perspectives about the teaching and learning of mathematics and the mathematics teacher's role. For example, they stressed the importance of promoting student-centred teaching methodologies and the use of several strategies and resources, in contrast to the teaching style they were used to when they were secondary students. Nevertheless, the study revealed different levels of rupture and of focus among these four beginning teachers.

Guilherme expressed a deep change in his perspectives about the nature of mathematics as a consequence of the readings and discussions that took place in the methods classes. He had been a very successful mathematics student in secondary school and at university, but began to see "another type" of mathematics and to rethink what it means to teach mathematics. This was a turning point for him and he started to see the teaching profession as a stimulating intellectual job, one that is constantly changing.

Rita and Susana changed their own visions about what it means to be a good mathematics teacher, one who developed good pedagogical content knowledge that focused not only on the students' success but also on achieving more significant mathematics learning. They came to see the teaching of mathematics as a much more demanding and complex profession than they thought it would be, namely that the teacher has to give attention to a lot of aspects beyond teaching the content. Cheila also recognized that her vision had been transformed and now considered that it is necessary to change old methodologies if students are to be more motivated to learn.

The teaching practicum that the four teachers experienced occupied a full year at a school and involved teaching two different mathematics classes. This was a time in which the teachers predominantly continued with the ideas they developed before, except for Cheila who reached a new turning point. Her expectations that the ideas she developed concerning "new methodologies" would have an impact on students' motivation remained unfulfilled. This situation caused many doubts about the possibility of putting in practice what she learned. It is worth noticing that among the four teachers, Cheila was the only one who felt that she did not have the support she needed from the mentor to work with her very low achieving students.

The main changes for these four teachers began when they had to face the first year of teaching on their own, in basic schools that did not have any induction programme for new teachers. Now they had to regard themselves as autonomous teachers. Rita and Guilherme came to understand that they could have an important role as teachers and not "merely" as mathematics teachers. Guilherme made every effort to know the students well and to attend to their various needs. Rita also clearly assumed the role of an educator, who wants to contribute to the social and personal development of students.

Cheila, at this point, expressed a great rupture with the ideas she associated with the university programme. She questioned the applicability of the programme's ideas in practice and developed a teaching style consistent with the one she experienced as a student and in which she succeeded. From there on, her major concern was for having professional stability and, consequently, maintaining a continuity in her perspectives and practices.

In Susana's case, there was an initial moment of continuity in the first year; however, as time went by she began to question her own perspectives through confrontation with other teachers' perspectives and through reflection on her incapacity to deal with some difficult situations in the classroom. Since she looked at the profession as her natural vocation, this tension created deep doubts about her professional and personal projects.

It is important to stress that most of these beginning teachers had very difficult positions in schools that were labelled as "unwanted". However, some of them were creative in terms of their identity development, one that was positive and congruent from their point of view.

Besides the teacher education programme, there are many conditions that appear to have contributed to the development of these different professional identities. It is interesting to note that Rita and Guilherme immediately became involved with continuing teacher education and, especially, Rita participated in a research group located at the Mathematics Teacher Association (APM, in Portuguese). In contrast, Cheila and Susana only participated in some short sessions in schools about specific aspects of the teachers' roles. Additionally, Cheila had no reference group and Susana was far way from those who constituted her reference group (her colleagues from the teaching practice).

These beginning teachers participated in the same teacher education programme but developed very contrasting professional identities (Oliveira identifies four different identity configurations). When these beginning teachers talked about the perspectives they developed in the programme, superficially they sounded quite similar. However, their teaching practices differed markedly. Teacher education discourse does not affect all prospective teachers in the same way, as they are different people, with diverse expectations, experiences and origins. This study also showed that their biographies can reveal much about their beliefs, values and knowledge about mathematics and its teaching.

NURTURING INDIVIDUAL PROSPECTIVE TEACHERS' GROWTH

Learning to be a mathematics teacher is a single trajectory, through multiple contexts (Perresini, Borko, Romagno, Knuth, & Willis, 2004), and involving many characters. However, in the research we analysed we focused on the learning of individual prospective (mathematics) teachers. Programmes that focus on *teacher education and research on teachers' beliefs* show sensitiveness to the individual prospective teacher. Usually in this research, "the student teacher is recognized as a learner and an active processor of knowledge", one who develops "systems of constructs through which they interpret their undergraduate experiences" (Llinares & Krainer, 2006, p. 430). However, in the need to theorize about these, research sometimes does not attend to the prospective teacher holistically as a person and to the social origins of his or her beliefs. It seems that research is now beginning to incorporate the fact that beliefs are also contextualized (Llinares & Krainer, 2006).

Studies on prospective teachers' knowledge focus on the individual, but quite often these do not show the *prospective teachers' perspectives about what they are learning and how*; neither do they explain the development of that knowledge, taking into account past and present personal experiences of prospective teachers. As Ponte and Chapman (in press) notice, it is rare for reflection on self to be addressed in research on the development of knowledge of mathematics teaching; it occurs mainly as "a by-product". Making tacit knowledge explicit would be an important element in their development as future mathematics teachers. In the case of prospective secondary mathematics teachers, with a strong mathematical background, it is common for them to "value mathematics as important and beautiful but lack a critical attitude to mathematics and to teaching itself". Elementary teachers often value educational goals but just use "mathematical weak conceptions" (Jaworski & Gellert, 2003, p. 843).

The recognition of the importance of linking theory and practice led many programmes to develop frameworks for *promoting learning in context*. There is now a growing body of research aiming to understand how prospective teachers "make sense of their beliefs, reflect, and learn while participating in field experiences" (Lloyd, 2005, p. 443).

Research has shown that many prospective teachers are receptive to the *reform ideas* that are presented in teacher education programmes at the universities, but interpret these differently. It seems that they develop a professional argot, phraseology typical of mathematics education, and some myths about classroom reform. When they try to change their role as teachers, they realize that this may involve taking on practices that differ the ones they were used to observe. But they often do not know how to develop new communication patterns in the classroom or to teach for conceptual understanding. Teacher educators clearly have a demanding task to help prospective teachers to assume their role in a new classroom setting and informed by new theories on learning.

The process of learning to teach in practice has to do with teachers' perceptions of their own knowledge, of what they are able to do or not do, of what in particular they think will benefit their students, and so on; and this can be seen as evolving their beliefs and their knowledge, as well as themselves as persons. *Prospective and beginning teachers' dispositions and identities* are receiving increasing research attention. There is a growing debate about the dispositions for teaching and efforts to define and assess them (Borko, Liston, & Whitcomb, 2007). Although, if we want to attend to the individuality of the prospective teacher regarded as a whole person, it is not fruitful to try to match his or her development with a list of dispositions. What some of the studies we analysed suggest is that the enormous difficulty involved in learning to teach in the current, challenging times, needs to be balanced by a deep consciousness about what it means to be a teacher.

The *paradox* for the prospective teacher (and consequently for teachers educators) is that teaching is a long term enterprise, meaning that the teacher's decisions depend upon other long term decisions and not just of those they can make during a limited period of time. Issues of conflict between prospective teachers' perspective and those of their mentors raise important ethical questions for teacher education, namely, how is it possible to create a good balance between promoting the development of a professional identity that is attuned to the educational aims of the institution and *respecting the professional autonomy of the mentors and of the schools were the practicum occurs*?

Research on prospective and beginning mathematics teachers reveals that they do not simple reproduce the institutionalized practices in which they teach and that it is possible for them to become *active agents of their own development* (Goos, 2005); this shows that they are re-interpreting the social conditions of their professional context "in the light of [their] own professional goals and beliefs" (p. 55). We have to recognize that initial teacher education is just the beginning of *a long journey of professional development for teachers*, and that the constitution of a professional identity is subject to multiple influences (personal and contextual), many of which teacher education can not fully anticipate. Becoming a mathematics teacher is not "a sudden move from novice to experienced practitioner on the completion of a module or the passing of a test" (Jaworski, 2006, p. 189).

We add some final words about some *challenges to teacher education*. A focus on the individual prospective teacher as learner has a strong parallel with the need for the teacher to make an effort to know individually the students in front of him or her. But this can be very difficult when teacher educators are responsible for dozens of prospective teachers (as also happens with school teachers and their students). The advancement of technology has opened new opportunities in teacher education. The use of multimedia can facilitate learning from practice. However, using these resources gives only a certain picture of mathematics teaching and is no substitute for real interaction with students in the classroom. The use of the Internet to promote virtual interaction is another possibility for teacher education but there is still much to understand about how people "perform" in these scenarios. At the same time, we observe in educational research an increasing interest in looking at learning as participating in communities of practice, and it becomes clear that it is not possible to study the individual prospective teacher's learning without considering the contexts where it takes place. However, in this chapter, we intended to illustrate how learning to teach is also an idiosyncratic process and to review research providing evidence for this. As the studies analysed in this chapter show, much of the research on initial teacher educator is done by the teacher educators themselves (see also Adler et al., 2005). Therefore, there is a strong perception that the knowledge accumulated can be used readily in the design and development of new programmes and courses and (most importantly) in the interactions between teacher educators and prospective teachers.

ACKNOWLEDGEMENTS

We wish to gratefully acknowledge the helpful comments and feedback on former versions of this chapter provided by Gilah Leder, Heinz Steinbring and Terry Wood, and the continued encouragement and feedback from Konrad Krainer.

REFERENCES

Adler, J., Ball, D., Krainer, K., Lin, F.-L., & Novotná, J. (2005). Reflections on an emerging field: Researching mathematics teacher education. *Educational Studies in Mathematics, 60*, 359–381.

Amato, S. A. (2006). Improving student teachers' understanding of fractions. In J. Novotná, H. Moraová, M. Krátká, & N. Stehlková (Eds.), *Proceedings of the 30th Conference of the International Group for the Psychology of Mathematics Education* (Vol. 2, pp. 41–48). Prague, Czech Republic: Charles University.

Ambrose, R. (2004). Initiating change in prospective elementary school teachers' orientations to mathematics teaching by building on beliefs. *Journal of Mathematics Teacher Education, 7*, 91–119.

Artzt, A. F. (1999). A structure to enable preservice teachers of mathematics to reflect on their teaching. *Journal of Mathematics Teacher Education, 2*, 143–166.

Blanton, M. L. (2002). Using an undergraduate geometry course to challenge pre-service teachers' notions of discourse. *Journal of Mathematics Teacher Education, 5*, 117–152.

Bobis, J., & Aldridge, S. (2002). Authentic learning contexts as an interface for theory and practice. In A. Cockburn & E. Nardi (Eds.), *Proceedings of the 26th Conference of the International Group for the Psychology of Mathematics Education* (Vol. 2, pp. 121–128). Norwich, UK: University of East Anglia.

Borko, H., Liston, D., & Whitcomb, J. (2007). Apples and fishes: The debate over dispositions in teacher education. *Journal of Teacher Education, 58*, 359–364.

Bowers, J., & Doerr, H. M. (2001). An analysis of prospective teachers' dual roles in understanding the mathematics of change: Eliciting growth with technology. *Journal of Mathematics Teacher Education, 4*, 115–137.

Davis, G. E., & McGoven, M. A. (2001). Jennifer's journey: Seeing and remembering mathematical connections in a pre-service elementary teachers' course. In M. van den Heuvel-Panhuizen (Ed.), *Proceedings of the 25th Conference of the International Group for the Psychology of Mathematics Education* (Vol. 2, pp. 305–312). Utrecht, the Netherlands: Freudenthal Institute, Utrecht University.

Ebby, C. B. (2000). Learning to teach mathematics differently: The interaction between coursework and fieldwork for preservice teachers? *Journal of Mathematics Teacher Education, 3*, 69–97.

Ensor, P. (2001). From preservice mathematics teacher education to beginning teaching: A study in recontextualizing. *Journal for Research in Mathematics Education, 32*, 296–320.

Goffree, F., & Oonk, W. (2001). Digitizing real teaching practice for teacher education programmes: The MILE approach. In F.-L. Lin & T. J. Cooney (Eds.), *Making sense of mathematics teacher education* (pp. 111–145). Dordrecht, the Netherlands: Kluwer Academic Publishers.

Gohier, C., Anadón, M., Bouchard, Y., Charbonneau, B., & Chevrier, J. (2001). La construction identitaire de l'enseignant sur le plan professionnel: Un processus dynamique et interactif [The construction of teacher's professional identity: A dynamic and interactive process]. *Revues des Sciences de l'Education, 27*(1), 1–27.

Goos, M. (2005). A sociocultural analysis of the development of pre-service and beginning teachers' pedagogical identities as users of technology. *Journal of Mathematics Teacher Education, 8*, 35–59.

Hannula, M. S., Liljedahl, P., Kaasila, R., & Rösken, B. (2007). Researching relief of mathematics anxiety among pre-service elementary school teachers. In J.-H. Woo, H.-C. Lew, K.-S. Park, & D.-Y. Seo (Eds.), *Proceedings of the 31st Conference of the International Group for the Psychology of Mathematics Education* (Vol. 1, pp. 153–157). Seoul, Korea: Seoul National University.

Herrington, A., Herrington, J., Sparrow, L., & Oliver, R. (1998). Learning to teach and assess mathematics using multimedia: A teacher development project. *Journal of Mathematics Teacher Education, 1*, 89–112.

Jaworski, B. (2006). Theory and practice in mathematics teaching development: Critical inquiry as a mode of learning in teaching. *Journal of Mathematics Teacher Education, 9*, 187–211.

Jaworski, B., & Gellert, U. (2003). Educating new mathematics teachers: Integrating theory and practice, and the roles of practising teachers. In A. Bishop, M. Clements, C. Keitel, J. Kilpatrick, & F. Leung (Eds.), *Second international handbook of mathematics education* (pp. 829–875). Dordrecht, the Netherlands: Kluwer Academic Publishers.

Johnsen Høines, M., & Lode, B. (2006). Positioning of a subject based and investigative dialogue in practice teaching. In J. Novotná, H. Moraová, M. Krátká, & N. Stehlková (Eds.), *Proceedings of the 30th Conference of the International Group for the Psychology of Mathematics Education* (Vol. 3, pp. 369–376). Prague, Czech Republic: Charles University.

Kaasila, R. (2002). "There's someone else in the same boat after all." Preservice Elementary Teachers' Identification with the Mathematical Biography of Other Students. In P. Martino (Ed.), *Current state of research on mathematical beliefs* (pp. 65–75). Italy: University of Pisa.

Kaasila, R. (2006). Reducing mathematics anxiety of elementary teacher students by handling their memories from school time. In E. Pehkonen, G. Brandell, & C. Winslow (Eds.), *Nordic*

Presentations at ICME 10 in Copenhagen. (Research Report 265; pp. 51–56). Finland: University of Helsinki.

Kaasila, R., Hannula, M. S., Laine A., & Pehkonen, E. (2006). Facilitators for change of elementary teacher student's view of mathematics. In J. Novotná, H. Moraová, M. Krátká, & N. Stehlková (Eds.), *Proceedings of the 30th Conference of the International Group for the Psychology of Mathematics Education* (Vol. 3, pp. 385–392). Prague, Czech Republic: Charles University.

Kinach, B. M. (2002). Understanding and learning-to-explain by representing mathematics: Epistemological dilemmas facing teacher educators in the secondary mathematics "methods" course. *Journal of Mathematics Teacher Education, 5,* 153–186.

Krainer, K. (2005). What is "good" mathematics teaching, and how can research inform practice and policy? *Journal of Mathematics Teacher Education, 8,* 75–81.

Langford, K., & Huntley, M. A. (1999). Internships as commencement: Mathematics and science research experiences as catalysts for preservice teacher professional development. *Journal of Mathematics Teacher Education, 2,* 277–299.

Lerman, S. (2001). A review of research perspectives on mathematics teacher education. In F. -L. Lin & T. J. Cooney (Eds.), *Making sense of mathematics teacher education* (pp. 33–52). Dordrecht, the Netherlands: Kluwer Academic Publishers.

Liljedahl, P. (2005). AHA! The effect and affect of mathematical discovery on undergraduate mathematics students. *International Journal of Mathematical Education in Science and Technology, 36*(2-3), 219–236.

Liljedahl, P., Rolka, K., & Rösken, B. (2007). Affecting affect: The reeducation of preservice teachers' beliefs about mathematics and mathematics teaching and learning. In W. G. Martin, M. E. Strutchens, & P. C. Elliott (Eds.), *The learning of mathematics. Sixty-ninth Yearbook of the National Council of Teachers of Mathematics* (pp. 319–330). Reston, VA: National Council of Teachers of Mathematics.

Llinares, S. (2003). Participation and reification in learning to teach: The role of knowledge and beliefs. In G. C. Leder, E. Pehkonen, & G. Törner (Eds.), *Beliefs: A hidden variable in mathematics education* (pp. 195-209). Dordrecht, the Netherlands: Kluwer Academic Publishers.

Llinares, S., & Krainer, K. (2006). Mathematics (student) teachers and teacher educators as learners. In A. Gutierrez & P. Boero (Eds.), *Handbook of research on the psychology of mathematics education: Past, present and future* (pp. 429–459). Rotterdam, the Netherlands: Sense Publishers.

Lloyd, G. M. (2005). Beliefs about the teacher's role in the mathematics classroom: One student teacher's explorations in fiction and in practice. *Journal of Mathematics Teacher Education, 8,* 441–467.

Lloyd, G. M. (2006). Preservice teachers' stories of mathematics classrooms: Explorations of practice through fictional accounts. *Educational Studies in Mathematics, 63,* 57–87.

Masingila, J. O., & Doerr, H. M. (2002). Understanding pre-service teachers' emerging practices through their analyses of a multimedia case study of practice. *Journal of Mathematics Teacher Education, 5,* 235–263.

Mason, J. (1998). Enabling teachers to be real teachers: Necessary levels of awareness and structure of attention. *Journal of Mathematics Teacher Education, 1,* 243–267.

McDuffie, A. M. (2004). Mathematics teaching as a deliberate practice: An investigation of elementary preservice teachers' reflective thinking during student teaching. *Journal of Mathematics Teacher Education, 7,* 33–61.

Mewborn, D. S. (1999). Reflective thinking among preservice elementary mathematics teachers. *Journal for Research in Mathematics Education, 30,* 316–341.

Morris, A. K. (2006). Assessing pre-service teachers' skills for analyzing teaching. *Journal of Mathematics Teacher Education, 9,* 471–505.

Moyer, P. S., & Milewicz, E. (2002). Learning to question: Categories of questioning used by preservice teachers during diagnostic mathematics interviews. *Journal of Mathematics Teacher Education, 5,* 293–315.

Munby, H., Russell, T., & Martin, A. K. (2001). Teachers' knowledge and how it develops. In V. Richardson (Ed.), *Handbook of research on teaching* (pp. 877–904). Washington, DC: American Educational Research Association.

Nicol, C., Gooya, Z., & Martin, J. (2002). Learning mathematics for teaching: Developing content knowledge and pedagogy in a mathematics course for intending teachers. In A. Cockburn & E. Nardi (Eds.), *Proceedings of the 26th Conference of the International Group for the Psychology of Mathematics Education* (Vol. 3, pp. 17–24). Norwich, UK: University of East Anglia.

Oliveira, H. (2004). *A construção da identidade profissional de professores de Matemática em início de carreira* [The construction of professional identity in beginning mathematics teachers]. Unpublished doctoral dissertation. University of Lisbon, Portugal.

Olson, J. C., Colasanti, M., & Trujillo, K. (2006). Prompting growth for prospective teachers using cognitive dissonance. In J. Novotná, H. Moraová, M. Krátká, & N. Stehlková (Eds.), *Proceedings of the 30th Conference of the International Group for the Psychology of Mathematics Education* (Vol. 4, pp. 281–288). Prague, Czech Republic: Charles University.

Pehkonen, E., & Pietilä, A. (2003). On relationships between beliefs and knowledge in mathematics education. In ERME (Ed.), *Proceedings of the 3rd Conference of the European Society for Research in Mathematics Education* (CD-ROM and On-line). Available: http://ermeweb.free.fr/CERME3/tableofcontents_cerme3.html

Peretz, D. (2006). Enhancing reasoning attitudes of prospective elementary school mathematics teachers. *Journal of Mathematics Teacher Education, 9,* 381–400.

Perresini, D., Borko, H., Romagno, L., Knuth, E., & Willis, C. (2004). A conceptual framework for learning to teach secondary mathematics: A situative perspective. *Educational Studies in Mathematics, 56,* 67–96.

Philipp, R. A., & Sowder, J. T. (2002). Using eye-tracking technology to determine the best use of video with prospective and practicing teachers. In A. Cockburn & E. Nardi (Eds.), *Proceedings of the 26th Conference of the International Group for the Psychology of Mathematics Education* (Vol. 4, pp. 233–240). Norwich, UK: University of East Anglia.

Pietilä, A. (2002). The role of mathematics experiences in forming pre-service elementary teachers' views of mathematics. In A. Cockburn & E. Nardi (Eds.), *Proceedings of the 26th Conference of the International Group for the Psychology of Mathematics Education* (Vol. 4, pp. 57–64). Norwich, UK: University of East Anglia.

Ponte, J. P., & Chapman, O. (in press). Preservice mathematics teachers' knowledge and development. In L. English (Ed.), *Handbook of international research in mathematics education* (2nd ed.). Mahwah, NJ: Lawrence Erlbaum Associates.

Rowland, T., Huckstep, P., & Thwaites, A. (2005). Elementary teachers' mathematics subject knowledge: The knowledge quartet and the case of Naomi. *Journal of Mathematics Teacher Education, 8,* 255–281.

Sánchez, V., & Llinares, S. (2003). Four student teachers' pedagogical reasoning on functions. *Journal of Mathematics Teacher Education, 6,* 5–25.

Schorr, R. Y. (2001). A study of the use of clinical interviewing with prospective teachers. In M van den Heuvel-Panhuizen (Ed.), *Proceedings of the 25th Conference of the International Group for the Psychology of Mathematics Education* (Vol. 4, pp. 153–160). Utrecht, the Netherlands: Freudenthal Institute, Utrecht University.

Sfard, A., & Prusak, A. (2005). Telling identities: The missing link between culture and learning mathematics. In H. L. Chick & J. L. Vincent (Eds.), *Proceedings of the 29th conference of the International Group for the Psychology of Mathematics Education* (Vol. 1, pp. 37–52). Melbourne, Victoria, Australia: University of Melbourne.

Shulman, L. (1987). Knowledge and teaching: Foundations of the new reform. *Harvard Educational Review, 57*(1), 1–14.

Skott, J. (2001). The emerging practices of a novice teacher: The roles of his school mathematics images. *Journal of Mathematics Teacher Education, 4,* 3–28.

Sowder, J. T. (2007). The mathematical education and development of teachers. In F. K. Lester, Jr. (Ed.), *Second handbook of research on mathematics teaching and learning* (pp. 157–223). Charlotte, NC: Information Age Publishing & National Council of Teachers of Mathematics.

Steele, D. F. (2001). The interfacing of preservice and inservice experiences of reform-based teaching: A longitudinal study. *Journal of Mathematics Teacher Education, 4*, 139–172.

Stehlíková, J. (2002). A case study of a university student's work analysed in three different levels. In A. Cockburn & E. Nardi (Eds.), *Proceedings of the 26th Conference of the International Group for the Psychology of Mathematics Education* (Vol. 4, pp. 241–248). Norwich, UK: University of East Anglia.

Szydlik, J. E., Szydlik, S. D., & Benson, S. R. (2003). Exploring changes in pre-service elementary teachers' mathematical beliefs. *Journal of Mathematics Teacher Education, 6*, 253–279.

Tirosh, D. (2000). Enhancing prospective teachers' knowledge of children's conceptions: The case of division of fractions. *Journal for Research in Mathematics Education, 31*, 5–25.

Uusimäki, S. L., & Kidman, G. (2004, July). *Challenging maths-anxiety: An intervention model.* A paper presented in TSG24 at ICME-10. (Available online at http://icme-organisers.dk/tsg24/Documents/UusimakiKidman.doc).

Uusimäki, S. L., & Nason, R. (2004). Causes underlying pre-service teachers' negative beliefs and anxietes about mathematics. In M. Høines & A. Fuglestad (Eds.), *Proceedings of the 28th Conference of the International Group for the Psychology of Mathematics Education* (Vol. 4, pp. 369–376). Bergen, Norway: University College.

Van Zoest, L., & Bohl, J. (2002). The role of reform curricular materials in an internship: The case of Alice and Gregory. *Journal of Mathematics Teacher Education, 5*, 265–288.

Walshaw, M. (2004). Pre-service mathematics teaching in the context of schools: An exploration into the constitution of identity. *Journal of Mathematics Teacher Education, 7*, 63–86.

Hélia Oliveira
Centro de Investigação em Educação da FCUL
University of Lisbon
Portugal

Markku S. Hannula
Department of Applied Sciences of Education
University of Helsinki
Finland

MARIE-JEANNE PERRIN-GLORIAN, LUCIE DEBLOIS, AND
ALINE ROBERT

2. INDIVIDUAL PRACTISING MATHEMATICS TEACHERS

Studies on Their Professional Growth

This chapter focuses on the professional growth of practising teachers. In the first part, two examples illustrating major trends of current research allow to launch the discussion. We then present our methodology and the main results from our review of literature. Finally, we conclude on three main issues and perspectives: 1) the change of paradigm proposed in practising teacher education poses new teaching problems, thus it seems important to study teaching in its context; 2) when teachers have to change because of an external constraint, some changes may occur, but they are not always the "wanted" ones; we need better understanding of deep components of practice; perhaps the study of the stabilization of practice during the first years of career may help progress; 3) it seems important to construct concepts or systems capable of taking into consideration the variety of teachers' work (from planning to classroom interactions).

INTRODUCTION

This chapter focuses on the professional growth of practising teachers. We are interested in the evolution of teachers' practice, knowledge and beliefs, as well as the constraints, dilemmas and difficulties they face in adapting their practice to students or to a new curriculum. Though the constructs and theoretical frameworks are often different, we distinguish *three main issues*: 1) How are teachers' conceptual, belief and knowledge systems organized in relation to their practice? 2) How are these systems to be changed in order to improve teaching? 3) How do teachers' practices change "naturally" and in what ways do teachers learn from their own practice? The first two of these questions are close to issues raised by Adler, Ball, Krainer, Lin, and Novotná (2005) in their survey on mathematics teacher education, whereas the third issue, at the core of our chapter, is scarcely addressed in the literature.

Part one of this chapter presents our general point of view regarding the problem. Two examples from our own recent research are included as a point of departure. We then specify the methodology we used in conducting our review of the literature. In the third and fourth parts, we state our research questions and present our results. We then move on to provide a more in-depth discussion of those issues with more recent research about actual practices and their

K. Krainer and T. Wood (eds.), Participants in Mathematics Teacher Education, 35–59.

development. Finally, we draw some provisional conclusions as to what new questions, concepts and methodologies might be considered.

THE PROBLEM

Our Point of View

One's learning as a mathematics teacher is a lifelong learning process which starts with one's own experiences as a learner of mathematics, later supported by both prospective and practising teacher training. In this chapter, we view professional growth as a *progressive transformation* of mathematics teachers' actual practice in relationship to their individual and professional experience, their knowledge and their beliefs or conceptions about mathematics and mathematics teaching. In the literature, terms such as teacher development, changes in teachers' practice or teachers' learning are often used indiscriminately, though they are not equivalent. For practising teachers, teacher development can be seen through the changes that occur in their practice. Nonetheless, recent research seems to indicate that teachers may learn about teaching, for example about student's logical development or challenging problems but not change their practices, or they may change their practices without really new thinking.

Behind the three research issues considered above, important questions arise:

1) Is it possible to study only beliefs, or knowledge, or practice? What relationships between these concepts are most relevant? For example, beliefs can influence practice, but practice can also influence beliefs. How can we study systems of beliefs and knowledge and their relationship to practice? Research issues depend on these implicit or explicit assumptions. Many models have been constructed to explain interactions between different views of teachers. In reviewing the literature, we see that during the last decade a shift has occurred from research describing one issue (beliefs, or knowledge or practice) to research taking greater account of complexity and the relationship of these constructs to context.

2) In what sense can we speak of professional growth? What constitutes good teaching? Very little research goes so far as to study the effect of teaching on students' learning. It looks like as if an implicit agreement exists about what is good teaching (see e.g., Wilson, Cooney, & Stinson, 2005) and such teaching produce students' best learning. In many studies, particularly in US, the implicit reference is to the NCTM standards without questioning its effect on students' learning, particularly in the case of socio-cultural differences between students. Another possible reference for professional development among research is the participation in a community of practice (and development of this participation). Otherwise, the reference may only be the researcher's conception of good teaching.

3) What is meant by "natural" change? The difficulty in accessing natural teacher growth without modifying it from outside may explain why there are so few studies on this topic (e.g., self-study, often from teacher educators or teachers involved in research projects). Teachers may decide themselves to register for a

practising teacher education course. This decision is an indication that they wish to improve their practice but the changes are influenced by the teacher education program and are not "natural".

4) The relevance of making a synthesis of questions and results achieved from very different theoretical perspectives and with different aims may be questioned. Theory may be a theorisation of practice: assumptions on learning and on effective teaching; in such case, research consists in elaborating and testing such a theory of practice. In other research, theory is a construct in order to analyse, understand and explain practice and relationships between teaching and learning, for any style of teaching. Sometimes, both positions co-exist in the same research, in particular in the case of collaborative research (e.g., Scherer & Steinbring, 2006). In this chapter, we consider mainly research the aim of which is to study professional practice in order to understand it and thus what may make it evolve.

Two Examples to Launch Our Discussion

Example 1: Enhancing our understanding of stability of practice. We refer here to a research which was done in 2004-2006 (Pariès, Robert, & Rogalski, in press). This work aims at identifying specific difficulties that experienced mathematics teachers' face when changing their own practices. In the following, we discuss one of the two cases presented in the article mentioned above.

This case investigates two lessons given by the same teacher at grades eight and nine in "ordinary" classes[1]. The lessons focused on the same kind of geometrical activities for both groups of students (the resolution of problems just after a lesson on a new theorem). To exhibit stability of practice both mathematical tasks and lesson management were analysed.

There was a real difference in how the tasks were proposed in these classes. In the first class, students had to conceive of some steps on their own before applying corresponding theorems (once the Pythagoras theorem, once the converse, and then a theorem on the sum of angles). In the second class, the problem applying Thales's theorem[2] was more direct. The difficulty, however, was to write "x" instead of a formal length "EM" in an equality. There were few differences in terms of classroom management. The activities explicitly organised by the teacher for her students and the order in which the activities are carried out are the same in both groups (drawing the figure, looking for a strategy and then for the resolution and correction). We note the similarity in the length of each activity (including the total), even if there are slight differences. At that point, it is important to assess the previous comment: this stability of classroom management has been confirmed by the teacher as typical for this kind of problem when she was asked about the representativeness of these videos. So we can assume that they represent the usual way of working for this teacher on analogous problems.

---

[1] Students work in class, at home and there are no special problems of discipline.
[2] The theorem of proportional lengths made by a parallel to one side of a triangle.

Table 1. Lesson plan (with time in minutes)

	On Pythagoras' theorem grade 8	On Thales' theorem grade 9		
Work organised by teacher for students		First question (1) beginning, (2) end	Second question	Total for the grade 8 class
Draw the geometrical figure	**6'**	Drawing **2'20**		More than **2'20**
Looking for a strategy to solve the problem	Individual then collective **8'30**	Collective (1) **5'30**	Collective **2'30**	**8'**
Looking for the resolution	Individual **4'30**	In two steps **2'**	Individual **2'10**	**4'10**
Correcting and recopying the correction	The teacher writes on the blackboard at students' dictation **9'**	Two students chosen by the teacher write successively on the blackboard **2'10 and 2'40**	One student writes on the blackboard **9'50**	Almost **15'**
Total	**28'**			**30'**

The relationship between tasks and the students' activity are different in the two lessons, not only in terms of the tasks themselves but also in terms of the teacher's management[3]. As the first problem, which can be more difficult than the second problem, required more steps, it was impossible for many grade 8 students to come up with something during the 8 minutes they had to look for a strategy. The teacher relied on some isolated students' proposals and finally explained the whole strategy to the students who, for the most part, did not find anything. She then wrote the three steps on the blackboard. The students then had to work on three easier tasks. Perhaps, if the teacher had allowed more time or if the students had had the possibility of working in small groups, more students would have begun to move in the direction of a resolution.

One can argue that the teacher does not mind changing the task in that way. It is not clear because the teacher's last sentence in grade 8 is "You see [...] you are able to solve a problem without intermediate questions." So, even if the teacher does not mind this reduction of students' activities, it does not change the fact that her (stable) management style is incompatible with letting students work by themselves on such complex activities. On the contrary, in grade 9, more students find the strategy. The difficulty of calculating with x is widely anticipated by the teacher and it seems that a lot of students get involved in it. Maybe the teacher's

---

[3] We use here the term "management" to precise the part of practice by which the teacher manages the students' mathematical activity.

management is well adapted to such a problem because this exercise was an old one for the teacher and the other problem was more recent, selected for the purpose of providing complex activities. What can be deduced from these analyses?

The stability of experienced mathematics teachers' practice concerns, first of all, the management of the session at the scale of lessons. In other words, *tasks are easier to change than management* (see e.g., Cogan & Schmidt, 1999). Even if tasks adopted by teachers for students change, due to, for example, new curricula or new standards, this does not ensure that the expected consequences for students' work occur, because of no variation in the way they choose to manage their classroom. In the case where students have to work in a precise way on some (new) tasks to benefit from new activities, as finding steps by themselves before applying a theorem, we can guess that nothing will occur in the class if the teacher's usual management does not let students work in a compatible way. Consequently, it may explain why it is so difficult for teachers to change their own practice. Maybe, the management of their practice is so stable that in order to change it has to be revealed by somebody else, for example, by mutual observation, and explicitly discussed to be questioned (see also Nickerson, this volume).

Example 2: Conditions leading to the transformations of the interpretation and the intervention. Previous research of DeBlois and Squalli (2001) leads to the study of how discussions among teachers may help them transform their understanding of their students and develop their practice.

A first study (DeBlois, 2006) was done with elementary school teachers concerning the errors contained in students' written products. It showed, for example, that when teachers compare the task to all the tasks usually proposed, they evaluate the influence of the student's work habits. This type of reflection makes the error "logical". It is no longer synonymous with a lack of attention on the part of the student. The error becomes an extension of the procedures known by students. This reflection then leads the teacher to choose a form of intervention that allows students to break with their usual work habits. This study was continued with teachers at the early high school level. Seminars allowed teachers to discuss the errors contained in students' work. At the beginning, teachers expressed themselves in an affirmative way when they described the students' production or when they talked about the teaching offered and other parts of environment to which they are sensitive. During the discussion, they were entering a process of dissociation from the teaching offered. This dissociation allowed them to review the tasks performed with and by the students in the classroom.

For example, four teachers (D, K, M, J) discussed a 13-year-old student's production (Figure 1). At first, one teacher could not find any justification to explain the strip diagram. Another teacher explained that/how he had worked on the vertical and horizontal diagrams with the students. He added that he informed the students about what could be asked. The problem exposed in the student's production became afterwards proof of confusion between the two elements of knowledge.

19. On demande à des élèves le nombre de frères et de soeurs qu'ils ont.
Construis un diagramme à bandes à l'aide de ces résultats.

Élèves de l'école Sainte-Marguerite	
Nombre de frères et de soeurs	Effectif
0	20
1	31
2	56
3	12
4	5
5	3
6	1

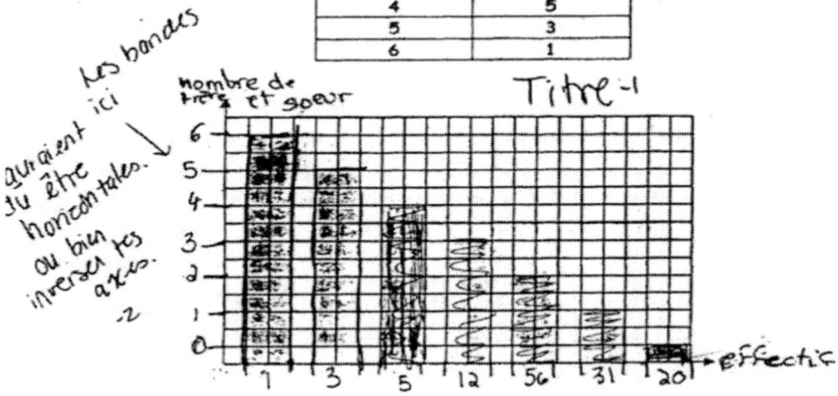

Figure 1. Student's production.

Time and a collective decision became the means of the student's understanding as shown in this excerpt:

D – I can impose you, [precise] what I want. I can say: trace the one that is appropriate and you will have to choose the one that is appropriate.
K – If you had shown the two of them, they could have mixed them up […].
D – Because different situations required two different diagrams.
D – Give a class showing the possibility of making a horizontal or vertical diagram and take a decision in group. In two groups, the choice of the strip's form was different, one chose the vertical diagram and the other chose the horizontal.

Other teachers considered the error as a way for students to regulate how to get good answers that, by itself, is part of the student's learning process.

M – Maybe they wanted to do a horizontal strip first? The zero should have been there.
M – It is possible. He could have changed his mind at the last minute.

The fact that a teacher brings out the notion of regulation weakens for the group the hypothesis of an automatism suggested at the beginning of the discussion. The research method undoubtedly influenced the discussion. In fact, asking teachers to describe their students' written products was above all an invitation that freed them from concerns they had. Indeed, the teachers' interpretations seemed to change as other possible clues concerning the origin of the error were explored. Thus, in this case, among the possible interventions, we find the wish of knowing the student's representation of a graphic and a diagram. This way, we can consider the discussion between colleagues as an environment for re-examining students' production.

In the excerpt studied, it was the *moments of intense interaction* that modified the teachers' interpretation and allowed the understanding of the student's production, resulting in an effect on the planned interventions. Their sensitivity appears mostly in regard to the particular learning conditions, to students' uncommon procedures and to institutional knowledge. The teachers agree that, despite the confusion that led to an inversion of the representation, the final result makes sense. The analysis shows that, from time to time, the researcher, while also playing her role as a mathematics teacher educator, uses teachers' affirmations as a starting point to call attention to other hypotheses or observable facts in the student's production which were ignored until then. This way, the interaction produced between teachers and the researcher played an important role in the process of transformation.

These two examples illustrate two major trends of current research: On the one hand, there are diagnoses of difficulties for transforming practice, they involve beliefs, classroom management, or cultural and institutional constraints. On the other hand, research presents some ways of overcoming these difficulties, including new concepts for analysing teachers' appropriation of teacher education.

OUR METHODOLOGY

In order to define the three *areas of research* mentioned at the beginning of this chapter, we started a *literature review* with the following interrelated questions in mind:
1. What is studied (practice, knowledge, beliefs, relations among them, how to change them, how they can change)? We also tried as much as possible to specify the cultural and political context as main factors of practice.
2. What factors are taken into account for professional growth and their effects (institutional or cultural factors: reforms, new technologies; later effects of previous training; research participation; individual factors: learning from practice)?
3. What theoretical framework, implicit or explicit hypotheses, and what methodologies are used to gain access to individual professional growth?
4. What are the findings? We will distinguish the results concerning primary and secondary school teachers. Indeed, their conditions are not the same, neither concerning mathematics (their learning of mathematics as students which may

influence their practice as teachers) nor with regard to teaching (the former teach many subjects and not only mathematics).

The *key words* used in our search of literature were: teachers' experience, teachers' beliefs, teachers' practice, teachers' learning, professional knowledge, and practices of mathematics teachers. We used also handbooks and synthesis articles as well as their bibliographies in selecting research concerning the professional development of practising teachers. Moreover, a variety of reviews were systematically studied. For the selected papers, we drew up a summary taking into account issues 1 to 4 above. This allowed us to define categories used to present the third and fourth parts.

RESEARCH QUESTIONS AND FIRST RESULTS

A Recent Emergence

The interest of scholars for teachers as object of study is recent. Fifteen years ago, Hoyles (1992) deplored the scarcity of teacher-focused research and appealed to develop it. Her request was granted: For example, Sfard (2005), Ponte and Chapman (2006) noticed a growing interest in this subject and a surprising growth of papers on teachers' practice since 1995 (see also Krainer, volume 4). Similarly, Margolinas and Perrin-Glorian (1997) noticed that research concerning teachers' action has developed in France since 1990 and a book on Teacher Education emerged from the first European meeting on Mathematics Education (Krainer, Goffree, & Berger, 1999).

Several reasons may explain this growing interest in teachers' practices and the way they can evolve: results that did not answer the teachers' questions but the researchers' questions; research did not consider enough constraints of the class. Thus, mathematics education researchers felt the need to better understand teachers' conceptions of mathematics teaching and their various constraints to conduct their teaching. These new questions required an extension of the theoretical frameworks. For example, in France where the question of the teacher was posed early, the theory of didactic situations in mathematics (Brousseau, 1997), particularly the notion of *milieu*, was refined to study "ordinary" classes. The teacher's action on[4] the *milieu* of a didactic situation is a key issue to understand his or her role in class (Bloch, 2002; Hersant & Perrin-Glorian, 2005; Margolinas, 2002; Margolinas, Coulange, & Bessot, 2005; Perrin-Glorian, 1999; Salin, 2002). Extending the notion of didactic transposition, a new framework emerged in order to help describe the organisation of study at school (Barbé,

---

[4] In the theory of didactical situations (Brousseau, 1997), the *milieu* of a didactic situation is the part of the context that can bring a feedback to student's actions to solve a problem. The teacher can act on the *milieu* bringing some new information or new equipment, for example, asking a question or giving a compass; acting on the milieu, he changes the knowledge needed to solve the problem. One can refer to Warfield (2006) for an introduction to this theoretical framework

Bosch, Espinoza, & Gascon, 2005; Bosch & Gascon, 2002; Chevallard, 1999; Chevallard, 2002). Other scholars endeavoured to model teachers' didactic action using a combination of these two theories (Sensevy, Mercier, & Schubauer-Leoni, 2000; Sensevy, Schubauer-Leoni, Mercier, Ligozat, & Perrot, 2005). The didactical and ergonomical twofold approach of Robert and Rogalski (2002, 2005) copes in another way with the complexity of practice.

In Quebec, different program reforms have led researchers to develop new contexts for practising teacher education. The theoretical frameworks of Schön (1983), Lave (1991), Erickson (1991), and Bauersfeld (1994), contributed to the development, experimentation and analysis of collaborative research (Bednarz, 2000). In this perspective, the teachers' practice is the starting point of the training. The didactic content is more a tool for training than a corpus of knowledge to be transmitted. In this way, teachers could develop a deep understanding of mathematical knowledge. Recently, Bednarz (2007) observed that research was suffering from an absence of a teacher-oriented database which allows for a thorough consideration of classroom situations.

At the same time, at the international level, sociocultural theories (D'Ambrosio, 1999) and references to Vygotsky's work were spreading as well as a new interest for teacher and students' interactions. Several models appeared; theoretical efforts were done to control the teacher's role or action inside theory in order to understand teacher's work. However, it is not sufficient to understand how to change practice; for that, it is necessary to understand teacher's work in and of itself. Thus, research concerning teacher change is even more recent, involving various questions and methods referring to psychological or sociological perspectives (Richardson & Placier, 2001). The recent 15th ICMI Study Conference on The Professional Education and Development of Teachers of Mathematics (2005) was a crucial moment to discuss this theme.

Understand Teachers' Practice and Teachers' Growth

Previous experience of learning and teaching strongly influences current teaching. Though we cannot separate beliefs, knowledge and practice to understand teachers' practice or teachers' growth, the aim of this section is to clarify these notions and their use to better understand the way practising teachers may evolve.

Beliefs. Research on beliefs was first carried out from psychological perspectives and beliefs were treated as cognitive phenomena (see e.g., Thompson, 1992). Some studies used questionnaires, others focused on describing teachers' beliefs or conceptions in relation to a particular aspect of teaching or learning mathematics, problem solving, students' errors or technology for many of those involving practising teachers. The results of these studies led researchers to appreciate the complexity of the notion of beliefs (Ernest, 1989; Jaworski, 1994; Mura, 1995).

More recently, their contextualised nature and their social origin were considered (see e.g., Gates, 2006; Leder, Pehkonen, & Törner, 2003; Llinares &

Krainer, 2006). Nevertheless, some scholars, for example in France (Robert & Robinet, 1996) referred earlier to social representations. Be that as it may, beliefs and attitudes about mathematics, mathematics teaching and the role of the teacher were regarded as a main factor influencing teachers' teaching and their learning processes about mathematics teaching (see also Oliveira and Hannula, this volume).

Knowledge. Many studies have attempted to know more about teachers' knowledge for teaching mathematics, and its effect on students' learning.

Early research showed that there was no clear relationship between the number and the level of mathematics courses completed by teachers and students' achievement. Then research focused on a specific mathematical content, identified deficiencies and misconceptions in teachers' mathematical content knowledge on many topics, generally for prospective teachers or primary school teachers. A number of papers point out explicitly implications for teacher education but the relationship with teaching was not evidenced. Thus researchers grappled with the question of what would constitute conceptual understanding for teachers and felt the need to extend the theorisation of teachers' mathematics knowledge by including teachers' knowledge of mathematics for teaching (Ball, Lubienski, & Mewborn, 2001; Ponte & Chapman, 2006).

Shulman (1986) was the first to call attention to a special kind of teacher knowledge that linked content and pedagogy: pedagogical content knowledge (PCK). Research into PCK identified the necessity of teachers' awareness on students' difficulties in specific subjects. Later, the notion of PCK was often combined with other theoretical constructs. Studies involving PCK showed an effort in establishing a critical perspective. For example, Ma's study (1999) described what she called "profound understanding of fundamental mathematics" to explain the difference between American and Chinese teachers. That said, Ball, Lubienski, and Mewborn (2001) claim that the descriptions of teachers' knowledge do not necessarily illuminate the knowledge that is critical to good practice. Moreover, distance remains between studies on teachers' knowledge and on teaching itself. Ball, Bass, Sleep, and Thames (2005) developed an extension of the notion of PCK. They identified four domains of which two are close to the Shulman's work: knowledge of students and content, knowledge of teaching and content, and two are new: common content knowledge and specialized content knowledge.

For Suurtamm (2004), professional development necessarily passes through a deepening of one's mathematical knowledge in order to answer the students' questions and to guide them in their exploration process. Many authors confirm this vision, by linking risk taking, self confidence, teamwork and the use of appropriate resources with teachers' professional development (Brunner et al., 2006; Carpenter & Fennema, 1989). Even (2003) recalls that insofar as learning is a personal construction, the construction of mathematical knowledge does not necessarily reflect instruction. Some common experiences (subjective and sociocultural) will favour a common signification contributing to deepen reflection.

Thus, the research has revealed the complexity of mathematical knowledge for teaching, its links with mathematical knowledge thus indicating "a shift away from regarding mathematical knowledge independent of context to regarding teachers' mathematical knowledge situated in the practice of teaching" (Llinares & Krainer, 2006, p. 432).

The research approach developed mainly in France around the basic notions of the Theory of Didactic Situations does not focus on actors but on teaching and relationships to mathematical knowledge. Rather than pedagogical content knowledge or knowledge on mathematics teaching, Margolinas et al. (2005) use the notion of "teacher's didactic knowledge". This notion is defined as part of teacher's knowledge "which is related to the mathematical knowledge to be taught". They prefer this notion because, as Steinbring (1998) has also stressed, mathematical knowledge and pedagogical knowledge cannot be separated for teaching. Indeed, crucial questions for teacher education now are 1) what special form of mathematical knowledge is fundamental for teaching? and 2) how can teachers not only acquire such knowledge in order to use it effectively in the classroom but go on developing it over the course of their teaching careers? We will see in part 4 how recent research addresses this question.

Practices. There is a large variety of studies on teachers' practices referring to various theoretical frameworks and methods. Some of them describe practice in terms of indicators such as amount of time spent on lesson development, types of problems selected during development, teacher's types of questioning and so on.

Other studies focus on the relationship between the structure of the lesson and the teachers' understanding of a specific mathematical content and others are biographical studies. Among them, some studies are linked to education reform efforts or to the quest for effective practices. There are also many studies at a microdidactic level which study classroom interactions, with an interest in the language used, the nature of classroom discourse, the role that the teacher plays in classroom discussions, the identification and characterisation of interaction patterns. We can notice that teachers' practices and research on teachers' practices strongly depend on the cultural and political context (e.g., Cogan & Schmidt, 1999). We also must consider results coming from international evaluations like TIMSS and PISA. These evaluations may have some influence on practices. For example, some countries may develop students' training in problem situations like PISA to have best performance. Thus, the teachers' practice, the curriculum and the studies could nowadays be influenced by international evaluation (Bodin, 2006; DeBlois, Freiman, & Rousseau, 2007).

Ponte and Chapman (2006) point out that the notion of practice used in research has evolved. Mostly regarded as actions or behaviours in early studies, practice includes later what the teacher does, knows, believes and intends. Boaler (2003) and Saxe (1999) consider the notion of stability and recurrence of practices. Saxe emphasizes the socially organised nature of these practices; Boaler considers not only activities but also norms. We consider with Ponte and Chapman (2006, p. 483) that "teachers' practices can be viewed as the activities they regularly conduct, taking in consideration their working context and their meanings and intentions".

Relations between Beliefs and Practices

Initially, it seemed that one way to improve practice was to improve beliefs and knowledge. But research has shown that a change in beliefs does not necessarily entail a change in practices especially for practising teachers. Many studies focused, directly or indirectly, on the relationship between beliefs or conceptions and practices. These studies found inconsistencies between them, particularly when teachers were faced with innovation, notably involving computers. Nevertheless, these inconsistencies may be apparent only. For example, Skott (2004) explains these inconsistencies in terms of the existence of the multiple motives of teachers' activity, experienced as incompatible. These inconsistencies may thus be seen as situations in which the teachers' priorities are dominated by other motives, maybe not immediately related to school mathematics, for example, developing students' self-confidence. Vincent (2001) and DeBlois and Squalli (2001) talked about preoccupations about the space and the time of learning. Moreover, Lerman (2001) criticises past research on beliefs and comparison with practice, including his own, because it does not take sufficiently *contexts* into account: for example, the interview context is different from class context. He suggests that "whilst there is a family resemblance between concepts, beliefs, and actions in one context and those in another, they are qualitatively different by virtue of these contexts" (Lerman, 2001, p. 36), and that "contexts in which research on teachers' beliefs and practices is carried out should be seen as a whole". More recently, Herbel-Eisenmann, Lubienski, and Id-Deen (2006) distinguish local and global changes, taking into account the importance of curricular context for local changes. Thus, students' and parents' expectations and desires as well as the curriculum materials may influence the teacher adopt local adaptations not really compatible with his global beliefs.

GROWTH AND LEARNING

What Actually Changes, What Resists? What Means Seem Effective?

Two main questions on practices strongly concern teacher education: (1) what constitutes good practice for students' effective learning? and (2) how can teachers' practice be improved? For the first question, research often gives an implicit answer supported by constructivist or socio-constructivist theories supporting practice that let a large place to students' action. For the second question, the research to better understand teachers' practice concludes on the complexity of teachers' practice so that it is now widely recognized that professional development programs that attempt to achieve real changes in classroom practices must address teachers' knowledge, beliefs and practice. However, the nature and genuineness of changes further complicates this question. The question of efficiency is very difficult to evaluate; actual and deep changes require time. Moreover, to find efficiency in students' achievement, one has to be sure that the planned changes in practices were achieved (Bobis, 2004; Sullivan, Mousley, & Zevenbergen, 2004). Other reasons could explain these difficulties: the methodology used, the paradigm adopted, the cultural factors and the context, and teachers' engagement.

Thus, an important methodological problem occurs to know what changes and what is resistant to change. How can we compare or measure changes that occur in teachers' beliefs, knowledge or practices? Teachers' answers to questionnaires are not easily interpretable into actual changes made. Class observation, more often used in recent research, is very time-consuming such that only a few cases can be studied. Some researchers adopt a mixed approach, asking teachers to react to class contexts, for example using video clips of classroom excerpts.

A common feature of reforms in mathematics education carried out in the last decades is the change in relative emphasis from mathematical products to processes, with a greater importance given to individual processes. The student is expected not only to learn predetermined concepts and procedures but also to become involved in genuinely creative individual and collective processes of investigating, experimenting, generalising, naming and formalising. This adaptation supposes a rather different and more difficult role for the teacher. The teacher has to adopt a certain interpretative stance; to engage in reflexive activity enabling him to a flexible use of interactions with the students, what Skott (2004) named "forced autonomy". He observed some novice teachers claiming teaching priorities inspired by the reform. Their classroom practices were in line with these priorities most of time but not at other moments, identified as critical incidents, where teachers are "playing a very different game than one of teaching mathematics". In this type of research, some recent work tries to specify new tasks for students or/and new tasks for teachers, to get students to become more engaged and more effective problem solvers (Doerr, 2006). Recent research also tries to describe the diversity of ways of adoption of this new "job", sometimes in relation with an appropriate (or hoped so) teachers' training program (Herbst, 2003). Even though teacher education programs have gained some positive results, much research highlights the difficulties for teachers to change their practices in a deep way.

Other recent work tries to understand the *difficulty to change mathematics teachers' practice*, and how their beliefs are implicated in a complex way in practices, at different levels, combined with social or cultural considerations. For example, Arbaugh, Lannin, Jones, and Park-Rogers (2006) studied 26 secondary teachers using a problems-based mathematics textbook *Core-Plus*. They conclude that adopting a problem-based textbook series and using it in a classroom is not enough, in itself, to have an effect on teacher instructional practices – to get them to teach in a more reform-oriented manner, according to the strength of previous habits and beliefs. Wilson, Cooney, and Stinson (2005) reveal some subtle aspects of these beliefs in what constitutes good mathematics teaching and how it develops for teachers: they find considerable overlap between the teachers' espoused beliefs and the writing in NCTM standards documents as well as important differences, linked to these teacher-centred/student-centred classroom conceptions. Moreover, the teacher's view and the researcher's view of change may be different. For example, Sztajn (2003) shows the way in which elementary school teachers adapt their practices to their students' needs, that is to what they think their students' needs are, and at the same time being certain that they are acting according to current reform visions adapted as much as possible to their specific students.

Thus, professional development efforts often result only in surface changes. We can notice with Tirosh and Graeber (2003) the importance of cultural factors and the environment of teachers. Some research reports success of individual teachers changing their practices though their colleagues do not (e.g., Koch, 1997). But successful change is more likely to occur when simultaneous attention is given to changing the system in which teachers work. Many studies have noted the value derived from discussions with colleagues who are experiencing similar concerns and can provide ideas for solving problems encountered in change (e.g., Krainer, 2001). Students themselves may resist (Brodie, 2000; Ponte, Matos, Guimarães, Leal, & Canavarro, 1994). Thus it may be easier to change practices with a program involving all the teachers in a given school (e.g., Sztajn, Alex-Saht, White, & Hackenberg 2004); nevertheless, volunteer teachers will change more easily; research projects often balance between these two options.

Indeed, student achievement is the main goal of the vast majority of efforts to change classroom practice and the main motive for teachers to try to do it, especially at a large scale (see e.g., large programs for primary schools in Australia: Bobis, 2004; Sullivan et al., 2004) or with low-achieving students in South Africa (Graven, 2004).

Taking into account the fact that *deep changes take a long time*, Franke, Carpenter, Levi, and Fennema (2001) also addressed the question why some teachers continue to develop their practices when teacher education programs are over. Their study, a follow-up of the Cognitive Guided Instruction (CGI) program for practising teachers (Carpenter & Fennema, 1989), shows that some teachers of this program were engaged in a generative growth. They suggest that focusing on students' thinking is a means for engaging teachers in continued learning and that helping teachers' collaboration with their colleagues can support it. Graven (2004), in a study in the Lave and Wenger's theoretical framework of community of practice, adds the notion of *confidence* as both a product and a process of learning, in relation to teacher learning as "learning as mastery". It seems that the notion of confidence could help particularly in this case, involving teachers with a low (sometimes even absent) mathematical background in their teaching preparation and students coming from low socio-cultural backgrounds. However, engaging teachers in learning to examine mathematical tasks using the Level of Cognitive Demand criteria supports both a growth in pedagogical content knowledge (ways of thinking about mathematical tasks) and a change in practice (choosing mathematical tasks) proved to be a non-threatening way to start teachers thinking more deeply about their practices (Arbaugh & Brown, 2005).

Nevertheless, an important condition is the teacher' involvement in the program during its unfolding and after it. Doerr and English (2006) show that the modelling tasks were actually a means used to bring about change in teachers' practices, even if that change is not the same for any two teachers. Wood (2001, p. 432) attempted to find out if teachers were actually learning by investigating their process of reflection, namely "how teachers use reflective thinking in their pedagogical reasoning and how their thinking relates to changes in teaching". She confirms that teachers develop differently while giving some insight into how this difference continues. But the challenge remains to explain why this development is different among teachers or to know if another choice in approach to teacher education would produce another effect. The study of Empson and Junk (2004) is devoted to an assessment of a training program for elementary teachers, novice and experienced teachers alike, based on knowledge of students' mathematics. It shows that teachers' knowledge of students' non-standard strategies is broadest and sometimes deepest in the chosen topic, even if it depends on the teachers; the teachers use information given in their training, some of them even extended their knowledge.

To change practices (in a broad sense), the importance of reflection on practice as well as collaboration and discussion among colleagues about concrete cases (for example excerpts of videos, particularly critical classrooms incidents) is nowadays stressed (e.g., Nickerson, this volume). Nevertheless, as Llinares and Krainer (2006, p. 444) comment:

> At the present time, we need to understand better the relationship between these instruments [reflection and collaboration] and teachers' different levels of development, as well as the changes in teachers' practice.

Spontaneous Changes. How Do Teachers Learn through Teaching?

Interest of scholars in the individual and spontaneous changes in teachers' practice is quite recent. Moreover, questions and methods used are different: Searching why and how teachers change without questioning if it is in a desirable direction (change is not always desirable, especially at the end of their career), studies have found that *teachers are always changing*. They refer mainly to psychological background and methods are often based on case studies looking for relationship between biography, professional experience and professional knowledge development. Results show mainly stability of style with certain flexibility. Large differences between teachers are observed, some of them being more able than others to frame puzzles stemming from practice (Richardson & Placier, 2001). For example, Sztajn (2003) analyses the case of Helen, an elementary school teacher with 31 years of teaching experience, who thinks that her mathematics teaching has greatly improved during her career. Nevertheless, the same fact may be seen as change for the teacher and as stability by the researcher if actually the students' activity is not really changed. Thus, Sztajn stresses the difference of scale between teachers' and researchers' views about change and the necessity for researchers to understand teachers from the teachers' point of view.

Most scholars share the view that teachers increase their understanding of learning and teaching mathematics indirectly from their practice, through years of participating in classroom life (Stigler & Hiebert, 1999). However, even though "direct and indirect learning are interrelated and depend on each other" (Zaslavsky, Chapman, & Leikin, 2003), little research concerns indirect practising teacher learning (embedded in practice). Such research may consist in self-analysis carried out by teacher educators of their own practice as teachers (e.g., Tzur, 2002) or joint analysis of a teacher and a researcher (e.g., Rota & Leikin, 2002) or analysis by a researcher of teacher's learning from class observation (Margolinas et al., 2005). Tzur (2002) conducted, as researcher-teacher, a teaching experiment in a third-grade classroom observing his own improvement of practice. His reflection is similar to Ma's (1999) and raises the question if and how a teacher (not researcher) can lead this kind of reflection in his class. Rota and Leikin (2002) studied the development of one elementary school beginning teacher's proficiency in managing a whole class mathematics discussion in an inquiry-based learning environment. They found a large *growth in flexibility* for the teacher, much more attentive to the students, without any professional development intervention, except the existence of their research. They also stress the difficulty of teaching a teacher when to apply a particular teaching action.

More research is needed on teachers' learning through teaching, especially for beginning teachers. However, some models explain how such learning may occur, and enhance in some way previous results, as they suggest that a teacher cannot "see" what he is not prepared to see. This explains that a deep professional growth cannot occur in some cases without some external interventions. For example, Zaslavsky et al. (2003, p. 880) refer to Steinbring's model (1998):

> According to this model, the teacher offers a learning environment for his or her students in which the students operate and construct knowledge of school mathematics in a rather autonomous way. This occurs by subjective interpretations of the tasks in which they engage and by ongoing reflection on their work. The teacher, by observing the students' work and reflecting on their learning processes, constructs and understanding, which enables him or her to vary the learning environment in ways that are more appropriate for the students. Although both the students' learning processes and the interactive teaching process are autonomous, the two systems are nevertheless interdependent. This interdependence can explain how teachers learn through their teaching.

Zaslavsky et al. (2003) extend this model to teacher educators' learning with one more layer.

Another model of teachers and teacher educators' development, strongly emphasising collaboration, is the co-learning partnership described by Jaworski (1997) and Bednarz (2000), in which "teachers and educators learn together in a reciprocal relationship of a reflexive nature". Margolinas et al. (2005), using a model extending Brousseau's work, carry out two case studies of lessons in which the teacher's didactical knowledge seemed insufficient for dealing with students' solutions and identified two kinds of teacher's learning.

Let us notice that the three quoted models also implicitly suggest that teachers learn more from their practice when they provide their students with a rich environment allowing for autonomous reflection. There is in some way a dialectic process with actions reciprocal to the usual ones: Students' learning   Teachers' learning   Teacher educators' learning. However, Margolinas et al. (2005) suggest that it may not be sufficient for general and stable learning.

CONCEPTS TO CONSIDER PROFESSIONAL GROWTH IN THE SYSTEM OF TEACHERS' WORK

As early as 1993, Ball recognized that the *tensions* (Cohen, 1990) and the *dilemmas* (Lampert, 1985) with which teachers are confronted, are the distinguishing features of teaching and must be treated throughout the teacher's career. The importance of the practice context and of the contextualised pedagogical contents has been acknowledged in relation to the restructuring of a repertoire of interventions (Brodie, 2000; Bednarz, 2000). Grossman, Smagorinsky, and Valencia (1999) use the concept of *appropriation* to determine the process by which a person adopts a pedagogical tool available in a particular social environment. The degree of appropriation depended on the congruence between the values, the experiences and the goals of the members of this culture. The American Institutes for Research recognize the influence of the length of the training in the transformation of teaching practices (Garet et al., 2001). This component permitted the emphasis on the mathematical and scientific contents and also to perceive a greater coherence between the teacher's objectives, the standards and the other teachers, and offered the opportunity for active learning. Finally, a direct relationship is established between what people know and the way they learned the knowledge and the practices.

To consider these components, a variety of concepts were used: dilemmas and tensions (Herbst, 2003; Suurtamm, 2004; Herbst & Chazan, 2003), constraints and conditions (Barbé et al., 2005; Robert & Rogalski, 2002; Roditi, 2006); the concept of practical rationality (Herbst & Chazan, 2003), and the concept of teachers' sensibility to a *milieu* (DeBlois, 2006).

Tensions and Dilemmas

Practising teacher education programs usually require a change of paradigm. Consequently, the teachers are often confronted with dilemmas that many studies have identified. Brodie (2000), Herbst (2003), and Suurtamm (2004) describe how a constructivist approach could create tensions and dilemmas. For example, questioning students makes their weaknesses more apparent. Experimenting new tasks with students requires paying attention to the explicitly expected product or to the new ideas which students may develop while engaged in the activity. The research of coherent evaluation methods according to the teaching practices, the time to explore, develop and find an appropriate curriculum and evaluation resources add to the tensions lived by the teachers.

These dilemmas concern the coordination to be accomplished between the new teaching practices and the contents to cover, the students' rhythm, the type of questions formulated by the teacher, the conciliation of norms, and "authentic" evaluation. Some conditions make it easier to cope with these dilemmas and tensions: collaboration between teachers (collegiality), adequate resources (e.g., time), school administration support.

Practical Rationality

The concept of *practical rationality* allows practitioners to use their acquired knowledge (knowledge, personal engagement) in a similar or different manner than the others and to describe the action in its context (Herbst & Chazan, 2003). This way, it becomes possible to predict the dilemmas which the teachers will be confronted with when they will engage themselves into actions activating these dispositions. Like the disposition network, activated in particular situations, it becomes possible to justify the presence of very different teaching styles according to the objective characteristics of the position of "mathematics teacher" compared with connected practices, but still different (e.g., teaching history, doing mathematics).

The concept of *didactical and ergonomical twofold approach*, developed in France by Robert and Rogalski (2002), seems to get closer to the concept of practical rationality. However, these authors seem to give more consideration to non premeditated actions than to those derived from practical rationality. Different components are identified and defined: cognitive, mediative, institutional, social, personal (Robert & Rogalski, 2002), and collective (Roditi, 2005, 2006).

Teachers' Sensibility

René de Cotret (1999) introduces the following distinction between *milieu* (Brousseau, 1997) and *environment* (Maturana & Varela, 1994): the environment relates to the observer's description of a situation and the milieu relates to the student's sensibility to this environment. DeBlois (2006) uses this distinction to develop the concept of "sensibility" of teachers to speak of their interpretation of this milieu (for the student). She observed teachers that were asked to interpret their students' errors in mathematics in order to examine the interpretative process and its influence on the choice of teaching strategies in a mathematics class. Four types of teachers' sensibilities (teaching, familiarity of the student with the task, students' understanding, curriculum and characteristics of the task) were identified. At that point, it was possible to recognize a relationship between a variety of interpretations of students' productions (attention, extension of students' procedures, students' ability, product of an interaction between student and the task) and kinds of teaching strategies (method of working, creation of a gap with the habits, reconsider exercises or manipulative, play with didactic variables).

When she analyses her data, Leikin (2006) prefers the notion of *awareness* to explain teachers' choices when they teach. She includes this notion in one of the two types of factors: momentary factors (reasoning, noticing and awareness) and preliminary factors (knowledge, abilities, and beliefs). These two concepts (sensibility and awareness) could help to understand the choice of teachers.

CONCLUSION

This review of literature shows how difficult it is to organize the variety of results and develop some conceptualisation. Nonetheless, we have identified *three main issues*. First, the change of paradigm proposed in practising teacher education poses new teaching problems. Research on mathematics teacher education shows the importance of flexibility, depth and connectedness of teachers' mathematical knowledge. It also shows how difficult it is for teachers to acquire such flexible knowledge and use it to manage students' learning in challenging classroom mathematics activities. Thus, it seems important to study teaching in its context (e.g., in relation with the students or within the larger social or political context).

Second, when teachers have to change because of an external constraint, reform, or new syllabus, it is often difficult for them, and research shows that whereas some changes may occur, they are not always the "wanted" ones. The difficulties often stem from the very stable imbrications between teachers' beliefs and knowledge, and social and institutional expectations as well as cultural context. Previous research had already shown that "isolated" changes are not sufficient to guarantee real improvement in practice. Some studies show that there are actually teachers who learn alone through their teaching, but these studies and inferences from other research lead us to believe that these improvements occur inside the teachers' previous "teaching style", for example, their beliefs and choices regarding contents and classroom management. Perhaps some progress will come from better understanding of the differences between this kind of improvement and a deeper transformation of practice: what indicators may help researchers assess this difference? A way to enlighten this issue may be to study more deeply how novice teachers' practice stabilizes during the first five years of their career. We meet here one of perspectives by Leikin (this volume) drawn from her analysis of research on education of prospective mathematics teachers. Such studies might give us evidence of different ways of improving practice according to the level of teaching (primary or secondary) and mixing different kinds of knowledge. Moreover, recent studies enable us to think that professional growth takes a long time and requires a collective investment and the implementation of specific new tasks to be used by students and/or teachers. However, due to the complexity of these elements of change and the length of time needed, it becomes even more difficult for research to assess progress.

Third, it seems important to construct concepts or systems capable of taking into consideration the variety of teachers' work (planning, analysis, classroom interactions, including relations with parents etc.). Perhaps some further development of research will occur when researchers are able to elaborate models of teachers' professional growth which involve mathematical development blended with teaching issues and are adaptable to individual specificity.

ACKNOWLEDGMENTS

The contribution of Lucie DeBlois was partly supported by Social Sciences and Humanities Research Council of Canada 410-2005-0406 and the revision of English language by DIDIREM-EA 1547 (Paris).

REFERENCES

Adler, J., Ball, D., Krainer, K., Lin, F.-L., & Novotná, J. (2005). Reflections on an emerging field: researching mathematics teacher education. *Educational Studies in Mathematics, 60,* 359–381.

Arbaugh, F., & Brown, C. A. (2005). Analyzing Mathematical tasks: a catalyst for change? *Journal of Mathematics Teacher Education, 8,* 499–536.

Arbaugh, F., Lannin, J., Jones, D., & Park-Rogers, M. (2006). Examining instructional practices in Core-Plus lessons: Implications for professional development. *Journal of Mathematics Teacher Education, 9,* 517–550.

Ball, D. L. (1993). With an eye on the mathematical horizon: Dilemmas of teaching elementary school mathematics. *Elementary School Journal, 93,* 373–397.

Ball, D. L., Bass, H., Sleep, L., & Thames, M. (2005). A theory of mathematical knowledge for teaching. *15th ICMI Study Conference: The Professional Education and Development of Teachers of Mathematics.* Lindoia. Brésil. http://stwww.weizmann.ac.il/G-math/ICMI/log_in.html

Ball, D. L., Lubienski, S. T., & Mewborn, D. S. (2001). Research on teaching mathematics: the unsolved problem of teachers' mathematical knowledge. In V. Richardson (Ed.), *Handbook of research on teaching* (4th ed., pp. 433–456). Washington, DC: American Educational Research Association.

Barbé, J., Bosch, M., Espinoza, L., & Gascon, J. (2005). Didactic restrictions on the teacher's practice: The case of limits of functions at Spanish high schools. *Educational Studies in Mathematics, 59,* 235–268.

Bauersfeld, H. (1994). Réflexions sur la formation des maîtres et sur l'enseignement des mathématiques au primaire. *Revue des sciences de l'éducation, 20*(1), 175–198.

Bednarz, N. (2000). Formation continue des enseignants en mathématiques: une nécessaire prise en compte du contexte. In P. Blouin & L. Gattuso (Eds.), *Didactique des mathématiques et formation des enseignants* (pp. 61–78). Mont-Royal, Québec, Canada: Éditions Modulo. Collection Astroïde.

Bednarz, N. (2007). Ancrage et tendances actuelles de la didactique des mathématiques au Québec: A la recherche de sens et de cohérence. *Colloque du Groupe de Didactique des Mathématiques.* Mai 2007. Rimouski, Québec, Canada.

Bloch, I. (2002). Différents niveaux de milieu dans la théorie des situations. In J. L. Dorier, M. Artaud, M. Artigue, R. Berthelot, & R. Floris (Eds.), *Actes de la 11ème Ecole d'été de didactique des mathématiques, Corps, 2001* (pp. 125–139). Grenoble, France: La Pensée Sauvage.

Boaler, J. (2003). Studying and capturing the complexity of practice: The case of the dance of agency. In N. Paterman, J. Dougherty, & J. T. Zilliox (Eds.), *Proceedings of the 27th Psychology of Mathematics Education International Conference* (Vol. 1, pp. 3–16). Honolulu, HI: University of Hawaii.

Bobis, J. (2004). For the sake of the children: Maintaining the momentum of professional development. In M. J. Hoines & A. B. Fulglestad (Eds.), *Proceedings of the 28th Psychology of Mathematics Education International Conference* (Vol. 2, pp. 143–150). Bergen, Norway: Psychology of Mathematics Education.

Bodin, A. (2006). Les mathématiques face aux évaluations nationales et internationales. *Repères-IREM* *65*, 55-89.

Bosch, M., & Gascon, J. (2001). Organiser l'étude: Théories et empiries. In J. L. Dorier, M. Artaud, M. Artigue, R. Berthelot, & R. Floris (Eds.), *Actes de la 11ème Ecole d'été de didactique des mathématiques, Corps, 2001* (pp. 23–40). Grenoble, France: La Pensée Sauvage.

Brodie, K. (2000). Mathematics teacher development and learner failure: Challenges for teacher education. *International Mathematics Education and Society Conference*. Portugal. 26–31. ERIC – # ED482653.

Brousseau, G. (1997). *Theory of didactical situations in mathematics. Didactique des mathématiques 1970–1990*. Dordrecht, the Netherlands: Kluwer Academic Publishers.

Brunner, M., Kunter, M., Krauss, S., Klusmann, U., Baumert, J., Blum, W., Neubrand, M., Dubberke, Th., Jordan, A., Löwen, K., & Tsai, Y.-M. (2006). Die professionelle Kompetenz von Mathematiklehrkräften: Konzeptualisierung, Erfassung und Bedeutung für den Unterricht. Eine Zwischenbilanz des COACTIV-Projekts. In M. Prenzel & L. Allolio-Näcke (Eds.), *Untersuchungen zur Bildungsqualität von Schule. Abschlussbericht des DFG-Schwerpunktprogramms* (pp. 54–83). Münster, Germany: Waxmann.

Carpenter, T. P., & Fennema, E. (1989). Building on the knowledge of students and teachers. In G. Vergnaud, J. Rogalski, & M. Artigue (Eds.), *Proceedings of 13th the Psychology of Mathematics Education International Conference* (Vol. 1, pp. 34–45). Paris: Bicentenaire de la révolution française.

Chevallard, Y. (1999). Pratiques enseignantes en théorie anthropologique. *Recherches en didactique des mathématiques, 19*, 221–266.

Chevallard, Y. (2002). Organiser l'étude : Structures et fonctions. Ecologie et régulation. In J. L. Dorier, M. Artaud, M. Artigue, R. Berthelot, R. Floris (Eds.), *Actes de la 11ème Ecole d'été de didactique des mathématiques, Corps, 2001* (pp. 3–22 and pp.41–56). Grenoble, France: La Pensée Sauvage.

Cogan, L., & Schmidt, W. (1999). An examination of instructional practices in six countries. In G. Kaiser, E. Luna, & I. Huntley (Eds.), *International Comparisons in Mathematics Education* (pp. 68–85). London: Falmer.

Cohen, D. K. (1990). A revolution in one classroom: The case of Mrs. Oublier. *Educational Evaluation and Policy Analysis, 12*, 327–345.

D'Ambrosio, U. (1999). Literacy, matheracy, and technocracy: A trivium for today. *Mathematical Thinking and Learning, 1*(2), 131–153.

DeBlois, L. (2006). Influence des interprétations des productions des élèves sur les stratégies d'intervention en classe de mathématiques. *Educational Studies in Mathematics, 62*, 307–329.

DeBlois, L., Freiman, V., & Rousseau, M. (2007) Influences possibles sur les programmes de recherches subventionnées. *Colloque du Groupe de didacticiens en mathématiques*. Rimouski, Québec, Canada.

DeBlois, L., & Squalli, H. (2001). Une modélisation des savoirs d'expérience chez des orthopédagogues intervenant en mathématiques. In G. Debeurme (Ed.), *Enseignement et difficultés d'apprentissage*. (pp.153–157). Sherbrooke, Canada: Les éditions du CRP.

Doerr, H. (2006). Examining the tasks of teaching when using students' mathematical thinking. *Educational Studies in Mathematics, 62*, 3–24.

Doerr, H., & English, L. (2006). Middle grade teachers' learning through students' engagement with modelling tasks. *Journal of Mathematics Teacher Education, 9*, 5–32.

Empson, L., & Junk, D. L. (2004). Teachers' knowledge of children's mathematics after implementing a student-centered curriculum. *Journal of Mathematics Teacher Education, 7*, 121–144.

Erickson, G. (1991). Collaborative inquiry and the professional development of science teachers. *The Journal of Educational Thought, 25*(3), 228–245.

Ernest, P. (1989). The impact of beliefs on the teaching of mathematics. In P. Ernest (Ed.), *Mathematics teaching: The state of the art* (pp. 249–254). New York: Falmer Press.

Even, R. (2003). What can teachers learn from research in mathematics education? *For the Learning of Mathematics, 23*(3), 38–42.

Franke, M. L., Carpenter, T. P., Levi, L., & Fennema, E. (2001). Capturing teachers' generative change: A follow-up study of professional development in mathematics. *American Educational Research Journal, 38*, 653–689.

Garet, M. S., Porter, A. C., Desimone, L., Birman, B. F., & Yoon, K. S. (2001). What makes professional development effective? Results from a national sample of teachers. *American Educational Research Journal, 38*, 915–945.

Gates, P. (2006). Going beyond belief systems: exploring a model for the social influence on mathematics teacher education. *Educational Studies in Mathematics, 63*, 347–369.

Graven, M. (2004). Investigating mathematics teacher learning within an in-service community of practice: The centrality of confidence. *Educational Studies in Mathematics, 57*, 177–211.

Grossman, P. L., Smagorinsky P., & Valencia, S. (1999). Appropriating tools for teaching English: A theorical framework for research on learning to teach. *American Journal of Education, 108*, 1–29.

Herbel-Eisenmann, B., Lubienski, S. T., & Id-Deen, L. (2006). Reconsidering the study of mathematics instructional practices: the importance of curricular context in understanding local and global teacher change. *Journal of Mathematics Teacher Education, 9*, 313–345.

Herbst, P. G. (2003). Using novel tasks in teaching mathematics: Three tensions affecting the work of the teacher. *American Educational Research Journal, 40*, 197–238.

Herbst, P., & Chazan, D. (2003). Exploring the practical rationality of mathematics teaching through conversations about videotaped episodes: the case of engaging students in proving. *For the Learning of Mathematics, 23*(1), 2–14.

Hersant, M., & Perrin-Glorian, M. J. (2005). Characterization of an ordinary teaching practice with the help of the theory of didactic situations. *Educational Studies in Mathematics, 59*, 113–151.

Hoyles, C. (1992). Mathematics teaching and mathematics teachers: A meta-case study. *For the Learning of Mathematics, 12*(3), 32–44.

Jaworski, B. (1994). *Investigating mathematics teaching*. New York: Falmer Press.

Jaworski, B. (1997). Tensions in teachers' conceptualisations of mathematics and of teaching. *Annual Meeting of the American Educational Research Association*. Chicago, IL. ERIC – # ED408151.

Koch, L. (1997). The growing pains of change: A case study of a third grade teacher. In J. Ferrini-Mundy & T. Schram (Eds.), *Recognizing and recording reform in mathematics education project: Insights, issues and implications*. Journal for Research in Mathematics Education, Monograph 8, (pp. 87–109). Reston, VA: National Council of Teachers of Mathematics.

Krainer, K. (2001). Teachers' Growth is more than the growth of teachers. The case of Gisela. In F.-L. Lin & T. J. Cooney (Eds.), *Making sense of teacher education* (pp. 271–294). Boston: Kluwer Academic Publishers.

Krainer, K., Goffree, F., & Berger, P. (1999). *European research in mathematics education I.3. On research in mathematics teacher education*. Osnabrück: Forschungsinstitut für Mathematik didaktik. http://www.fmd.uni-osnabrueck.de/ebooks/erme/cerme1-proceedings/cerme1-group3.pdf

Lampert, M. (1985). How do teachers manage to teach? Perspectives on problems in practice. *Harvard Educational Review, 55*, 178–194.

Lave, J. (1991). Acquisition des savoirs et pratiques de groupe. *Sociologie et Sociétés, 23*(1), 145–162.

Leder, G., Pehkonen, E., & Törner, G. (Eds.). (2003). *Beliefs: A hidden variable in Mathematics Education?* Dordrecht, the Netherlands: Kluwer Academic Publishers. See particularly the paper of F. Furinghetti & E. Pekhonen.

Leikin, R. (2006). Learning by teaching: The case of Sieve of Eratosthenes and one elementary school teacher. In R. Zazkis & S. Campbell (Eds.), *Number theory in mathematics education: Perspectives and prospects* (pp. 115–140). Mahwah, NJ: Erlbaum

Lerman, S. (2001). A review of research perspectives on mathematics teacher education. In F.-L. Lin & T. J. Cooney (Eds.), *Making sense of teacher education* (pp. 33–52). Boston: Kluwer Academic Publishers.

Llinares, S., & Krainer, K. (2006). Mathematics (student) teachers and teacher educators as learners. In A. Guttierez & P. Boero (Eds.), *Handbook of research on the psychology of mathematics education. Past, present and future* (pp. 429–459). Rotterdam, the Netherlands: Sense Publishers.

Ma, L. (1999). *Knowing and teaching elementary mathematics: Teacher's understanding of fundamental mathematics in China and in the U.S.* New Jersey: Lawrence Erlbaum Associates.

Margolinas, C. (2002). Situations, milieux, connaissances. Analyse de l'activité du professeur. In J. L. Dorier, M. Artaud, M. Artigue, R. Berthelot, & R. Floris (Eds.), *Actes de la 11ème Ecole d'été de didactique des mathématiques, Corps, 2001* (pp.141–155). Grenoble, France: La Pensée Sauvage.

Margolinas, C., Coulange, L., & Bessot, A. (2005). What can the teacher learn in the classroom? *Educational Studies in Mathematics, 59,* 205–234.

Margolinas, C., & Perrin-Glorian, M. J. (1997). Editorial: Les recherches sur l'enseignant en France, *Recherches en didactique des mathématiques, 17*(3), 7–15.

Maturana, H., & Varela, F. (1994). *L'arbre de la connaissance.* Paris: Addison-Wesley.

Mura, R. (1995). Images of mathematics held by university teachers of mathematics education. *Educational Studies in Mathematics, 28,* 385–399.

Pariès, M., Robert, A., & Rogalski, J. (in press). Analyses de séances en classe et stabilité des pratiques d'enseignants de mathématiques expérimentés en seconde. *Educational Studies in Mathematics.*

Perrin-Glorian, M. J. (1999). Problèmes d'articulation de cadres théoriques: l'exemple du concept de milieu. *Recherches en Didactique des Mathématiques, 19*(3), 279–321.

Ponte, J. P., & Chapman, O. (2006). Mathematics teachers' knowledge and practices. In A. Guttierez & P. Boero (Eds), *Handbook of research on the psychology of mathematics education. Past, present and future* (pp. 461–494). Rotterdam, the Netherlands: Sense Publishers.

Ponte, J. P., Matos, J. F., Guimarães, H. M., Leal, L. C., & Canavarro, A. P. (1994). Teachers and students' views and attitudes towards a new mathematics curriculum: A case study. *Educational Studies in Mathematics, 26,* 347–365.

Richardson, V., & Placier, P. (2001). Teacher change. In V. Richardson (Ed.), *Handbook of research on teaching* (4th ed., pp. 905–947). Washington, DC: American Educational Research Association.

Robert, A., & Robinet, J. (1996). Prise en compte du méta en didactique des mathématiques. *Recherches en Didactique des Mathématiques, 16*(2), 145–175.

Robert, A., & Rogalski, J. (2002). Le système complexe et cohérent des pratiques des enseignants de mathématiques: une double approche. *La revue canadienne de l'enseignement des sciences des mathématiques et des technologies, 2*(4), 505–527.

Robert, A., & Rogalski, J. (2005). A cross-analysis of the mathematics teacher's activity. Example in a French 10th-grade class. *Educational Studies in Mathematics, 59,* 269–298.

Roditi, E. (2005). *Les pratiques enseignantes en mathématiques: Entre contraintes et liberté pédagogique.* Paris: l'Harmattan.

Roditi, E. (2006). Une formation pour la pratique et par la pratique, des hypothèses sur la formation continue. *Colloque international "Espace Mathématique Francophone 2006",* Université de Sherbrooke (Canada).

Rota, S., & Leikin, R. (2002). Development of mathematics teachers' proficiency in discussion orchestration. In A. D. Cockburn & E. Nardi (Eds.), *Proceedings of the 26th Psychology of Mathematics Education International Conference* (Vol. 4, pp. 137–144). Norwich, UK: University of East Anglia.

Salin, M. H. (2002). Repères sur l'évolution du concept de milieu en théorie des situations. In J. L. Dorier, M. Artaud, M. Artigue, R. Berthelot, & R. Floris (Eds.), *Actes de la 11ème Ecole d'été de didactique des mathématiques, Corps, 2001* (pp. 111–124). Grenoble, France: La Pensée Sauvage.

Scherer, P., & Steinbring, H. (2006). Noticing children's learning processes – Teachers jointly reflect on their own classroom interaction for improving mathematics teaching. *Journal of Mathematics Teacher Education, 9,* 157–185.

Schön, D. A. (1983). *The reflective practitioner.* New York: Basic Books.

Sensevy, G., Mercier, A., & Schubauer-Leoni, M. L. (2000). Vers un modèle de l'action didactique du professeur. A propos de la course à 20. *Recherches en didactique des mathématiques, 20*(3), 263–304.

Sensevy, G., Schubauer-Leoni, M. L., Mercier, A., Ligozat, F., & Perrot, G. (2005). An attempt to model the teacher's action in the mathematics. *Educational Studies in Mathematics, 59,* 153–181.

Sfard, A. (2005). What could be more practical than good research? On mutual relations between research and practice of mathematics education. *Educational Studies in Mathematics, 58*, 393–413.

Shulman, L. S. (1986). Those who understand: Knowledge growth in teaching. *Educational Researcher, 15*(2), 4–14.

Skott, J. (2004). The forced autonomy of mathematics teachers. *Educational Studies in Mathematics, 55*, 227–257.

Steinbring, H. (1998). Elements of epistemological knowledge for mathematics teachers. *Journal of Mathematics Teacher Education, 1*, 157–189.

Stigler, J., & Hiebert, J. (1999). *The teaching gap: Best ideas from the world's teachers for improving education in the classroom.* New York: The Free Press.

Sullivan, P., Mousley, J., & Zevenbergen, R. (2004). Describing elements of mathematics lessons that accommodate diversity in student background. In M. J. Hoines & A. B. Fulglestad (Eds.), *Proceedings of the 28th Psychology of Mathematics Education International Conference* (Vol. 4, pp. 257–264). Bergen, Norway: Psychology of Mathematics Education.

Suurtamm, C. A. (2004). Developing authentic assessment: Case studies of secondary school mathematics teachers' experiences. *The Canadian Journal of Science, Mathematics and Technology Education, 4*, 497–513.

Sztajn, P. (2003). Adapting reform ideas in different mathematics classrooms: Beliefs beyond mathematics. *Journal of Mathematics Teacher Education, 6*, 53–75.

Sztajn, P., Alex-Saht, M., White, D. Y., & Hackenberg, A. (2004). School-based community of teachers and outcome for students. In M. J. Hoines & A. B. Fulglestad (Eds.), *Proceedings of the 28th Psychology of Mathematics Education International Conference* (Vol. 4, pp. 273–280). Bergen, Norway: Psychology of Mathematics Education.

Thompson, A. (1992). Teachers' beliefs and conceptions: A synthesis of the research. In D. A. Grouws (Ed.), *Handbook of research on mathematical teaching and learning* (pp. 127–146). New York: Macmillan.

Tirosh, D., & Graeber, A. (2003). Challenging and changing mathematics teaching classrooms practices. In A. J. Bishop, M. A. Clements, C. Keitel, J. Kilpatrick, & F. K. S. Leung (Eds.), *Second international handbook on mathematics education* (pp. 643–687). Dordrecht, the Netherlands: Kluwer Academic Publishers.

Tzur, R. (2002). From theory to practice: Explaining successful and unsuccessful teaching activites (case of fractions). In A. D. Cockburn & E. Nardi (Eds.), *Proceedings of the 26th Psychology of Mathematics Education International Conference* (Vol. 4, pp. 297–304). Norwich, UK: University of East Anglia.

Vincent, S. (2001). Le trajet du 'savoir à enseigner' dans les pratiques de classe. Une analyse de points de vue d'enseignants. In Ph. Jonnaert & S. Laurin (Eds.), *Les didactiques des disciplines. Un débat contemporain* (pp. 210–239). Sainte-Foy, Canada: Presses de l'Université du Québec.

Warfield, V. (2006). *Invitation to didactique.* http://www.math.washington.edu/~warfield/Didactique.html

Wilson, P. S., Cooney, T. J., & Stinson, D. W. (2005). What constitutes good mathematics teaching and how it develops: Nine high school teachers' perspectives. *Journal of Mathematics Teacher Education, 8*, 83–111.

Wood, T. (2001). Learning to teach mathematics differently: Reflection matters. In M. van den Heuvel-Panhuizen (Ed.), *Proceedings of the 25th Psychology of Mathematics Education International Conference* (Vol. 4, pp. 431–438). Utrecht, the Netherlands: Freudenthal Institute.

Zaslavsky, O., Chapman, O., & Leikin, R. (2003). Professional development in Mathematics Education. Trends and tasks. In A. J. Bishop, M. A. Clements, C. Keitel, J. Kilpatrick, & F. K. S. Leung (Eds.), *Second international handbook on mathematics education* (pp. 877–915). Dordrecht, the Netherlands: Kluwer Academic Publishers.

Marie-Jeanne Perrin-Glorian
Equipe DIDIREM
Institut Universitaire de Formation des Maîtres, Université d'Artois
France

Lucie DeBlois
Centre de recherche sur l'intervention et la réussite scolaire (CRIRES)
Faculté des sciences de l'éducation, Université Laval
Canada

Aline Robert
Equipe DIDIREM
Institut Universitaire de Formation des Maîtres, Université de Cergy-Pontoise
France

SECTION 2

TEAMS OF MATHEMATICS TEACHERS
AS LEARNERS

ROZA LEIKIN

3. TEAMS OF PROSPECTIVE MATHEMATICS TEACHERS

Multiple Problems and Multiple Solutions

In this chapter, I first address four interrelated problems that mathematics teacher educators (MTEs) are currently facing in the education of prospective mathematics teachers (PMTs): (1) The importance of challenging mathematics and PMTs' limited experience in challenging mathematics; (2) Changing approaches to mathematics teaching and the resistance to change in teaching; (3) The need to intermingle the different components of teachers' knowledge in teacher education; and (4) The difficulty of becoming a member of a community of practice. To analyse a variety of solutions that MTEs suggest for these problems when working with teams of PMTs, I provide in a second part a comparative analysis of 30 studies focusing on diverse issues integrated in PMT education programmes. Finally, I make connections between the problems outlined in the chapter and the solutions discussed in the observed studies. The argument presented in the chapter is that even though many solutions are suggested and proven to be effective in solving some of the outlined problems, we are still lack of evidence that those solutions are ample for preparing PMTs to become members of the communities of practice they join. I suggest that combining the various solutions proposed for the education of teams of teachers in various studies is necessary in order to prepare PMTs to be effective mathematics teachers.

PROBLEMS IN THE EDUCATION OF PMTS

This chapter is based on *two main positions*: first, teaching is a *complex system* that includes interrelated and mutually dependent elements such as teachers, students, curriculum, textbooks, school management, students' families, local settings, and other factors that effect classroom procedures; second, teaching is a *cultural activity*, reflected in knowledge and beliefs that guide behaviour and determine the expectations of the participants. The chapter also assumes that prospective teachers should be prepared to teach in ways that would allow students to fulfil their learning potential, and that the mathematical challenge is an irreducible element of mathematics education. Based on these assumptions and on the analysis of the research literature, I outline *four interrelated problematic issues* in the education of prospective mathematics teachers.

K. Krainer and T. Wood (eds.), Participants in Mathematics Teacher Education, 63–88.

The Importance of Challenging Mathematics and PMTs' Limited Experience in Challenging Mathematics

The learners' intellectual potential is a multivariable function of ability, motivation, belief, and learning experiences (National Council of Teachers of Mathematics, 1995). Principles of "developing education" (Davydov, 1996), which integrate Vygotsky's (1978) notion of ZPD (Zone of Proximal Development) and Leontiev's (1983) theory of activity, claim that to fulfil the learners' mathematical potential the leaning environment must involve *challenging mathematics*. A mathematical challenge is an interesting mathematical difficulty that a person can overcome (Leikin, 2007). Mathematical challenge is subjective because it depends on the learner's potential.

The importance of the mathematical challenge and its student-dependence in teaching and learning is reflected in Jaworski's *Teaching Triad* that synthesizes three core elements: the management of learning, sensitivity to students, and mathematical challenge (Jaworski, 1992, 1994). Brousseau (1997), in his Theory of Didactical Situation, claimed that one of the central responsibilities of a teacher is devolution of good (challenging) tasks to learners. Both the teaching triad and the theory of didactical situation stress that teachers ought to provide each and every student with learning opportunities that fit their abilities and motivate their learning.

Mathematical challenges may appear in different forms in mathematics classrooms. These can be *proof tasks* where solvers must find a proof, *definition tasks* in which learners are required to define concepts, or *investigation tasks*. One way of helping teachers to use challenging mathematics in their classes is to provide them with appropriate learning material (e.g., a textbook), making a large number of challenging tasks available to them (Barbeau & Talor, 2005); but merely providing teachers with ready-to-use challenging mathematics activities is not sufficient for their implementation: teachers should be aware of the importance of mathematical challenges and convinced about them, and they should feel safe (mathematically and pedagogically) when dealing with this type of mathematics (Holton et al., in press). Furthermore, teachers should have autonomy in employing this type of mathematics in their classes (Krainer, 2001; Jaworski & Gellert, 2003). They should be able to choose mathematical tasks themselves create those tasks, change them so that they become challenging and stimulating, and naturally they must be able to solve these problems.

But despite the importance of teacher awareness of the role of mathematical challenge in teaching and learning, prospective teachers often have *limited experience* in challenging mathematics, and sometimes have strong negative feelings about it (Gellert, 1998, 2000). In other cases, PMTs find challenging mathematical activities interesting and encouraging, but are not sure whether these activities are applicable to students. These views are connected to novice teachers' inclinations to rely on their procedural understanding of mathematics when making pedagogical decisions about mathematical challenges (Borko et al., 1992) or when planning or discussing their ideas for teaching (Berenson et al., 1997). Many PMTs encounter difficulties in coping with challenging mathematics themselves, and their beliefs about the nature of mathematical tasks contradict the character of the tasks they are asked to solve (Cooney & Wiegel, 2003).

Changing Approaches to Mathematics Teaching and the Resistance to Change in Teaching

The beginning of the 21st century is full of ever better and more advanced technological tools. In a changing world, invention and progress can be anticipated and developed only by human beings with rich imagination, deep and broad knowledge, and solid proficiency. In a changing world, learning and teaching environments, informational resources, interpersonal communications, and the roles of teachers and students in the classroom adapt constantly to the latest modifications. Mathematics education is a typical example of a subject that experiences ongoing, multifaceted change, manifest in the shift toward the dynamic and investigative nature of mathematical tasks, toward multiple uses of technological tools for teaching and learning, and toward the dialogic learning environment (Lagrange, Artigue, Laborde, & Trouche, 2003).

Inquiry and experimentation are basic characteristics of the development of mathematics, science, and technology. Inquiry (experimentation) tasks in mathematics classrooms are usually challenging, cognitively demanding, and enable highly motivated work by students (e.g., Yerushalmy, Chazan, & Gordon, 1990). Borba and Villarreal (2005, pp. 75–76) stressed that the "experimentation approach gains more power with the use of technological tools" by providing learners with the opportunity to propose and test conjectures using multiple examples, obtain quick feedback, use multiple representations, and become involved in the modelling process.

Educational technologies such as computers and graphic calculators can be viewed as cultural tools that reorganize cognitive processes and transform social practices in the classroom (Borba & Villarreal, 2005; Goos, 2005). These tools can provide a vehicle for incorporating new teaching roles ranging from the authoritative "master" to the collaborative "partner" (Goos, Galbraith, Renshaw, & Geiger, 2003) and influence the mathematics curriculum (Wong, 2003).

As approaches to teaching and learning mathematics change, the nature of mathematical discourse and socio-mathematical norms changes as well (e.g., Cobb & Bauersfeld, 1995; Wood, 1998; Wells, 1999). The shift toward the dialogic nature of learning is grounded mainly in Vygotsky's (1978) theory of meaning making as the result of the learners' communicative experiences. This approach to learning and teaching is based on theories that go beyond cognitive views of learning (e.g., Brousseau, 1997; Cobb & Bauersfeld, 1995; Jaworski, 1994; Lave & Wenger, 1991; Steinbring, 1998; Wells, 1999). In this context, teaching can be considered as a spiral process that facilitates the students' autonomous learning and includes planning of learning opportunities for students, presenting challenging tasks, monitoring the students' handling of the tasks, and reflecting on learning and teaching.

As a complex system, teaching is stable and resistant to change (Cogan & Schmidt, 1999). As a result, changing approaches to school teaching are beset by many pitfalls and difficulties (e.g., Lampert & Ball, 1999; Tirosh & Graeber, 2003). As is true with any cultural activity, teaching is learned through participation in activities involving learning and teaching (Stigler & Hiebert, 1998). In part, future teachers learned to teach when they were prospective teachers with certain perspectives on teaching and learning. When they are challenged by new teaching approaches, PMTs are often unenthusiastic and reluctant to adopt new practices and express preferences for the teaching methods used by their own teachers (Cooney, Shealy, & Arvold, 1998; Hiebert, 1986; Lampert & Ball, 1999). Education programmes have a special role in supporting educational reform by developing teachers' knowledge and beliefs (Llinares & Krainer, 2006).

The Need to Intermingle the Different Components of Teachers' Knowledge in Teacher Education

Teachers' knowledge and beliefs determine their decision making at all stages of teaching (Ball & Cohen, 1999; Cooney, et al., 1998; Even & Tirosh, 1995; Shulman, 1986; Thompson, 1992). The complexity of teachers' knowledge within the context of the complexity of teaching itself is one of the main problems in the education of PMTs (Llinares & Krainer, 2006). To demonstrate this complexity, I use a 3D model of teacher knowledge (Leikin, 2006) that combines three main perspectives adopted by researchers in discussing teachers' knowledge: *kinds of knowledge* (Shulman, 1986), *conditions of knowledge* (Scheffler, 1965), and *sources of knowledge* (Kennedy, 2002).

From the perspective of the *kinds of teacher knowledge* (Shulman, 1986), teachers' subject-matter knowledge (SMK) comprises the PMTs' own knowledge of mathematics and of the philosophy and history of mathematics. Teachers' pedagogical content knowledge (PCK) includes knowledge of how students cope with mathematics and knowledge of the appropriate learning setting. Ball and Cohen (1999) discussed "mathematics knowledge for teaching" that allows teachers to unpack their SMK in order to develop deep and robust mathematical knowledge in students. Teachers' curricular content knowledge (CCK) includes knowledge of different types of curricula and understanding the different approaches to teaching. Under conditions of changing approaches to school mathematics, this type of knowledge can endow teachers with flexibility in shifting among various curricular approaches.

Kennedy (2002) classified teachers' knowledge according to the *sources of knowledge development*. *Systematic knowledge*, she argued, is acquired first through personal experiences as school students, then through participation in courses for teachers, reading professional literature, and interacting with colleagues. *Prescriptive knowledge* is acquired through institutional policies and is manifest in tests, accountability systems, and texts of a diverse nature. In contrast, *craft knowledge* is developed largely through experience. This type of knowledge relates to teachers as members in a community of practitioners, and is based mainly on teachers' interactions with their students and on teachers' reflections on these interactions.

The distinction between knowledge and beliefs as *conditions of teacher knowledge* started with Scheffler (1965) and has been presented in the works of mathematics education researchers (e.g., Thompson, 1992; Cooney et al., 1998). Knowledge has operational power whereas beliefs are of propositional nature solely. An individual has proofs for the facts that belong to his/her knowledge, whereas beliefs are accepted without proof. The additional distinction between formal and intuitive knowledge is consistent with the views of Atkinson and Claxton (2000), who discussed teachers as *intuitive practitioners*, and differentiated between teachers' intuitive knowledge as determining actions that cannot be premeditated and their formal knowledge, which has to do mostly with planned teacher actions.

Professional development programmes must be consistent with the complex structure of teacher knowledge. The complexity of professional development programmes lies in searching for a reasonable balance between mathematics and pedagogy and in connecting between them (Peressini, Borko, Romagnano, Knuth, & Wills, 2004). The balance between systematic and craft modes of development is also important because if teachers develop their own mathematical understanding in a systematic mode, only practice can persuade them that implementation of this type of mathematics in the classroom is valid (Leikin & Levav-Waynberg, 2007). Because PMTs lack experience as teachers, pedagogical and craft knowledge are among the most challenging issues in the professional development of prospective mathematics teachers.

The Difficulty of Becoming a Member of a Community of Practice

From the social perspective, teachers are considered to be *members of communities of practice* characterized by common norms, routines, sensibilities, artefacts, and a vocabulary that are the result of the situated nature of the teachers' practice (Lave, 1996; Lave & Wenger, 1991). This practice is embedded in a cultural enterprise that is also a complex system of the beliefs about society, educational policies, curricular requirements, assessments, and the school environment (e.g., Stigler & Hiebert, 1999). Teachers' understanding of mathematics and pedagogy within the community of practice is bounded by socially constructed webs of beliefs that determine the teachers' perception of what needs to be done (Roth, 1991; Brown, Collins, & Duguid, 1989).

The community of mathematics teachers is usually regarded as one of learners who *continually reflect on their work* and make sense of their history, practice, and other experiences (Lave & Wenger, 1991). In other words, teacher knowledge develops socially within communities of practice, and in turn determines these practices. The situation of PMTs is very different from that of practising teachers. When PMTs begin their studies, they are (in the best case) *members of a team*. Krainer (2003) maintains that

"Teams" (and project groups) are mostly selected by the management, have pre-determined goals and therefore rather tight and formal connections within the team. [In contrast,] "communities" are regarded as self selecting, their members negotiating goals and tasks. People participate because they personally identify with the topic. (p. 95)

PMTs may find that they are simultaneously *members of different teams* in the different courses they attend. One of the purposes of educational programmes is to develop the norms, routines, sensibilities, artefacts, and vocabulary that will help PMTs join their future professional communities. But PMTs rarely emerge from their mathematics teacher preparation programme as members of these communities. Moreover, they realize that many teachers work more or less individually, some of them collaborate because the department or school challenges them to do so; in general, it is rather rare, that teachers really take part or form self-selected communities of practice. Furthermore, when starting their teaching in a school in which a group of mathematics teachers abide by different norms than the ones taught and learned in the programme, they often return to their point of departure (e.g., Peressini et al., 2004). PMTs should be prepared for integration into the collectives they join – especially into those that adopt ideas contrary to those stressed in their teacher education programme. As newcomers they must take an active part in advancing those groups towards communities, prompting innovations, making communities creative and adapting to changes in society and culture.

In sum, preparatory programmes for PMTs must answer various complex and sometimes contradictory questions. They should be aimed at developing new generations of teachers ready to teach new generations of students in a changing world. They must develop the PMTs' mathematical understanding to enable them to approach challenging mathematical tasks successfully, design tasks creatively, and be flexible in the implementation of the tasks in their classes. Teacher programmes should prepare PMTs to teach in ways that are different from those in which they learned as students. They need to prepare PMTs to be effective, confident, and creative users of new educational approaches, rich in technological tools (Goos, 2005). PMTs should become acquainted with approaches useful for studying their own teaching practice as well as that of others, and in analysing the effects of teaching on learning. They must aim at generating enthusiasm, intuitions, and beliefs about the introduction of challenging mathematics in school in the form of reform-oriented pedagogy.

DIVERSITY OF SOLUTIONS SUGGESTED BY RESEARCH ON PMT EDUCATION

MTEs offer a wide range of courses and programmes for the professional development of PMTs, aimed at solving the problems described above. Corresponding research on knowledge, beliefs, and the education of PMTs is characterized by the diversity of focal points, types of knowledge involved, level of mathematics addressed, and the research tools used in the investigations. In this subchapter, I present a review of 30 studies exploring the education of PMTs'. The choice of the studies was based on the two main issues: (1) the studies focused on the education of *prospective teachers as members of teams*, (2) they analysed development of teachers' knowledge, skills or beliefs rather then examined their knowledge as a in its present condition. The selected papers were published between 1998 and 2007 in *Educational Studies in Mathematics* (ESM), the *Journal of Mathematical Behavior* (JMB), and the *Journal of Mathematics Teacher Education* (JMTE). Table 1 summarizes the following characteristics of the 30 papers:

- *Type of knowledge* (skills, beliefs): The distinction was mainly between research focused on SMK and PCK.
- *Level of PMT participants*: This column addresses teachers in elementary school, secondary school, and other populations involved in the studies. At times, the relation between these characteristics is apparent. For example, in the first category, studies focusing on SMK were conducted with secondary school PMTs, whereas studies focusing on PCK involved primary school PMTs.
- *Number of participants*: most of the studies were performed with one group of PMTs who participated in a specific course; several were case studies reporting on a small number of participants; and some involved a large number of PMTs who completed a research questionnaire. Note that studies based on a small number of participants (N=1, 2, 3) were included in the review because the selected PMTs were representatives of teams.
- *The setting in which the study was performed*: for example, mathematics course (MC), didactic course (DC), or teaching practicum (TP). This column also includes information about the "mathematics of change" in a computer-based environment.
- *Research tools*: for example, individual interviews, examples from video- and audio-recordings, artefacts of the students' activities, individual journals, and written questionnaires.
- *Focal issues of the research*: these characteristics are detailed further in this subchapter with respect to the findings of the studies under consideration.

Note, that some of the authors did not report all these characteristics, which accounts for empty cells in the table.

The studies are divided into several categories with respect to the roles PMTs play in the research interventions and the balance between systematic and craft modes of development implemented in the courses. The categories are not mutually exclusive, and some studies can belong to more than one category. Moreover, other categorizations are possible (e.g., Cooney & Wiegel, 2003; Jaworski & Gellert, 2003), but the focus of the present analysis is on the balance between *mathematics* and *pedagogy* on one hand, and between *systematic* and *craft modes of learning* on the other.

Table 1

Development through Personal Experiences as Learners

Applying context-based approaches to course design (CD)

Article	Journal	Type of knowledge	PMT level	No. of PMTs	Setting	Research tools	Focus of the study
1. Cavey & Berenson (2005)	JMB	SMK PCK	secondary	1	LPS	Case study 1-Int	CD, growth in understanding right triangle trigonometry
2. Furinghetti (in press)	ESM	SMK PCK	secondary	15	DC designing learning sequences	I-Int Observation	CD, how history affects the construction of teaching sequences in algebra
3. Heaton & Mickelson (2002)	JMTE	SMK PCK	primary	44	MC statistics	I-Int Observation	CD, statistical knowledge, views on teaching statistics, project-based learning
4. Lavy & Bershadsky (2003)	JMB	SMK	secondary	28	DC (2 lessons)	I-Int Observation (protocols)	Types of participant-generated problems, mathematical difficulties
5. Nicol (2002)	ESM	SMK PCK	primary	22	Connect SMK and work place	G-int, I-Int PMT journals Researcher field notes	CD, style of teaching, changing PMTs' belief that they must reproduce the style of mathematics teaching seen in their school days
6. Philippou & Christou (1998)	ESM	SMK PCK	primary	427	DC history	Questionnaire 1- Int	CD, identifying and changing PMT attitudes and beliefs about math
7. Taplin & Chan (2001)	JMTE	SMK PCK	primary	28	DC problem-based learning	Group discussion Journals	CD, student attitudes toward problem-based learning and critical pedagogical incidents

Article	Journal	Type of knowledge	PMT level	No. of PMTs	Setting	Research tools	Focus of the study
8. Wubbels, Korthagen, & Broekman (1997)	ESM	SMK PCK	secondary	18	DC realistic math	Longitudinal study comparing two courses Quest, I-Int, video	CD, student and teacher views of mathematics and mathematics education, more inquiry oriented approach
9. Zbiek & Conner (2006)	ESM	SMK PCK	primary	17	MC modelling	I-Int, video, audio, artifacts	CD, how mathematical understandings can develop while learners engage in modelling tasks
Socio-mathematical norms and psychological processes							
10. Blanton (2002)	JMTE	SMK PCK	secondary	11	MC geometry discourse	Observation, video	CD, notions about mathematical discourse
11. McNeal & Simon (2000)	JMB	SMK PCK	primary	26	MC constructivist TE	Observation, video	Mathematical and pedagogical development, processes of negotiation of norms and practices
12. Szydlik, Szydlik, & Benson (2003)	JMTE	PCK	primary	177	MC norms	Survey I-Int	Beliefs about the nature of mathematical behaviour
13. Tsamir (2005)	JMTE	PCK SMK	second	38	DC - intuitive rules	Lessons, video, audio	CD, awareness of the role of intuitive rules, learning math
14. Tsamir (2007)	ESM	PCK SMK	second	32	DC - intuitive rules	Lessons, video, audio	CD, awareness of the role of intuitive rules, learning math
15. Ponte, Oliveira, & Varandas (2002).	JMTE	Professional knowledge and identity	Attitude test of use of information technology	160	DC - Internet and DGE	Observation, reflective discussions	CD, awareness of the role of intuitive rules, learning math

Focusing on the Teaching Process

Using multimedia cases (MCA)

Article	Journal	Type of knowledge	PMT level	No. of PMTs	Setting	Research tools	Focus of the study
16. Doerr & Thomson (2004)	JMTE	PCK	Secondary PMTs T-educators	28 4	DC MCA	Questionnaire, I-Int observation, field notes	CD, use of cases, teacher educators' decisions
17. Masingila & Doerr (2002)	JMTE	PCK			DC after TP	Class observation, student notes, final paper, questionnaire instructor journals, researcher field notes	MCA for using students' thinking in guiding classroom experience
18. McGraw, Lynch, Koc, Budak, & Brown (2007)	JMTE	PCK	Secondary PMTs Practising Teachers Mathematicians Teacher educators	8 5 4 4	LS MCA	Observation, videos transcripts of dialogs, semi-structured interview	Online and face-to-face discussions, classroom implementation of tasks, task characteristics and appropriateness, developing content, and pedagogical content knowledge
19. Morris (2006)	JMTE	PCK	primary	30	Individual work sessions videotaped lessons	Written analysis of lesson, student learning, source of problem	Ability to collect evidence about students' learning, ability to analyse and revise instruction
20. Santagata, Zannoni, & Stigler (2007)	JMTE	PCK	secondary	144	DC (videotaped lessons)	Pre/post-assessment	What do PMTs learn from the analysis of videotaped lessons? How to measure PMTs' analysis ability and its improvement

Teaching individual students (TIP)

Article	Journal	Type of knowledge	PMT level	No. of PMTs	Setting	Research tools	Focus of the study
21. Ambrose (2004)	JMTE	SMK PCK	primary	15	MC - TIP	Surveys, I-int: pre/post, written work, field notes	Changes in beliefs and skills
22. Bowers & Doerr (2001)	JMTE	SMK PCK	secondary	26	MC - TIP Math worlds software	Participant works, written reflections on teaching, daily journals (AHA! Insights)	Thinking: as learners (about math with computers); as teachers about students' thinking
23. Crespo (2000)	JMTE	PCK	primary		DC - Letter exchange with 4th grade students	Journals: reflection on activities, case reports	(Changes in) learning about students' thinking, interpretive practices
24. Lee (2005)	JMTE	PCK	second	3	DC - TIP teaching math with technology	Videos, written works (PMTs' and students')	Teacher's role in facilitating students' math problem solving with technological tool

Teaching practicum (TP)

Article	Journal	Type of knowledge	PMT level	No. of PMTs	Setting	Research tools	Focus of the study
25. Blanton, Berenson, & Norwood (2001)	JMTE	PCK TE	middle school	1	TP	Case study, observation, episode-based interviews, journals	Supervision in teacher education
26. Goos (2005)	JMTE	PCK skills	secondary	4 of 18	TP	Survey, whole-class interviews, 4 case studies	Working with technology
27. Nicol (1999)	ESM	PCK	primary	14 of 34	MC - TP	Course video, PMT journals, TE journals	Learning to teach (what appears to be problematic)
28. Nicol & Crespo (2006)	ESM	PCK use of textbooks	primary	4 of 33	MC - TP	I-Int, pre, med, post, course work, class observation	Learning to teach (use of textbooks and teaching)
29. Rowland, Huckstep, & Thwaites (2005)	JMTE	SMK PCK	primary	12	TP	24 videotaped lessons	Contribution of knowledge to teaching
30. Walshaw (2004)	JMTE	PCK, skills	primary	72	TP	Questionnaire about recent teaching practice experience, discussion	Instances of teaching knowledge in production, as interpreted by prospective teachers

Development through Personal Experiences as Learners

These studies examined the education of PMTs through *personal learning experiences* and reflection on those experiences. These studies assumed that PMTs should be involved in authentic mathematical activities in order to develop SMK and PCK, to advance the understanding of constructivist socio-mathematical norms, of the uses of technology in mathematics education, and of awareness of psychological issues in the teaching and learning of mathematics. Studies in this category analysed PMT development through participation in mathematical, didactic, or psychological courses that integrated different approaches to teaching and learning mathematics. Courses in this category can be subdivided into two groups: applying context-based approaches to course design and focusing socio-mathematical norms and psychological processes.

Applying context-based approaches to course design. Based on the assumption that PMTs need a context that would allow them to look in a different way at the topics they will be teaching, the studies in this group suggest a *context-based course design.* Most of the studies were carried out within the framework of didactics of mathematics courses. Among the contexts that were proposed for the course design, we find the history of mathematics (Furinghetti, in press; Philippou & Christou, 1998), project-based learning within a statistical context (Heaton & Mickelson, 2002), realistic mathematics (Wubbels, Korthagen, & Broekman, 1997), mathematical modelling (Zbiek & Conner, 2006), right triangle trigonometry (Cavey & Berenson, 2005), mathematics in a workplace (Nicol, 2002), and problem-based learning (Taplin & Chan, 2001).

These studies demonstrated that a context-based design of courses for PMTs was effective when using content previously unknown to the PMTs. For example, in Zbiek and Conner's study the objectives of the course included both learning mathematical modelling and learning to develop and implement application problems and mathematical modelling tasks in future classrooms. They found that the course opened opportunities for PMTs to grow as "knowers and doers" of curricular mathematics. Furinghetti analysed how history affected the construction of teaching sequences in algebra based on activities carried out at the "Laboratory of Mathematics Education". The aim of the course was to equip PMTs with understanding of the cognitive roots of the concepts and processes that their future students were going to encounter in algebra. The study showed that the integration of history in school mathematics inspired variability in strategies of teaching, and that the fact that students had not had specific preparation in the history of mathematics opened diverse opportunities for the development of prospective teachers' SMK and PCK.

Overall, these studies demonstrated that as a result of systematic implementation of the suggested context-based approaches in the courses for teams of prospective teachers the changes that took place in the PMTs' knowledge and beliefs occurred both in the field of mathematics and pedagogy. At the same time, these studies did not ask whether these learning experiences were powerful enough to equip PMTs with norms that will help PMTs join their future professional communities.

Socio-mathematical norms and psychological processes. The studies in this group acknowledged the importance of involving PMTs in authentic activities focusing particular socio-mathematical norms. The motivation of these studies was to design undergraduate experiences organized around reform-minded ways of teaching in order to close the gap between reform-oriented mathematics and the PMTs previous mathematical experiences and conceptions about mathematics and the teaching of mathematics. Two main modes of course design can be observed here. The first one – a *mathematical mode* – in which PMTs' learning through challenging mathematical experiences leads to the development of both SMK and PCK (e.g., Blanton, 2002; McNeal & Simon, 2000). The second one – *a didactic mode* – in which MTEs emphasize changes in approaches to teaching mathematics, leading to the development of both PCK and SMK through PMTs' experiences with innovative pedagogy (Szydlik, Szydlik, & Benson, 2002).

The results of these studies show that changes in socio-mathematical norms in PMTs' courses influence their conceptions of mathematics teaching. Blanton (2002) showed that the undergraduate mathematics classroom offers a powerful framework for PMTs to practice, articulate, and collectively reflect on reform-minded ways of teaching. The study demonstrated that participants construct an image of discourse as an active collective process by which students build mathematical understanding and develop their ability to participate in such discourse. McNeal and Simon (2000) noted that, in the beginning, most prospective teachers were uncomfortable with the mathematics of the course both as learners and as future teachers. They argued that the constitution of a classroom micro-culture supports knowledge development and demonstrated how through participation in the course, students develop a new relationship with mathematics. Examining the processes by which PMTs negotiated norms and practices, the researchers identified and elaborated categories of interaction central to the ongoing negotiation of new norms and practises, and illustrated how each of these categories of interaction contributed to the process of negotiation. Szydlik, Szydlik, and Benson, (2002) found that participants' beliefs became more supportive of autonomous student behaviours. Participating PMTs attributed their changes in beliefs to classroom norms that included mathematical explorations, expanding problem-solving methods, and the requirement for explanation and argumentation. All these studies stressed once again that cognitive development requires a social context in which mathematical activities support such development (McNeal & Simon, 2000).

In contrast with the above studies, Tsamir's (2005, 2007) studies examined courses from a psychological perspective. Tsamir addressed the accumulating knowledge of secondary school PMTs in a course from the psychological point of view of mathematics education, explicitly including the intuitive rules theory.

Tsamir demonstrated that emphasis on the psychological processes involved in mathematics learning and teaching allowed advancing PMTs' knowledge of both SMK and PCK types.

The mutual relationships between mathematics and pedagogy (including the didactic and psychological aspects) appear clearly in the studies of this category. Regardless of whether PMTs participate in mathematical, didactic, or psychology courses, both SMK and PCK are developed at once. It may suggested that by attending to the two types of knowledge explicitly, MTEs can develop both PMTs' knowledge and their awareness of the importance of mathematical challenges and pedagogical approaches in teaching and learning mathematics.

As members of teams of PMTs' the participants of the observed studies advanced in their views on socio-mathematical norms, changed their attitudes towards "different mathematics" or "new pedagogy" and sometimes were shown to develop their mathematical expertise. Moreover, the learning teams when involved in challenging learning experiences transformed into communities of learners. Through the participation in "unusual" mathematical activities prospective teachers developed shared values, norms, routines, appreciation of the role of mathematical discussion for the development of mathematical understanding (e.g., Blanton, 2002; McNeal & Simon, 2000). Still, the question of PMTs' readiness to join their future communities of practice was not addressed. Additionally, Santagata, Zannoni, and Stigler (2007) found PMTs often found innovative teaching approaches to be too abstract and unrealistic (e.g., MTEs often hear PMTs saying: *"We learned the other way, and why do we need this?"* or *"These experiences are good for us as future teachers but not for our future students"*).

Thus, the content of the courses should be well connected to the classroom context in which PMTs are going to apply that knowledge. It is a common belief that in order to bridge the gap between the PMTs' previous experience and the desired outcome of their education, programmes for them must include field experiences where prospective teachers are exposed to the complexity of the classroom and to the reality of having to implement alternative approaches.

Focusing on the Teaching Process

Prospective mathematics teachers must be offered more authentic teaching-related experiences to prepare them for the complexity and challenges of the school context (e.g., Darling-Hammond, 1997). The studies in this category explored courses in which PMTs were involved in *analysing teaching processes*. Courses for PMTs vary in the way in which they enable PMTs to learn form experience, whether they are based on others' teaching experiences (exposure to examples of teaching) or on one's own: (a) using multimedia cases, (b) teaching individual students, or (c) making teaching practice an integral part of each educational programme for PMTs. The use of video cases may be considered a transition from pure learning of mathematics and pedagogy to learning from the teaching experiences of other teachers. These studies maintain that observation and systematic analysis of video cases and videotaped lessons are effective professional development tools. Another group of studies deals with the teaching of individual students and reflection on those experiences within a team and can be considered as an intermediate stage between systematic and craft modes of development. Although PMTs are not in a classroom, they interact with students and learn from these interactions. The last category is that of teaching practicum. These studies examine the PMTs' involvement in school teaching as individuals with sequencing discussion of the teaching experiences in a team. The authors analyse the process of learning to teach, supervision in the course of practicum, and the contribution of knowledge to teaching.

Using multimedia cases. Research on video cases continues earlier research that examined the use of text-based cases in teacher education (e.g., Barnett, 1991; Shulman, 1992; Stein, Smith, Henningsen, & Silver, 2000). The rationale for the implementation of video cases includes several considerations. First, it is difficult to find sufficient high-quality classrooms for placements; a careful choice of video cases can expose PMTs to good teaching. Second, video cases or complete videotaped lessons serve as a basis for group discussion, the development of shared norms, and reflective thinking on the students' mathematical thinking (see also Seago, this volume). Third, videotaped classroom episodes or whole-class procedures can develop PMTs' critical evaluation of classroom practice. Fourth, videos can be played repeatedly to enable a depth of reflection and analysis that are often impossible to achieve in live observations. Overall, the various uses of videos allow teacher education programmes to face the challenge of developing PMTs' conceptual understanding of how students understand subject matter and how it should be introduced to them (Hiebert, Gallimore, & Stigler, 2002).

Studies on the implementation of multimedia cases demonstrated the following outcomes: (1) PMTs were able to learn from video cases about students' learning, to analyse the effects of instruction, and to revise the initial instruction (McGraw et al., 2007); (2) providing ways to measure PMTs' ability to analyse video cases and the improvement of this ability along the course (Santagata, Zannoni, & Stigler, 2007); (3) characterizing ways in which video-cases are used by MTEs and the relationship between the PMTs' background and experiences and their uses of video cases (Doerr & Thomson, 2004); (4) demonstrating the potential of the case studies for developing PMTs' ability to analyse critically classroom episodes (Masingila & Doerr, 2002).

These studies showed that video cases have a positive effect on the development of PMTs' knowledge and skills and identified the complexity of diverse processes involved in this development. They stressed once again the complexity of noticing (in the sense of Mason, 2002) and the diversity of the focuses of attention: the mathematics of the tasks, the interaction between teacher and students, and the issues related to whole-class discussions (McGraw et al., 2007; Morris, 2006). The studies showed that PMTs analyse dilemmas and tensions revealed in teaching recorded in video-cases based on their own perspectives on teaching (Masingila & Doerr, 2002).

Overall, video-case studies may be seen as a preparatory stage in PMTs' experiences of analysing teaching practice. I suggest considering video-case courses as exemplifying an *experimental mode* of professional development. By analysing other teachers' craft experiences in laboratory conditions PMTs develop tools and skills for analysing their own teaching practice. The analysis of video-cases performed in systematic mode, under the guidance of MTEs, leads future teachers to important inferences about the nature of teacher-student interactions and their role in the students' knowledge development. These experiences evolved PMTs' understanding of the complexity of teaching. As members of teams, through analysis of the video-cases, PMTs developed sensibilities and a vocabulary that should prepare them to future teaching practice, and help them to enter there future communities (e.g., Morris, 2006; Doerr & Thomson, 2004).

It should be noted that video-case studies analysed primarily the impact of the use of video-cases on PMTs' knowledge of pedagogy. In these studies, little attention has been paid to PMTs' learning of mathematics. Additionally, the question of whether in their personal teaching interactions with students PMTs will be able to use the knowledge and skills advanced through the analysis of video-cases remains open until PMTs experience the teaching settings in person.

Teaching individual students. As an intermediate stage between video-cases and teaching practicum, mathematics educators incorporate the teaching of individual students, complemented by reflective analysis of their experiences within teams. A diversity of focal issues appears in this group of studies. For example, Bowers and Doerr (2001) and Lee (2005) analysed secondary PMTs' thinking about the "mathematics of change" in a computer-based environment, working individually with young children. Crespo (2000) explored PMTs' learning about student thinking by analysing their interpretations of the students' works by PMTs engaged in interactive mathematics letter exchanges with fourth-grade students.

A variety of findings associated with learning through teaching individual students have been reported. PMTs were surprised to find mathematics teaching to be more difficult than they had thought, and inferred that providing children with time to think when solving mathematical problems was an irreducible component of teaching (Ambrose, 2004). PMTs' foci of attention changed as their roles changed: as students they were curious about reconceptualising the mathematical theorem they learned, whereas as teachers they built on their students' explanations and on the role of the technological tools (Bowers & Doerr, 2001). PMTs tended to use their problem-solving approaches in their pedagogical decisions: they asked questions that would guide students to their own solution strategies; recognized their struggle in facilitating students' problem solving, and focused on improving their interactions with students. PMTs used technological representations to promote students' mathematical thinking, and used technological tools in ways consistent with the nature of their interactions with students (Lee, 2005). PMTs' interpretations of students' works developed in the course of their experiences: in the beginning, PMTs attended to the correctness of students' answers and later they focused on meaning; they started from quick and conclusive evaluation and shifted to a more complex, thoughtful, and tentative approach.

Overall, the studies that analysed PMTs' teaching experiences with individual students demonstrated advance in PMTs' understanding of the teaching process. Instructing individual students helped break the well-known *conviction loop*: to implement new pedagogical approaches, teachers must be convinced of the suitability of those approaches in their work with students and, at the same time, to be convinced of the suitability of those approaches they have to implement them in school. Experiencing teaching with individual students allowed PMTs to feel more confident and to gain those convincing experiences. By discussing these experiences with their team-mates, PMTs realized they all had common difficulties, surprises, unexpected events and satisfaction. Did PMTs, only when teaching, begin to understand that teaching was complex and required different levels of attention? Only in craft mode PMTs started feeling what it meant to be flexible in teaching and sensitive to the students. The role of teams in these courses was to enhance PMT's reflective skills, to provide them with mutual support, and sharpen their critical reasoning.

Teaching practicum. Teaching practicum is one of the professional development settings that enable PMTs to make the connection between learning and teaching, but requires negotiation between the school and the college or university culture. Practicum is a course in which the knowledge of content and pedagogy learned in systematic mode is implemented, and craft knowledge is developed almost for the first time in the PMTs' professional career. The teachers find themselves teaching individually school students and then discussing those experiences with supervisors or team-mates. I suggest that courses of this type are representative of another mode of professional development: implementation mode.

Several studies performed in the last decade analysed the effects and characteristics of diverse components of teaching practicum on the professional development of PMTs. These studies explored the role of university supervision (Blanton, Berenson, & Norwood, 2001); pedagogical practices and beliefs about integrating technology into the teaching of mathematics (Goos, 2005); ways in which PMTs employ their knowledge of mathematics and pedagogy in their teaching (Rowland et al., 2005); issues that PMTs find problematic in teaching mathematics and changes in the types of questions PMTs ask students (Nicol, 1999); and the use of textbooks in learning to teach mathematics (Nicol & Crespo, 2006). Nicol (1999) showed that PMTs – as a result of experiences gained in practicum – began to consider students' thinking and to create spaces for inquiry through the types of questions they posed. PMTs also began to see and hear possibilities for mathematical exploration that evolved as their relationship with mathematics and students changed. Nicol and Crespo (2006) showed that PMTs' attempts to modify textbook lessons posed pedagogical, curricular, and mathematical questions that were not easily answered by reference to textbooks or teacher's guides. Findings indicated that practicum could challenge prospective teachers to be creative and flexible users of curriculum materials.

In this group, we also find studies that constructed theoretical models and tools (e.g., Goos, 2005; Rowland et al., 2005). Goos (2005) theorized PMTs' learning using the notions of Zone of Proximal Development (ZPD), Zone of Free Movement (ZFM, possible teaching actions), and Zone of Promoted Action (ZPA, the efforts of a teacher educator that are needed to promote particular teaching skills or approaches). Using these concepts and the mutual relationships between them, Goos demonstrated a variety of relationships between a range of personal and contextual factors that influence the formation of the PMTs' identity as teachers.

The study by Rowland et al. (2005) proposed a set of four units as a framework for lesson observation and mathematics teaching development. The four units were: foundation, transformation, connection, and contingency. *Foundation* refers to teachers' awareness of purpose, the theoretical underpinning of learning and pedagogy, and the use of various tools. *Transformation* refers to knowledge-in-action as revealed in manner in which the teacher's own meanings are transformed to enable students to learn, including the use of analogies and examples. The teachers perform *connections* between different meanings and descriptions of particular concepts or between alternative ways of representing concepts and carrying out procedures. *Contingency* is revealed by the ability of the teacher to respond appropriately to contributions by students during a teaching episode.

Overall, the studies on teaching practicum involved various issues and participants in the process of learning-to-teach. The studies analysed primarily PMT's pedagogical skills and beliefs, including their understanding of students (and their errors), teaching with technological tools, and the use of textbooks. Note that these studies paid little attention to the development of SMK in the process of teaching or to the extent to which PMTs implemented in practice the material that had been studied in systematic mode. The role of the teams in the teaching practicum courses was especially important for the development of PMTs' reflective and analytical skills (e.g., Nicol, 1999). The prospective teachers when discussing their teaching experiences were exposed to the variety of views on teaching profession, could reify their own position, learn from own and others' "mistakes". Teaching practicum got PMTs closer to the communities of practice that they would join in near future.

THE DIVERSITY OF SOLUTIONS AND QUESTIONS THAT REMAIN OPEN

MTEs face inherent *dilemmas* and *challenges* when preparing teachers for work in classrooms. The studies described above demonstrated the *diversity of solutions* that MTEs use in order to solve various issues in teacher education and to support prospective mathematics teachers' conceptual changes. In a majority of the studies under consideration, these solutions took the form of various professional development tools that MTEs integrated in the courses designed for PMTs. Their effectiveness was shown by analysing changes in PMTs' knowledge, beliefs, and attitudes. Other studies designed theoretical models and tools that may be effective in analysing and describing changes in teachers' knowledge and beliefs. In this subchapter, I return to the problems highlighted in the first subchapter and outline further research questions associated with the education of PMTs.

Attending to the Centrality of the Mathematical Challenge

Most of the studies that examined PMTs' development through their personal learning experiences included mathematical challenge among those experiences (e.g., McNeal & Simon, 2000; Taplin & Chan, 2001; Zbiek & Conner, 2006). Little attention has been paid, however, to the concept of mathematical challenge itself, although this meta-mathematical awareness is complex and crucial for the ability to design and analyse a lesson effectively (e.g., Holton et al., in press). I suggest that the notion of "mathematical challenge" as a meta-mathematical and psychological concept may serve as a springboard for the development of PMTs' knowledge and beliefs. The following questions are important for advancing their beliefs in the importance of the mathematical challenge:

What are the PMTs' conceptions of the mathematical challenge and its role in teaching and learning mathematics? How can programmes for teams of PMTs foster these conceptions so that PMTs would be eager to implement them in their future practice? How can these programmes promote PMT's expertise in solving challenging mathematical tasks and their capability of choosing and designing those tasks for teaching?

Attending to Changing Approaches in Mathematics Teaching and Learning

PMTs' mathematical knowledge and beliefs about mathematics and about teaching mathematics are influenced significantly by their experiences in learning mathematics long before they decided to become teachers (Cooney et al., 1998). PMTs bring these experiences to their teacher education programmes in the form of conceptions, and are expected to make changes in their views of mathematics and pedagogy. I suggest that the ideas of conceptual change theory found in science education (Posner, Strike, Hewson, & Gertzog, 1982) may be useful in addressing this issue. Conceptual change acknowledges the importance of prior knowledge to learning and considers both the enrichment of existing cognitive structures and their substantial reorganization (Schnotz, Vosniadou, & Carretero, 1999). Such reorganization is conceptualised as being motivated by *dissatisfaction* with the initial conception and by the *intelligibility, plausibility,* and *fruitfulness* of the new conception (Posner et al., 1982). When teaching PMTs about learning alternative approaches to teaching mathematics, MTEs must reconceptualise their initial views on teaching and learning.

Most of the studies reviewed in this chapter showed the effectiveness of integrating alternative approaches to mathematics teaching and learning within courses or programmes for PMTs. They argued that that programmes focused on alternative approaches to teaching and learning mathematics must require from

PMTs to experiment with these approaches with their students (Hiebert, Morris, & Glass, 2003), and to analyse and discuss these experiments (e.g., Bowers & Doerr, 2001; Crespo, 2000; Lee, 2005; Goos, 2005; Nicol, 1999). But in order to be able to experiment the alternative approaches, PMTs must encounter conceptual change in the field of pedagogy or of mathematics. Thus, beyond what has been achieved already in the reviewed studies, the following questions can be raised to further analyse and strengthen PMTs' learning in the various university and college programmes:

What are the ways in which PMTs can achieve dissatisfaction with their initial conceptions of school mathematics and mathematics teaching? How can courses for teams of PMTs advance their perception of the new approaches as intelligible, plausible, and fruitful for teaching?

Attending to the Complexity of PMTs' Knowledge

Most of the studies described course design and examined its effectiveness. The courses differed in the balance between systematic modes of development (through learning) and craft modes (through teaching), between knowledge and beliefs, between mathematics and pedagogy. From this perspective, and together with the analysis of the research provided in the second subchapter, I suggest that there are *four main modes of professional development* that vary with respect to explicit versus implicit goals, the balance between mathematics and pedagogy, the role of challenging content, and the mechanisms of teachers' knowledge development. These are the *mathematical*, *pedagogical* (didactic or psychological), *experimental*, and *implementation modes*.

Combinations of different modes can be achieved by PMTs' participation in the courses belonging to different modes within a programme, or through the integration of different modes in one particular course for teachers. For example, such integration is present in studies that combine experimental and mathematical modes (Ambrose, 2004; Bowers & Doerr, 2001), mathematical and implementation modes (Nicol, 1999; Nicol & Crespo, 2006), or pedagogical and implementation modes (Masingila & Doerr, 2002). Balancing between craft and systematic modes is especially important: whereas systematic knowledge provides a stable base for the development of craft knowledge, only craft knowledge contains the necessary convictions and beliefs about the applicability of what has been learned systematically. The balance between systematic and craft modes can help solve the "conviction loop" (see above).

Answering the following questions would further advance the design of the programmes for the professional development of PMTs:

What combinations of systematic and craft modes of development are most effective in the courses for PMTs? What combinations of mathematics and pedagogy are the most effective in the preparation of PMTs? How can the different modes be integrated so that they support each other?

Becoming a Member of a Community of Practice

All the studies reviewed in this chapter explicitly or implicitly acknowledged the importance of integrating newcomers in the school system. Llinares and Krainer (2006) and Peressini et al. (2004) stressed that the process of recontextualization of what has been learned in teacher education programmes for prospective teachers into what will be taught in the classroom is extremely important. There is not enough evidence that the professional development of PMTs prepares them for such integration and recontextualization. And there is not enough evidence that PMTs who changed their views about approaches to mathematics teaching and learning will implement these approaches in their future classes.

When they first begin to teach school, teachers usually learn from more experienced teachers. At the same time, experienced teachers can learn from the newcomers how to change mathematics teaching and learning so that it fits better the new reality, new technologies, and the latest cultural artefacts and advances. It is unclear, however, to what extent future teachers are ready to be adaptive agents of these approaches. When beginning their teaching careers, new teachers grasp the conflict between systematic knowledge (constructed in the teacher education programme) and the prescriptive knowledge they develop within the school system. They usually find it hard to cope with the complexity of the system, and with the gap between what has been learned in teacher education and the reality of the school. Longitudinal studies that could answer the following question may further advance teacher education programmes:

What are the springboards and pitfalls in the transitions from systematic to experimental learning, from experimental learning to teaching practicum, and from teaching practicum to the real classroom? How, when educated in teams, PMTs may be prepared to become members of communities of practices?

Gaining a better understanding of the factors that promote and hamper the professional development of PMTs will support MTEs in their complex task of preparing their students for teaching careers at all grade levels.

REFERENCES

Ambrose, R. (2004). Initiating change in prospective elementary school teachers' orientation to mathematics teaching by building on beliefs. *Journal of Mathematics Teacher Education, 7*, 91–119.

Atkinson, T., & Claxton, G. (2000). *The intuitive practitioner: On the value of not always knowing what one is doing.* Buckingham, UK: The Open University Press.

Barbeau, E. J., & Taylor P. J. (2005). Challenging mathematics in and beyond the classroom. Discussion document of the ICMI Study 16. http://www.amt.edu.au/icmis16.html

Barnett, C. (1991). Building a case-based curriculum to enhance the pedagogical content knowledge of mathematics teachers. *Journal of Teacher Education, 42*, 263–272.

Berenson, S. B., Valk, T. V. D., Oldham, E., Runesson, U., Moreira, C. Q., & Broekman, H. (1997). An international study to investigate prospective teacher's content knowledge of the area concept. *European Journal of Teacher Education, 20*, 137–150.

Blanton, M. L. (2002). Using an undergraduate geometry course to challenge pre-service teachers' notions of Discourse. *Journal of Mathematics Teacher Education, 5*, 117–152.

Blanton, M. L., Berenson, S. B., & Norwood, K. B. (2001). Exploring a pedagogy for the supervision of prospective mathematics teachers. *Journal of Mathematics Teacher Education, 4*, 177–204.

Borba, M. C., & Villarreal, M. (2005). *Humans-with-Media and reorganization of mathematical thinking: Information and communication technologies, modeling, experimentation and visualization.* US: Springer.

Borko, H., Eisenhart, M., Brown, C. A., Underhill, R. G., Jones, D., & Agard, P. C. (1992). Learning to teach hard mathematics: Do novice teachers and their instructors give up too easily? *Journal for Research in Mathematics Education, 23*, 194–222.

Bowers, J., & Doerr, H. M. (2001). An analysis of prospective teachers' dual roles in understanding the mathematics of change: Eliciting growth with technology. *Journal of Mathematics Teacher Education, 4*, 115–137.

Brousseau, G. (1997). *Theory of didactical situations in mathematics.* Dordrecht, the Netherlands: Kluwer.

Brown, J. S., Collins, A., & Diguid, P. (1989). Situated cognition and the culture of learning. *Educational Researcher, 1*, 32–41.

Cavey, L. O., & Berenson, S. B. (2005). Learning to teach high school mathematics: Patterns of growth in understanding right triangle trigonometry during lesson plan study. *Journal of Mathematical Behavior, 24*, 171–190.

Cobb, P., & Bauersfeld, H. (1995). *The emergence of mathematical meaning: Interaction in classroom cultures.* Hillsdale, NJ: Erlbaum.

Cogan, L., & Schmidt, W. H. (1999). An examination of instructional practices in six countries. In G. Kaiser, E. Luna, & I. Huntley (Eds.), *International Comparison in Mathematics Education* (pp. 68–85). London, UK: Falmer.

Cooney, T. J. (1994). Teacher education as an exercise in adaptation. In D. B. Aichele & A. F. Coxford (Eds.), *Professional development for teachers of mathematics. 1994 Yearbook* (pp. 9–22). Reston, VA: National Council of Teachers of Mathematics.

Cooney, T. J., Shealy, B. E., & Arvold, B. (1998). Conceptualizing belief structures of preservice secondary mathematics teachers. *Journal for Research in Mathematics Education, 29*, 306–333.

Cooney, T., & Wiegel, H. (2003). Examining the mathematics in mathematics teacher education. In A. J. Bishop, M. A. Clements, D. Brunei, C. Keitel, J. Kilpatrick, F. K. S. Leung (Eds.), *The Second International Handbook of Mathematics Education* (pp. 795–828). Dordrecht, the Netherlands: Kluwer.

Crespo, S. (2000). Seeing more than right and wrong answers: Prospective teachers' interpretations of students' mathematics works. *Journal of Mathematics Teacher Education, 3*, 155–181.

Darling-Hammond, L. (1997). *Doing what matters most: Investing in quality teaching.* New York: National Commission on Teaching & America's Future.

Davydov, V. V. (1996). *Theory of developing education.* Moscow, Russia: Intor (in Russian).

Doerr, H. M., & Thomson, T. (2004). Understanding teacher educators and their pre-service teachers through multi-media case studies of practice. *Journal of Mathematics Teacher Education, 7*, 175–2001.

Even, R., & Tirosh, D. (1995). Subject-matter knowledge and knowledge about students as source of teacher presentations of the subject-matter. *Educational Studies in Mathematics, 29*, 1–20.

Furinghetti, F. (in press). Teacher education through the history of mathematics. *Educational Studies in Mathematics.*

Goos, M. (2005). A socio-cultural analysis of the development of pre-service and beginning teachers' pedagogical identities as users of technology. *Journal of Mathematics Teacher Education, 8*, 35–59.

Goos, M., Galbraith, P., Renshaw, P., & Geiger, V. (2003). Perspectives on technology- mediated learning in secondary school mathematics classrooms. *Journal of Mathematical Behavior, 22*, 73–89.

Heaton, R. M., & Mickelson, W. T. (2002). The learning and teaching of statistical investigation in teaching and teacher education. *Journal of Mathematics Teacher Education, 5*, 35-59.

Hiebert, J., Gallimore, R., & Stigler, J. W. (2002). A knowledge base for the teaching profession: What would it look like and how can we get one? *Educational Researcher, 31*, 3–15.

Hiebert, J., Morris, A. K., & Glass, B. (2003). Learning to learn to teach: An "experiment" model for teaching and teacher preparation in mathematics. *Journal of Mathematics Teacher Education, 6,* 201–222.

Holton, D., Cheung, K.-C., Kesianye, S., de Losada, M., Leikin, R., Makrides, G., Meissner, H., Sheffield, L., & Yeap, B. H. (in press). Teacher development and mathematical challenge. In E. J. Barbeau & P. J. Taylor (Eds.), *ICMI Study-15 Volume: Mathematical challenge in and beyond the classroom.*

Jaworski, B. (1992). Mathematics teaching: What is it? *For the Learning of Mathematics, 12,* 8–14.

Jaworski, B. (1994). *Investigating mathematics teaching: A constructivist enquiry.* London: Falmer.

Jaworski, B., & Gellert, U. (2003). Educating new mathematics teachers: Integrating theory and practice, and the roles of practicing teachers. In A. J. Bishop, M. A. Clements, D. Brunei, C. Keitel, J. Kilpatrick, F. K. S. Leung (Eds.), *The second international handbook of mathematics education* (pp. 829–875). Dordrecht, the Netherlands: Kluwer.

Kennedy, M. M. (2002). Knowledge and teaching. *Teacher and teaching: Theory and practice, 8,* 355–370.

Krainer, K. (2001). Teachers' growth is more than the growth of individual teachers: The case of Gisela. In F.-L. Lin & T. J. Cooney (Eds.), *Making sense of mathematics teacher education* (pp. 271–293). Dordrecht, the Netherlands: Kluwer.

Krainer, K. (2003). Teams, communities and networks (editorial). *Journal of Mathematics Teacher Education, 6,* 93–105.

Lagrange, J.-B., Artigue, M., Laborde, C., & Trouche, L. (2003). Technology and mathematics education: a multidimensional overview of recent research and innovation. In A. J. Bishop, M. A. Clements, D. Brunei, C. Keitel, J. Kilpatrick, F. K. S. Leung (Eds.), *The second international handbook of mathematics education* (pp. 237–269). Dordrecht, the Netherlands: Kluwer.

Lampert, M., & Ball, D. (1998). *Teaching, multimedia, and mathematics: Investigations of real practice. The practitioner inquiry series.* New York: Teachers College Press.

Lampert, M., & Ball, D. (1999). Aligning teacher education with contemporary K-12 reform visions. In L. Darling-Hammond & G. Sykes (Eds.), *Teaching as the learning profession. Handbook of policy and practice* (pp. 33–53). San Francisco: Jossey-Bass.

Lave, J., & Wenger, E. (1991). *Situated learning: Legitimate peripheral participation.* Cambridge, UK: Cambridge University Press.

Lavy, I., & Bershadsky, I. (2003). Problem posing via "what if not?" strategy in solid geometry – A case study. *Journal of Mathematical Behavior, 22,* 369–387.

Lee, H. S. (2005). Facilitating students' problem solving in a technological context: Prospective teachers' learning trajectory. *Journal of Mathematics Teacher Education, 8,* 223–254.

Leikin, R., & Levav-Waynberg, A. (accepted). Solution spaces of multiple-solution connecting tasks as a mirror of the development of mathematics teachers' knowledge. *Canadian Journal of Science, Mathematics and Technology Education.*

Leikin, R. (2006). Learning by teaching: The case of the Sieve of Eratosthenes and one elementary school teacher. In R. Zazkis & S. Campbell (Eds.), *Number theory in mathematics education: Perspectives and prospects* (pp. 115–140). Mahwah, NJ: Lawrence Erlbaum.

Leikin, R. (2007). Habits of mind associated with advanced mathematical thinking and solution spaces of mathematical tasks. In D. Pitta-Pantazi & G. Philippou (Eds.), *Proceedings of the Fifth Conference of the European Society for Research in Mathematics Education – CERME-5* (pp. 2330–2339) (CD-ROM and On-line). Available: http://ermeweb.free.fr/Cerme5.pdf

Leikin, R., & Dinur, S. (2007). Teacher flexibility in mathematical discussion. *Journal of Mathematical Behavior, 26,* 328–347.

Leontiev, L. (1983). *Analysis of activity.* Vestnik MGU (Moscow State University), Vol. 14: Psychology.

Llinares, S., & Krainer, K. (2006). Mathematics (student) teachers and teacher educators as learners. In A. Gutiérrez & P. Boero (Eds.), *Handbook of research on the psychology of mathematics education. Past, present and future* (pp. 429–459). Rotterdam, the Netherlands: Sense Publishers.

Masingila, J. O., & Doerr, H. M. (2002). Understanding pre-service teachers' emerging practices through their analyses of a multimedia case study of practice. *Journal of Mathematics Teacher Education, 5*, 235–263.

Mason, J. (2002). *Researching your own practice: The discipline of noticing*. New York: Falmer.

McGraw, R., Lynch, K., Koc, Y., Budak, A., & Brown, C. A. (2007). The multimedia case as a tool for professional development: An analysis of online and face-to-face interaction among mathematics pre-service teachers, in-service teachers, mathematicians, and mathematics teacher educators. *Journal of Mathematics Teacher Education, 10*, 95–121.

McNeal, B., & Simon, M. A. (2000). Mathematics culture clash: Negotiating new classroom norms with prospective teachers. *Journal of Mathematical Behavior, 18*, 475–509.

Morris, A. K. (2006). Assessing pre-service teachers' skills for analyzing teaching. *Journal of Mathematics Teacher Education, 9*, 471–505.

National Council of Teachers of Mathematics (NCTM). (1995). Report of the NCTM task force on the mathematically promising. *NCTM News Bulletin, 32*.

National Council of Teachers of Mathematics (NCTM) (2000). *Principles and standards for school mathematics*. Reston, VA: NCTM.

Nicol, C. (1999). Learning to teach mathematics: Questioning, listening, and responding. *Educational Studies in Mathematics, 37*, 45–66.

Nicol, C. (2002). Where's the math? Prospective teachers visit the workplace. *Educational Studies in Mathematics, 50*, 289–309.

Nicol, C. C., & Crespo, S. M. (2006). Learning to teach with mathematics textbooks: How preservice teachers interpret and use curriculum materials. *Educational Studies in Mathematics, 62*, 331–355.

Peressini, D., Borko, H., Romagnano, L., Knuth, E., & Wills, C. (2004). A conceptual framework for learning to teach secondary mathematics: A situative perspective. *Educational Studies in Mathematics, 56*, 67–96.

Philippou, G. N., & Christou, C. (1998). The effects of a preparatory mathematics program in changing prospective teachers' attitudes towards mathematic. *Educational Studies in Mathematics, 35*, 189–206.

Ponte, J. P., Oliveira, H., & Varandas, J. M. (2002). Development of pre-service mathematics teachers' professional knowledge and identity in working with information and communication technology. *Journal of Mathematics Teacher Education, 5*, 93–115.

Portnoy, N., Grundmeier, T. A., & Graham, K. J. (2006). Students' understanding of mathematical objects in the context of transformational geometry: Implications for constructing and understanding proofs. *Journal of Mathematical Behavior, 25*, 196–207.

Posner, G. J., Strike, K. A., Hewson, P. W., & Gertzog, W. A. (1982). Accommodation of a scientific conception: Towards a theory of conceptual change. *Science Education, 66*, 211–227.

Rowland, T., Huckstep, P., & Thwaites, A. (2005). Elementary teachers' mathematics subject knowledge: the knowledge quartet and the case of Naomi. *Journal of Mathematics Teacher Education, 8*, 255–281.

Santagata, R., Zannoni, C., & Stigler, J. W. (2007). The role of lesson analysis in pre-service teacher education: an empirical investigation of teacher learning from a virtual video-based field experience. *Journal of Mathematics Teacher Education, 10*, 123–140.

Scheffler, I. (1965). *Conditions of knowledge. An introduction to epistemology and education*. Glenview, IL: Scott, Foresman & Company.

Schnotz, W., Vosniadou, S., & Carretero, M. (1999). *New Perspectives on Conceptual Change*. UK: Pergamon.

Schön, D. A. (1983). *The reflective practitioner: How professionals think in action*. New York: Basic Books.

Shulman, L. S. (1986). Those who understand: Knowing growth in teaching. *Educational Researcher, 5*, 4–14.

Shulman, L. S. (1992). Towards a pedagogy of cases. In J. H. Shulman (Ed.), *Cases Methods in Teacher Education* (pp. 1–30). New York: Teachers College Press.

Stein, M. K., Smith, M. S., Henningsen, M. A., & Silver, E. A. (2000). *Implementing standards-based mathematics instruction: A casebook for professional development*. New York: Teachers College Press.

Steinbring, H. (1998). Elements of epistemological knowledge for mathematics teachers. *Journal of Mathematics Teacher Education, 1*, 157–189.

Stigler, J. W., & Hiebert, J. (1998). Teaching is a cultural activity. *American Educator*, Winter 1998.

Stigler, J. W., & Hiebert, J. (1999). *The teaching gap: Best ideas from the world's teachers for improving education in the classroom.* New York: The Free Press.

Szydlik, J. E., Szydlik, S. D., & Benson, S. R. (2002). Exploring changes in pre-service elementary teachers' mathematical beliefs. *Journal of Mathematics Teacher Education, 6*, 253–279.

Taplin, M., & Chan, C. (2001). Developing problem-solving practitioners. *Journal of Mathematics Teacher Education, 4*, 285–304.

Thompson, A. (1992). Teachers' beliefs and conceptions: A synthesis of the research. In D. A. Grouws (Ed.), *Handbook for research on mathematics teaching and learning* (pp. 127–146). New York: Macmillan.

Tirosh, D., & Graeber, A. O. (2003). Challenging and changing mathematics classroom practices. In A. J. Bishop, M. A. Clements, C. Keitel, J. Kilpatrick, & F. K. S. Leung (Eds.), *The second international handbook of mathematics education* (pp. 643–687). Dordrecht, the Netherlands: Kluwer.

Tsamir, P. (2005). Enhancing prospective teachers' knowledge of learners' intuitive conceptions: The case of same A–same B. *Journal of Mathematics Teacher Education, 8*, 469–497.

Tsamir, P. (2007). When intuition beats logic: prospective teachers' awareness of their same sides – Same angles solutions. *Educational Studies in Mathematics, 65*, 255–279.

Vygotsky, L. S. (1978). *Mind in society: The development of higher psychological processes.* Cambridge, MA: Harvard University Press.

Walshaw, M. (2004). Pre-service mathematics teaching in the context of schools: An exploration into the constitution of identity. *Journal of Mathematics Teacher Education, 7*, 63–86.

Wells, G. (1999). *Dialogic inquiry: Towards a sociocultural practice and theory of education.* Cambridge, UK: Cambridge University Press.

Wong, N.-Y. (2003). Influence of technology on the mathematics curriculum. In A. J. Bishop, M. A. Clements, D. Brunei, C. Keitel, J. Kilpatrick, F. K. S. Leung (Eds.), *The second international handbook of mathematics education* (pp. 271–321). Dordrecht, the Netherlands: Kluwer.

Wood, T. (1998). Alternative patterns of Communication in Mathematics classes: Funnelling or Focusing. In H. Steinbring, A. Sierpinska, & M. G. Bartolini-Bussi (Eds.), *Language and communication in the mathematics classroom* (pp. 167–178). Reston, VA: NCTM.

Wubbels, T., Korthagen, F., & Broekman, H. (1997). Preparing teachers for realistic mathematics education. *Educational Studies in Mathematics, 32*, 1–28.

Yerushalmy, M., Chazan, D., & Gordon, M. (1990). Mathematical problem posing: Implications for facilitating student inquiry in classrooms. *Instructional Science, 19*, 219–245.

Zaslavsky, O., Chapman, O., & Leikin, R. (2003). Professional development of mathematics educators: Trends and tasks. In A. J. Bishop, M. A. Clements, D. Brunei, C. Keitel, J. Kilpatrick, F. K. S. Leung (Eds.), *The second international handbook of mathematics education* (pp. 875–915). Dordrecht, the Netherlands: Kluwer.

Zaslavsky, O., & Leikin, R. (2004). Professional development of mathematics teacher-educators: Growth through practice. *Journal of Mathematics Teacher Education, 7*, 5–32.

Zbiek, R. M., & Conner, A. (2006). Beyond motivation: Exploring mathematical modeling as a context for deepening students' understandings of curricular mathematics. *Educational Studies in Mathematics, 63*, 89–112.

Roza Leikin
Faculty of Education
University of Haifa
Israel

SUSAN D. NICKERSON

4. TEAMS OF PRACTISING TEACHERS

Developing Teacher Professionals

The focus of this chapter is on teams of practising teachers brought together in formally arranged situations organized by management, such as, subject coordinators, school-based or district-based administrators. The chapter begins with a description of the goals for developing teacher professionals. I then illustrate the current practice of professional development of the past ten years with examples from several countries. Common aspects are evident in the structure of the professional development programmes. A case study brings the issues of the complexity of studying practising teachers into focus. Finally, I use these examples to explicate the message about teams and relevant environment, framed in terms of inter-dependence and the co-constructed context.

GOALS FOR DEVELOPING TEACHER PROFESSIONALS

Current reform initiatives mainly initiated by the National Council of Teachers of Mathematics (1989) call for changes in the "core dimensions of instruction" (Spillane, 1999; Spillane & Zeuli, 1999). Mathematics teachers are expected to establish in their classrooms "communities of learners" where students explore mathematics in depth and teachers facilitate students' mathematical learning. Students are expected to construct mathematics for themselves and develop a means of determining the appropriateness of solutions and procedures based on arguments used to justify the solutions and procedures. This vision of mathematics learners suggests students make meaning of mathematics and comprises a corresponding emphasis on achievement for all students (Stein, Silver, & Smith, 1998; Tirosh & Graeber, 2003). This theme of more learner-centred and conceptually-focused instructional practice is international in scope with mathematics progressively seen as a critical competency for greater numbers of more diverse students (Adler, 2000; Adler, Ball, Krainer, Lin, & Novotná, 2005).

A common goal of teacher development programmes, therefore, is to develop support for student thinking by helping teachers develop interactive and dialogic contexts for learning and promoting students' thinking with appropriate questions and statements (Sowder, 2007). Teachers' learning to teach for student understanding must integrate knowledge of: mathematics content (including concepts, processes, and methods of inquiry); student thinking (understanding the ways in which students thinking could develop); and instructional practice (nature and effects of their teaching) (Carpenter, Blanton, Cobb, Franke, Kaput, &

K. Krainer and T. Wood (eds.), Participants in Mathematics Teacher Education, 89–109.

McClain, 2004; Jaworski & Wood, 1999). Teachers, often having only been participants in a classroom with a traditional or an instrumental approach to mathematics teaching, are expected to teach in ways they themselves have not experienced. Therefore, many professional development programmes have as a goal assisting teachers in paradigmatic shifts in epistemology and instructional practice. The goals of supporting changes in teachers' practice, philosophy, and beliefs is fundamentally based in the notion that changed practice, raised awareness, and changes in beliefs about mathematics, mathematics teaching, and learning can result in a more effective environment for student learning (Jaworski & Wood, 1999).

This chapter focuses on professional development experiences for *teams* of practising mathematics teachers; in particular, teams are mostly selected by management, with pre-determined goals, which therefore create rather tight and formal connections within the team (Krainer, 2003). Although teams may develop into collaborative communities, they are not inherently so. Teams of practising mathematics teachers may consist of school-based groups or teachers drawn from across a school district or region. Subject-coordinators, school-based or district-based administrators are examples of management that bring a team together within a formal structure. Teacher educators' and management's choice of what to offer or require is shaped by a perception of teachers' needs, by the larger context in which schooling occurs, and resources (human, social, and capital) committed to such endeavours (Borasi & Fonzi, 2003; Nickerson & Brown, 2008). Individual teacher participant's decision to participate is affected by factors such as his or her perception of meaningfulness, feasibility, work demands, management and collegial support (Kwakman, 2003). Although teams of mathematics teachers are mostly selected by management for work structured towards predetermined goals, in practice, the goals and structure of the work are equally affected by teachers' and managements' participation and the design of successful professional development can and should evolve and change (Loucks-Horsley, Hewson, Love, & Stiles, 1998). As such, the professional development programmes in which teams of teachers are engaged is the joint construction of the teacher educators who design it, administrators and management who decide what to offer or require, and the teachers who choose the programmes and the manner in which they agree to participate (Borasi & Fonzi, 2003). In this same sense, context is not deterministic but *interactively constructed* among the participants (Jones, 1997).

Therefore, the mathematics teacher professional development programmes as constituted are reflective of the specific political and cultural contexts in which they are embedded. Cooney and Krainer (1996) describe how the nature of the programmes for practising mathematics teachers is constructed from macro problems and micro problems. Macro problems emanate from society in general and are related to economics, politics, culture, and language. Micro problems are directly related to problems within mathematics teacher education, such as curricula or teacher training. The design of professional development programmes is reflective of an attempt to address both macro and micro problems.

For example, national initiatives affect policy and privilege some foci in the distribution of resources. Mathematics teachers' professional development in many Western countries is motivated by having not compared well to other countries in international comparisons of students' mathematics achievement in the 1990s. Consequently, the governments, for example, New Zealand, Australia, some European countries and the United States responded to such rankings with an impetus to improve student achievement (see e.g., Bobis et al., 2005; Borasi, Fonzi, Smith, & Rose, 1999; Keitel & Kilpatrick, 1999). Some countries have a focus on repairing inadequate prospective teachers' preparation, which includes the mathematical knowledge of teachers and, in the case of South Africa, extends to reconstruction of identity (Adler & Davis, 2006). In other countries, mathematics education and consequently professional development programmes for teachers are shaped by the goal of eradicating economic and technological disparity (Atweh & Clarkson, 2001; Tirosh & Graeber, 2003). Thus, teams of teachers are, by definition, engaged in professional development structured as top-down implementations. As such, political, social, and economic concerns contribute to the structure of mathematics professional development for teams of teachers.

The nature of mathematics teacher professional development is also shaped by the mathematics education community's beliefs about mathematics, mathematics teaching, and learning. For example, Ball (1997) discusses mathematics education reform in the United States as based on concern about students' achievement in mathematics and current economic, political, and social pressures for greater numbers of students who can use mathematics competently. Yet, the reform is also shaped by our ideas of what constitutes mathematics learning and knowledge. Constructivist learning theories permeate new directions for teacher professional development experiences (Ball, 1997). In many teacher education programmes around the world, teachers are seen as constructors of knowledge with a need for opportunities for reflection in order to learn (Cooney & Krainer, 1996). Teacher educators of practising teachers acknowledge the challenge of paradigmatic changes in instructional practice, the need to make connections between professional development and work on site, and the benefits to teachers of substantial support from colleagues (see e.g., Knight, 2002; Putnam & Borko, 2000; Tirosh & Graeber, 2003).

What follows is a survey of studies of professional development programmes and approaches that illustrate current themes of mathematics teacher professional development for teams of teachers in many countries. Approaches to professional development are frequently characterized according to the content of the workshops or focus of the work with teachers (see e.g., Borasi & Fonzi, 2003; Kilpatrick, Swafford, & Findell, 2001; Sowder, 2007). Most studies of teacher development adopt an individual teacher as the unit of analysis, describing changes in an individual teacher's knowledge of mathematics, beliefs, or instructional practice (e.g., Cohen, 1990; Sowder & Schappelle, 1995). From another perspective, professional development is a social matter, enhancing collective capability (Knight, 2002). This perspective on teacher development situates teachers' work in context and views professional development as the building of communities of collaborative, reflective practice, wherein teachers are joined with colleagues to create effective mathematics environment for their students' learning (McClain & Cobb, 2004; Stein, Silver, & Smith, 1998).

Researchers have identified some of the critical aspects of effective professional development. Notable among these is the need to *foster collaboration to encourage the formation of communities* of collegial learners (e.g., Borasi & Fonzi, 2003; Wilson & Berne, 1999), to *involve administrators and other stakeholders* as they are critical to arranging resources (e.g., Gamoran, Anderson, & Ashmann, 2003; Krainer, 2001), and the need to *carefully consider alignment with the organizational context* in which these teachers work (e.g., McClain & Cobb, 2004; Sowder, 2007; Stein & Brown, 1997; Walshaw & Anthony, 2006). In what follows, I describe several professional development programmes that illustrate the importance of organizational factors and joint activities when teams of practising teachers are engaged in professional development (Krainer, 2001). This survey is intended to highlight these themes while simultaneously revealing the breadth of possible paths.

PROFESSIONAL DEVELOPMENT WITH TEAMS OF PRACTISING TEACHERS WITHIN THE WORK OF TEACHING

Although the structure of the mathematics professional development described here varies with regard to length and focus and in the manner in which the goals are addressed, the central goal of these programmes is to support practising teachers in reorganizing their instructional practice to become more learner-centred and conceptually focused. Teachers learning to teach in a manner that supports student understanding means that professional development often focuses on engaging teachers in doing mathematics, understanding student thinking and the ways in which it develops, and scaffolding attempts at changed instructional practice.

Teacher education programmes have focused on and continue to focus on the central aspect of teachers' knowledge of mathematics (Jaworski & Wood, 1999; Sowder, 2007). This knowledge of mathematics is framed more broadly than understanding concepts. The mathematical knowledge needed by teachers encompasses the ability to use knowledge of mathematics to foster effective learning for students (Adler & Davis, 2006; Ball & Bass, 2000). One important line of research of the last decade concerns the nature of the mathematical knowledge needed for teaching, which in turn influences the design of teacher education as mathematics teacher educators try to provide opportunities to learn these specialized ways of learning and knowing mathematics (Adler & Davis, 2006). Thus, the programmes with a mathematical focus encompass concepts, process, methods of inquiry, beliefs about mathematics and mathematics learning. In some countries, professional development has a focus on initiating an alternative conception with regards to mathematics teaching and learning (see e.g., Farah-Sarkis, 1999; Mohammad, 2004; Murray, Olivier, & Human, 1999).

As an example, in the context of South Africa, the practising teachers and the administrator placed limits on the time available for professional development.

Murray et al. (1999) describe a two-day workshop attended by primary (K-3, 5-8 year olds) mathematics teachers and head of subject upper elementary teachers in South Africa. Within this narrow window of time, teacher educators had a goal of changing teachers' perceptions of mathematics "[...] and equipping teachers for radically different classroom practice" (Murray et al., 1999, p. 33). Given the teachers' impoverished preparation consisting of traditional mathematics experiences and low self-perception of mathematical ability, the teacher educators tried to address, in their workshop, perceptions of how mathematics is learned and used, as well as the teachers' perceptions of their own mathematical ability. By posing problems that were challenging to teachers and then supporting reflection on their experiences as learners, the designers hoped to justify a problem-centred approach to teaching and to share information to support teachers in establishing a problem-centred classroom. Murray et al. (1999) noted the importance of engaging teachers in mathematical activities that suggested different solution strategies and were aligned to the syllabus. The format encouraged reflection and connections to students' views in similar activities, and the development of a vision of the teacher's role in fostering a problem-centred approach to learning mathematics.

The teachers' evaluations of the workshop suggested that the activities were successful in providing a vision of a "starting place" in their own classrooms. Teachers who perceived themselves as mathematically weak reported being deeply moved by their experience with mathematical sense-making. While the real test of the workshop's success was in changed instructional practice, the authors believed that the fundamental groundwork was laid. They acknowledged that the challenge of changed practice is ultimately highly dependent on factors such as supervisor and peer support. The teams of practising teachers were brought together with persons who were heads of mathematics in their schools to develop a vision of how mathematics is learned with understanding and the role of the teacher in supporting this understanding. After participation, the teachers requested more opportunities for professional development of longer duration.

In stark contrast to the time available with practising South African teachers, teacher educators in Israel describe an extensive programme for practising middle and high school mathematics teachers and mathematics department chairpersons. Each round of the *Kidumatica* programme consisted of full-day weekly meetings for three years, and had a goal of raising the level of teachers' content knowledge and of promoting collaboration among teachers teaching at different grade levels. Fried and Amit (2005) describe a "spiral" activity employed to provide opportunities for teachers to see a problem situation developed for different grade levels. A single problem situation was illustrated and modified for each of seventh through eleventh grades. The teacher educators addressed a perceived problem in instructional practice wherein teachers tended to present problems as one-dimensional entities that embody a single technique or concept. The team met for a portion of the time into large across-grade groups to encourage reflective professional conversations. These conversations were not just about a particular task, but rather concerned the links between the mathematics for students of different grades or achievement levels.

One of the goals of arranging across-grade groups was to knit together a broad mathematics teaching community within an individual school and a region. Fried and Amit (2005) stressed the importance of the multiple perspectives brought by a broad grade-level range of teachers both to develop a deeper, connected understanding of the mathematics and also to develop respectful relationships with colleagues across the grade spectrum. The professional development enhanced collective capability of the team in understanding the range of mathematics connections and challenged the notion that if one understands the concepts at a higher level, then one has the mathematical knowledge needed for effectively teaching it to lower middle-grade students.

A number of professional development initiatives are characterized by the central goal of making students' thinking the focus of and the impetus for teachers' reflection on their own instructional practice (e.g., Fennema et al., 1996; Loucks-Horsley et al., 1998; Sowder, 2007; Zaslavsky, Chapman, & Leikin, 2003). Teaching mathematics for understanding requires knowledge of students and how their mathematical thinking develops. Examining student thinking focuses teachers' attention on the consequences of instructional practices and provides opportunities to understand the discrepancies between what students understand and what teachers wish them to learn (Loucks-Horsley et al., 1998). Teachers can then build upon the concepts and skills expressed in student thinking, using it to guide instructional decisions.

Whitenack, Knipping, Novinger, Coutts, and Standifer (2000) report on a team of practising primary teachers brought together to learn about students' thinking. There were three phases to the programme; in the first phase, the practising primary teachers were part of a larger district-wide group invited to hear two presentations by pre-eminent mathematics educators who addressed issues of teaching and learning mathematics with understanding and creating a learning environment for all students to engage in meaningful mathematics. The teacher educators sent out a district-wide invitation to all K-2 teachers requesting they submit an application to participate in the programme. The professional developers worked with a K-7 district mathematics coordinator, who had a rich history with some of the teacher participants, to plan sessions (Whitenack, personal communiqué).

During the second phase, 27 practising teachers participated in a one-week summer institute. Participants viewed videotapes of students being interviewed while engaged in mathematical problem solving then discussed the videos in terms of students' number development. A mini-case study assignment was designed as a culminating activity for the summer institute. In contrast to case-based professional development formats wherein teachers analyse and discuss a presented case, teachers in the summer institute were asked to work with a partner to develop mini-case studies of students' thinking. The videos included examples of six students (5-9 years old) solving various problems. For example, teachers could select to investigate the strategies used by one child or identify instances in which several students using the same strategy. This provided an opportunity for teachers to develop hypotheses about the strategies students used and the kind(s) of mathematical reasoning such solutions required and conjectures about what it means for students to know and do mathematics.

During the third phase, the project team met with teachers for eight 3-hour sessions during the first four months of the school year. These meetings afforded opportunities for teachers to share new ideas they were exploring, and to reflect on instructional materials that might support students' understanding of place value, multiplication, division, and geometrical concepts. The teachers designed and conducted interviews with students from their own classes and implemented lessons that addressed concepts that had surfaced during interview sessions. The mathematics teacher educators worked with the district mathematics coordinator as a means to support teachers' learning about students' thinking. Participation in the project facilitated peer collaboration focused around an analysis of students' thinking, and scaffolded teachers' trying on new lenses for looking at the student work by assisting teachers embedded in the work of teaching.

Another professional development approach involving teacher-teams was also based on the belief that increasing teacher's awareness of students' thinking contributes to improvement in teaching, however in this case with middle and secondary level students. Tirosh, Stavy, and Tsamir (2001) developed a research-based seminar to introduce a theory that would assist practising middle school and high school teachers in understanding and predicting students' responses to mathematical and scientific tasks. During the course of the seminar, teachers were first introduced to the *Intuitive Rules Theory*, used to explain how students react in similar ways to mathematical and scientific tasks. Teachers learned about how incorrect answers involving comparison and subdivision tasks can be explained by this theory, the educational implications of this theory, and then they engaged in discussions of teaching by analogy and conflict. Specific examples of research in the context of the intuitive rules are discussed. Finally, each teacher was asked to select a topic and define research questions either to conduct a micro-study related to validating a known or identifying a new intuitive rule, or the development and assessment of teaching interventions to counter unproductive intuitive rules. Members of the group met weekly to collectively discuss each other's proposals and research questions. Several teachers collectively analysed data and presented the results to the others. Although the team of practising teachers met with experts outside of the teaching community with an initial structured agenda, in the final phase they selected an investigation related to the work of their teaching. These practising teachers collectively developed a new lens for collaborative inquiry into student reasoning.

Thus far, the programmes discussed illustrate professional development that is grounded in and related to the work of teachers' own teaching and involving collaboration with outside experts. The programmes are reflective of the growing realization of the importance of involvement of *heads of department* or other stakeholders. They illustrate different means of support toward reorganization of instructional practice, often by asking teachers to "try out" aspects of practice that they are encouraged to "take back" to the classroom. The following programmes I describe are more integral to the institutions in which the teachers work. In each of these cases, a level of professional development and scaffolded attempts at changed instructional practice occur at the level of the school and within the site. Two programmes for Australian teachers focused on the use of research-based frameworks for young students' number learning in the early years of schooling, an assessment interview to profile a child's knowledge, and whole-school approaches to professional development.

The two initiatives, Count Me In Too (CMIT) in New South Wales and the Victorian Early Numeracy Research Project (ENRP), had two goals: to help teachers understand students' mathematical development and to improve students' achievement in mathematics. A key aspect of CMIT was the Learning Framework in Number (LFIN) developed by Wright (1994) and based on Les Steffe's psychological model of the development of students' counting-based strategies (Bobis et al., 2005). Teachers were assisted in using an assessment to profile a student's knowledge across the spectrum of key components of LFIN; this profile was then be used to guide instruction. Typically, the programme involved a district mathematics consultant and a team of three to five teachers from each school with the district mathematics consultant assisting in planning. The project expanded from a pilot in 1996 in 13 schools to almost 1700 schools by 2003. One initial obstacle to implementing CMIT was the misalignment between the programme's content and the national syllabus. In 2002, a new syllabus was released which was closely aligned with the CMIT project. During this time, the focus in the professional development on number extended to include a measurement strand and a space (geometry) strand (Bobis et al., 2005).

With a similar focus on the use of research-based frameworks, the Victorian Early Numeracy Research Project (ENRP), which ran for three years from 1999-2002, introduced teachers to a framework of growth points in young students' mathematical learning developed by the project leaders (Bobis et al., 2005). This included five or six growth points in each strand of Number, Measurement, and Space. Similarly, it involved a task-based assessment interview, and a multi-level professional development programme aimed at developing a common "lens" through which teachers could view students' reasoning in multiple settings. The professional development programme involved engagement at national, regional, and school levels.

The ENRP involved approximately 250 teachers from 35 project schools. The support for teachers formally occurred on three levels, state, regional and school, (Bobis et al., 2005). All 250 teachers from the state of Victoria met with the research team each year for five full days spread across the year. The focus of these meetings was on understanding the research framework, the interview, as well as appropriate classroom strategies, content, and activities to meet the needs of their students. At the regional level, teachers gathered on four or five occasions each year usually for two hours after school. These meetings brought together three to five school "professional learning" teams and were facilitated by a member of the university research team. Teams were made up of all Prep-2 teachers (teachers of students 5-8 years old) in each school, an early numeracy coordinator, the principal and the early year's literacy coordinator in some schools. The meetings focused on sharing particular activities or approaches, mathematical content, and an articulation of the tasks to be completed before the group met again. Finally, at the school or classroom level, the cluster coordinator spent time on teaching, observing, and planning. The coordinator at each school conducted regular meetings of the "professional learning team" to facilitate communication, maintain continuity and focus.

Researchers examined the nature of the work of the professional learning teams by analysing coordinators' "significant event" folio entries in which they reflected on current mathematics education issues at their school. Other data sources were interviews of the coordinators and surveys administered to principals of the participating schools. The professional learning teams varied in size, operation, and meeting frequency. Some teams had the same team members and coordinator across the three years of the project, others had a transient team and some had a different coordinator each year (State of Victoria, 2003). Early in the project, professional learning teams were enthusiastic, yet somewhat overwhelmed by the requirements of project participation, while the student interviews provided insight into students' thinking, the information also proved daunting for teachers. The teams became aware of and were initially uncomfortable with the notion that there were many different approaches to teaching. Eventually, teams acknowledged common goals for students while accepting professional differences in teaching. In the beginning of each subsequent year, the enculturation of new team members was seen as a major challenge. The further the project progressed, the greater became the discrepancy between the "oldtimers" and the "newcomers". The coordinators worked within limited release time to address this discrepancy but the strategies and success in mediating this varied across sites. However, both principals and coordinators noted increased dialogue around mathematics with more willingness to share ideas, opinions, and resources. The researchers concluded that the teams served an important role in supporting teachers in improving the teaching of mathematics (State of Victoria, 2003).

These two programmes were motivated by national government interest in a remedy for poor achievement in mathematics in international comparisons. The initiatives drew on research-based learning frameworks that describe a trajectory or pathway of students' early mathematical learning. The frameworks and assessment tools provided teachers with a common lens for discussions across groups. Both programmes were whole-school approaches to professional development with outside experts and site-based coordinators supporting teachers' practice.

Many professional development programmes of the past decade engage teachers in concrete examination of instructional practice more broadly considered than student thinking alone. Chissick (2002) described a three-year professional development programme for secondary mathematics teachers in Israel. The goal was to change the instructional practices of teachers toward a use of innovative instructional practices, including more prominent use of technology and promotion of teamwork. Teams from 13 schools were assigned a "facilitator" for one day a week for three years, and the school's head of mathematical department worked with the facilitator to lead weekly training workshops on innovative instructional practices and to assist teachers in experimenting with new instructional practices and technology. The facilitators and department heads received support for their leadership role in monthly meetings.

Chissick (2002) investigated effective implementation of reform mathematics teaching practices, effective use of technology and increased teamwork in mathematics teaching. The teachers, head of departments, and school heads were asked to complete structured and semi-structured questionnaires. Additional data collected included weekly reports from project facilitators and field notes of observations of meetings. Chissick reported significant change in teamwork culture and some changes in classroom practice (specifically the use of more open-ended tasks and more student-centred teaching). This study also explored teachers' views of themselves as learners. Case studies at two of the schools provided more in-depth data analysis and a closer look at a few teachers that included classroom observations, interviews regarding teacher beliefs and attitudes toward change, mathematics and mathematics teaching, personal history and self esteem. Thus, this research included a focus on an individual's role in implementation.

Another trend of the past ten years has been an effort to take successful models of practising teacher professional development and use them with a team of practising teachers. Here I focus on successful professional development for teachers in East Asia adopted for use in the United States. Teacher development in Japan, called *kenshu*, describes peer collaboration, review and critique of actual lessons; this is often referred to as "Lesson Study" (see Yoshida, Volume 1). The first thing teachers generally do is establish a lesson study goal. Study lessons are collaboratively planned by about four to six teachers, implemented by one teacher (usually the teaching is videotaped and observation notes are taken) and afterward the lesson is discussed. Administrators and principals participate in this discussion because they are considered "peers". The participants discuss their observations and decisions about how to improve the lesson. An invited observer provides an "outside prospective". An outside observer is most often an instructional superintendent, an individual appointed by prefectures to regularly visit schools and advise teachers in a region. The outside advisor can also be a university expert or teacher on leave hired to provide professional development (Fernandez & Yoshida, 2004). In Japan, practising teachers organize the most common type of professional development with the formation of a study promotion committee drafting a yearly study plan, which is the negotiated with the teachers at different grade levels. There are also interschool programmes organized by district-wide subject area associations of teachers (Shimahara, 2002).

Lesson study as practiced in Japan can be obligatory or voluntary. For example, one type of obligatory programme is an internship for beginning teachers. Internships are legally required for teachers and provide a one-year probation wherein beginning teachers have reduced responsibilities and a mentor who is selected from among experienced teachers. As part of the internship, interns observe mentor teachers teaching and implement study lessons before their more experienced colleagues. The beginning teachers learn and practice the different roles of the teacher in teaching a lesson (Shimizu, 1999). The internship is designed by the prefectural education centre or local board (Shimahara, 2002; Yoshida, 2002). Though there are obligatory top-down initiatives, lesson study in Japan is embedded in the culture of teaching (Shimahara, 2002). Three premises are used as organizing principles for Japanese professional development. The first is that teaching is a collaborative, peer-driven process that can be improved through this process. The second is that peer planning is critical to teaching. The third is that teachers' active participation is a critical element of professional development and teaching. Although these premises constitute the normative framework of Japanese professional development, school-based teacher professional development varies a great deal depending upon the leadership of teachers in the local context and the level of teaching (Shimahara, 2002). In general, lesson study is utilized more at the elementary school level and is less common at the secondary level.

On the basis of their growing understanding of how lessons are conducted and prepared in Japanese classrooms, Hiebert and Stigler (2000) suggested that educators in the US consider a form of lesson study to build professional knowledge; thus variations of lesson study are rapidly proliferating across the country (Chokski & Fernandez, 2004; Fernandez, 2005). As lesson study comes to be viewed as effective approach to professional development, school and district administrators select this structure as a means to provide a professional development experience connected to the classroom work of teachers. Because collaboration is not part of the culture of teaching in the US, management and teacher educators need to bring teachers together to engage them in lesson study. Lessons study requires management to assist with scheduling, allocating funding and arranging for substitute teachers and these endeavours are often initially obligatory for teams of teachers.

Podhorsky and Fisher (2007) described a lesson study implementation in an elementary school in a low socio-economic area, offered in response to No Child Left Behind (NCLB) legislation, a high stakes accountability programme. Lesson study was selected because it provides a collaborative environment for teachers to focus on curriculum and student learning to facilitate an increase in student achievement. Teacher participants (30 teachers of grades 1-5) met weekly for roughly a year to plan, teach, and critique lessons. The participants were also part of a university class, but the approach became one that was implemented school-wide. The school administrator at the time was very involved (Fisher, personal communiqué, June, 2007).

The teachers were observed as they engaged in lesson study and were interviewed individually and in focus groups. Teachers and school site administrators were surveyed using Likert-scale questionnaires assessing perceptions of this model of professional development. From the surveys and interviews we learn about the participants' perspectives on the strengths and challenges of the lesson study process within their context. The strengths of lessons study as identified by the teachers included: an emphasis on meaningful lessons; an impetus for implementing short and long term goals; and a focus on student assessment. Teachers also cited the benefits of the community aspect of participation in lesson study, increased reflection on teaching practices, and excellent preparation for attaining national teaching certification. The challenges of implementing lesson study in this urban school were the planning time required for the research lesson and, in particular, the significant amount of time required outside of the school setting. Lesson study requires common preparation periods with grade-level teams, common curriculum, and external guidance in conducting lesson study; resources not readily available to teams of practising teachers in other schools throughout the United States. However, this situation is slowly changing. According to a survey conducted in 2004, a majority of US lesson study groups met at least once a week, most during the school day (Chokshi & Fernandez, 2004). As lesson study becomes part of the culture of teaching in the US, it can evolve into a more teacher-led process of professional development.

In another approach to professional development, teams of practising teachers are often brought together to implement challenging curriculum. Balfanz, MacIver, and Byrnes (2006) reported on a study of the first 4-years of a mathematics reform project, the Talent Development Middle School Model Mathematics (TD) programme, which was initiated in three, high-poverty urban US middle schools in the context of whole school reform. This programme included professional development that was directly linked to implementation of three reform mathematics curricula in grades 5 through 8 (10-13 year olds). The mathematics reform (curricula, corresponding professional development and whole school initiative) was instigated to meet the national milestones of the federal No Child Left Behind (NCLB) legislation. The professional development approach was that of providing "model lessons" using the curricula.

The professional development was led by peer teachers and experienced users of the curricula and took place over three days of summer training that was followed by monthly 3-hour workshops on Saturdays. The monthly sessions were focused on lessons that would be taught in the participants' classes the following month. The facilitator guided the teachers as participants through the upcoming lesson and modelled important aspects, including the mechanics of the activities, questioning and then providing an opportunity for the participant teachers to ask questions and discuss with each other past experiences of teaching. The teachers also had substantial implementation support in the form of curriculum coaches that spent 1-2 days a week at a school helping teachers in their classrooms. The curriculum coach co-taught, modelled, assisted with lesson planning, provided feedback and worked with the teachers to make modifications to the curriculum to address his or her students' specific needs. By the completion of the fourth year of the initiative, two teacher leaders from each school were ready to help with on-site implementation. Part of the teacher-leader training involved shadowing the curriculum coaches in their work with teachers.

Even with all of the support structured into this programme, high levels of implementation were difficult to achieve. Across the four years of the study, about two-thirds of the teachers achieved the minimum recommended hours of professional development each year. The initial goal of having teachers' complete instruction in the use of 6 to 8 units of each grade level's instructional materials was not achieved. Two-thirds to three-fourths of the classrooms in these high-poverty middle schools obtained at least a medium-level of implementation, but with significant variation across sites. Of significance to this discussion, the Balfanz et al. (2006) noted important factors of institutional context that may have affected the implementation: school leadership; scheduling; staffing and resources. As an example, during the four years of the reported intervention, only one school of the three had the same principal and one school had three principals, with varying degrees of commitment to the programme. Staffing patterns changed as the administration either successfully or unsuccessfully provided the resources, and assigned or reassigned teachers. Teacher turnover was one of the biggest challenges; by the fourth year of the study only 31% to 59% of the homerooms across the three schools had mathematics taught by a teacher who had participated in the reform effort all four years.

Summary

The studies described illustrate themes of mathematics professional development for teams of practising teachers in several countries. The programmes are structured toward predetermined goals of improving student achievement by constructing effective mathematics environments for student learning. Consequently, the focus is often on developing understanding of connections among concepts and topics in mathematics, increasing awareness of students' mathematical thinking and the pathways of development, and supporting teachers' changing instructional practice. Whether the approaches to professional development involve engaging teachers in doing mathematics, or examining student thinking, or introducing lesson study as a mechanism for improving teaching, or modelling the teaching of reform curriculum, some common themes have emerged. Here we see, teams of practising teachers engaged in programmes structured to foster collaboration, including not just peers but heads of departments and other significant site leaders. The programmes illustrate a growing awareness of the critical role of alignment with organizational context (see Cobb & Smith, this volume). The following case study is an example of these common themes and importantly, illustrates that the goals and structure of the work are equally affected by teachers' and managements' participation.

CO-CONSTRUCTED CONTEXT: A CASE OF MATHEMATICS SPECIALISTS

The story that emerges from the studies on teams of practising teachers across multiple school sites is one of differential enactment for seemingly similar programmatic activities, highlighting the co-constructed nature of the professional development experience. I have chosen a case study for elaboration. The case study describes a programme designed to assist teachers in becoming mathematics specialists. The initiative emerged in a context of addressing poor student achievement at a local level. The focus was on engaging a team of teachers in doing mathematics and supporting reorganization of their instructional practices. Several school districts and universities in the United States have partnered to develop professional development programmes for mathematics specialists, individuals with specialized preparation in mathematics (see e.g., Nickerson & Moriarty, 2005; *The Journal of Mathematics and Science*, 2005). Mathematics specialists can have work assignments such as a lead teacher or coach. In some specialist work assignments, teachers may teach only mathematics or they may teach mathematics and one other subject, such as science. In this way, teachers can focus on being knowledgeable or expert in the teaching and learning of one, or at most two, subjects.

Nickerson and Moriarty (2005) described an initiative in which 32 upper-elementary teachers in a large urban school district in the United States were hired as additional staff at eight low-achieving schools. The teachers, as the only teachers of mathematics in these schools, travelled from classroom to classroom with carts of materials "visiting" other teachers' classes to teach three mathematics classes, each lasting 90 minutes. During their first year of teaching as a mathematics specialist, they participated in a professional development programme that had a focus on building teachers' knowledge of mathematics and mathematics for teaching with connections to practice. The principals arranged for shared professional development time at each school site. The 60-90 minutes each day was intended to facilitate teacher's sustained growth in knowledge and practice. The teachers met for two weeks one summer and then about three hours a week for one year in coursework designed to help teachers reconceptualize the mathematics they were teaching and to deepen understanding of mathematics pedagogy. The coursework also entailed teachers' learning about how students' mathematical thinking develops. Coursework and on-site activities provided opportunities for reflecting on practice by engaging in collaborative reflective teaching cycles and an analysis of student work, their own and from research. In addition, the mathematics specialists had on-site coaching support from the teacher educators about once a week.

Furthermore, the coursework, site-based support, and daily, shared professional development time was intended to facilitate teachers' sustained, generative growth in content knowledge and practice. Like other programmes described in this chapter, this team of practising teachers was brought together by administrators with pre-determined goals. The professional development was in support of a larger reform initiative, and was planned with the school district mathematics instructional team. The designers of the initiative had the expectation that the provision of these resources would promote the formation of teachers' professional communities of collaborative, reflective practice. Nickerson and Moriarty (2005) used the construct of teachers' professional community as defined by Secada and Adajian (1997). Teachers' professional communities are described along four dimensions: (1) shared sense of purpose, (2) co-ordinated effort to improve students' mathematical learning, (3) collaborative professional learning, and (4) collective control over decisions affecting the mathematics programme. The researchers undertook an analysis of teachers' activities and experiences as situated within institutions as opposed to a structural analysis (Cobb & McClain, 2001).

Based on an analysis of a number of data sources including weekly field-notes of teacher educators and researchers regarding visits to schools, interviews with teachers and mathematics administrators, teachers' written coursework and reflections, teachers' mathematics exams, a survey regarding curriculum implementation, and an interview with the school district leadership team. Nickerson and Moriarty (2005) investigated the relationship of professional development, encompassing both formal and informal sources of support, to teachers' knowledge and practice. Nickerson and Moriarty (2005) reported that professional communities formed at some sites and not others. Five aspects of teachers' professional lives emerged as significant in the formation and strength of teachers' professional community: (1) the relationship the mathematics teachers had with the school administration and other classroom teachers, (2) the respect for and access to the knowledge of other mathematics teachers, (3) the presence or absence of a teacher leader at the site, (4) a shared base of mathematical and pedagogical knowledge, and (5) shared high teachers' expectation for students. The strength and nature of teachers' professional community is significant in local interpretation of reform and the development of collective professional values and goals (see e.g., Talbert & Perry, 1994).

One important aspect of teachers' professional lives was the relationship that a team had with a principal and other teachers at the site. The teachers applied for positions at particular schools. The school principals made the hiring decisions. At a few schools, the teachers were at the site and were encouraged to apply while other principals hired all the staff from outside. School-based administrators were able to align resources for the teaching of mathematics – choosing teams of participants, arranging shared professional development time at each site, and facilitating the teams' ability to exercise collective control over decisions concerning the mathematics programme. The other teachers further contributed to or hindered the formation of a shared vision. At some sites, administrators arranged for minimal shared professional development time that was sometimes overtaken by other responsibilities. There was evidence of administrators who did not understand the goals of the initiative and inhibited the power of teachers to make decisions regarding the mathematics programme.

A second important aspect related to teachers developing respect for and access to the knowledge of other mathematics teachers because it involves teachers seeing themselves as members of a community with contributions to make to the collective capabilities (Nickerson & Moriarty, 2005). This sense of self as a valuable member of a team contributed to collaborative professional learning at some sites. However, one team of teachers expressed a view that they were implementing school district mandates and spent little time together unless mandated by an outside presence. A third important aspect was the presence or absence of a teacher leader who appeared to play a fundamental role in supporting collaborative professional learning and shaping a shared sense of purpose. A fourth important aspect was teachers' mathematical knowledge that appeared to affect their collective control over decisions regarding the mathematics programme and their ability to effectively discuss instruction and student learning. Teacher teams differed in how they spent the professional development time together. Some teachers used the time to help each other with mathematics and to share the successes and failures of their classes. Other teams used the time to look ahead, prioritize topics, and examine mathematics across grades. Finally, and significantly, shared high expectations for students were successfully jointly constructed by some teams and administrators and not others.

The goals and structure of the work were equally affected by teachers' and managements' participation. Teacher educators and administrators designed an initiative shaped by administrator's selection of team participants and alignment of resources. The programme was jointly constructed by teachers' sense of self as a mathematics teacher, teachers' respect for others' contributions, and their ability to effectively discuss instruction and student learning. Teacher educators and school district administrators designed the initiative, local site administrators decided what to require, and the teachers who chose the mathematics specialist programmes shaped the initiative by their varying and evolving participation. The case study suggests that the *fostering of collaboration, the involvement of administrators, and the alignment of organizational context do not individually account for differential enactment* and point to the complexity of studies on teams of practising teachers.

STUDYING TEACHER DEVELOPMENT IN CONTEXT

The focus in this chapter has been on studies of the approaches to professional development for teams of teachers, with a particular focus on the past ten years. Issues of political, social, and economic significance contribute to the structure of mathematics professional development for teams by providing resources for reform curricula, new technologies, and orienting administrators' focus on mathematics. This survey of studies of the past decade highlights the nature of professional development approaches for teams of teachers. The studies illustrate an aim of fostering collaboration among colleagues around central issues such as developing a common lens for viewing and discussing students' early learning, connections among mathematical content areas, and improving instructional practice. The studies of the past decade reveal increasing involvement of management, principals, heads of department and other stakeholders, as part of crafting the vision of effective mathematics teaching. Furthermore, these studies speak to the need to align programmes with the organizational context in which teachers work.

The research that has emerged from the studies point to the complexity and highlight the interdependence of institutional context, relevant management, and teachers themselves as learners. Teams brought together to foster formation of communities of collaborative learners are affected by and affect the different ways that teachers participate in the team. Likewise, as Krainer (2001, p. 282) suggested the management's vision and alignment of resources critically affects and is affected by institutional context:

Principals and other important stakeholders such as regional subject coordinators or superintendents with different roles and functions in school system, have their own ideas and beliefs about the nature of learning, teaching, mathematical knowledge, and reform. [...] it is essential to pay more attention to their role in the professional development of teachers, both practically and theoretically.

The research in social context suggests the importance of consistent intentions and motives among teacher educators, administrators, and teachers (Cobb & McClain, 2001). Yet, many of these initiatives describe multiple layers of administrators, wherein the administrators who decided what to require were distinct from the site administrators who are proximate to teachers. As a district superintendent describes (Nickerson & Brown, 2008, p. 20):

> We've got. I don't know. We've got 1, 2, 3 partnerships over 26 teachers right now. We've challenged principals next year that they all will have at least one partnering teacher when school starts in September. Principals are uncomfortable with that because they have to figure out how to make that happen. We challenge them to make that happen. We think, you know, trust us. In the end you will be glad you did.

Although management selected or required the programmes required, several researchers described the varying degrees of commitment by the administrators that work most closely with teachers (see e.g., Balfanz et al., 2006; Nickerson & Moriarty, 2005; Walshaw & Anthony, 2006).

In closing, we must acknowledge that the nature of the professional development programmes for teams of practising mathematics teachers is reflective of different contexts. There are differences in the issues for developed western countries with substantial resources directed to large-scale recruitment of teams of teachers and developing countries with limited time and resources. Whatever the nature of these professional development programmes, as Perrin-Glorian, DeBlois, and Robert (this volume) conclude, it is important to study teaching within the larger societal and political context and to recognize that when practising teachers must change because of external reforms, it can be very difficult to integrate new instructional practices with institutional and social expectations. This suggests that mathematics educators and researchers can learn much by taking up the challenge of understanding the complex interrelationships among teachers, peers, teacher educators, administrators, and institutional contexts.

REFERENCES

Adler, J. (2000). Conceptualizing resources as a theme for teacher education. *Journal of Mathematics Teacher Education, 3*, 205–224.

Adler, J., Ball, D., Krainer, K., Lin, F.-L, & Novotná, J. (2005). Reflections on an emerging field: Researching mathematics teacher education. *Educational Studies in Mathematics, 60*, 359–381.

Adler, J., & Davis, Z. (2006). Opening another black box: Researching mathematics for teaching in mathematics teacher education. *Journal for Research in Mathematics Education, 37*, 270–296.

Atweh, B., & Clarkson, P. (2001). Internationalization and globalization of mathematics education: Toward an agenda for research/action. In B. Atweh, H. Forgasz, & B. Nebres (Eds.), *Sociocultural* research on mathematics education: An international perspective (pp. 77–94). Mahwah, NJ: Lawrence Erlbaum Associates.

Ball, D. L. (1997). Developing mathematics reform: What don't we know about teacher learning – but would make a good working hypothesis. In S. N. Friel & G. W. Bright (Eds.), *Reflecting on our work: NSF teacher enhancement in K-6 mathematics* (pp. 77–111). Lanham, MD: University Press of America.

Ball, D. L., & Bass, H. (2000). Interweaving content and pedagogy in teaching and learning to teach: Knowing and using mathematics. In J. Boaler (Ed.), *Multiple perspectives on mathematics teaching and learning* (pp. 83–104). Westport, CT: Ablex Publishing.

Balfanz, R., MacIver, D., & Byrnes, V. (2006). The implementation and impact of evidence-based mathematics reforms in high-poverty middle schools: A multi-site, multi-year study. *Journal for Research in Mathematics Education, 37*, 33–64.

Bobis, J., Clarke, B., Clarke, D. M., Thomas, G., Wright, R., Young-Loveridge, J., & Gould, P. (2005). Supporting teachers in the development of young children's mathematical thinking: Three large scale cases. *Mathematics Education Research Journal, 16*(3), 27–57.

Borasi, R., & Fonzi, J. (2003). *Professional development that supports school mathematics reform.* Foundations series of monographs for professionals in science, mathematics and technology education. Arlington, VA: National Science Foundation.

Borasi, R., Fonzi, J., Smith, C. F., Rose, B. J. (1999). Beginning the process of rethinking mathematics instruction: A professional development program. *Journal of Mathematics Teacher Education, 2*, 49–78.

Carpenter, T. P., Blanton, M. L., Cobb, P., Franke, M. L., Kaput, J., & McClain, K. (2004). *Research report: Scaling up innovative practices in mathematics and science.* Madison, WI: National Center for Improving Student Learning and Achievement in Mathematics and Science.

Chissick, N. (2002). Factors affecting the implementation of reform in school mathematics. In A. Cockburn & E. Nardi (Eds.), *Proceedings of the 26th Conference of the International Group for the Psychology of Mathematics Education* (Vol. 2, pp. 248–256). Norwich, UK: University of East Anglia.

Chokshi, S., & Fernandez, C. (2004). Challenges to importing Japanese lesson study: Concerns, misconceptions, and nuances. *Phi Delta Kappan, 85*, 520–525.

Cobb, P., & McClain, K. (2001). An approach for supporting teachers' learning in social context. In F.-L. Lin & T. J. Cooney (Eds.), *Making sense of mathematics teacher education* (pp. 207–231). Dordrecht, the Netherlands: Kluwer Academic Publishers.

Cohen, D. K. (1990). A revolution in one classroom: The case of Mrs. Oublier. *Educational Evaluation and Policy Analysis, 12*, 327–345.

Cooney, T. J., & Krainer, K. (1996). Inservice mathematics teacher education: The importance of listening. In A. J. Bishop, K. Clements, C. Kietel, J. Kilpatrick, & C. Laborde (Eds.), *International handbook of mathematics education* (Part 2, pp. 1155–1185). Dordrecht, the Netherlands: Kluwer Academic Publishers.

Farah-Sarkis, F. (1999). Inservice in Lebanon. In B. Jaworski, T. Wood, & S. Dawson (Eds.), *Mathematics teacher education: Critical international perspectives* (pp. 42–47). Philadelphia, PA: Falmer Press.

Fennema, E., Carpenter, T. P., Franke, M. L., Levi, M., Jacobs, V., & Empson, S. (1996). A longitudinal study of learning to use children's thinking in mathematics instruction. *Journal for Research in Mathematics Education, 27*, 403–434.

Fernandez, C. (2005). Lesson study: A means for elementary teachers to develop the knowledge of mathematics needed for reform-minded teaching? *Mathematical Thinking and Learning, 7*, 265–289.

Fernandez, C., & Yoshida, M. (2004). *Lesson study: A Japanese approach to improving mathematics teaching and learning.* Mahweh, NJ: Lawrence Erlbaum Associates.

Fried, M., & Amit, M. (2005). A spiral task as a model for in-service teacher education. *Journal of Mathematics Teacher Education, 8*, 419–436.

Gamoran, A., Anderson, C. W., & Ashmann, S. (2003). Leadership for change. In A. Gamoran, C. W. Anderson, P. A. Quiroz, W. G. Secada, T. Williams, & S. Ashmann (Eds.), *Transforming teaching in math and science: How schools and districts can support change* (pp. 105–126). New York: Teachers College Press.

Hiebert, J., & Stigler, J. W. (2000). A proposal for improving classroom teaching: Lessons from the TIMMS video study. *Elementary School Journal, 101,* 3–20.

Jaworski, B., & Wood, T. (1999). Themes and issues in inservice programmes. In B. Jaworski, T. Wood, & S. Dawson (Eds.), *Mathematics teacher education: Critical international perspectives* (pp. 125–147). Philadelphia, PA: Falmer Press.

Jones, D. (1997). A conceptual framework for studying the relevance of context in mathematics teachers' change. In E. Fennema & B. S. Nelson (Eds.), *Mathematics teachers in transition* (pp. 131–154). Mahwah, NJ: Lawrence Erlbaum Associates.

Keitel, C., & Kilpatrick, J. (1999). The rationality and irrationality of international comparative studies. In G. Kaiser, E. Luna, & I. Huntley (Eds.), *International comparisons in mathematics education* (pp. 242–257). London: Falmer Press.

Kilpatrick, J., Swafford, & B. Findell (Eds.). (2001). *Adding it up: Helping children learn mathematics.* Washington, DC: National Academy Press.

Knight, P. (2002). A systemic approach to professional development: Learning as practice. *Teaching and Teacher Education, 18,* 229–241.

Krainer, K. (2001). Teachers' growth is more than the growth of individual teachers: The case of Gisela. In F.-L. Lin & T. J. Cooney (Eds.), *Making sense of mathematics teacher education* (pp. 271–293). Dordrecht, the Netherlands: Kluwer Academic Publishers.

Krainer, K. (2003). Editorial: Teams, communities, & networks. *Journal of Mathematics Teacher Education, 6,* 93–105.

Kwakman, K. (2003). Factors affecting teachers' participation in professional learning activities. *Teaching and Teacher Education, 19,* 149–170.

Loucks-Horsley, S., Hewson, P. W., Love, N., & Stiles, K. E. (1998). *Designing professional development for teachers of mathematics.* Thousand Oaks, CA: Corwin Press.

McClain, K., & Cobb, P. (2004). The critical role of institutional context in teacher development. In M. Høines & A. Fuglestad (Eds.), *Proceedings of the 28th Conference of the International Group for the Psychology of Mathematics Education* (Vol. 3, pp. 281–288). Bergen, Norway: University College.

Mohammad, R. F. (2004). Practical constraints upon teacher development in Pakistani schools. In M. Høines & A. Fuglestad (Eds.), *Proceedings of the 28th Conference of the International Group for the Psychology of Mathematics Education* (Vol. 2, pp. 359–366). Bergen, Norway: University College.

Murray, H., Olivier, A., & Human, P. (1999). Teachers' mathematical experiences as links to children's needs. In B. Jaworski, T. Wood, & S. Dawson (Eds.), *Mathematics teacher education: Critical international perspectives* (pp. 33–41). Philadelphia, PA: Falmer Press.

National Council of Teachers of Mathematics (1989). *Curriculum and evaluation standards for school mathematics.* Reston, VA: Author.

Nickerson, S. D., & Brown, C. (2008). *How resources matter in teacher professional development.* Unpublished manuscript.

Nickerson, S. D., & Moriarty, G. (2005). Professional communities in the context of teachers' professional lives: A case of mathematics specialists. *Journal of Mathematics Teacher Education, 8,* 113–140.

Podhorsky, C., & Fisher, D. (2007). Lesson study: An opportunity for teacher led professional development. In T. Townsend & R. Bates (Eds.), *Handbook of teacher education: Globalization, standards, and professionalism in times of change* (pp. 445–456). Dordrecht, the Netherlands: Springer.

Putnam, R. T., & Borko, H. (2000). What new views of knowledge and thinking say about research on teaching and learning? *Educational Researcher, 29,* 4–15.

Secada, W., & Adajian, L. (1997). Mathematics teacher's change in the context of their professional communities. In E. Fennema & B. S. Nelson (Eds.), *Mathematics teachers in transition* (pp. 193–219). Mahwah, NJ: Lawrence Erlbaum Associates.

Shimahara, N. K. (2002). *Teaching in Japan: A cultural perspective.* New York: Routledge Falmer.

Shimizu, Y. (1999). Aspects of mathematics teacher education in Japan: Focusing on teacher roles. *Journal of Mathematics Teacher Education, 2,* 107–116.

Sowder, J. T. (2007). The mathematical education and development of teachers. In F. K. Lester, Jr. (Ed.), *Second handbook of research on mathematics teaching and learning* (pp. 157–224). Charlotte, NC: Information Age Publishing and National Council of Teachers of Mathematics.

Sowder, J. T., & Schappelle, B. P. (Eds.). (1995). *Providing a foundation for teaching mathematics in the middle grades.* Albany, NY: State University of New York Press.

Spillane, J. P. (1999). External reform initiatives and teachers' efforts to reconstruct their practice: The mediating role of teacher's zones of enactment. *Journal of Curriculum Studies, 31*(2), 143–175.

Spillane, J. P., & Zeuli, J. S. (1999). Reform and teaching: Exploring patterns of practice in the context of national and state mathematics reforms. *Educational Evaluation and Policy Analysis, 21,* 1–27.

State of Victoria Department of Education and Early Childhood Development (2003). Early Numeracy Research Project Final Report.Online.www.sofweb.vic.edu.au/eys/num/ENRP/wholeschdes/plts.htm

Stein, M. K., & Brown, C. (1997). Teacher learning in social context: Integrating collaborative and institutional processes in a study of teacher change. In E. Fennema & B. S. Nelson (Eds.), *Mathematics teachers in transition* (pp. 155–191). Mahwah, NJ: Lawrence Erlbaum Associates.

Stein, M. K., Silver, E. A., & Smith, M. S. (1998). Mathematics reform and teacher development. In J. Greeno & S. V. Goldman (Eds.), *Thinking practices in mathematics and science learning* (pp. 17–52). Mahwah, NJ: Lawrence Erlbaum Associates.

Talbert, J. E., & Perry, R. (1994). *How department communities mediate mathematics and science education reforms.* Paper presented at the annual meeting of the American Education Research Association, New Orleans, LA, April.

The Journal of Mathematics and Science: Collaborative Explorations (2005). Vol. 8.

Tirosh, D., & Graeber, A. O. (2003). Challenging and changing mathematics teaching classroom practices. In A. J. Bishop, M. A. Clements, C. Keitel, J. Kilpatrick, & F. K. S. Leung (Eds.), *Second international handbook of mathematics education* (pp. 643–687). Dordrecht, the Netherlands: Kluwer Academic Publishers.

Tirosh, D., Stavy, R., & Tsamir, P. (2001). Using the intuitive rules theory as a basis for educating teachers. In F.-L. Lin & T. J. Cooney (Eds.), *Making sense of mathematics teacher education* (pp. 73–85). Dordrecht, the Netherlands: Kluwer Academic Publishers.

Walshaw, M., & Anthony, G. (2006). Numeracy reform in New Zealand: Factors that influence classroom enactment. In J. Novotná, H. Moraová, M. Krátká, & N. Stehlíková (Eds.), *Proceedings of the 30th Conference of the International Group for the Psychology of Mathematics Education* (Vol. 5, pp. 361–368). Prague, Czech Republic: Charles University.

Whitenack, J. W., Knipping, N., Novinger, S., Coutts, L., & Standifer, S. (2000). Teachers' mini-case studies of children's mathematics. *Journal of Mathematics Teacher Education, 3,* 101–123.

Wilson, S. M., & Berne, J. (1999). Teacher learning and the acquisition of professional knowledge: An examination of research on contemporary professional development. In A. Iran-Nejad & P. D. Pearson (Eds.), *Review of Research in Education, 24* (pp. 173–209). Washington DC: American Educational Research Association.

Wright, R. (1994). A study of the numerical development of 5-year-olds and 6-year-olds. *Educational Studies in Mathematics, 26,* 25–44.

Yoshida, M. (2002). Framing lesson study for U.S. Participants. In H. Bass, Z. Usiskin, & G. Burrill (Eds.), *Studying classroom teaching as a medium for professional development: Proceedings of a U.S.-Japan workshop* (pp. 58–66). Washington, DC: National Academy Press.

Zaslavsky, O., Chapman, O., & Leikin, R. (2003). Professional development of mathematics educators: Trends and tasks. In A. J. Bishop, M. A. Clements, C. Keitel, J. Kilpatrick, & F. K. S. Leung (Eds.),

Second international handbook of mathematics education (pp. 877–917). Dordrecht, the Netherlands: Kluwer Academic Publishers.

Susan D. Nickerson
Department of Mathematics and Statistics
San Diego State University
USA

FOU-LAI LIN AND JOÃO PEDRO DA PONTE

5. FACE-TO-FACE LEARNING COMMUNITIES OF PROSPECTIVE MATHEMATICS TEACHERS

Studies on Their Professional Growth

Focusing on participants in mathematics teacher education, this chapter focuses on face-to-face learning communities of prospective teachers. Important elements of a learning community synthesized from the literature are addressed in the starting section and used as a frame for discussion in the final section. Two cases from Taiwan and Portugal, which comprise prospective teachers for secondary and elementary schools, are presented. Examples of learning communities both initiated by participants and created by institutional arrangements are given, with consideration for their outer contexts. The process and product of learning from one another within a community from the two cases are synthesized with respect to the inner issues of face-to-face learning communities.

INTRODUCTION

The responsibility of mathematics teachers is to foster students' learning. However, teachers and prospective teachers are also learners. In particular, prospective teachers have to learn how to carry out their job and later, as practising teachers, need to learn to deal with new mathematics topics, technologies, needs from students, and demands from curriculum and society. Both teachers and prospective teachers learn – in practice – for practice, and – from practice. For prospective teachers, this includes not only teaching practice in school contexts, but also learning practice during university courses and in informal situations. They learn as they carry out the activities set up in the courses of their teacher education programme and during field work as they design instructional units and educational materials and tasks, observe classroom situations, interview students and work together with their colleagues and supervisors.

In this chapter, learning is viewed as both an individual and a social process. People learn as they interact with the physical and social world and as they reflect on what they do. Therefore, learning originates from the activity of an individual carried out in a given social context (Lerman, 2001). Prospective teachers learn from their activity and their reflection on their activity, and such learning takes place in a variety of places, as they interact with others, notably their university

K. Krainer and T. Wood (eds.), Participants in Mathematics Teacher Education, 111–129.

teachers, colleagues, school mentors, school students, and other members of the community.

A *learning community* is a special context in which practising teachers and prospective teachers may learn. The most important feature of a learning community is that its members learn from one another. There may be differences in age, experience, status, and professional roles, but the unifying element is that all assume that they are learners; they are keen to learn together and, most importantly, to learn from the others.

These learning communities may take a variety of forms. They may develop from a group that developed habits of working together or a group that was particularly constituted for the purpose of learning or carrying out some project. Such a group may be formed spontaneously by the initiative of its participants, or may be created by some institutional arrangement. Therefore, the group of mathematics teachers in a school, formed on a purely administrative basis, may become a learning community if the teachers begin valuing the fact that the participants can learn a great deal from each other. Similarly, a class for prospective teachers, that by itself is a highly contrived setting, can constitute a learning community if the instructor and the prospective teachers develop relationships of learning from each other (Jaworski, 2004).

People may work together in a variety of ways, either competitively or collaboratively. For example, they may constitute teams, that "are mostly selected by the management, have pre-determined goals and therefore rather tight and formal connections within the team" (Krainer, 2003, p. 95); In contrast, communities "are regarded as self-selecting, their members negotiating goals and tasks. People participate because they personally identify with the topic" (p. 95). A group that begins as a team may develop a working culture that transforms it into a community. Learning is generally regarded as a key element in becoming a member of a community but it may also be regarded as an important feature of the activity of the whole community. Therefore, a learning community is a community where learning is valued as an important outcome of the groups' activity.

The notion of learning community in many respects is close to that of *discourse community*. For example, for Putnam and Borko (1997), a discourse community is a group of people that learned to think, talk, and act in a similar way – in our case, as mathematics teachers. The authors suggest that prospective teachers can model joint cognitive activities, doing "careful analysis of the cognitive roles played by each participant" (p. 1276). Another related notion is that of *community of practice* (Lave & Wenger, 1991), where newcomers learn from old-timers by participating in the tasks that relate to the practice of the community and, with time, newcomers move from peripheral to full participation. Still another related notion is that of *inquiry community* (Jaworski, 2005), in which a group of professionals question their existing practices and explore alternative practices. In this chapter, we use the notion of learning community because our focus is on prospective teachers' face-to-face learning in formal and informal teacher education activities.

Diversity and heterogeneity among the participants of a learning community often make it difficult to find a common language, to adjust purposes and ways of working. However, such diversity may be very beneficial to the work of the community. As Ponte et al. (in press) highlight, different experiences, viewpoints, and expertise may make the group more powerful in identifying and generating solutions to deal with relevant issues, thus leading to quite significant learning from the participants. For example, Clark and Borko (2004) describe how a community was generated in a professional development institute for middle-school mathematics teachers that focused on algebra content knowledge. In their view, the participants at the beginning formed a rather diverse group but the tasks proposed on the first day of the institute fostered their active participation in activities such as "explaining and clarifying ideas, building off of others' ideas, admitting weaknesses, giving praise to others, and laughing" (p. 229), that the authors regard as indicators of the establishment of a community.

Working with colleagues, aiming at professional learning, is also an essential part of the model proposed by Hiebert, Morris, and Glass (2003, pp. 211–212) for generating and accumulating knowledge for teaching and for teacher education (and we may see prospective teachers and practising teachers both involved in this process):

> Becoming a professional teacher, in our view, means drawing from, and contributing to, a shared knowledge base for teaching. It means shifting the focus from improving as a teacher to improving teaching. This requires moving outside the individual classroom, surmounting the insularity of the usual school environment, and working with colleagues with the intent of improving the professional standard for daily practice. This also requires redirecting attention from the teacher to the methods of teaching. It is not the personality or style of the teacher that is being examined but rather the elements of classroom practice.

Jaworski and Gellert (2003) indicate that, to teach effectively, prospective teachers need to integrate different kinds and layers of knowledge. Such knowledge develops through the work of the university and school, of prospective teachers and their university tutors, mentors and other teachers. In their view, all the participants involved, including prospective teachers, may contribute to this development: "all participants are learners, their roles developing in relation to their critical evaluation of them" (p. 270).

Ponte et al. (in press) indicate that there are *four key issues* in learning communities. The first is the *purpose* of the group and its relation to the personal purpose of its members. In fact, a very important condition for one person to learn is his or her wanting to learn and, similarly, a very important condition for one group to learn is its desire to learn. Therefore, we need to consider the purposes that led to the creation of the group, to what brought people to the group and how they identify with the purposes of the group. And, of course, we need to consider the fact that the group's purposes change with time. The second issue concerns the *knowledge* that develops from the activity of the community based on shared practices. We need to pay attention to what participants are really learning and how they learn it. Is it superficial or significant knowledge? The third issue is *how learning happens* in the group. Do group activities involve intensive moments of studying, discussing, and reflecting, or are the participants mostly carrying out routine activities? Is learning developed through negotiating meanings and sharing reflections or just by memorizing and imitating the others? Finally, the fourth issue concerns the *roles and relationships* of the participants. In a learning community, the mutual involvement and commitment of members to the progress of the group are essential features (Ponte et al., in press):

> The learning community is stifled if some members do not feel confident enough to expose their concerns, do not ask for help, and refrain from participation in the group or if, on the contrary, other members participate "too much", occupying all space, helping others too much or in an improper way, etc. A proper style of leadership is a critical element to the working of any group [...]. There are always participants that play a more prominent role in one stage or another of any group, but the group itself may establish a collective leadership, assuming the most important decisions after a thorough discussion of the issues, and a distributed leadership for practical activities, assigning specific group members the conduction of such or such activity.

The development of e-learning and other distance education settings generated a great deal of interest in learning communities for practising and prospective teachers (Llinares & Valls, 2007; Ponte, Oliveira, Varandas, Oliveira, & Fonseca, 2007; Borba & Gadanidis, this volume). However, much less attention has been paid to face-to-face learning communities of prospective teachers; this is the focus in this chapter (see also Llinares & Oliveiro, this volume). We begin by presenting two case studies that illustrate learning communities for prospective teachers as learners. The first, from Taiwan shows how prospective secondary and elementary teachers form learning communities to study for exams, and the second one, from Portugal, illustrates the different learning communities to which a prospective teacher may belong during their teacher education programme.

A CASE FROM TAIWAN

In this section, the social and political contexts of prospective teacher education in Taiwan are described. Based on the specific conditions under which prospective teachers are certified, certain learning communities are formed.

The Supply of Prospective Teachers in Taiwan Exceeds the Demand

According to the statistical data of 2006 annual reports on teacher education (Dai, Kuo, Yang, Lin, & Wei, 2006), 72 universities and colleges with teacher education programmes, in general, a two years study, graduated a total of 17,000 certified elementary and secondary school teachers. Among them, about 4,000 were selected by schools as regular teachers. From the 13,000 of prospective teachers who were not selected, about 2,500 are teaching in schools as substitute teachers and more than 10,000 do not have any teaching position in schools. These teachers are named "stray teachers" by the media for the fact that they are certified as teachers but are not hired by any school. This has become a social issue.

The social status of teachers in Taiwan is relatively moderate; teachers are generally deemed as middle class. Their initial salary is about 30% more than that in almost all other jobs; those who specialize in humanities may even exceed other humanity-related jobs by 80%. Teaching is generally a lifelong career. With a stable pay, few change for another career as the Taiwanese society has an unstable economy. A reliable job with a good retirement system is attractive to young people. A teacher qualified to retire will have a monthly pension that is 85% to 95% of his or her original pay. Therefore, it is likely that a teacher with 30 years seniority would receive retirement pension for another 30 years. These incentives attract many distinguished youngsters to teacher education programmes. Besides, low birth-rate and concomitant low population growth rate in Taiwan bring about a decrease every year in the number of people in each age group, from the maximum of about 420,000 births in 1976, to a minimum of 205,000 births in 2006. Due to this, the number of school-age children lessens each year, and so does the demand for teachers. While the demand for teachers declines, the incentives for people to become teachers remain strong. Under such circumstances, when the number of certified prospective teachers that graduate is not efficiently limited, the supply of teachers naturally exceeds the demand.

Examination for Teacher Certification

Owing to the new social issue of "stray teachers", the Ministry of Education set a limit on enrolling students for teacher education programmes. At the same time, the Ministry of Education started to evaluate these programmes. The ones that score low would have their enrolment decreased at first. Two years later, they would be re-evaluated. The ones that fail to pass the evaluation would have to close their education programmes. In addition, the Ministry of Education instigated an examination for teacher certification. Before 2005, prospective teachers became certified teachers once they completed the teacher education programme which included one year of teaching practice in school. Since 2005, however, the period of teaching practice for prospective teachers was cut in half, and the examination for teacher certification was added and administered by the Ministry of Education. Those who pass the exam receive the teacher's certificate.

The examination for teacher certification comprises of four subjects: Mandarin-Chinese; general education theory and system; youth (child) development and counselling; and secondary (elementary) curricula and pedagogy. Words inside and outside of parentheses are the subject names for elementary school teachers and secondary school teachers respectively. In 2006, there were 7,857 persons registered for taking the exam; 4,595 of them passed it, which means a passing rate of 58% (Dai et al., 2006).

Examination for Teacher Selection

Following the examination for teacher certification, those who get the teacher certification attend the examination for teacher selection held in each of the 23 counties and cities. The examinations for senior high school teacher selection are hosted by each school. There are two phases to the selection exam. The first phase tests the prospective teachers' content knowledge (e.g., mathematics teachers will have an exam on mathematics). Those who pass the first phase can proceed to the second phase, which is a teaching demonstration and interviews. Generally speaking, on average, each elementary level prospective teacher takes more than three examinations for teacher selection. The number of those that obtain a teaching position is between 1% and 2% of the total. Secondary school teachers are a little better off. The ratio of those that obtained a new teaching position is around 5% to 6% in 2006.

Du Shu Hui (讀書會), Learning Communities for Exams

In the following, we regard the prospective teacher education programmes at National Taiwan Normal University. In mathematics education, the university prepares for the examinations for teacher certification and teacher selection as well as for the entrance examination for graduate schools. Personal communication with colleagues and prospective teachers about how the graduates prepare for the examinations mentioned above, indicated that active students usually form Du Shu Hui (讀書會), or learning communities. Prospective teachers participating in Du Shu Hui are more likely than others to pass these examinations. Du Shu Hui are usually initiated by one or several *students*. The motive of initiating a Du Shu Hui is to prepare for certain examinations. Many of these Du Shu Hui last nearly a whole year. Under the present social and political contexts of Taiwan, these prospective teachers, in order to further their education or to become teachers, form their Du Shu Hui as a learning strategy. The interactions and the norms for interacting, the knowledge sharing, the operation of collaborative learning, and the outcome and feedback of the learning communities are interesting issues in terms of social dimension.

Du Shu Hui is a Chinese noun (讀書會) meaning *study group*. If translated literally, Du means to read, Shu means books and Hui means meeting. According to the definition of learning community given by Krainer (2003), Du Shu Hui is a learning community in that:

– Du Shu Hui are self-selecting, their members negotiate goals and tasks.
– Prospective teachers participate because they personally identify with the topic.

The following is an overview of some Du Shu Hui we picked out as examples of how these work as learning communities.

Method of collecting data. In order to understand prospective teachers' Du Shu Hui, a structured interview was conducted in November, 2007. The structure of the interviews consists of three parts: the incentives and goals for setting up learning communities, their organizational operation, and the outcomes and reflection of these communities.

Subjects from departments of mathematics (education) in three universities, two for elementary school teachers and one for secondary school teachers were selected and interviewed. One of the mathematics educators from the departments of these subjects conducted the interviews. Each interview lasted about 30 to 40 minutes.

Four Examples of Du Shu Hui. After being certificated, most of prospective secondary mathematics teachers take examinations either for teacher selection or for further study in graduate institutes, majoring in mathematics or mathematics education. In the examination for secondary mathematics teacher selection, solving pedagogical mathematics problems, designing instruction units and 15-minute teaching demonstration are the main activities. From the data we collected, we chose three Du Shu Hui, each of which respectively focused on one of the three activities during their community meetings. A brief description of the Du Shu Hui are shown in Table 1. This table also shows one Du Shu Hui which focused on studying advanced mathematics for entrance examination of graduate institute.

Some specific features of each Du Shu Hui are described as following. During each community meeting, the five members of the Du Shu Hui *teaching demonstration* took turns to demonstrate 15 minutes teaching. The other four members could spend as much time as they wanted on commenting others' teaching demonstration. They are *critical friends* (Jaworski, 1999) to each other. During the interview with Shi-An, he reflected that "I was influenced by other members. They helped me rectify my teaching approach. This is rather important. I wouldn't have passed the exam if not for the rectification." and "everyone has blind spots. The members helped me see mine."

In Du Shu Hui on *designing instruction units*, the reason there were only two members was that each one would like to design more instruction units to understand more fully the teaching content. One of them has to travel more than 100 kilometres to meet the other at a café each week. Both of them were selected as senior high school mathematics teachers in the summer of 2007. Though they are teaching in different schools, they remain close friends. One member reflected in the interview that: "Now, whenever I have problems concerning teaching I talk it over with Wen-Rong. We discuss about issues including mathematical contents, teaching method, and developing test items."

In the Du Shu Hui for *solving pedagogical mathematics problems*, four members are still in their fifth practicum year. They meet one whole day a week. They are solving pedagogical mathematics problems appeared in previous examinations for teacher selection. Because one of them practice teaching at the best gifted class in Taiwan, tough problems very often are assigned to those gifted students to do; afterwards they discuss students' answers and learn from those students. The community implicitly consists of not only the four prospective teachers but also the class of more than 40 mathematically gifted senior high school students. Those gifted students are also learning by solving problems. The members we interviewed expressed that "One of us has very good understanding of mathematical concepts. His clear linking of geometry and algebra made a great impact on me." and "One of us has excellent conceptual generic examples; they are inspiring."

Table1. Examples of Du Shu Hui, prospective secondary teachers

Activity	Du Shu Hui for exams			
	Teaching demonstration	**Designing instruction units**	**Advanced mathematics**	**Solving pedagogical mathematics problems**
Goal	To pass teacher selection	To pass teacher selection	To join graduate study	To pass teacher selection
Members	5	2	4	4
Duration	September 2006 ~June 2007	December 2006 ~March 2007	November 2006 ~March 2007	March 2007~on going
Frequency	1 weekly meeting (3-4 hours each)	Saturday morning biweekly (3-4 hours each)	2 meetings weekly (3-4 hours each)	A whole day per week
Mode	Took turns to practice teaching (15 min/person) + commented on others' demonstration	Discussed over their pre-written instruction units	- divided the textbook content by schedule - took turns to lecture - collected hard questions and solved by a particular member - focused on doing test questions before the exam	- do past exam questions (2~3 exam papers) during each meeting - (20 min. demonstration+others comment) × 4 - discuss the tough questions assigned to the gifted students
Outcome	All passed	All passed	3 joined graduate study; 1 became a teacher	will take exams in 2008

In the Du Shu Hui for *advanced mathematics*, the four members started to take turns to give lectures. But gradually most of tough problems in the textbook were collected to be solved by one of the members. He became a preceptor for the community. He himself expressed that: "It is only by explaining the texts to others in detail does one know where his/her weaknesses lie. Other people's criticisms and opinions help one to find misunderstandings of texts. This is the best part during the discussions."

Three of them passed the entrance exam for mathematics graduate institute, the other one passed the exam for teacher selection. Two members were interviewed and expressed that: "By attending this learning community, the members have more incentives to study because they oversee each others' progress – one would be urged to study when seeing others do so." The advantage of keeping the community small is: "They could hear their peers share any mathematical thoughts. They were impressed by some of the brilliant thoughts."

Examples of Learning Communities of Prospective Elementary Teachers

After interviewing prospective mathematics teachers from two education colleges that educate elementary school teachers, it is found that learning communities in these schools are not as common as in NTNU. It is worth investigating whether these students are less keen on taking the exams due to low passing rates (1% to 2%) or the university traditions (10 years ago prospective teachers from these colleges were assigned teaching positions after they graduated). However, 30 of the graduates (about 5% of the total graduates) from National Taipei University of Education, one of the two universities interviewed, passed the examination for elementary teacher selection of year 2007. There were about 300 vacant positions in 2007. NTUE had a celebration for the graduates' "good performance". Some of the students of NTUE said that they joined a school club named "Math Camp". The objective of Math Camp is that during summer and winter vacations the participants go to elementary schools in remote areas to provide social service for the students there. The organization and operation of Math Camp basically follow Krainer's definition of learning communities (2003). The following are brief reports of the interviews.

In Table 2 is a brief description of two learning communities of prospective elementary teachers: Math Camp and Du Shu Hui for enhancing understanding mathematics. We will further describe some specific features of those two communities as follows.

In the *Math Camp community*, prospective elementary teachers are practising school organizational operation. Members are put into groups of five to ten and organized in structure similar to a school administrative system. Particularly, each member is designing mathematics activities. During community meetings, they discuss over each member's design of activities. Those activities intend to implement to an elementary school for the children there during summer and winter vocation. The schools chosen for running a math camp are in remote districts. A group of them reflected that

> By trying to design various mathematical learning activities, we acquire knowledge that is not in the elementary mathematics teacher education program. Since the camp is held in different places every year, we learn about regional differences. For example, we have seen the cultural diversities in the

students of Hakka village schools and coastal Min-Nan schools. These divergences contribute to the differences in students' response in learning. This helps us know that it is necessary and important to teach students in accordance with their aptitude.

Table 2. Examples of Du Shu Hui, prospective elementary teachers

Activity	Du Shu Hui	
	Math camp	**Enhancing mathematics understanding**
Goal	To learn mathematics teaching, obtain collaboration experiences, and enhance member-to-member relationships	To enhance undergraduate mathematics understanding
Members	5-10 per group (to recruit new members yearly)	11 (10 sophomores + 1 junior)
Duration	All the year round	September 2007~ (during school terms)
Frequency	Fixed time, once a week	3 hour-meeting, once a week
Mode	- hold mathematics camps for elementary school children during summer and winter vacation - activity design, activity execution, and novice member training	- the junior takes position as the instructor; the sophomores discuss over his or her instruction
Outcome	- members relationship enhanced - knowledge in the non-elementary mathematics curriculum acquired - cultural diversities learned	- the junior: the only one to pass the first quiz - concentration on studying raised

The Du Shu Hui for enhancing *undergraduate mathematics understanding*, ten sophomores and one junior mathematics education students have participated. The community meeting have developed in the way that the junior student takes position as the instructor which others discuss over what he or she speaks. It seems that an instructorship is often developing whenever a community is focused on advanced mathematics. The junior student responded to the interviewer that

I have to go through the texts and questions in advance and then teach the others during each meeting. While I teach I examine whether I was on the right track. I have gained more than others during the process (teaching becomes learning). Among the members I was the only one to pass the first quiz.

Furthermore, he expected that "Hope that the sophomores would go over the questions before each meeting, otherwise they would not have much progress."

A CASE FROM PORTUGAL

Teacher Education in Portugal

The political and social situation of Portugal bears some resemblances but also important differences to that of Taiwan. Like Taiwan, in Portugal the population is aging and declining and every year the need for teachers decreases, both at the primary and secondary school levels. Recently, there was a national effort to universalize education and thus new institutions were created to supply the necessary teachers; there was a shortage in many school subjects, including mathematics. Teaching was then became an attractive career, as it not only provided a reasonable salary but also had unique features of flexibility, reduced weekly schedule and extra holidays in Christmas, Easter and Summer. All this changed dramatically in the last few years. The shortage is over and now there is a large surplus, with many unemployed teachers that can do not find a place in schools. The weekly schedule was extended and teachers are now required to participate in school activities even when students are absent. The government has announced an external mathematics exam to ascertain if the teachers to be recruited have the necessary mathematical competence. The Government also decided to adopt the Bologna framework,[1] and revised the structure of teacher education. Programmes to prepare school teachers take five years (for secondary school candidates) or four and a half years (for primary) to complete and teachers now get a professional masters' degree. Professional practice (or practicum) in schools was reshaped to consist of about three-fourths of a year from one full year) but prospective teachers now have to write an extended report to conclude their study.

These changes are taking place at this moment in time; thus it is too early to know what the effects will be. So far, the main noticeable effect is a decrease in the number of teacher candidates, especially at the secondary school level – due to the large number of unemployed teachers and also the long period of time that it took the government to certify the new study plans that were submitted by all teacher education institutions.

The Teacher Education Programme of the Faculty of Sciences, University of Lisbon

The prospective mathematics teacher education programme of the Faculty of Sciences of the University of Lisbon prepares for teaching at grades 7 to 12. This five-

---

[1] The Bologna framework is a movement of general reform in higher education in Europe, also including some non-European countries, aiming to promote student mobility, programme comparability and renewal of teaching and learning processes.

year programme, as it happens in other countries, has a three-stage model: (i) During the first three years, prospective teachers follow scientific-oriented courses (covering the standard branches of pure and applied mathematics, with emphasis in advanced algebra and infinitesimal analysis); (ii) In the fourth year they take educational courses, some addressing general educational issues (pedagogy, psychology, sociology, history, and philosophy of education) and some others dealing with mathematics education issues (mathematics curriculum, instructional materials, classroom work, assessment, and teaching number, algebra, geometry, statistics and probability); and (iii) The most important part of the fifth year is a supervised practicum in a school. During the first three years, with only a few exceptions, prospective teachers take the same courses as pure mathematics majors. During the fourth year, the programme seeks to provide prospective teachers with theoretical frameworks to analyse educational issues with special attention to current problems, and to provide the essential elements to plan and carry out the daily activity of a mathematics teacher. It also puts prospective teachers in contact with educational practice through two fieldwork courses (one in each semester). The fifth year, the programme includes a year long practicum, during which prospective teachers are responsible for teaching in one class and become progressively involved in all aspects of the professional activity of a mathematics teacher. The programme still includes other elements that complete the educational, scientific, cultural, and ethic preparation of prospective mathematics teachers. Elements for the following examples were drawn from different studies carried out by the second author, as part of a research programme in teacher education.

Face-to-Face Learning Communities in Regular Courses

Within this programme, prospective teachers have several opportunities to constitute face-to-face learning communities. Each course, during the first four years, either in mathematics or in educational subjects, has made such possibility implicit. Often, prospective teachers create informal groups to study, to work on assignments, or to carry out more extended tasks. In the fourth year, most education courses explicitly encourage these groups and some of them constitute rather stable communities of prospective teachers that tackle in turn the tasks related to different courses. One of the most interesting opportunities for prospective teachers to constitute learning communities is provided in the fourth year by the fieldwork course *Pedagogical Actions of Observation and Analysis.*[2] In each semester, the course runs for 3 hours a week, providing an opportunity for prospective teachers to reflect about educational phenomena based on school observations. The aim is that they begin to regard these phenomena from the point of view of the teacher and to develop their capacity of observation and reflection about educational situations. Contrary to all other disciplines of the programme, this one does not have a fixed

---

[2] In Portuguese, Acções Pedagógicas de Observação e Análise (APOA).

curriculum. Its activity is mostly based on observing and reflecting about observations and is jointly undertaken by prospective teachers and instructors. Given the nature of the work, the classes have between 12 and 16 prospective teachers. Group work – involving usually three or four prospective teachers – is the most common working pattern used all through the year. Visits to the school are first prepared, then carried out, and later discussed in classes at the university. Prospective teachers present in class the results of extended observations on issues of their choice. The most usual form of classroom interaction is informal discussion with active participation by prospective teachers. The role of the instructor is to propose tasks and to lead discussions. Each semester ends with presentation and discussion of projects (in oral and written form).

The group of 12 to 16 prospective teachers, together with the instructor, constitutes a learning community. Several factors contribute to that. The fact that there is no prescribed curriculum enables that the planning of work be carried out in a flexible way with the contribution of all participants. Since the activity extends for a full academic year, there is plenty of time for the participants to get to know each other and to adjust to the working requirements of this course. Most of the prospective teachers experienced working in small groups from the time when they were in high school. They now come back to this kind of activity for which most of them adjust rather quickly. The balance between the moments of working as a whole group and in small groups of 3-4 elements, all with their own more specific division of labour, has proved adequate for carrying out tasks such as observing, recording data, analysing observations, and reflecting.

A study by Ponte and Brunheira (2001) indicates how some prospective teachers regard this activity:

While I circulated in the corridors, among pupils, teachers, and staff, I had the opportunity to look at things differently and see things that I had never noticed before. (Beatriz)

This visit [to the school] [...] now made me enter a world that I already knew, but with other eyes, in another role, a little [as I will do] in the future as a teacher. I no longer felt like a pupil although I [still] do not feel like a teacher. (Ana)

The observation allowed us to look at the classroom in a completely different way, a "teacher's" look. It was there that we began paying more attention to the type of class, to the physical conditions, to the teacher's methodology, to the pupils' reactions. (Eduardo)

Although I left secondary school 5 years ago I can already see that it went through great changes [...]. (Dora)

The practicum in the fifth year constitutes another important event in this programme. The prospective teacher, together with one, two, or three other colleagues is assigned to a school. He or she is responsible for teaching two classes, and at the same time participates in seminars and other activities with his/her supervisors from the school and the university. In each school, a micro learning community is formed by this small group of prospective teachers and the school supervisor. The university supervisor is not present on a daily basis but tends to become more of an external consultant. The practicum plays an essential role in developing the professional competencies of the teacher candidate and in supporting the construction of his or her professional identity, and promoting a reflective and active professional attitude.

The different practicum groups, together with their supervisors, meet regularly about once a month. This large group (its size may vary from 30 to 50 or even 70 participants) plans the programme of work for the year, discusses issues that emerge from the activity of the practicum groups, and invites outside experts (sometimes a secondary school mathematics teacher) to carry out seminars on specific topics. The most important activity is the meeting organized for the end of the year, with a format similar to that of a mathematics teachers' professional meeting, in which prospective teachers present to each other some aspects of their work, through posters, oral communications, and workshops.

The practicum group constitutes another kind of learning community, especially when there are collaborative relationships between the prospective teachers and the supervisors that provide the appropriate challenge and support. For many prospective teachers, the practicum is the most important element in their teacher education programme; this is understandable, since it provides a *confrontation* with the reality of practice, requiring the mobilization, revision, and integration of previous knowledge developed in separate experiences and leading to the development of new practical knowledge necessary to conduct the professional activity. One prospective teacher, Nélia (the study is described in Ponte et al., 2007), indicates that one of the aspects that contributed to the success of her practicum was the fact that she already worked with her two colleagues in many university courses. She also indicates that at her school there were two other mathematics practicum groups and there was a good collaboration among all of them.

An Informal Face-to-Face Learning Community Setting

Nélia reports that, as a prospective teacher in the last two years of her studies, she participated in a research project in mathematics education. This project, conducted by a university mathematics teacher educator, involved practising and prospective teachers as well as a large group of doctoral students. Overall, the project had about 40 members organized in different sub teams that provided intensive activity of planning research studies, collecting data, presenting seminars, writing and discussing papers; thus this was another important learning community in Nélia's professional journey:

> In this project we have several themes, we analyse several things. Besides maintaining a contact with on-going research [...] it is an opportunity to talk to people with rather different backgrounds. Therefore, we have a meeting once a month and in those meetings we may share the experiences concerning classroom practice as well as concerning research. Therefore we may al-

ways talk to somebody, share our questions with somebody, know what the others are doing, what questions they also have, and this keeps my inquiry attitude active, that leads me searching for more things [for my practice].

It is interesting to note how this project had a profound impact on this prospective teacher. The formal activities of the project were important, as were the informal contacts with other members and especially the work that she carried out in collaboration with her close colleagues.

In summary, this mathematics teacher education programme provides several opportunities for prospective teachers to participate in different face-to-face learning communities. These communities vary in size, from very small to rather large groups, vary in the intensity of their activity, and also vary in the extent to which they support prospective teachers' learning. The most successful learning communities seem to be those that combine some sort of *formal aims and structure* with a significant *flexibility* in carrying out the activities and involve *different levels of working* together from small groups for undertaking specific tasks to large groups for sharing and discussing more general issues.

CONCLUSION AND DISCUSSION

In order to make sense of learning communities for prospective mathematics teachers, the *outer contexts* and *inner issues* need to be considered. In the following, we focus on these two aspects separately.

The Outer Contexts of Face-to-Face Learning Communities

A learning community often is rooted meaningfully in its *outer context*. On the one hand, different functions of communities may be established with respect to different relations of supply and demand of beginning mathematics teachers within a society. Popularly established Du Shu Hui with the goal of preparing for examinations in the case from Taiwan resulted from the outer context of a supply of teachers far greater than available teaching positions. However, whenever the supply is less than the demand, establishment of a face-to-face learning community often is created by institutional arrangement akin to a team and then transformed into a community. The case from Portugal provided an example of learning communities that were organized along such approach. An educational system in which an over-supply of teachers exists, prospective teacher education programmes are naturally extended to include the need for students to perform well on examinations for teacher certification and teacher selection. Various types of learning activities may take place from each component in such a programme: participating within a learning community is one such activity. Examples of learning communities taking place in regular courses, research projects and teaching practices are shown to be major activities as in the case from Portugal. Thus, the two cases, Taiwan and Portugal, provide a diversified set of examples of learning communities with regard to the outer contexts of the different relations of the societal need for teachers, and the components in a broader sense of prospective teacher education programme.

The Inner Issues of Face-to-Face Learning Communities

Four *inner issues* for learning communities were identified by Ponte et al. (in press) at the beginning of this chapter. However, a more fundamental principle is that, in both the cases from Taiwan and Portugal, apart from each of distinct goals for learning, were similar learning communities in the sense that the prospective teacher participants were learners that learned from one another. The following provides a synthesis from the examples of the learning communities given by the two cases mentioned according to the four inner issues.

The *first issue* is the *purpose* of the group and its relation to the personal purpose of its members. The cases of Taiwan and Portugal both illustrate that the aim of the learning communities is for the professional learning of prospective teachers by generating and accumulating knowledge about teaching and teacher education, as is indicated by the model proposed by Hiebert et al. (2003). The members of the learning communities in these cases did participate in framing their tasks. This is clear in the case of Taiwan. In the Portuguese case, prospective teachers from the field-based course *Pedagogical Actions of Observation and Analysis* learned through the process of observing and reflecting on educational situations, as well during their practicum activities and in the research project. In all cases the tasks were negotiated by participants with teacher educators or project leaders.

The *second issue* concerns the *knowledge* that develops from the activity of the learning community based on shared practices. Learning activities within a learning community can be sequentially separated into three phases: entry, interacting and reflecting. Professional knowledge of teaching can be distinguished into *practice knowledge* and *thought knowledge*. Practice knowledge is context-dependent and has to be gained from real teaching practice (Goffree & Oonk, 2001). Thought knowledge is revealed when one is thinking about teaching without facing students. At the entry phase of learning communities provided by the Portuguese fieldwork course, participants focused on practice knowledge. In Taiwan, at the entry phase of Du Shu Hui for examinations, participants designed instruction units and demonstrated teaching which focused on thought knowledge. To what extent that different entry knowledge might influence the knowledge that is generated and accumulates during interacting and reflecting phases is worth further investigation. For example, at the entry phase, participants in the Math Camp designed various mathematical learning activities for implementing in a school; thus they focused on thought knowledge. Participants reflected on the fact that they saw the cultural diversities in students from different cultural backgrounds. These variations contributed to the differences in students' responses in situations of school learning. The knowledge participants of Math Camp generated was "local knowledge of teaching" that could not be generated outside the practice (see e.g., Krainer, 2003, p. 98). The prospective teachers indicated from these learning communities that they acquired knowledge that was not included in the elementary mathematics teacher education programme.

The *third issue* concerns *how learning happens* in the group. This crucial issue is somehow related to the *fourth issue* that concerns the *roles and relationships* of the participants. The roles and relationships of participants in a community might change simply by making adjustments in their operation. Such changes are necessary in order to meet the members' interests and learning needs. Let us regard, for example, the Du Shu Hui for Advanced Mathematics and the Du Shu Hui for Enhancing Mathematics Undergraduate Understanding: Each of these two learning communities had one member that had a greater mathematical competence than the others. Both began with equal competence among the participants such that they criticized each other and helped each other solve problems, but evolved to a learning activity which was dominated by a student superior in mathematical competence taking over as the leader. This is most evident in the Du Shu Hui for Enhancing Mathematics Undergraduate Understanding. Among the members, the junior student played the role as an instructor. What he learned during the process of instruction is that he became aware of what he did not understand, which he then discussed with other members. This is how learning happened in a community with a definite leadership.

In the case of Portugal, the learning communities were study groups of school courses and a research project. The prospective teachers in these communities were learning through an open and flexible discourse among them. For example, the study groups in the field-based course had no fixed curriculum, enabling a flexible planning of work with the contribution of all participants. And as the prospective teacher who participated in a research project described there was plenty of opportunity to talk to others, know what they were doing, learn about their questions, and thus cultivate an inquiry stance.

Learning may happen through reflecting on critical friends' comments in the interacting phase of a community's meetings. In the Du Shu Hui for examinations, prospective teachers started to learn together collaboratively. During the interviews, some prospective teachers expressed that the closer to the days of examination for teacher selection, the participants became aware that they were indeed competitors for the sparse number of teaching positions. However, they further expressed that this competitive relationship among participants did not change the operation within the learning community, particularly, the role of being a critical friend to one another on teaching demonstrations and in the analysis of instruction units. This regulation of operation showed that the relationship of critical friends between participants remained in the Du Shu Hui despite the competition for limited teaching positions.

ACKNOWLEDGEMENTS

The first author thanks Yuh-Chyn Leu, Yuan-Shun Lee and Wen-Xiu Xu for conducting interviews and Yu-Ping Chang and Jia-Rou Hsieh for preparing the manuscripts of cases from Taiwan.

REFERENCES

Bohl, J. V., & Van Zoest, L. R. (2002). Learning through identity: A new unit of analysis for studying teacher development. In A. Cockburn & E. Nardi (Eds.), *Proceedings of the 26th Conference of the International Group for the Psychology of Mathematics Education* (Vol. 2, pp. 137–144). Norwich, UK: School of Education and Professional Development, University of East Anglia.

Clark, K., & Borko, H. (2004). Establishing a professional learning community among middle school mathematics teachers. In M. Høines & A. Fuglestad (Eds.), *Proceedings of the 28th Conference of the International Group for the Psychology of Mathematics Education* (Vol. 2, pp. 223–230). Bergen, Norway: University College.

Dai, G. N., Kuo, L. S., Yang, H. R., Lin, Z. Z., & Wei, M. H. (Eds.). (2006). *Yearbook of teacher education statistics Republic of China*. Taipei, Taiwan: Ministry of Education.

Goffree, F., & Oonk, W. (2001). Digitizing real teaching practice for teacher education programmes: The MILE approach. In F.-L. Lin & T. Cooney (Eds.), *Making sense of mathematics teacher education* (pp. 111–145). Dordrecht, the Netherlands: Kluwer Academic Publishers.

Hiebert, J., Morris, A. K., & Glass, B. (2003). Learning to learn to teach: An "experiment" model for teaching and teacher preparation in mathematics. *Journal of Mathematics Teacher Education, 6*, 201–222.

Jaworski, B. (2004). Grappling with complexity: Co-learning in inquiry communities in mathematics teaching development. In M. J. Høines & A. B. Fuglestad (Eds.), *Proceedings of the 28th Conference of the International Group for the Psychology of Mathematics Education* (Vol. 1, pp. 17–36). Bergen, Norway: University College.

Jaworski, B. (2005). Learning communities in mathematics: Creating an inquiry community between teachers and didacticians. In R. Barwell & A. Noyes (Eds.), *Research in mathematics education, Papers of the British Society for Research into Learning Mathematics* (Vol. 7, pp. 101–120). London: BSRLM.

Jaworski, B. (1999). Teacher education through teachers' investigation into their own practice. In K. Krainer, F. Goffree, & P. Berger (Eds.), *Proceedings of the first conference of the European Society for Research in Mathematics Education* (Vol. 3, pp. 201–221). Osnabrueck, Germany: Forschungsinstitut für Mathematikdidaktik.

Jaworski, B., & Gellert, U. (2003). Educating new mathematics teachers: Integrating theory and practice, and the roles of practicing teachers. In A. J. Bishop, M. A. Clements, C. Keitel, J. Kilpatrick, & F. K. S. Leung (Eds.), *Second international handbook of mathematics education* (pp. 829–875). Dordrecht, the Netherlands: Kluwer Academic Publishers.

Krainer, K. (2003). Editorial: Teams, communities & networks. *Journal of Mathematics Teacher Education, 6*, 93–105.

Lave, J., & Wenger, E. (1991) *Situated learning: Legitimate peripheral participation*. Cambridge, UK: Cambridge University Press.

Lerman, S. (2001). A review of research perspectives in mathematics teacher education. In F.-L. Lin & T. Cooney (Eds.), *Making sense of mathematics teacher education* (pp. 33–52). Dordrecht, the Netherlands: Kluwer Academic Publishers.

Llinares, S., & Valls, J. (2007). *The building of pre-service primary teachers' knowledge of mathematics teaching: Interaction and online video case studies*. Research Paper for Department of "Innovación y Formación Didáctica". University of Alicante, Spain.

Ponte, J. P., & Brunheira, L. (2001). Analysing practice in preservice mathematics teacher education. *Journal of Mathematics Teacher Development, 3*, 16–27.

Ponte, J. P., Guerreiro, A., Cunha, H., Duarte, J., Martinho, H., Martins, C., Menezes, L., Menino, H., Pinto, H., Santos, L., Varandas, J. M., Veia, L., & Viseu, F. (2007). A comunicação nas práticas de jovens professores de Matemática [Mathematics teachers' classroom communication practices]. *Revista Portuguesa de Educação, 20*(2), 39–74.

Ponte, J. P., Oliveira, P., Varandas, J. M., Oliveira, H., & Fonseca, H. (2007). Using ICT to support reflection in pre-service mathematics teacher education. *Interactive Educational Multimedia, 14,* 79–89.

Ponte, J. P., Zaslavsky, O., Silver, E., Borba, M. C., van den Heuvel-Panhuizen, M., Gal, H., Fiorentini, D., Miskulin, R., Passos, C., Palis, G., Huang, R., & Chapman, O. (in press). Tools and settings supporting mathematics teachers' learning in and from practice. In D. Ball & R. Even (Eds.), *ICMI Study Volume: The professional education and development of teachers of mathematics.* New York: Springer.

Putnam, R. T., & Borko, H. (1997). Teacher learning: Implications of new views of cognition. In B. J. Bridlde, T. L. Good, & I. F. Goodson (Eds.), *International handbook of teachers and teaching* (Vol. 2, pp. 1223–1296). Dordrecht, the Netherlands: Kluwer Academic Publishers.

Fou-Lai Lin
Department of Mathematics
National Taiwan Normal University
Taiwan

João Pedro da Ponte
Departamento de Educação da Faculdade de Ciências
University of Lisbon
Portugal

SECTION 3

COMMUNITIES AND NETWORKS
OF MATHEMATICS TEACHERS
AS LEARNERS

STEPHEN LERMAN AND STEFAN ZEHETMEIER

6. FACE-TO-FACE COMMUNITIES AND NETWORKS OF PRACTISING MATHEMATICS TEACHERS

Studies on Their Professional Growth

In this chapter we examine the research on and by mathematics teachers working together on their practice. We examine both groups of teachers within a school, that we are calling face-to-face communities, as well as wider networks across schools, in regions or even national initiatives. We give examples of research and we raise a range of issues that call for consideration when embarking on the use of such networks and communities. Of particular concern is the sustainability of such work beyond the engagement of teachers in research or professional development activities. By "sustainability" we mean the lasting continuation of achieved benefits and effects of a project or initiative even after its termination (DEZA, 2005). We draw on the literature and our own experiences to suggest critical factors that may lead to sustainability. It may be the case, we suggest, that teachers need to engage in some type of research mode with issues that face them on a regular basis. The difficulties of sustainability might suggest more systematic support at state level for learning communities engaging in such activity in every school and across school networks.

INTRODUCTION

Researching practice in teacher groups within a school, when this takes place, may take a number of forms and serve different purposes and goals. It is perhaps not unusual to find mathematics departments in high schools wanting to analyse their student achievement data to identify areas for development. There are likely to be experiments with new resources that may be examined systematically. In general, though, we must say that teachers in most countries at all levels are under increasing pressure of expectations and demands, with performance management criteria, targets for students' achievements and other constraints. Time for systematic research by teachers is difficult to find, even when the will is there. It is therefore particularly important to identify what has and is being done in this area in order to inform others of the feasibility of such work and to provide some evidence of teachers' experience in researching their practice as members of a community.

In this chapter, we will examine the literature on communities of practising mathematics teachers to identify the kinds of organisational structures that have been established, the issues that have been identified for development, the aims of

K. Krainer and T. Wood (eds.), Participants in Mathematics Teacher Education, 133–153.

the initiatives, methodologies, and outcomes. *Sustainability* is a key issue in such initiatives, particularly where the initial motivation is for higher study or driven by a research project rather than the more intrinsic goal of improvement of teaching and learning *per se*. We will also discuss the sustainability of professional development projects and identify *communities* and *networks* as key factors fostering the long-term impact of such initiatives.

WITHIN-SCHOOL COMMUNITIES

Perhaps the most extensive framework for the study of teaching and learning is the *Lesson Study* (see also Yoshida, volume 1; Nickerson, this volume) which has been implemented in Japan for many years as a method for teachers' professional development and taken up more recently in the US (Stigler & Hiebert, 1999; Lewis & Tsuschida, 1998; Fernandez & Yoshida, 2004; Puchner & Taylor, 2006). There are also cases in which Japanese teachers provided support to US teachers to engage in Lesson Study (e.g., Fernandez, Cannon, & Chokshi, 2003). Briefly, lesson study involves a group of teachers in a school analysing in great depth how to improve specific lessons within particular topics, such that over a period of time the way concepts are taught changes. Initial development of a lesson will typically be followed by one teacher teaching the revised lesson, observed by the other teachers. They meet subsequently to review what happened, make further changes, and possibly teach the re-revised lesson again.

Other studies in the US (see also e.g., Peterson, 2005) have investigated the impact of Lesson Study on prospective teachers and indicated that this can support growth in understanding of what to teach which can, in turn, lead to growth in understanding of how to teach (Cavey & Berenson, 2005). Puchner and Taylor (2006) found that the Lesson Study work can have an impact on teacher efficacy since teachers have the potential to discover through their lesson planning that their work does have an impact on their students' engagement and learning activities in class. In a major review of the potential of lesson study to contribute to instructional achievement Lewis, Perry, and Murata (2006, p. 3) suggest that we have few examples of full Japanese lesson study cycles on which to base research and development:

> Yoshida's (1999) dissertation case of mathematics lesson study in a Japanese elementary school (which formed the basis for Stigler's and Hiebert's chapter on lesson study and is now available in Fernandez & Yoshida, 2004); and a case of science lesson study in a Japanese elementary school [...].

Lewis, Perry, and Murata (2006) call for more detailed exemplars, which can help us try to understand the mechanisms and cycles of design-based research. The bibliography of review indicates, however, that whilst these deep studies are not yet available, a great deal of work is taking place using Lesson Study, in mathematics and other curriculum subjects.

There is a long tradition of *action research* in education amongst practising teachers (see Krainer, 2006a; Benke, Hošpesová, & Tichá, this volume) with the aim of improving one's own teaching, drawing inspiration from Lewin (1948) and Schön (1983). The goal of action research is to bring about change in one's own setting, be that classroom, department or indeed whole school (Stenhouse, 1975; Elliott, 1978). Generalisability is not a major concern, site-specificity is recognised as what matters. As such, the action research movement, which "can be traced back to Stenhouse's (1975, p. 142) reconceptualisation of curriculum development from an objectives to a process model" (Adler, 1997, p. 88) saw itself as, first, making educational research relevant to the classroom and, second, as giving teachers a voice in research, indeed *the* voice in research, as teachers were claiming power over what was researched and by whom, and the right to make the decisions over what the research was intended to change. It was, for some teachers, a response to the university researcher who came into their classroom, recorded some data, and then went away to publish in journals which no teacher read, in the furtherance of their career. There are strong links between action research and *reflective practice* (Leitch & Day, 2000), whereby in the act of teaching one reflects and acts, usually unconsciously, called reflection-*in*-action, and later perhaps one reflects *on* action (Schön, 1983), this latter leading to a recognition of the need to change something, coming therefore into line with action research. One might describe action research as reflection-*on*-reflection-*on*-action. It is intentionally set against an instrumental or technical view of action research. A search of the leading relevant journal *Educational Action Research* reveals very few studies in mathematics education although the approach is known within the community (e.g., Crawford & Adler, 1996; Lerman, 1994). The two articles in the 2006 issue of the *Journal of Mathematics Teacher Education* by Goodell (2006) and Stephens (2006) draw on reflective practice and action research in their studies of prospective teachers' learning and their own practice, indicating that teacher educators can find action research a fruitful research orientation to support prospective teachers' learning. Goodell refers to the approach she took to her own practice as a teacher educator as *self-study* but this also has very similar features to action research, this latter term being more present in the mathematics education research literature (Schuck, 2002; Dinkelman, 2003). Stephens (2006) demonstrates the role of prospective teachers' reflections on their students' learning for developing awareness of their own mathematics.

To return to the way in which teachers' action research can be more than instrumental or technical, the revolutionary potential of action research was taken up by Carr and Kemmis (1986). They used Habermas's (1970) three-fold classification of social action: technical; practical; or emancipatory and they emphasised the need to take an emancipatory approach, which called for collective action to change education. However, action research is today often motivated by higher study goals or it may be instigated by engagement in research projects, usually in collaboration with university researchers. The sustainability of action research beyond the course of study or after the researchers leave, or if the funding runs out is clearly an issue, one we take up later in this chapter.

We must note here also the external drivers for face-to-face researching communities. We have indicated that the regulatory systems of education in many countries have restricted teachers' freedom to engage in research in their departments on their pedagogy, curriculum, assessment or other aspects. Conversely, that same regulatory system in many countries (e.g., UK, the Netherlands) is requiring schools to produce development plans for school improvement and in most cases preparing those plans and acting on them devolves to departments. This can be an opportunity for subject-specific quality development and quality assurance that will have to be taken on board and acted upon by senior management in the schools. We report below on some research in this area. It may well be that a community may develop from the work called for by the regulatory system.

In general, we might note that cooperation between mathematics teachers for the improvement of their pedagogy and their students' learning is possibly less common than in other school subjects because of the tendency to teacher autonomy (Lortie, 1975), particularly in mathematics. However, Visscher and Witziers (2004) examined the performance of school students in mathematics differentiated by how cooperatively mathematics departments in those schools operated, using a six-point scale for assessing the form and degree of cooperation. "A positive relationship was found between departmental policy, on the one hand, and student achievement on the other" (p. 796).

EXAMPLES

To this point, we have set out some theoretical considerations in relation to teachers working together in face-to-face communities and networks to change mathematics teaching and learning. In this section we will present some examples of within-school research and across-school projects on mathematics teaching and learning. It is our intention to select examples that highlight *key features of successful groups*, "success" being defined locally, that is, by the participants themselves. It seems to us that it is in the spirit of the theme of this chapter that we do not judge particular initiatives by objectively developed measures, if such measures could be developed at all, but by the subjective evaluations of the participants, both university staff and teachers. We will "collect" together the key features from each of the examples and, following a review of the literature and of other initiatives, we will present them all, emphasising what, for us, are the most critical factors that enable the success of any programme to be sustained beyond the end of the specific project, namely the establishment of communities or networks.

In the first three examples, all of face-to-face communities, we have chosen ones that among them cover the main possibilities in terms of initiation of such networks. The first example was the initiative of a group of teachers in a school, the second is a mutual collaboration between university researchers and school teachers, and the third is the initiative of university researchers. Our fourth example sets the scene for the study and analysis of across-school networks which follows.

Example 1

Arbaugh (2003) describes her work with a study group. A study group is defined as "a group of educators who come together on a regular basis to support each other as they work collaboratively to both develop professionally and to change their practice" (p. 141). A mathematics department chair in a US high school contacted the university researcher, Fran Arbaugh, for support in the department's development of a way of teaching geometry that was more student-centred and inquiry-based than their current practice. Over a period of six months the group met ten times, drawing on what is called the Mathematics Task Framework (Stein, Smith, Henningsen, & Silver, 2000) which "focuses on the levels of cognitive demand required by mathematical tasks and the various phases tasks pass through in their instructional use" (p. 142). The seven teachers who participated throughout reported that they valued the development of community and relationships that supported their learning. They particularly benefited from sharing experiences about aspects of their teaching, such as managing whole-class discussion, and appreciated the way the group worked, whereby no one person dominated, as is usually the case in other forms of education for practising teachers. They talked of the opportunity to think things through, to question and to experiment. They all spoke about how the study group enabled them to bring the theories, as used in the research community and practice together, facilitated by the research articles provided by Arbaugh. There is clear evidence of curriculum reform and change and a growing sense of their professionalism. One teacher commented (Arbaugh, 2003, p. 153):

> I'd not spent a lot of reflection time before. When I did, I mainly thought of how the kids could learn better. Now I look at things I could do to help them learn better. I look more at how I can create an opportunity for them to learn.

Key features of the success of this activity, according to Arbaugh, were the financial support that enabled the teachers to be free from their teaching to hold the meetings and the fact that the teachers were all from the same school. Arbaugh highlighted the tension for herself between being the expert needed to introduce new content and the autonomy and empowerment that teacher groups needed to really benefit from working within a community. Arbaugh notes that the group continued alone for a further year to work on algebra. We find it interesting that there is no mention of action research in the article, even though the research seems to have followed that approach. Features of the activity not mentioned specifically by Arbaugh but important for this review are the focus on content-specific material and the opportunity for addressing pedagogical content knowledge.

Example 2

We have referred to Japanese Lesson Study above. A modified version, called Action Education, has been developed and used in China (Huang & Bao, 2006). These authors, in designing their approach, argued that the established and well-known benefits of Lesson Study can be, and need to be, enhanced by the participation of experts who can provide input on new content and on pedagogic issues, whilst the control of what is changed and improved in the mathematics lesson remains in the hands of the teachers. In their model, the process begins with a teacher teaching a lesson, with a focus on an issue that requires reflection and examination, in front of a group of other teachers and experts (Huang & Bao, 2006, p. 280):

> A fundamental feature of "Action Education" is that the unfolding of the program is mediated within the community by the whole process of developing an exemplary lesson (Keli), including the lesson planning, lesson delivery and post-lesson reflection, and lesson-re-delivery [...] a collaborative group (the Keli group) that consists of teachers and researchers is established through discussion between researchers and a group of interested teachers.

Huang and Bao locate their approach within the literature on action research. It is a requirement of the whole learning process that the teacher group writes a narrative article that summarises their experiences, the changes, and their findings. The authors give an example of work on teaching Pythagoras' Theorem in which the group was formed from teachers in the school and a group of researchers from the local university. The teachers were aware that using an inductive approach to the proof tends to fail due to the problems of measurement, whilst expecting students to find a proof for themselves is unreasonable. They designed a series of lessons around the following diagram and the associated proof of Pythagoras' Theorem:

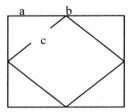

Figure 1. Diagram for the proof of Pythagoras' Theorem.

Using a series of worksheets building from numerical examples to the general, students' learning was scaffolded to a proof of the theorem.

The findings of the study revealed a number of interesting and important changes. The first to be commented upon in the article is the change in what Huang and Bao (2006, p. 290) call the teaching paradigm:

> Through a comparison of the time distribution between the previous lesson and the revised lessons in terms of teacher talk, teacher-student interaction, student exploration and student practice, it was found that the time for teacher talk, and student practice went down from 51.2% to 26.7%, and from 28.2%

to 3.2%, respectively, while the times for teacher-student interaction, and student exploration went up from 16.8% to 23.5% and from 3.8% to 46.6%, respectively.

They argue also that students learnt not only the proof but also why it constitutes a proof. They go on to illustrate the teachers' reflections and hence their learning through Keli. In their conclusions, Huang and Bao (2006, p. 295) point to some of the problems faced by this approach to development for practising teachers:

> [...] where do the qualified experts come from? How to organize a practice community including teachers and researchers? How to re-schedule the teaching program for doing Keli without disturbing the normal teaching program? How to simplify the Keli model for use by teachers, so that the phases of the model can be easily understood and implemented effectively by teachers?

They also emphasise the importance of the role of the expert:

> It also shows that the expert's roles and follow-up action are important for participating teachers' professional learning and changes in classroom practice (p. 295).

Key features, beyond those mentioned by the authors, are the focus on both content and pedagogical knowledge and skills and an open, learner-centred implementation component.

Example 3

Drawing on a situated theory of learning, Kazemi and Franke (2004, p. 205) describe the work of a group of teachers across a year examining their students' work in an attempt to develop their understanding of their students' mathematical thinking. They work with a notion of *transformation of participation* in studying the change in the teachers over that time.

> The transformation of participation view takes neither the environment nor the individual as the unit of analysis. Instead, it holds activity as the primary unit of analysis and accounts for individual development by examining how individuals engage in interpersonal and cultural-historical activities.

The intervention was the initiative of the university researchers and was based on pilot work using the Cognitively Guided Instruction (CGI) approach (Carpenter, Fennema, Franke, Levi, & Empson, 1999). The researcher, called facilitator in the paper, worked with the teachers to choose a common problem, modified by each teacher to suit her or his students. The group then met to discuss the strategies their students had used, and what those strategies revealed about their students' thinking. The researcher might add some findings from research, and assist the teachers in seeing commonalities and differences between their own findings and the research.

139

Data were collected of the group meetings and in the classrooms. Kazemi and Franke (2004, p. 213) highlight:

Two major shifts in teachers' workgroup participation emerged from our analyses. The first shift in teachers' participation centered around attending to the details of children's thinking. This shift was related to teachers' attempts to elicit their students' thinking and to their subsequent surprise and delight in noticing sophisticated reasoning in their students' work. The second shift in teachers' participation consisted of developing possible instructional trajectories in mathematics that emerged because of the group's attention to the details of student thinking.

As *Key Features* for teachers' learning, Kazemi and Franke emphasise two factors in particular as mediators of teachers' learning: the role of the facilitator in guiding their reflections and appropriate use of the students' work as material upon which to reflect. Interestingly also, from our point of view, is the indication by the authors that the initiative was sustained beyond the year of interaction with the facilitator. From our point of view we would add: the focus on both content and pedagogical knowledge and skills; an open, learner-centred implementation component; and the prolonged duration of the activity.

Example 4

Background. The Austrian Ministry of Education put in place the project IMST ("Innovations in Mathematics, Science, and Technology Teaching"; see Krainer, 2007; Pegg & Krainer, this volume). The project represents a nation-wide support system in the areas of mathematics, science and technology as well as related subjects. This project is working on the levels of professional, school, and system development, integrates systematically the principles of evaluation, gender sensitivity, and gender mainstreaming, and comprises several central programmes. One of these programmes is the setting up and supporting of *Regional and Thematic Networks* of teachers and schools. While the concept of Regional Networks is targeted at local and regional level, the Thematic Networks aim for cooperation between teachers across the whole nation. These Regional and Thematic Networks were successively established in 2004 and have gained importance in recent years, as they enable the economical use of available human and material resources. Beyond this, the establishment of such networks is expected to facilitate the setting of regional subject-related or cross-subject goals which direct the support in the teaching of mathematics, science and technology. Each Regional or Thematic Network is coordinated by a steering group, consisting of teachers, university staff, school authorities, and further relevant persons (Krainer, 2005). More than 8000 teachers have already participated in network meetings.

The implementation of Regional and Thematic Networks aims at three goals: (a) enhancement of attractiveness and quality of teaching and school development; (b) professional development of teachers; (c) increased numbers of participating teachers and schools by enhancing regional and national communication structures. The design of the networks is based on several principles: (a) utilisation of existing human, institutional and material resources; (b) accountability of participating persons and organisations; (c) target-oriented thinking and acting together with systematic evaluation (balance of action and reflection); and (d) autonomous thinking and acting of persons or organisations in close interplay with the shared goals and principles (balance of autonomy and networking). In cooperation with school authorities and universities, teachers are implementing innovative projects aimed at these goals and principles (Rauch & Kreis, 2007).

In the focus: The thematic geometry network. Recent technological development and innovation processes show impact on the teaching and learning of mathematics as well as on teacher education (see e.g., Llinares & Oliveira, this volume; Borba & Gadanidis, this volume). For example, the increasing number of accessible internet resources and miscellaneous packages of CAD (computer aided design) software are changing the context of teaching and learning geometry. This change tends to result in several consequences. On the one hand, in Austrian secondary schools descriptive geometry is not part of mathematics and represents an independent subject. The development of new technologies leads to fundamental changes in the subject's curriculum, which in turn have to be implemented by the teachers. On the other hand, the implementation of these new contents and techniques requires highly skilled teachers. Even though many secondary mathematics teachers are highly engaged and innovative, they often lack knowledge and practice regarding these new issues, simply because in Austria hardly any descriptive geometry courses for teachers' professional development are offered.

To address these issues and to support the concerned teachers, the ADG (the professional association of geometry in Austria) decided to implement action by establishing the Thematic Geometry Network, a face-to-face network of practicing mathematics (in particular geometry) teachers and teacher educators interested in subject-didactics (Gems, 2007). This is seen as a step towards becoming an Austrian Educational Competence Centre (AECC). So far in Austria six such centres are established, among these is one for mathematics education. The geometry network was created in November 2005 and aims at improving communication between descriptive geometry teachers, quick and direct exchange of information concerning recent subject-related development, and the organisation of a database containing professional development programmes and expert pools. The spirit and guiding idea of the Thematic Geometry Network is characterised by shared intentions and goals, mutual trust and respect, voluntary participation, and a common exchange principle.

On a concrete level, the network designs, initiates, implements, and evaluates various projects. All activities are coordinated by the network's steering group, consisting of teachers representing participating school types and levels. This group acts as both an inward central administrative network node (e.g., for planning meetings or distributing learning materials), and an outward contact point (e.g., providing information or handling public relations). The steering group together with different subgroups on national, regional, and local level frame the structure of the network (Müller & Gems, 2006). The Thematic Geometry Network initiates and organises annual nation wide meetings of geometry teachers: Within the scope of these "subject didactics days" the teachers and working groups share information and ideas concerning geometry teaching and learning, curriculum, prospective teacher training, and professional development.

Various working groups within the network deal with issues concerning geometry. One particular group prepares the content, curriculum, and implementation of a modified initial teacher training model. Another working group develops and provides support and assistance regarding 3D-CAD-software for students and teachers by designing and offering online tutorials and examples. A third group coordinates CAD modelling contests for students of secondary schools on regional and national levels. Yet another working group provides and maintains a touring geometry exhibition that contains objects, working and experimental stations, as well as concomitant information and material. In the future, the Thematic Geometry Network intends, on the one hand, to deepen and consolidate the actual projects and, on the other hand, to expand its activities by focussing on issues of competences, standards, assessment, and evaluation. In particular, by becoming a competence centre (AECC) the network could serve as a support structure for practicing teachers (Gems, 2007).

There are two *Key Features* for the success of this network initiative. The first is the existence of teacher leaders that are willing to overcome the lack of an adequate support system for teachers' professional development. The second is the window of opportunity when IMST offered the establishment of Thematic Networks. In short: It is a combination of internal human resources and external support.

KEY FACTORS IN FOSTERING SUSTAINABILITY OF PROFESSIONAL DEVELOPMENT

Rationale for Examining Sustainability

Most reform projects are initiated to enhance the quality of teaching and learning in the specific setting of schools and across regions and nations. Ingvarson, Meiers, and Beavis (2005, p. 2) state that

> Professional development for teachers is now recognised as a vital component of policies to enhance the quality of teaching and learning in our schools. Consequently, there is increased interest in research that identifies features of effective professional learning.

In particular, the formation of face-to-face communities and networks, as described in the examples above, is seen as one of the most promising ways to reach the goal of enhanced teacher quality. In the next section, the following questions are addressed: 1) "What kinds of effects on teacher quality are possible?" and 2) "How can this impact be sustained?"

The expected effects of such projects by both the facilitators and the participants are not only related to the professional development of individual teachers to improve teacher quality, but also to the enhancement of the quality of whole schools, regions and nations. Expected outcomes are not only focused on short-term effects that occur during or at the end of the project, but also on long-term effects that emerge (even some years) after the project's termination (Peter, 1996). The desideratum of all such projects and community building activities for providing teachers support and qualification is to enhance the learning of students. As Mundry (2005) states, "We recognize professional development as a tool focused on improving student outcomes" (p. 2); "Funders, providers, and practitioners tend to agree that the ultimate goal of professional development is improved outcomes for learners" (Kerka, 2003, p. 1). This strategy, to achieve change at the level of students (improved outcomes) by fostering change at the teachers' level (professional development and community building), is based on the assumption of a causal relationship between students' and teachers' classroom performance, "high quality professional development will produce superior teaching in classrooms, which will, in turn, translate into higher levels of student achievement" (Supovits, 2001, p. 81). Even though a variety of external factors influence students' outcomes (e.g., the socio-economic background of students' parents), the above mentioned hypothesis was verified in several studies such as Fennema and Loef (1992). Hattie (2003) states, "It is what teachers know, do, and care about which is very powerful in this learning equation" (p. 2).

Most evaluations and impact analyses of professional development are formative or summative in nature; they are conducted during or at the end of a project and exclusively provide results regarding short-term effects. Apart from these findings which are highly relevant for critical reflection of the terminated project and necessary for the conception of similar projects in the future, an analysis of sustainable effects is crucial and the central goal of professional development; "too many resources are invested in professional development to ignore its impact over time" (Loucks-Horsley, Stiles, & Hewson, 1996, p. 5). But this kind of sustainability analysis is often missing because of a lack of material, financial and personal resources. "Reformers and reform advocates, policymakers and funders often pay little attention to the problem and requirements of sustaining a reform, when they move their attention to new implementation sites or end active involvement with the project" (McLaughlin & Mitra, 2001, p. 303). Despite its central importance, research on this issue is generally lacking (Rogers, 2003) and, "Few studies have actually examined the sustainability of reforms over long periods of time" (Datnow, 2006, p. 133). Hargreaves (2002, p. 120) summarises the situation as follows:

> As a result, many writers and reformers have begun to worry and write about not just how to effect snapshots of change at any particular point, but how to sustain them, keep them going, make them last. The sustainability of

educational change has, in this sense, become one of the key priorities in the field.

Levels of Impact

When analysing possible effects of professional development, the question of possible levels of impact arises. Which levels of impact are possible and/or most important? How can impact be classified? Ball (1995) points out that teacher educators and facilitators should take a "stance of inquiry and experimentation" (p. 29) themselves regarding these questions of impact. Recent literature provides some information as to the answers to these two questions; the following levels of impact are identified (Lipowsky, 2004):

- *Teachers' knowledge:* This level includes different taxonomies of teachers' knowledge (e.g., subject knowledge and general and subject-specific pedagogical knowledge; e.g., Shulman, 1987), or attention-based knowledge (Ainley & Luntley, 2005), including knowledge about learning and teaching processes, assessment and evaluation methods and classroom management (Ingvarson et al., 2005).
- *Teachers' beliefs:* This level includes a variety of different aspects of beliefs about mathematics, and its teaching and learning (Leder, Pehkonen, & Törner, 2002), as well as the perceived professional growth, the satisfaction of the participating teachers (Lipowsky, 2004), perceived teacher efficacy (Ingvarson et al., 2005) and the teachers' opinions and values (Bromme, 1997). Shifter and Simon (1992) highlight that change of teachers' beliefs is indeed common and desired, but is not necessarily an accomplished goal.
- *Teachers' practice:* At this level, the focus is on classroom activities and structures, teaching and learning strategies, methods or contents (Ingvarson et al., 2005).
- *Students' outcomes:* This level is related to professional development's central task, the improved learning and consequential results for students (Kerka, 2003; Mundry, 2005; Weiss & Klein, 2006).

Classification and Analysis of Impact

Classification and analysis of impact is based on two major types of effects: short-term effects that emerge during or at the end of a project; and, long-term effects that occur after the project's termination. Effects that are both short-term and long-term are considered by some to be sustainable. However, as Fullan (2006) points out, short-term effects are "necessary to build trust with the public or shareholders for longer-term investments" (p. 120). Although short-term effects are important and it may be that it is only possible to accomplish short-term impact, this does not provide for sustainable impact and the result would be to "win the battle, [but] lose the war" (p. 120), because sustainability, in this case, means the lasting continuation of achieved benefits and effects of a project or initiative beyond the termination of a professional development project or effort (DEZA, 2005). Hargreaves and Fink (2003) state, "Sustainable improvement requires investment in building long term capacity for improvement, such as the development of teachers' skills, which will stay with them forever, long after the project money has gone" (p. 3). Moreover, analysis of sustainable impact should not be limited to effects that were planned at the beginning of the project; it is important to examine the unintended effects and unanticipated consequences that were not known at the beginning of the project (Rogers, 2003; Stockmann, 1992).

Factors Fostering Sustainability

To give an overview and to summarise the literature concerning factors contributing to and fostering the sustainability of change, the following four elements of professional development projects are used to classify these factors: *participating teachers*, *participating facilitators*, the *project or initiative* itself, and the *context* that embedded the first three elements (Borko, 2004). Rice (1992) states that "these factors relate to the nature of teachers as people, schools as organisations and change processes themselves including many variables which facilitate or constrain change" (p. 470). Finally, we argue that the core factors fostering sustainability are *community building* and *networking*.

Participating teachers. A professional development project should meet the teachers' needs and interests (Clarke, 1991; Peter, 1996) and it should be coherent with teachers' other learning activities (Garet, Porter, Desimone, Birman, & Yoon, 2001), fit into the context in which they operate, and provide direct links to teachers' curriculum (Mundry, 2005). The teachers should be involved in the conception and implementation of the project; this allows teachers to develop an affective relationship towards the project by developing teachers' ownership in the proposed change (Clarke, 1991; Peter, 1996); it prepares and supports them to serve in leadership roles (Loucks-Horsley et al., 1996); and it focuses on the teachers' possibility to influence their own development process (empowerment) (Harvey & Green, 2000). These features act to facilitate attendance and trust, which in turn affects the teachers' future decisions concerning their development process. This ends up in a spiral process, which continually enhances the level of teachers' empowerment.

An "inquiry stance" is another factor that fosters impact on sustainability (Farmer, Gerretson, & Lassak, 2003, p. 343; Jaworski, this volume). Teachers understand their role as learners in their own teaching process and try to understand, reflect, and improve their practice. This stance requires professional and personal maturity as well as the possibility to critically reflect one's own decisions and activities (Farmer et al., 2003). This notion was also used by Cochran-Smith and Lytle (1999, p. 289) when describing the attitude of teachers who participate in communities towards the relationship of theory and practice:

"Teachers and student teachers who take an inquiry stance work within inquiry communities to generate local knowledge, envision and theorise their practice, and interpret and interrogate the theory and research of others".

Participating facilitators. Similar to the teachers, are also the participating facilitators of the professional development programme. They also should take a "stance of inquiry" (Ball, 1995, p. 29) towards their activities, reflect on their practice and evaluate its impact (Farmer et al., 2003). In addition, another important factor is the facilitators' knowledge, understanding, and whether they have a well-defined image of effective learning and teaching (Loucks-Horsley et al., 1996).

Project or initiative. Each innovation, intervention, or project (e.g., the formation of communities and networks) is unique regarding its design. Therefore, impact analysis needs to include these differences in organisational and structural characteristics. Rogers (2003) studied the process of *diffusion of innovations* and pointed out that the impact of an innovation depends on several characteristics (Relative Advantage, Compatibility, Complexity, Trialability, and Observability). Fullan (2001) also described similar characteristics (Need, Clarity, Complexity, Quality and Practicality) that influence the acceptance and impact of innovative processes.
- *Relative Advantage:* This includes the individually perceived advantage of the innovation (which is not necessarily the same as the objective one). An innovation with greater relative advantage will be adopted more rapidly (Rogers, 2003).
- *Compatibility* and *Need* denote the degree to which the innovation is perceived by the adopters as consistent with their needs, values and experiences (Fullan, 2001; Rogers, 2003).
- *Complexity* and *Clarity* indicate the adopter's perception of how difficult the innovation is to be understood or used (Rogers, 2003) which relates to concomitant difficulties and changes (Fullan, 2001). Thus, more complex innovations are adopted rather slowly, compared to less complicated ones. *Clarity* (Fullan, 2001) supports reducing complexity and perceiving advantages.
- *Trialability* means the possibility of potential adopters to experiment and test the innovation on a limited basis. Divisible innovations that can be tested in small steps therefore, represent less uncertainty and will be adopted as a whole more rapidly (Rogers, 2003).
- *Quality and Practicality* makes an impact on the change processes. High quality innovations that are easily applicable in practice are more rapidly accepted (Fullan, 2001).
- *Observability:* The more the results of the innovation are visible to other persons (e.g., parents, principals) and organisations, the more likely the innovation is accepted and adopted (Rogers, 2003).

For example, if face-to-face communities and networks are expected to make an impact, they should provide a high level of relative advantage, should meet the teachers' needs and their goals, and structures should be clearly and easily understandable, they should be practical and usable, of high quality and their results should be visible to others.

Context. The particular importance of the school context that embeds participating teachers, participating facilitators, and the project or initiative itself, as a factor fostering the sustainability of innovations and change processes is well documented (e.g., Fullan, 1990; McNamara, Jaworski, Rowland, Hodgen, & Prestage, 2002; Noddings, 1992; Owston, 2007). Teachers promoting change (e.g., by participating in face-to-face communities and networks) need administrative support and resources (McLaughlin & Mitra, 2001). Support from outside the school by parents or the district policy is also an important factor (McLaughlin & Mitra, 2001; Owston, 2007). Moreover, school-based support can be provided by students and colleagues (Ingvarson et al., 2005; Owston, 2007), and in particular by the principal (Clarke, 1991; Fullan, 2006; Krainer, 2006b). As Owston (2007) states, "Support from the school principal is another essential factor that contributes to sustainability" (p. 70). Moreover, to foster sustainability not only at the individual (teacher's) level but also at the organisational (school's) level, Fullan (2006) proposes a new type of leadership that "needs to go beyond the successes of increasing student achievement and move toward leading organizations to sustainability" (p. 113), and calls these leaders "system thinkers in action". In particular, these school leaders should "widen their sphere of engagement by interacting with other schools" (p. 113) and should engage in "capacity-building through networks" (p. 115).

Community building and networking as key factors fostering sustainability. The review of the literature on sustainability of structures for developing teaching and learning indicates that there is a great deal of research on factors that can lead to such initiatives continuing beyond the initiation stage. There is plenty of evidence to demonstrate that the community as a whole and the participants in particular benefit and learn from any initiatives to develop the teaching and learning of mathematics. That such projects may be initiated by higher level study, the research interests of university faculty or the immediate needs of teachers in a school or network of schools is the nature of the professional educational environment in most *countries*.

Research findings, illustrated in large part by the examples given above, indicate that there are several characteristics of successful initiatives; we are particularly interested here in features that might foster the sustainability of a professional development programme or project: it should focus on content knowledge (Garet et al., 2001; Ingvarson et al., 2005), use content-specific material (Maldonado, 2002), and provide teachers with opportunities to develop both content and pedagogical content knowledge and skills (Loucks-Horsley et al., 1996; Mundry, 2005).

Moreover, an effective professional development initiative includes opportunities for active and inquiry-based learning (Garet et al., 2001; Ingvarson et al., 2005; Maldonado, 2002), authentic and readily adaptable student-centered mathematics learning activities, and an open, learner-centered implementation component (Farmer et al., 2003). Further factors fostering the effectiveness and sustainability of the programme are: prolonged duration of the activity (Garet et al., 2001; Maldonado, 2002), ongoing and follow-up support opportunities (Ingvarson et al., 2005; Maldonado, 2002; Mundry, 2005), and continuous evaluation, assessment, and feedback (Ingvarson et al., 2005; Loucks-Horsley et al., 1996; Maldonado, 2002).

In particular, research indicates that *communicative and cooperative activities* represent key factors fostering sustainable impact of professional development programmes. This general result is supported by several authors and studies, even if the categories used to describe these activities are different: Clarke (1991), Peter (1996), and Mundry (2005) point to cooperation and joint practice of teachers, Loucks-Horsley et al. (1996) and Maldonado (2002) highlight the importance of learning communities, McLaughlin and Mitra (2001) identify supportive communites of practice, Arbaugh (2003) refers to study groups, and Ingvarson et al. (2005) stress professional communities as factors contributing to the sustainability of effects. In particular, providing rich opportunities for collaborative reflection and discussion (e.g., of teachers' practice, students' work, or other artifacts) presents a core feature of effective change processes (Clarke, 1991; Farmer et al., 2003; Hošpesová & Tichá, 2006; Ingvarson et al., 2005; Park-Rogers et al., 2007). In this regard, research findings, exemplified by some of the authors in our examples, point to the issue of power relations between the external facilitator(s) and the teachers in the school. There is no one prescription for the best form of such relations, but it is clear that teachers must feel themselves empowered and autonomous and that the expert(s) play a role that supports their work rather than dominates it. Once again, this issue recalls the motivation of the action research movement but with the emphasis on collaboration and cooperation, not one of excluding the academic. Both, internals and externals need to be regarded as experts.

Reducing the long list of key features, on the basis of the examples we have given above as illustrative of the field, we suggest that there is evidence to show that large scale, centralised projects across schools, such as the Thematic Geometry Network, are sustainable. Within-school developments such as lesson study are also sustainable provided that the developments are supported by school resources (time being the most important) and that they are seen by the teachers as what they choose to do for the improvement of their mathematics teaching and their students' learning, because they see the benefits and the impact.

We believe that the job of a teacher should incorporate a *lifelong process of learning* about and developing one's teaching and two examples of sustainable structures, lesson study and Thematic Geometry Network, are indications of what works. Not all centralised interventions are benign of course, but where the participants (teachers in the main but also students and school managers), see the benefits of on-going research and development, sustainability is possible.

CONCLUSION

Reviewing the work we have described and analysed in this chapter, we end here with some final, concluding observations:

- There are few examples of either face-to-face or cross-school networks research when compared to the rest of the body of research on mathematics teacher education.
- Where there are examples, the effects seem to be extremely positive on teachers' perspectives and understanding and, where there is evidence, on students' achievements.
- Providing the opportunity for time out of the classroom for meetings may be a key to success but is costly.
- Engagement of academics as experts appears to be crucial, at least because when teachers do research as a group without an academic it may not be written up and disseminated. In addition, teachers' groups often call for support in aspects of research activity, such as access to literature, research design and data analysis.
- Community building and networking represent the core factors fostering sustainable impact of professional development programmes.
- In order to go deeper with these observations, we unquestionably need more research on how fruitful initiatives can be sustained.
- Whether dissemination of the outcomes and experiences of one network can or will be taken up by another network or by individual teachers remains an unresolved question. If it is the case that teachers' change and growth, perhaps what we should call *teacher learning*, only takes place when teachers engage in these activities themselves and not through reading the work of others, we may need to radically re-think and advocate that systematic national initiatives foster learning communities in *every* school as part of its work.

REFERENCES

Adler, J. (1997). Mathematics teacher as researcher from a South African Perspective. *Educational Action Research, 5*, 87–103.

Ainley, J., & Luntley, M. (2005). What teachers know: The knowledge base of classroom practice. In M. Bosch (Ed.), *Proceedings of the Fourth Congress of the European Society for Research in Mathematics Education* (pp. 1410–1419). Sant Feliu de Guíxols, Spain: European Research in Mathematics Education.

Arbaugh, F. (2003). Study groups as a form of professional development for secondary mathematics teachers. *Journal of Mathematics Teacher Education, 6*, 139–163.

Ball, D. L. (1995). Developing mathematics reform: What don't we know about teacher learning – but would make good working hypotheses? *NCRTL Craft Paper, 95*(4). (ERIC Document Reproduction Service No. ED399262).

Borko, H. (2004). Professional development and teacher learning: Mapping the terrain. *Educational Researcher, 33*(8), 3–15.

Bromme, R. (1997). Kompetenzen, Funktionen und unterrichtliches Handeln des Lehrers [Expertise, tasks and instructional practice of teachers]. In F. Weinert (Eds.), *Enzyklopädie der Psychologie. Band 3. Psychologie des Unterrichts und der Schule* (pp. 177–212). Göttingen, Germany: Hogrefe.

Carpenter, T. P., Fennema, E., Franke, M. L., Levi, L., & Empson, S. B. (1999). *Children's mathematics: Cognitively guided instruction.* Portsmouth, NH: Heinemann.

Carr, W., & Kemmis, S. (1986). *Becoming critical: Education, knowledge and action research.* London: Falmer Press.

Cavey, L. O., & Berenson, S. B. (2005). Learning to teach high school mathematics: Patterns of growth in understanding right triangle trigonometry during lesson plan study. *Journal of Mathematical Behavior, 24,* 171–190.

Clarke, D. M. (1991). *The role of staff development programs in facilitating professional growth.* Madison, WI: University of Wisconsin.

Cochran-Smith, M., & Lytle, S. (1999). Relationships of knowledge and practice: Teacher learning in communities. *Review of Research in Education, 24,* 249–305.

Crawford, K., & Adler, J. (1996). Teachers as researchers in mathematics education. In A. Bishop & C. Keitel (Eds.), *The international handbook on mathematics education* (pp. 1187–1206). Dordrecht, the Netherlands: Kluwer Academic Publishers.

Datnow, A. (2006). Comments on Michael Fullan's, "The future of educational change: System thinkers in action". *Journal of Educational Change, 7,* 133–135.

DEZA / Direktion für Entwicklungshilfe und Zusammenarbeit. (2005). Glossar deutsch. Bern: DEZA.

Dinkelman, T. (2003). Self-study in teacher education: A means and ends tool for promoting reflective teaching. *Journal of Teacher Education, 54,* 6–18.

Elliott, J. (1978). What is action research in schools? *Journal of Curriculum Studies, 10,* 355–357.

Farmer, J., Gerretson, H., & Lassak, M. (2003). What teachers take from professional development: Cases and implications. *Journal of Mathematics Teacher Education, 6,* 331–360.

Fennema, E., & Loef, M. L. (1992). Teachers' knowledge and its impact. In D. Grouws (Ed.), *Handbook of research on mathematics teaching and learning* (pp. 147–164). New York: Macmillan.

Fernandez, C., Cannon, J., & Chokshi, S. (2003). A US-Japan lesson study collaboration reveals critical lenses for examining practice. *Teaching and Teacher Education, 19,* 171–185.

Fernandez, C., & Yoshida, M. (2004). *Lesson study: A Japanese approach to improving mathematics teaching and learning.* Mahwah, NJ: Lawrence Erlbaum Associates.

Fullan, M. (1990). Staff development, innovation and institutional development. In B. Joyce (Ed.), *Changing school culture through staff development* (pp. 3–25). Alexandria, VA: Association for Supervision and Curriculum Development.

Fullan, M. (2001). *The new meaning of educational change* (3rd edition). New York: Teachers College Press.

Fullan, M. (2006).The future of educational change: System thinkers in action. *Journal of Educational Change, 7,* 113–122.

Garet, M., Porter, A., Desimone, L., Birman, B., & Yoon, K. (2001). What makes professional development effective? Results from a national sample of teachers. *American Educational Research Journal, 38,* 915–945.

Gems, W. (2007). *Thematisches Netzwerk "Geometrie" in der Sekundarstufe 1* [The thematic geometry network in lower secondary school]. Bericht 2007. Saalfelden, Klagenfurt, Austria: IUS.

Goodell, J. E. (2006). Using critical incident reflections: A self-study as a mathematics teacher educator. *Journal of Mathematics Teacher Education, 9,* 221–248.

Habermas, J. (1970). Towards a theory of communicative competence. In H. P. Dreitzel (Ed.), *Recent sociology, No. 2.* New York: Macmillan.

Hargreaves, A. (2002). Sustainability of educational change: The role of social geographies. *Journal of Educational Change, 3,* 189–214.

Hargreaves, A., & Fink, D. (2003). Sustaining leadership. *Phi Delta Kappan, 84*, 693–700.

Harvey, L., & Green, D. (2000). Qualität definieren [Defining quality]. *Zeitschrift für Pädagogik, Beiheft, 41*, 17–37.

Hattie, J. (2003, October). *Teachers make a difference. What is the research evidence?* Paper presented at the Australian Council of Educational Research conference: Building Teacher Quality. Melbourne, Australia.

Hošpesová, A., & Tichá, M. (2006). Qualified pedagogical reflection as a way to improve mathematics education. *Journal of Mathematics Teacher Education, 9*, 129–156.

Huang, R., & Bao, J. (2006). Towards a model for teacher professional development in China: Introducing Keli. *Journal of Mathematics Teacher Education, 9*, 279–298.

Ingvarson, L., Meiers, M., & Beavis, A. (2005). Factors affecting the impact of professional development programs on teachers' knowledge, practice, student outcomes and efficacy. *Education Policy Analysis Archives, 13*(10), 1–28.

Kazemi, E., & Franke, M. L. (2004). Teacher learning in mathematics: Using student work to promote collective inquiry. *Journal of Mathematics Teacher Education, 7*, 203–235.

Kerka, S. (2003). Does adult educator professional development make a difference? *ERIC Myths and Realities, 28*, 1–2.

Krainer, K. (2005). IMST3 – A sustainable support system. In Austrian Federal Ministry of Education (Ed.), *Austrian Education News 44* (pp. 8–14). Vienna: Austrian Federal Ministry of Education.

Krainer, K. (2006a). Editorial: Action research and mathematics teacher education. *Journal of Mathematics Teacher Education, 9*, 213–219.

Krainer, K. (2006b). How can schools put mathematics in their centre? Improvement = content + community + context. In J. Novotná, H. Moraová, M. Krátká, & N. Stehlíková (Eds.), *Proceedings of 30th conference of the international group for the psychology of mathematics education* (Vol. 1, pp. 84–89). Prague, Czech, Republic: Charles University.

Krainer, K. (2007). *Beiträge von IMST zur Steigerung der Attraktivität des MNI-Unterrichts in Österreich* [Contributions of IMST² to enhance the attractiveness of mathematics and science education in Austria]. Unpublished manuscript.

Leder, G., Pehkonen, E., & Törner, G. (2002). *Beliefs: A hidden variable in mathematics education?* Dordrecht, the Netherlands: Kluwer Academic Publishers.

Leitch, R., & Day, C. (2000). Action research and reflective practice: Towards a holistic view. *Educational Action Research, 8*, 179–193.

Lerman, S. (1994). Reflective practice. In B. Jaworski & A. Watson (Eds.), *Mentoring in the education of mathematics teachers* (pp. 52–64). Lewes, UK: Falmer Press.

Lewin, K. (1948). Action research and minority problems. In G. W. Lewin (Ed.), *Resolving social conflicts* (pp. 201–216). New York: Harper & Row.

Lewis, C., Perry, R., & Murata, A. (2006). How should research contribute to instructional achievement? The case of lesson study. *Educational Researcher, 35*(3), 3–14.

Lewis, C., & Tsuschida, I. (1998). A lesson is like a swiftly flowing river: How research lessons improve Japanese education. *American Educator, Winter,* 14–17 & 50–52.

Lipowsky, F. (2004). Was macht Fortbildungen für Lehrkräfte erfolgreich? [What makes professional development successful?]. *Die deutsche Schule, 96*, 462–479.

Lortie, D. C. (1975). *School teacher: A sociological study*. Chicago: University of Chicago Press.

Loucks-Horsley, S., Stiles, K., & Hewson, P. (1996). Principles of effective professional development for mathematics and science education: A synthesis of standards. *NISE Brief, 1*(1), 1–6.

Maldonado, L. (2002). *Effective professional development. Findings from research*. Retrieved 12.1.2007 from www.collegeboard.com.

McLaughlin, M., & Mitra, D. (2001). Theory-based change and change-based theory: Going deeper, going broader. *Journal of Educational Change, 2*, 301–323.

McNamara, O., Jaworski, B., Rowland, T., Hodgen, J., & Prestage, S. (2002). *Developing mathematics teaching and teachers*. Unpublished manuscript.

Müller, T., & Gems, W. (2006). *Thematisches Netzwerk "Geometrie" in der Sekundarstufe I* [The thematic geometry network in lower secondary school]. Mattsee, Klagenfurt, Austria: IUS.

Mundry, S. (2005). *What experience has taught us about professional development.* National Network of Eisenhower Regional Consortia and Clearinghouse.

Noddings, N. (1992). Professionalization and mathematics teaching. In D. Grouws (Ed.), *Handbook of research on mathematics teaching and learning* (pp. 197–208). New York: Macmillan.

Owston, R. (2007). Contextual factors that sustain innovative pedagogical practice using technology: An international study. *Journal of Educational Change, 8,* 61–77.

Park-Rogers, M., Abell, S., Lannin, J., Wang, C., Musikul, K., Barker, D., & Dingman, S. (2007). Effective professional development in science and mathematics education: Teachers' and facilitators' views. *Journal of Science and Mathematics Education, 7,* 507–532.

Peter, A. (1996). *Aktion und Reflexion – Lehrerfortbildung aus international vergleichender Perspektive* [Action and reflection – Teacher education from an international comparative perspective]. Weinheim, Germany: Deutscher Studien Verlag.

Peterson, B. (2005). Student teaching in Japan: The lesson. *Journal of Mathematics Teacher Education, 8,* 61–74.

Puchner, L. D., & Taylor, A. R. (2006). Lesson study, collaboration and teacher efficacy: Stories from two school-based math lesson study groups. *Teaching and Teacher Education, 22,* 922–934.

Rauch, F., & Kreis, I. (2007). Das Schwerpunktprogramm "Schulentwicklung": Konzept, Arbeitsweisen und Theorien [The priority programme 'school development': Concept, functions, and theories]. In F. Rauch & I. Kreis (Eds.), *Lernen durch fachbezogene Schulentwicklung* (pp. 37–58). Vienna, Austria: StudienVerlag.

Rice, M. (1992). Towards a professional development ethos. In B. Southwell, B. Perry, & K. Owens (Eds.), *Space – The first and final frontier. Proceedings of the fifteenth annual conference of the mathematical research group of Australasia* (pp. 470–477). Sydney, Australia: MERGA.

Rogers, E. (2003). *Diffusion of innovations.* New York: Free Press.

Schön, D. A. (1983). *The reflective practitioner.* New York: Basic Books.

Schuck, S. (2002). Using self-study to challenge my teaching practice in mathematics education. *Reflective Practice, 3,* 327–337.

Shifter, D., & Simon, M. (1992). Assessing teachers' development of a constructivist view of mathematics learning. *Teaching and Teacher Education, 8,* 187–197.

Shulman, L. (1987). Knowledge and teaching: Foundations of the new reform. *Harvard Educational Review, 57,* 1–22.

Stein, M. K., Smith, M. S., Henningsen, M. A., & Silver, E. A. (2000). *Implementing standards-based mathematics instruction: A casebook for professional development.* New York: Teachers College Press.

Stenhouse, L. (1975). *An introduction to curriculum research and development.* London: Heinemann.

Stephens, A. C. (2006). Equivalence and relational thinking: Preservice elementary teachers' awareness of opportunities and misconceptions. *Journal of Mathematics Teacher Education, 9,* 249–278.

Stigler, J., & Hiebert, J. (1999). *The teaching gap: Best ideas from the world's teachers for improving education in the classroom.* New York: Free Press.

Stockmann, R. (1992). *Die Nachhaltigkeit von Entwicklungsprojekten* [The sustainability of development projects]. Opladen, Germany: Westdeutscher Verlag.

Supovitz, J. (2001). Translating teaching practice into improved student achievement. In S. Fuhrman (Ed.), *From the capitol to the classroom. Standards-based reforms in the states* (pp. 81–98). Chicago: University of Chicago Press.

Visscher, A. J., & Witziers, B. (2004). Subject departments as professional communities? *British Educational Research Journal, 30,* 785–800.

Weiss, H., & Klein, L. (2006). Pathways from workforce development to child outcomes. *The Evaluation Exchange, 11*(4), 2–4.

Yoshida, M. (1999). *Lesson study: A case of a Japanese approach to improving instruction through school-based teacher development.* Unpublished doctoral dissertation, University of Chicago, Chicago.

Stephen Lerman
Department of Education
London South Bank University
United Kingdom

Stefan Zehetmeier
Institut für Unterrichts- und Schulentwicklung
University of Klagenfurt
Austria

SALVADOR LLINARES AND FEDERICA OLIVERO

7. VIRTUAL COMMUNITIES AND NETWORKS OF PROSPECTIVE MATHEMATICS TEACHERS

Technologies, Interactions and New Forms of Discourse

The chapter discusses the use of communication technologies and the development of new forms of discourse in the context of prospective mathematics teachers' learning. Two key ideas are identified from current studies and used to frame the processes that are generated when prospective teachers use new communication tools: the notion of community and the features of knowledge building processes and discourses, within a sociocultural framework. Three examples are discussed in details: creating and sustaining virtual communities and networks, constructing meaning through online interactions, writing and reading blogs and videopapers. Finally, the chapter draws together key factors that should be considered when computer-supported communication tools are introduced in mathematics teacher education and that seem to shape the characteristics of online interactions, construction of knowledge and creation and support of communities of practice.

INTRODUCTION

The use of information and communication technologies in Higher Education and in initial teacher education programmes has increased over the last few years. A range of new computer-based communication tools are now available for teacher educators to adapt and transform into pedagogical tools aimed at developing new approaches to teacher education (Blanton, Moorman, & Trathen, 1998; Mousley, Lambdin, & Koc, 2003). *Communication tools* are tools that typically handle the capturing, storing, and presentation of communication, usually written but increasingly including also audio and video. They can also handle mediated interactions between a pair or group of users.[1] Communication tools can be either synchronous or asynchronous, and include bulletin boards, e-mail, chats, virtual video-based cases, computer-mediated conferences and forums. These tools can be embedded in interactive learning environments that support the creation of virtual communities and networks. These new communication tools not only facilitate access to information, but also have the potential to change the personal and social relations amongst individuals and the way we understand the process of becoming a mathematics teacher (e.g., knowledge and identity, Borba & Villareal, 2005).

---

[1] http://en.wikipedia.org/wiki/Social_software

K. Krainer and T. Wood (eds.), Participants in Mathematics Teacher Education, 155–179.

Current studies explore a number of ways in which communication tools can be used in the context of teacher education. Nowadays, new technologies can be used to support *interaction* among prospective teachers. For example, computer-mediated communication may provide support for *online discussions* (Byman, Järvela, & Häkkinen, 2005) during problem solving activities or for the creation of virtual communities. New communication tools such as forum and bulletin boards allow extension of classroom boundaries and provide opportunities to develop skills that might enable prospective teachers to learn from practice and develop *knowledge-building practices* (Derry, Gance, Gance, & Schaleger, 2000). Bulletin boards and online discussion also enable content-related communication including course materials, resources and activities and are used by prospective teachers as source of support for their development. Questions are generated about the *social and cognitive effects* of interactions in this online social space. In particular, it is interesting to look at how different forms of participation may operate towards mediating meanings in conversations within prospective teachers' learning. In these social interaction spaces, reciprocal understanding and the process of becoming a member of a community support the possibilities of taking and sharing different perspectives that require an understanding of others' points of view when they join in the same activity. By using new communication tools, *new forms of discourse* are emerging, as for example argumentative discourse, videopapers and blogs, which are used both as tools to represent and communicate knowledge, practice and research in a new form but also as tools for prospective teachers' reflection, self-reflection and assessment and for sharing good practice.

The question of how these new forms of discourse and new forms of participation operate to mediate meaning construction in conversations and to create and sustain virtual communities is central to our understanding of the contribution of interactive learning environments and new communication tools in teacher education. In this sense, learning in collaborative settings is based on the assumption that learners engage in specific discourse activities and that learning stems from the relationship between the nature of the participation and the content of these discourses (learning is seen as becoming a member of a community that shares knowledge, values and skills). This situation assumes that computer-mediated communication is a tool used to mediate prospective teacher learning and reflective thinking and that it can mediate and transform teachers' experiences (Blanton et al., 1998).

The introduction of new communication tools in mathematics teacher education is *generating new research questions* and is calling for new analytical procedures. What emerges from the literature is on the one hand the scarcity of research in this area, and, on the other hand, the attempts to use theoretical constructs from sociocultural perspectives of learning to explain the processes taking place when these tools are implemented. Common features to current studies are the description of the activities and assignments tackled by prospective teachers, the enumeration of the messages exchanged and the subsequent development of analytic categories drawing on discourse analysis (Schrire, 2006; Strijbos, Martens, Prins, & Jochems, 2006). Research also suggests that prospective teachers should learn how to contextualise these tools as learning means rather than using them in isolated initiatives. When these communication tools are used as mediators in prospective teachers' learning then some issues are generated about the nature of this kind of learning. Mathematics educators are attempting to provide claims about both the individual and collective construction of meaning in communities and on the relationship between discourse and knowing. Another important point for discussion is what role these tools play in relation to the specific nature of mathematical knowledge and knowledge of mathematics education.

The chapter is structured taking into account these general features emerging from current studies on the use of tools and the creation of virtual communities and networks in the context of teacher education. In the second subchapter, we describe how the sociocultural perspective on mathematics teachers' learning is being used in current research studies. We identify two key ideas that can help us understand the generated processes: the notion of *community* and the features of *knowledge building processes and discourses*. These ideas underline different aspects of learning that are considered in those studies: learning as identity (becoming), learning as practice (doing) and learning as meaning (experience). Three examples of experiences with three different tools are introduced and discussed separately. Although we use a common theoretical framework to frame the three examples, each subchapter will highlight the specificities that each tool brings to the framework, as emerging from the literature. The third subchapter focuses on how virtual communities are created and sustained (learning as identity, becoming). The next subchapter deals with the question of how online interactions support the construction of meanings when prospective mathematics teachers are involved in solving specific learning tasks (learning as meaning, doing); and the fifth subchapter focuses on how the use of new forms of communication and discourse (blogs and videopapers) supports prospective mathematics teacher learning (learning as meaning, how experience becomes knowledge through discourse). Finally, in the last subchapter we discuss some emerging issues and suggest ideas for further research in mathematics teacher education.

USING SOCIOCULTURAL PERSPECTIVES TO INTERPRET PROSPECTIVE TEACHERS' LEARNING

Sociocultural theories of learning and development offer useful conceptual tools for studying prospective teachers' learning when new communication technologies are introduced in mathematics teacher education. This perspective views learning both as a process of meaning construction and as a process of participation in mathematics teaching practices (Greeno, 1998; Lerman, 2001; Llinares & Krainer, 2006). Sociocultural theories underline the social processes underpinning learning and consider that learning is mediated by participation in social processes of knowledge construction scaffolded by social artefacts or tools. These tools can be both technical tools and conceptual tools and are considered mediators of learning interactions in educational settings. Two notions appear to be essential when analysing the learning and development of prospective mathematics teachers: the notion of "communities" and the notion of "knowledge building" practices in interactions.

Communities of Learning

Communities of learning are formed by people who engage in a process of collective learning in a shared domain of human endeavour. The emergence and sustainability of some kind of community among prospective teachers seems to be an important mechanism in the process of becoming a mathematics teacher and in the transition from a university context to a professional context. The idea of community of practice introduced by Wenger (1998) in relation to learning in apprenticeship situations might be a useful analytical tool, but its translation to a context in which teaching is a deliberate process, as is the case in teacher education, is not an easy task (Graven & Lerman, 2003) and has fostered the necessary differentiation between communities, teams and networks (Krainer, 2003).

One of the main features of the notion of communities of practice is that they are groups of people who share a concern for something they do and learn how to do it better as they interact on a regular basis. One relevant aspect in this characterisation is the notion of sharing a goal, as for example acquiring knowledge, skills and dispositions that are necessary to teach mathematics. An institutional context assumes the intentionality of learning and the existence of an expert or facilitator, but from a general perspective the definition of a community of practice according to Wenger allows for, but does not assume, intentionality or the existence of a facilitator. Although this constitutes a theoretical difference between how mathematics educators may use this notion and how this notion is used in other contexts, the construct of "community" provides new avenues that may help understand better prospective teacher learning and offers suggestions for teacher educators about how to design opportunities for learning. In the context of teacher education, learning is the reason why the prospective teachers come together, therefore teacher education programmes should define a shared domain of interest, as for example learning to analyse mathematics teaching in terms of student learning. In addition, this goal can also be considered as a framework for teacher preparation programmes that aim at helping prospective teachers learn how to teach from studying teaching (Hiebert, Morris, Berk, & Jansen, 2007), how to interpret classroom practices (Morris, 2006; Sherin, 2001), or how to conceptualise a contemporary view of mathematics teaching (Lin, 2005). So, at the very least, the intentionality should be explicit when mathematics teacher educators use this approach to think about the process of becoming a mathematics teacher and to design opportunities for learning.

Three characteristics need to be fulfilled so that communities of practice emerge and are sustained and collaborative learning processes are knowledge productive (Wenger, McDermott, & Snyder, 2002): (i) a focus on shared interests and domain, (ii) the involvement in joint activities, discussions and sharing of information, (iii) the development of a shared repertoire of resources (experiences, stories, tools, ways to address recurrent problems).

The first characteristic of a community of practice is the existence of *a shared domain of interest* that generates the idea of membership as a commitment to the domain. In the case of prospective mathematics teachers, we should see these conditions as part of the process of becoming a mathematics teacher, and so, of the process of generating ways of seeing the activity of mathematics teaching with a teacher's eye. Sometimes, this process is supported by reflections on the actions and experience of others through video-cases that encourage prospective teachers to participate in and reflect on discourse centred on mathematical ideas (Lin, 2005; Seago, this volume). In this process of learning to analyse teaching in terms of student learning, prospective teachers can generate a shared competence that characterises them as teachers. Hiebert et al. (2007, p. 47) conjectured the features of this domain in terms of four skills and knowledge "rooted in the daily activity of teaching, that when deployed deliberatively and systematically, constitute a process of creating and testing hypotheses about cause-effect relationships between teaching and learning during classroom lessons".

Recently, information and communication technologies have been used to develop this characteristic of a community of practice. In the process of induction of primary mathematics teachers in professional communities, the constitution of an online mathematics community may provide both opportunities for sharing and communicating and access to quality resources (Dalgarno & Colgan, 2007; Goos & Benninson, 2008).

The second characteristic of a community of practice is the way in which the members pursuing their interest in their domain engage in *joint activities and discussions* as a way of sharing information and building relationships that enable them to learn from each other. Analysis of mutual engagement amongst prospective teachers when they are solving specific tasks has pointed out that what is really important is identifying how, through mutual engagement, the prospective teachers define tasks and develop meanings for the different elements of mathematics teaching. The key characteristic "interact and learn together" is being introduced in the design of web-based learning environments (Wade, Niederhauser, Cannon, & Long, 2001), since it is considered that interaction and cognitive engagement during online discussion are critical for constructing new knowledge (McGraw, Lynch, Koc, Budak, & Brown, 2007; Zhu, 2006). From this perspective, communication tools can begin to mediate prospective teachers' thoughts, actions and interactions.

Finally, the third characteristic of a community of practice is the development of *a shared repertoire* of resources, experiences, representations, tools and ways of addressing professional problems linked to mathematics teaching. Developing different ways to analyse teaching and to notice and interpret classroom interactions, or to interpret students' mathematical thinking is a process in which prior experience and beliefs are entwined. However, by using an instructional scaffolding process, it is possible that prospective teachers develop new ways of conceptualizing mathematics teaching. For example, Lin (2005) argues that the prospective teachers in his research, when constructing pedagogical representations, were able to articulate students' difficulties with a specific topic from multiple perspectives.

New Forms of Discourse and Knowledge Building

According to the sociocultural perspective about teacher learning (Wells, 2002), "knowledge building" has to do with ways in which prospective teachers are engaged in meaning making with others in an attempt to extend and transform their collective understanding. In this sense, knowledge building involves constructing, using and progressively improving different representational artefacts with a concern for systematicity, coherence and consistency (García, Sánchez, Escudero, & Llinares, 2006; Llinares, 2002; Sánchez, García, & Escudero, 2006). From this perspective, knowing is the intentional activity of prospective teachers who make use of and produce representations in a collaborative attempt to understand and transform their world (Wells, 2002). According to Wells (2002), the experience needs to be extended and reinterpreted through collaborative knowing, using the informational resources and representational tools of the wider culture, in our case mathematics education.

Knowledge construction in collaborative settings is based on the assumption that learners engage in specific discourse activities and that the nature of the participation and content of this discourse is related to the knowledge thereby constructed (Sfard, 2001; Wells, 2002). We use and adapt here the notion of *Discourses* as developed by Gee (1996, p. viii), according to whom Discourses are "ways of behaving, interacting, valuing, thinking, believing, speaking, and often reading and writing that are accepted as instantiations of particular roles (or types of people) by specific groups of people".

Prospective teachers might create points of focus around which the negotiation of meaning and reciprocal understanding become organised by generating processes such as noticing, representing, naming, describing, interpreting, using and so on, what Wenger (1998) calls *reification*. The process of reification shapes the prospective teachers' experience of creating "objects" about mathematics education that they use to notice and interpret mathematics teaching and learning.

Some research has shown that the construction of knowledge and the development of the skills needed in order to generate a more complex view of teaching is a process in which the interrelationship and integration of ideas about teaching and learning are progressively included in the analysis and reflection by prospective teachers (Garcia et al., 2006; Sanchez et al., 2006; van Es & Sherin, 2002). These ideas are viewed as "tools to think about" and handle mathematics teaching and learning situations. The progressive use of theoretical ideas as conceptual tools in activities of analysing and interpreting teaching and learning situations, and the progressive modification in the type of participation in the spaces set up for social interaction are manifestations of the knowledge construction process (Derry et al., 2000). Here we are paying special attention to the activity of knowing through making and using representational artefacts (e.g., the theoretical information provided in online discussions) as a means of guiding joint action and of enhancing collective understanding (as can be seen in the creation of a videopaper). The new interaction and communication tools (such as virtual debates, bulletin board discussions, videopapers, blogs) contribute to generating an ongoing discourse amongst prospective teachers that enables viewing "the said" as a knowledge artefact that contributes to the collaborative knowledge building of the participants in the activity. These new forms of discourse generated by the currently available communication tools use *"writing"* as an instrument for collaborative reflection and as a tool for inquiry. The new "type of text" generated by these communication tools can be used as an "improvable object" that favours the generation of a progressive discourse that acts as the focus of collaborative knowledge building (Wells, 2002).

CREATING AND SUSTAINING COMMUNITIES OF LEARNING

The use of communication technologies in teacher education has seen an attempt by researchers to develop a view of teacher learning as a social and cultural phenomenon. Within this framework, some teacher educators are now studying the role played by virtual learning communities through the use of electronic discussion boards. In particular, recent studies look at how these new communication tools support professional reflection, how communities are established and supported through online and face-to-face interactions, and what type of support an online community formed by prospective teachers and practising teachers can provide to prospective teachers (Dalgarno & Colgan, 2007; Goos & Benninson, 2008; Schuck, 2003).

Schuck (2003) argues the role played by computer-mediated conferencing (e.g., electronic conferencing boards[2]) in challenging prospective mathematics teachers' beliefs and poses the question of how teacher educators should express an opinion or suggest a course of action. In Schuck's study, a group of prospective primary teachers were encouraged to post questions to a forum, either about the use of technology or about the content of the course they were studying, with the aim of developing their understanding of mathematics and of mathematics teaching. The analysis of how the prospective teachers used the forum and of the content of the messages posted in the discussion board showed that the use of the forum to achieve this objective was irregular and that the role played by the students varied. Although there were prospective teachers who did not participate in the forum, for those who used the forum the discussions were useful to encourage reflection, to share teaching experiences without having to be on campus, and they also encouraged the process of justifying and explaining points of view. Because of these reasons, Schuck argues that *accessibility to a forum* is an important factor in developing a community of learners. This author raises the issue of whether participation should be compulsory due to the benefits identified, but in the end

---

[2] Electronic conference boards are web-based conferencing tools.

proposes that the reasons not to participate should also be respected. In this last case, the prospective teachers should value the participation in the forum as an alternative way of learning. Another issue to take into account is the *level of structure* imposed on the use of and participation in bulletin boards. Questions that emerge from the study are: what conditions may restrict the use of bulletin boards and the free exchange of ideas, what conditions may determine the emergence of a community and what should be the role of mathematics teacher educators in supporting or suggesting new avenues.

Also working with prospective primary teachers, Dalgarno and Colgan (2007) examine what is the support provided by an online mathematics community to prospective teachers. In their study, a group of prospective primary mathematics teachers sought opportunities to continue their professional development through a forum that they could access once they were out in schools after graduation. The needs identified by the prospective teachers were: discussion with experts, access to suggestions and help about mathematics content and to mathematical resources selected by the experts for use in the classroom (repository of exemplars and resources), having a place where they could share lesson plans and activities that they themselves had created (repository of novice teachers' ideas about teaching and learning). An online community called Connect-ME was created and was constituted by prospective teachers and beginning teachers. Connect-ME offered a means to meet the expressed needs through mixed-method delivery mechanisms. According to Dalgarno and Colgan (2007, p. 12), the online community Connect-ME provided novice teachers "with a safe, communicative community for sharing resources and ideas and an environment where they can proactively seek the help they need".

This also highlights the significance of *emotional and personal connections.* Dalgarno and Colgan suggest three essential elements that help sustain this type of connections: (i) the initial community members should have a personal link to, and a loyalty and respect for, the project facilitator; (ii) the facilitator should continue to communicate with all members of the online community even after they graduate; and (iii) the online forum should be created and developed at the "grassroots level", but its growth ought to be the results of previous personal connections.

Goos and Benninson (2004, 2008) also study the interface between secondary school mathematics prospective teachers and beginning teachers and how such type of community is established and maintained through online and face-to-face interaction. These researchers look at an online community of practice established via Yahoo! Groups[3] with the aim to: encourage sessions and professional discussion outside class times and during the practicum periods; provide continuing support, by remaining accessible to its members after graduation. One characteristic of this website was that the authors imposed minimal structure on communication. Goos and Benninson are in fact interested to know how and why

---

[3] http://uk.groups.yahoo.com/

prospective teachers and beginning teachers might choose to use this form of communication.

One participation structure linked to the bulletin board that Goos and Benninson considered interesting was the fact that prospective teachers used the bulletin board to organise and negotiate the agenda of a debriefing session to take place after they returned to university. Prospective teachers from different cohorts, beginning teachers and teacher educators attended this debriefing session, discussing pedagogical challenges, identifying sources of assistance, and comparing the effectiveness of different teaching approaches. Afterwards, the bulletin board was used to provide a summary of the debriefing session for those who had been unable to participate. This internship debriefing session was organised the following year too, which is what Goos and Benninson interpret as the beginning of a professional routine and a part of the *shared history* of the community.

Goos and Benninson (2004, 2008) also suggest a possible factor that might have influenced the creation and sustainability of this community, for example, their own role in shaping the interactions between the participants by offering models of online professional exchanges through forwarding messages from other e-mail discussion lists used by mathematics teachers, encouraging prospective teachers to share teaching resources and their mathematics teaching experiences.

The studies mentioned in this subchapter start shading light on the processes of creating and sustaining communities of practice through online environments. Four factors that emerge are: (i) the provision of *accessible and flexible* online forums, discussions and bulletin boards which can be appropriated and adapted to satisfy the teachers' needs; (ii) the *participation of both prospective and practising teachers* to the same community, *together with "experts"*, which may enable the construction of professional knowledge and practices, together with the creation of a shared repertoire of mathematics resources; (iii) the *co-existence of online and face-to-face interactions*, which also enables the creation of emotional and personal connections that foster continuous participation in the exchanges and discussions and the development of a shared history; and (iv) the *provision of models* of professional exchanges and interactions to get the teachers started and provide an initial structure for the discussion.

ONLINE INTERACTION AND KNOWLEDGE BUILDING

The question of how forms of participation operate to mediate meanings in conversations is central to our understanding about the role of interactive learning environments in teacher education. Research on knowledge construction in collaborative settings is based on the assumption that learners engage in specific discourse activities and that the nature of the participation and the content of these discourses are related to knowledge construction (Llinares, 2002; McGraw et al., 2007; Santagata, Zannoni, & Stigler, 2007). From the point of view of sociocultural perspectives on learning, it is assumed that prospective teachers construct arguments in interaction with their partners in order to build knowledge about mathematics teaching, as well as to develop the skills needed to learn from practice.

Llinares and his colleagues designed several learning environments considering this theoretical perspective and using "design experiments" as a methodological approach (Callejo, Valls, & Llinares, 2007; Cobb, Confrey, DiSessa, Lehrer, & Schauble, 2003; Llinares, 2004). Figure 1 displays the web-structure of one of these learning environments integrating video-clips of mathematics teaching, asynchronous computer mediated discussion, theoretical information related to the given task and links to written essays about mathematics teaching (Valls, Llinares, & Callejo, 2006). This particular design gives prospective teachers the opportunity to engage in the process of meaning making with other colleagues, in an attempt to extend and transform their collective understanding in relation to some aspects of a jointly undertaken activity. Video-clips or teaching vignettes are used to situate the individual cases in the context of classroom practices. In addition, this web-learning environment provides prospective teachers with theoretical information and questions aimed to generate online discussions and to promote an inquiry orientation towards the observation of mathematics teaching (which is one of the objectives of teacher education).

Figure 1. Structure of the web-based learning environment integrating video-clips, theoretical papers, social interaction spaces (online debate) and possibility of writing essays about mathematics teaching.

The adopted approach creates a setting in which prospective teachers come together in a virtual collaborative action and interaction setting. The website allows them to watch videos and to download reports in text format (transcription of the lesson in the video-clip, the activities used by the teacher during the lesson, and documents with theoretical information about the characteristics of mathematics teaching), at any time and from anywhere by logging in the learning environment.

In the study described in Llinares and Valls (2007), the prospective primary teachers had the chance to observe aspects of a mathematics lesson from different perspectives, starting from their own initial conceptions (based on their experience) and moving onto positions in which they use conceptual elements introduced in the training programme (theoretical information). The progressive use of the conceptual tools in the online discussions about the analysis and the interpretation of the teaching and learning situations and the progressive change in the way students participated in the spaces set up for social interaction, are manifestations of the development of the skills needed to learn from practice and of the knowledge construction process. What was emphasised in the design of the learning environments in Llinares and Valls' study was the activity of knowing through making and using representational artefacts (the provided theoretical information) as means of guiding prospective teachers' joint action and enhancing collective understanding through online discussions. The relationship between online interaction and the construction of meaning is rooted in the assumption that the semiotic process through which the ideas are formulated and communicated towards the achievement of a goal during an activity is part of the construction of meanings.

This organisation of the learning environments attempts to reflect the progressive and evolutionary nature of the process of construction of the knowledge needed for teaching (Goffree & Oonk, 2001) and of the required skills to learn from practice, in which conceptual tools are progressively integrated in the activities of analysis and reflection (Garcia et al., 2006). In this web-learning environment, when prospective primary teachers contributed to the online discussion they had to interpret the preceding contributions and to formulate a new contribution extending, questioning or qualifying what had already been said. Such progressively generated discourse mediated knowing. For example, in the exchanges below the prospective primary teachers refined and amplified previous contributions about how the idea of equity should be understood in the classroom context, when they analysed a video-clip in which a primary teacher managed the interactions among primary students posing problems from a commercial brochure.

I do not entirely agree (LUISA – 12:05:00 09/01/2006)

I partly agree with the comments made by my colleagues Estefanía and Ángela, but although all the students participate and interact, the teacher did not carry out her task properly. The role of the teacher in the classroom is to get everyone to share while working on the problem (which I think she does, like my colleagues). But the teacher, in my opinion, does not pay attention to what the children say, nor does she show any real interest in their suggestions. During the class, two other children offer possible data to help in solving the problem. One boy says that there are 14 chocolates in the box, and another says there are 50. The teacher ignores these two children's suggestions, and proceeds to solve the problem using only the supposed existence of 8 chocolates. In my opinion she should have paid more attention to these two children and should also have solved the problem using their data. Not doing the exercise in this manner means that she does not respect the principle of fairness, because she has not listened to the contributions made by two of the children.

To LUISA (ANGELA – 14:28:06 09/01/2006)

In one way you are right. The teacher does not accept all the children's proposals for the problem, she only accepts that of the child who suggests 8 chocolates. At one point in the video the teacher says "There could be 8 chocolates, or there could be more [...]" and "8 chocolates is a number which might be the one, or it could be different [...]", so I think that by saying that, she is trying to show that she has paid attention to the other opinions, but as she can't put all of them on the blackboard she decided to concentrate on the number proposed by one of the children, simply in order to set up the problem and solve it. I think that if the video were to continue and the teacher were to approach the problem again she would pay attention to a different child, and that if she required more data, she would use those suggested by several different children.

The interactions amongst the prospective primary teachers, motivated by other students' contributions, were *increasingly focused* – in this case on the notion of equity as a valued-added dimension in teaching that can promote understanding – indicating that the structure of this type of environments, including the contexts and the activities, seemed to encourage the prospective primary teachers to engage in meaning making with others in an attempt to extend and transform their collective understanding of mathematics teaching.

The study confirms that interaction occurs among prospective primary teachers when it is generated by a given task, which in this case was the analysis of mathematics instruction and of its effects on children's mathematical competence. The tasks and online discussions were intentionally integrated into the course in order to lead to a high degree of interaction. Llinares and Valls (2007) argue that the focus on shared interest helped the prospective teachers to engage in the joint activities of identifying and analysing different aspects of mathematics teaching thus enabling them to construct a shared understanding of the situation.

The activities that were designed within these online learning environments required the prospective primary teachers to *identify* key aspects in a mathematics lesson and *interpret* them, something that seemed to encourage interaction. Here the role of the theoretical information was to help prospective teachers to begin to "notice" (Pea, 2006). From Wells' (2002) theoretical perspective, the process of knowledge-building is based on the assumption that students are engaged in specific discourse activities related to knowledge acquisition through discussions in which they focus on issues directly related to their future teaching. The interactions in the online discussions showed how the prospective teachers' initial personal interpretations could progressively be modified to construct common knowledge, when they perceived the ideas about mathematics teaching as functional in relation to the task that they had to undertake.

These findings suggest that the different types of task and conditions of online discussion in the learning environments in which prospective primary teachers participated (the discussion questions and the video-clips) seem to exert an influence on the nature of the interaction (Schrire, 2006). The results of Llinares and Valls' analysis imply that the degree of prospective teacher involvement in interactive processes is related to the type of task intended to justify their participation in online discussions. Different structural factors that seemed to contribute to the construction of meaning were clear established goals with thematic prompts, and time to write.

The existence of clear goals with thematic prompts seems to support the hypothesis that prospective teachers should use online discussions as a tool in their learning environments. That is to say, prospective primary teachers should consider participation in online discussions to be useful and beneficial for carrying out assigned tasks. The findings suggest that prospective primary teachers could identify in the task a focus on a shared interest – the goal – that justified their engagement in joint activities, and considered the online discussions as social spaces in which it was possible to develop a shared repertoire of experiences, tools and ways of addressing the analysis of videotaped case studies (Wenger, 1998). In this context, the personal interpretations were questioned and clarified in the online discussion, and assumptions and inferences were challenged in an attempt to construct a communal answer supported by common knowledge. This process was given further importance by the fact that the progressive discourse was conducted in writing.

The questions for discussion that were set in the learning environment led the prospective primary teachers to respond to each others' messages, agreeing or disagreeing about different points of view. This enhanced their ability to see things from another's viewpoint and they began to develop a more complex view of teaching, as could be inferred from messages that became more focused on the specific topics over time (Byman et al., 2005) showing that writing was used as a tool for collaborative reflection where the text of the messages acted as an "improvable object" to the focus of collaborative knowledge building (Wells, 2002).

In another context, McGraw et al. (2007) uses *discussion prompts* to stimulate critical analysis in a multimedia case and facilitate online discussions. In the project described by McGraw at al., online forums were used to discuss a multimedia case amongst prospective mathematics teachers, practising mathematics teachers, mathematicians and mathematics teacher educators. The analysis of the messages posted in the online forums and of the transcripts of the face-to-face discussions identified episodes of dialogic interaction in which individuals explicitly responded to the ideas and opinions of the previous writers. McGraw and her colleagues suggest that integration in discussion groups of members with different perspectives and level of experience enabled the generation of multiple episodes of dialogic interaction in each discussion group. Moreover, the interplay between theoretical and practical knowledge as a manifestation of knowledge building was evidenced by movements in the discussions between case specific observations and more general observations or use of theoretical knowledge. In relation to this last aspect, the variations in level of noticing in the different members of the group – prospective teachers, practising teachers, mathematicians, teacher educators – seemed to influence the development of knowledge.

Summing up, two characteristics emerge as relevant as concerns online interactions and knowledge building: (i) providing *structured guidance* through tasks and discussion questions with thematic prompts seems to enable the participants in online discussions to reflect on and integrate multiple aspects of teaching; (ii) prospective teachers might benefit from engaging in discussions with *more knowledgeable persons*, grounded in a case of classroom practice, that can be accessed through an online environment from anywhere at anytime. The interaction amongst the multiple perspectives that may emerge, and be made explicit in the written messages appearing in the online discussions, from people with different levels of knowledge while "seeing" the same multimedia case, is vital to meaning making and knowledge construction.

NEW FORMS OF DISCOURSE THAT SUPPORT PROSPECTIVE TEACHER LEARNING: BLOGS AND VIDEOPAPERS

The relationship between the forms of discourse and knowledge building needed to become a mathematics teacher and the emergence of communities when new tools such as blogs and videopapers are used in mathematics teacher education have recently become an object of research (Beardsley, Cogan-Drew, & Olivero, 2007; Makri & Kynigos, 2007; Nemirovsky, DiMattia, Ribeiro, & Lara-Meloy, 2005; Olivero, John, & Sutherland, 2004; see also Borba & Gadanidis, this volume).

Blogs are (personal or organisational) web pages organised by dated entries whose items are links, commentaries, papers, personal thoughts and ongoing discussions. Blogs are considered as learning spaces with digital, sharable, and reusable entities that can be used for learning and are available to prospective teachers anytime and anywhere (learning objects). Recently, research interest has emerged about the potential and possible roles of blogs in the professional development of mathematics teachers and about the necessary relation between the use of these new tools of communication and the intentionality of their use in mathematics teacher education (Makri & Kynigos, 2007). Makri and Kynigos focus their research on the ways in which prospective teachers write about both their subject and its pedagogy and study the discourse that is developed in teachers' blogs. In Makri and Kynigos' course the prospective teachers were given writing tasks addressing their epistemological and pedagogical beliefs and their subject related knowledge (e.g., the pedagogical value of using software in mathematics). The prospective teachers were encouraged to publish their answers on a blog and comment on the work of their peers by sharing opinions and engaging in discussion.

The prospective teachers in this study used the explanatory and expository genres and their writings showed a structured cognitive presence since they combined factual knowledge and conceptual and theoretical knowledge which emerged collaboratively. The researchers suggest that the use of the blog introduced changes in the social orchestration of the course at an affective, interactive and cohesive level. Although research of this type is still recent, Makri and Kynigos identify different profiles of prospective teachers in relation to the emerging forms of social interaction indicating the degree of appropriation of the blog by the prospective teachers. The three profiles identified, blog enthusiasts, blog frequent visitors and blog sceptics, indicate that it is necessary to study in depth the changing social practices and roles and the new role of the instructor, as it has also been pointed out by studies on creating and sustaining communities of practice (Schuck, 2003). The sociocultural perspectives of learning assume that the social context affects the nature of learning activities, so when the social context is modified by introducing new forms of social interaction on the web it is assumed that this will influence the capacity to engage prospective teachers in collaborative activity, reflection, knowledge sharing and debate.

Besides tools that facilitate social interaction through writing, such as blogs, other multimodal tools that integrate different forms of discourse in the same environment, such as videopapers, are beginning to be investigated in the context of teacher education. Videopapers[4] (for an example, see Figure 2) are multimedia documents that integrate and synchronise different forms of representation including text, video and images, in one single non-linear cohesive document (Nemirovsky et al., 2005; Olivero et al., 2004).

Combining the video with the text in a videopaper creates a fluid document that is more explicit than the text or video alone, while remaining contained and controlled by the author. Since their initial development in 1998 as an alternative genre for the production, use, and dissemination of educational research, research has investigated their potential and use in a variety of contexts ranging from teacher education to professional development to research collaborative practices (e.g., Barnes & Sutherland, 2007; Beardsley et al., 2007; Galvis & Nemirovsky, 2003; Nemirovsky, Lara-Meloy, Earnest, & Ribeiro, 2001; Smith & Krumsvik, 2007).

---

[4] Videopapers are created with the free software VideoPaper Builder 3 (Nemirovsky et al., 2005), downloadable from http://vpb.concord.org

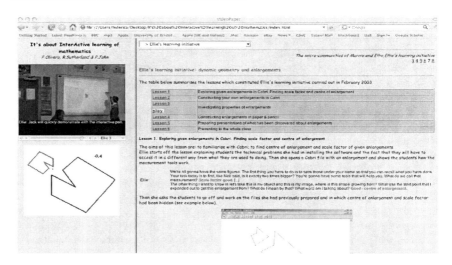

Figure 2. Screen shot from a videopaper.

Considering *videopapers as "products"*, Olivero et al. (2004) discuss the role they might have in teacher education and how they might support the representation and development of communities of practice where new ideas can be expressed and experienced. Reading about new and innovative approaches to teaching and learning can influences prospective teachers' beliefs and principles and impact on the process of "becoming a teacher", but reading does not provide any re-assuring image where the action is modelled vicariously. Moreover, prospective teachers might also lack the confidence to experiment if they have few realistic models to work from. Videopapers can provide prototypical instances of (innovative) practices combined with a range of supporting warrants. The study[5] reported in Olivero et al. (2004) uses videopapers as a way to represent and communicate innovative uses of ICT in mathematics teaching, based on research findings, to both prospective and practising mathematics teachers. After reading one of these videopapers, a teacher typically comments:

> What is going on in classrooms is being communicated and it does make the project look real, real pictures in real classrooms. Seeing it, helps you to make sense out of it and gives you real models that you know are more than just tips for teachers.

Such videopapers were seen as "more than tips for teachers" as they afforded the opportunity to develop a different kind of knowledge for teaching – knowledge not of "what to do next", but rather "knowledge of how to interpret and reflect on

---

[5] More information about the project can be found in Sutherland et al. (2004).

classroom practices" (Sherin, 2004, p. 17), because of the interplay between theoretical and practical knowledge they incorporated. Similarly to Valls et al. (2006), the teachers appreciated the theoretical knowledge embedded in the videopaper as a tool that could help them "notice" relevant practices, meanings, knowledge in the video:

> I have shown this to a number of teachers in Bristol – maths teachers – I was working with, they wanted something stimulating on proofs. So I did it but they wanted the bit on the research reading and the thinking cut out because they thought teachers would find it irrelevant and too time consuming. That's a problem because the thinking and the discussing and reading were so important. They are missing out […] well sort of missing out parts of the story.

Another teacher continues explaining how he thinks this kind of videopapers can be useful to teachers, who, thanks to the videopaper, would benefit from the results of the research project, in which the teachers collaborated with the researchers, even without being part of it:

> So they [teachers] would benefit I would hope from coming into my classroom, well we can't afford that because we can't get supply cover so they can watch my classroom instead [through the video in the videopaper]. They would benefit from talking to Tim [researcher], well they can't do that but they can understand what he is trying to say [through the text in the videopaper]. And they'd benefit from having my lesson plan which we worked on but they can adapt it for themselves. So they have everything – even the research evidence backing up the principles and practice. And also they can see the outcome, which is very important. If you do this they would do this, and this is the reason why we're doing it, this is me doing it and this is what they produce at the end.

This quote suggests how in this case the videopaper is a tool that may afford the creation of and provide a space for the representation of communities of practice that bring together researchers, practising teachers and prospective teachers.

Another project (Armstrong et al., 2005; Barnes & Sutherland, 2007) looks at the creation of videopapers to represent a collaborative research process in which both researchers and teachers interpreted classroom episodes within a series of mathematics and science lessons. Similarly to what McGraw et al. (2007) found in relation to the discussion of multimedia case studies, having people with different knowledge and expertise looking at the same data provides the possibility for different understandings of a lesson to be put forward and productively interact to create knowledge. The subsequently created videopaper embodies this process, enabling the multiple perspectives to coexist and to be grounded in the reality of the classroom (Galvis & Nemirovsky, 2003). While these projects see the process of creating a videopaper as an individual process, Zahn et al. (2006, p. 738) describe a pilot project on collaborative learning through advanced video technologies and analyse the use of the DIVER system[6] by prospective teachers:

> DIVER is based on the notion of a user *diving* into videos, for example, creating new points of view onto a source video and commenting on these by writing short text passages. Diving on video performs an important action for establishing common ground that is characterised as *"guided noticing"*.

The "diving" process can be shared and collaboratively developed.

Although videopapers are mainly seen as objects or "products", research has shown that what is also important in terms of the development of prospective teachers' knowledge are the phases of *actively creating a videopaper*. A number of studies look at the use of videopapers as a reflective learning tool for prospective teachers in different subjects (including mathematics) and its advantages and disadvantages over more conventional use of videos, observation tasks and assignments (Beardsley et al., 2007; Daniil, 2007; Lazarus & Olivero, 2007), adopting very similar methodologies. In these projects, groups of prospective teachers were asked to choose one lesson from those they taught in their teaching practice and create a videopaper showing self-reflection on their practice, as an alternative to the traditional assignment that consisted of writing an essay with the same aim. All studies demonstrate the profound insight that is possible when teachers use a medium, like videopapers, that allows them to represent and share the vitality of their classrooms by means of capturing, preserving, and representing events in ways that connect with their world, where different forms of knowledge are continually being juxtaposed, as opposed to traditional text-based documents (Olivero et al., 2004). Videopapers offer an easy to use tool for teachers to create commentaries around teaching episodes, including reflection on their own practice and reference to the underpinning theoretical ideas. This provides an essential medium for teachers to help them improve their understanding and interpretation of their practice (Carraher, Schliemann, & Brizuela, 2000; Derry et al., 2000; Pea, 2006), leading to knowledge construction and meaning making.

Research also shows that the process of creating a videopaper is crucial in supporting teacher reflection and is qualitatively different from simply watching a video from a whole lesson to reflect on one's practice (Daniil, 2007; Lazarus & Olivero, 2007). These studies shows that it was the *editing process*, for example, the process of *having* to select relevant clips to discuss, that fostered prospective teachers' reflection, by initiating a more analytical process that might not necessarily happen if they had just watched a whole lesson without needing to produce a written text. Besides, the multimodal character of videopapers suggests that the process of meaning making and knowledge construction, through reflection, comes from the two modes (video and text) together.

---

[6] http://www.diver.stanford.edu

Besides the process of creating a videopaper, also the process of *reading a videopaper* has been an object of research. Video has been used in teacher education and professional development in different forms since its introduction in the 1960s (Sherin, 2004). However, watching a video without text is different from reading a videopaper. Reading a videopaper can be described as a dialogue between the reader and the author through the text, the video clips and the Play buttons that refer the reader to particular clips while reading the text. Smith and Krumsvik (2007) present the analysis of the reading processes of and discussion around a videopaper integrating key educational theories that prospective teachers are normally exposed to. Video illustrations of these theories, taken from the authors' own teaching practice, are incorporated in the videopaper. This videopaper was read by prospective teachers, teacher educators, and researchers in conferences. Smith and Krumsvik argue that this way of using videopapers contributes to bringing together communities that would not normally exchange ideas around teaching; they also found that the prospective teachers appreciated the fact that the practice field was brought to the university and the fact that they could "see" the reality of the profession rather than just "hear" about it.

Overall we can say that videopapers *mediate reflection on practice* and therefore enculturation in the mathematics teaching community for both the creator and the reader. The mediation occurs through the multimodal character of videopapers, which enables the processes of becoming, doing and experiencing. Videopapers crystallise the reflection of the teacher creating them, through video and text, and stimulate reflection in the teachers reading them, through the dialogue and interaction with the video and the text created by the author. Multiple perspectives are elicited, so contributing to the development of professional vision and knowledge of mathematics teachers.

The tools discussed in this subchapter differ from the online learning environments previously described in that they are artefacts that are constructed by the prospective teachers themselves, with the purpose of representing knowledge and eventually communicating and sharing it, as opposed to given artefacts within which students may interact. Therefore, what emerges as important is the process of writing a blog or creating a videopaper, first as *private tools* embodying personal reflections and representing what is "seen" and "noticed" and then as *public tools* communicating and sharing these reflections with others. The collaborative aspect of these tools resides in this double face (creating and communicating) and in the interactive process of reading a blog or videopaper, through which multiple perspectives are elicited around a shared context, represented for example by the video clip in a videopaper. Because these forms of discourse are relatively new, they need to be gradually appropriated by both writers and readers before they can really become an integral part of teaching and learning processes.

EMERGING PERSPECTIVES AND FUTURE VIEWPOINTS

In the previous subchapters, we have identified key factors that should be considered when computer-supported communication tools are introduced in mathematics teacher education and that seem to shape the characteristics of online interactions, construction of knowledge and creation and support of communities of practice.

The *first key factor* is the *level of structure imposed on the context of communication* in the community and in the designed learning environment. The form in which the activities in online interaction spaces are structured and the establishment of clear goals, seem to mediate the process of knowledge building in interactive learning environments and the creation and sustainability of communities of practice. In some cases, allowing prospective teachers to build a space that meets their needs helps the emergence of the sense of belonging to a community and supports its sustainability over time (Goos & Benninson, 2004). Here, the emergent design of the community contributed to its sustainability by allowing the prospective teachers to define their own professional goals and values. In this case "communities" emerge since prospective teachers have more freedom to share their interests.

However, in other contexts, it was the pre-determined structure of the activity in which prospective teachers were engaged that contributed to the development of reflective dialogue, as for example in the learning environments integrating online discussions and the analysis of segments of mathematics teaching. A structural factor that seems to influence the involvement of prospective teachers in this type of learning environment was that the prospective teachers had a clear understanding of the goal of the activity (Llinares & Valls, 2007). In this intervention in a mathematics methods course, the object of reflection that the prospective teachers had to focus on was made salient since the initial phase and the conditions were public. In this case, the thematic prompts given to the prospective primary teachers seemed to contribute to the development of a shared understanding of the situation. Another characteristic that determined the level of participation of the prospective teachers was the nature of the questions posed and the theoretical information included in the learning environment (thematic prompts). The nature of the questions posed in the learning environment contributed to keep the messages focused and to generate different interactions that favoured the reification of meaning about mathematics teaching as a knowledge building process. But a common aspect of all the interactions generated in different social interaction spaces is that the activity towards the analysis of mathematics teaching or the identification of one-self as belonging to a community of practice were mediated by tools, like written text and technological tools (bulletin boards, online discussions, writing in a blog, creating a videopaper). Prospective teachers indicated that having to write and think about the different issues posed also contributed to generating a reciprocal understanding and a sense of belonging to a community. One thing that research has begun to point out is that the type of participation and the reification processes in these new learning environments seem to be dependent on the structure of the activity in which prospective teachers are engaged (Zhu, 2006). But the focus on a shared interest helps prospective teachers to engage in the joint activities enabling them to share the understanding of a given situation (Llinares & Valls, 2007).

The *second key factor* to our understanding of prospective teacher learning is the *role played by new communication tools and by the nature of the generated discourse*. Communication through forums, bulletin boards, blogs or videopapers mediates the process of becoming (learning as identity), doing (learning as practice) and experience (learning as meaning) of the prospective mathematics teachers. The sociocultural perspective on teacher learning underlines the role played by the artefacts built by prospective teachers as communication instruments. The prospective teachers' written contributions in an online discussion, the process of creating a videopaper or a blog as a way of communicating their understanding of facts and situations mediate the process of knowledge building and, in some cases, the sense of belonging to a community. The important thing is that individuals might come to understand a topic better, share resources or have opportunities to define their own professional goals and values, when they have to write in order to communicate to others – writing for others using the new ways of communication that new technologies provide. Writing, as a manifestation of the use of the new available communication technologies, is understood from this perspective as a tool for collaborative reflection and, at the same time, problem solving. Therefore, "writing" about a topic is considered to be a powerful way of knowing. Posting a message in an online discussion, exchanging ideas and experiences in bulletin boards, creating a videopaper in a reflective context, or creating blogs as ways of sharing knowledge and resources through a progressive discourse that takes place in "writing", constitute the spaces where prospective teachers' personal interpretations are questioned and clarified in an attempt to construct "common knowledge". The "text" created within these news ways of communicating functions as an improvable object, that provides the focus for progressive discourse and simultaneously embodies the progress made; this might allow prospective teachers to become acquainted with and understand the topic they are writing about and can be seen as a dialogic process of knowledge (Andriessen, Erkens, van de Laank, Peters, & Coirier, 2003; Wells, 2002). In these new contexts, discourse enables the development and articulation of shared values.

In summary, the introduction of information and communication technologies in teacher education also involves the development of sociocultural perspectives on learning that provide new avenues through which teacher educators may attempt to understand the process of becoming a mathematics teacher. Despite the scarcity of research on the topic, the studies discussed in this chapter have shed light on key factors related to the introduction and use of these new tools. Questions have emerged too and these call for further research.

ACKNOWLEDGEMENTS

The contribution of S. Llinares was supported by Ministerio de Educación y Ciencia, Dirección General de Investigación, Spain, under grant no. SEJ2004-05479.

REFERENCES

Andriessen, L., Erkens, G., van de Laank, C., Peters, N., & Coirier, N. (2003). Argumentation as negotiation in electronic collaborative writing. In J. Andriessen, M. Baker, & D. Suthers (Eds.), *Arguing to learn: Confronting cognition in computers-supporters collaborative learning environment* (pp. 79–115). Dordrecht, the Netherlands: Kluwer Academic Publishers.

Armstrong, V., Barnes, S., Sutherland, R., Curran, S., Mills, S., & Thompson, I. (2005). Collaborative research methodology for investigating teaching and learning: The use of interactive whiteboard technology. *Educational Review, 57*(4), 457–469.

Barnes, S., & Sutherland, R. (2007, August/September). *Using videopapers for multi-purposes: Disseminating research practice and research results.* Paper presented at the 12th Biennial Conference for Research on Learning and Instruction, Budapest, Hungary.

Beardsley, L., Cogan-Drew, D., & Olivero, F. (2007). Videopaper: bridging research and practice for pre-service and experienced teachers. In R. Goldman, R. D. Pea, B. Barron, & S. J. Derry (Eds.), *Video research in the learning sciences* (pp. 479–493). Hillsdale, NJ: Lawrence Erlbaum Associates.

Blanton, W. E., Moorman, G., & Trathen, W. (1998). Telecommunications and teacher education: A social constructivist review. In P. D. Pearson & A. Iran-Nejad (Eds.), *Review of research in education* (pp. 235–276). Washington, DC: American Educational Research Association.

Borba, M., & Villareal, M. (2005). *Humans-with-media and the reorganization of mathematical thinking. Information and communication technologies, modeling, experimentation and visualization.* New York: Springer.

Byman, A., Järvela, S., & Häkkinen, P. (2005). What is reciprocal understanding in virtual interaction? *Instructional Science, 33,* 121–136.

Callejo, M. L., Valls, J., & Llinares, S. (2007). Interacción y análisis de la enseñanza. Aspectos claves en la construcción del conocimiento professional [Interaction and analaysis of teaching. Key aspects in the construction of professional knowledge]. *Investigación en la Escuela, 61,* 5–21.

Carraher, D., Schliemann, A. D., & Brizuela, B. (2000). *Bringing out the algebraic character of arithmetic.* Paper presented at the Videopapers in Mathematics Education conference, Dedham, MA.

Cobb, P., Confrey, J., Disessa, A., Lehrer, R., & Schauble, L. (2003). Design experiments in educational research. *Educational Researcher, 32*(1), 9–13.

Dalgarno, N., & Colgan, L. (2007). Supporting novice elementary mathematics teachers' induction in professional communities and providing innovative forms of pedagogical content knowledge development through information and communication technology. *Teaching and Teacher Education, 23,* 1051–1065.

Daniil, M. (2007). *The use of videopapers from Modern Foreign Language student teachers as a tool to support reflection on practice.* Unpublished Master's thesis, University of Bristol, Bristol, UK.

Derry, Sh. J., Gance, S., Gance, L. L., & Schaleger, M. (2000). Toward assessment of knowledge-building practices in technology-mediated work group interactions. In E. Lajoie (Ed.), *Computers as cognitive tools. No more walls.* (Vol. 2, pp. 29–68). Mahwah, NJ: Lawrence Erlbaum Associates.

Galvis, A., & Nemirovsky, R. (2003). *Sharing and reflecting on teaching practices by using VideoPaper Builder 2.* Paper presented at the World Conference on E-Learning in Corporate, Government, Healthcare, and Higher Education 2003, Phoenix, Arizona, USA. http://www.editlib.org/index.cfm?fuseaction=Reader.ViewAbstract&paper_id=12304&from=NEW DL (accessed on 18 October 2007).

García, M., Sánchez, V., Escudero, I., & Llinares, S. (2006). The dialectic relationship between research and practice in mathematics teacher education. *Journal of Mathematics Teacher Education, 9,* 109–128.

Gee, G. P. (1996) *Social linguistics and literacies: Ideology in discourses.* London: RoutledgeFalmer

Goffree, F., & Oonk, W. (2001). Digitizing real teaching practice for teacher education programmes: The MILE approach. In F.-L. Lin & T. Cooney (Eds.), *Making sense of mathematics teacher education* (pp. 111–146). Dordrecht, the Netherlands: Kluwer Academic Publishers.

Goos, M., & Benninson, A. (2004). Emergence of a pre-service community of practice. In I. Putt, R. Faragher, & M. McLean (Eds.), *MERGA27. Mathematics education for the third millennium: towards 2010* (pp. 271–278). James Cook University: Australia.

Goos, M., & Benninson, A. (2008). Developing a communal identity as beginning teachers of mathematics: Emergence of an online community of practice. *Journal of Mathematics Teacher Education, 11,* 41–69.

Graven, M., & Lerman, S. (2003). Book review. Wenger, E. (1998) Communities of practice: Learning, meaning and identity. Cambridge, UK: Cambridge University Press. *Journal of Mathematics Teacher Education, 6,* 185–194.

Greeno, J. (1998). The situativity of knowing, learning, and research. *American Psychologist, 53,* 5–26.

Hiebert, J., Morris, A., Berk, D., & Jansen, A. (2007). Preparing teachers to learn from teaching. *Journal of Teacher Education, 58,* 47–61.

Krainer, K. (2003). Editorial. Teams, communities & networks. *Journal of Mathematics Teacher Education, 6,* 93–105.

Lazarus, E., & Olivero, F. (2007, August/September). *Using video papers for professional learning and assessment in initial teacher education.* Paper presented at the 12th Biennial Conference for Research on Learning and Instruction, Budapest, Hungary.

Lerman, S. (2001). A review of research perspectives on mathematics teacher education. In F.-L. Lin & T. Cooney (Eds.), *Making sense of mathematics teacher education* (pp. 33-52). Dordrecht, the Netherlands: Kluwer Academic Publisher.

Lin, P. (2005). Using research-based video-cases to help pre-service primary teachers conceptualize a contemporary view of mathematics teaching. *International Journal of Science and Mathematics Education, 3,* 351-377.

Llinares, S. (2002). Participation and reification in learning to teach. The role of knowledge and beliefs. In G. Leder, E. Pehkonen, & G. Törner (Eds.), *Beliefs: A hidden variable in mathematics education* (pp.195–210). Dordrecht, the Netherlands: Kluwer Academic Publishers.

Llinares, S. (2004). *Building virtual learning communities and the learning of mathematics student teacher.* Invited Regular Lecture Tenth International Congress for Mathematics Education (ICME), Copenhagen, Denmark.

Llinares, S., & Krainer, K. (2006). Mathematics (student) teachers and teacher educators as learners. In A. Gutierrez & P. Boero (Eds.), *Handbook of research on the psychology of mathematics education: Past, present and future* (pp. 429–459). Rotterdam, the Netherlands: Sense Publishers.

Llinares, S., & Valls, J. (2007). The building of preservice primary teachers' knowledge of mathematics teaching: interaction and online video case studies. *Instructional Science,* DOI: 10.1007/s11251-007-9043-4.

Makri, K., & Kynigos, C. (2007). The role of blogs in studying the discourse and social practices of mathematics teachers. *Educational Technology & Society, 10(1),* 73–84.

McGraw, R., Lynch, K., Koc, Y., Budak, A., & Brown, C. (2007). The multimedia case as a tool for professional development: An analysis of online and face-to-face interaction among mathematics pre-service teachers, in-service teachers, mathematicians, and mathematics teacher educators. *Journal of Mathematics Teacher Education, 10,* 95–121.

Morris, A. (2006). Assessing pre-service teachers' skills for analyzing teaching. *Journal of Mathematics Teacher Education, 9,* 471–505.

Mousley, J., Lambdin, D., & Koc, Y. (2003). Mathematics teacher education and technology. In A. J. Bishop, M. A. Clements, C. Keitel, J. Kilpatrick, & F. K. S. Leung (Eds.), *Second international handbook of mathematics education* (pp. 395–432). Dordrecht, the Netherlands: Kluwer Academic Publishers.

Nemirovsky, R., DiMattia, C., Ribeiro, B., & Lara-Meloy, T. (2005). Talking about teaching episodes. *Journal of Mathematics Teacher Education, 8*, 363–392.

Nemirovsky, R., Lara-Meloy, T., Earnest, D., & Ribeiro, B. (2001). Videopapers: Investigating new multimedia genres to foster the interweaving of research and teaching. In M. van den Heuvel-Panhuizen (Ed.), *Proceedings of the 25th Conference of the International Group for the Psychology of Mathematics Education* (Vol. 3, pp. 423–430). Utrecht, the Netherlands: Freudenthal Institute, Utrecht University.

Olivero, F., John, P., & Sutherland, R. (2004). Seeing is believing: Using videopapers to transform teachers' professional knowledge and practices. *Cambridge Journal of Education, 34*(2), 179–191.

Pea, R. D. (2006). Video-as-data and digital video manipulation techniques for transforming learning science research, education and other cultural practices. In J. Weiss, J. Nolan, J. Hunsinger, & P. Trifonas (Eds.), *The international handbook of virtual learning environments* (Vol. 2, pp. 1321–1394). Amsterdam, the Netherlands: Springer.

Sánchez, V., García, M., & Escudero, I. (2006). Elementary presevice teacher learning levels. In J. Novotná, H. Moraová, M. Krátká, & N. Stehlková (Eds.), *Proceedings of the 30th Conference of the International Group for the Psychology of Mathematics Education* (Vol. 5, pp. 33–40). Czech Republic: Charles University in Prague.

Santagata, R., Zannoni, Cl., & Stigler, J. (2007). The role of lesson analysis in pre-service teacher education: An empirical investigation of teacher learning from a virtual video-based field experience. *Journal of Mathematics Teacher Education, 10*, 123–140.

Schrire, S. (2006). Knowledge building in asynchronous discussion groups: Going beyond quantitative analysis. *Computers & Education, 46*, 49–70.

Schuck, S. (2003). The use of electronic question and answer forums in mathematics teacher education. *Mathematics Education Research Journal, 5*, 19–30.

Sfard, A. (2001). There is more than discourse than meets the ears: looking at thinking as communicating to learn more about mathematical learning. *Educational Studies in Mathematics, 46*, 13–57.

Sherin, M. G. (2001). Developing a professional vision of classroom events. In T. Wood, B. S. Nelson, & J. Warfield (Eds.), *Beyond classical pedagogy. Teaching elementary school mathematics* (pp. 75–93). Mahwah, NJ: Lawrence Erlbaum Associates.

Sherin, M. G. (2004). New perspectives on the roleof video in teacher education. In J. Brophy (Ed.), *Using video in teacher education* (pp. 1–28). Oxford, UK: Elsevier Ltd.

Smith, K., & Krumsvik, R. (2007). Video papers – A means for documenting practitioners' reflections on practical experiences: The story of two teacher educators. *Research in Comparative and International Education, 2*(4), 272–282.

Strijbos, J., Martens, R., Prins, F., & Jochems, W. (2006). Content analysis: What are they talking about? *Computers & Education, 46*, 29–48.

Sutherland, R., Armstrong, V., Barnes, S., Brawn, R., Gall, M., Matthewman, S., Olivero, F., Taylor, A., Triggs, P., Wishart, J., & John, P. (2004). Transforming teaching and learning: Embedding ICT into every-day classroom practices. *Journal of Computer Assisted Learning Special Issue, 20*(6), 413–425.

Valls, J., Llinares, S., & Callejo, M. L. (2006). Video-clips y análisis de la enseñanza. Construcción del conocimiento necesario para enseñar matemáticas [Video-clips and analysis of teaching. Construction of the necessary knowledge to teach mathematics]. In M. C. Penalva, I. Escudero, & D. Barba (Eds.), *Conocimiento, entornos de aprendizaje y tutorización para la formación del profesorado de matemáticas* [Knowledge, learning environments and tutoring in mathematics teacher education] (pp. 25–43). Granada, Spain: Proyecto Sur, España.

Van Es, E., & Sherin, M. G. (2002). Learning to notice: Scaffolding new teachers' interpretations of classroom interactions. *Journal of Technology and Teacher Education, 10*(4), 571–596.

Wade, S., Niederhauser, D., Cannon, M., & Long, T. (2001). Electronic discussions in an issues course. Expanding the boundaries of the classroom. *Journal of Computing in Teacher Education, 17*(3), 4–9.

Wells, G. (2002). *Dialogic inquiry. Towards a sociocultural practice and theory of education.* Cambridge, UK: Cambridge University Press.

Wenger, E. (1998). *Communities of practice: Learning, meaning, and identity.* Cambridge, UK: Cambridge University Press.

Wenger, E., McDermott, R., & Snyder, W. (2002). *Cultivating communities of practice: A guide to managing knowledge.* Harvard, MA: Harvard Business School Press.

Zahn, C., Hesse, F., Finke, M., Pea, R., Mills, M., & Rosen, J. (2006). Advanced digital video technologies to support collaborative learning in school education and beyond. In T. Koschmann, D. Suthers, & T. Chan (Eds.), *Proceedings of the 2005 Conference on Computer Support for Collaborative Learning* (pp. 737–742). Mahwan, NJ: Lawrence Erlbaum Associates.

Zhu, E. (2006). Interaction and cognitive engagement: An analysis of four asynchronous online discussions. *Instructional Science, 34,* 451–480.

Salvador Llinares
Departamento de Innovación y Formación Didáctica,
University of Alicante
Spain

Federica Olivero
Graduate School of Education,
University of Bristol
United Kingdom

MARCELO C. BORBA AND GEORGE GADANIDIS

8. VIRTUAL COMMUNITIES AND NETWORKS OF PRACTISING MATHEMATICS TEACHERS

The Role of Technology in Collaboration

The collaboration of practising teachers in a virtual environment introduces the technology tools themselves both as mediators and as participants – as co-actors – in the collaborative process. Although there is a growing literature on the collaboration of practising teachers, the role of virtual technology tools is typically not addressed. In this chapter, we turn our attention to two cases, one in Brazil and one in Canada, as we explore how tools mediate and interact in the way teachers collaborate and construct knowledge. A challenge in this exploration is that technological tools change dramatically over short periods of time. Some aspects of teachers' online learning that are brought to light by the two cases from Brazil and Canada are: (1) virtual collaboration can happen in very different ways and using very different tools and methods; (2) online technology tools can transform abstract mathematics objects like polygons into tangible objects of communal attention and action; (3) collaborative knowledge construction tools like wikis help re-shape the collaborative process and transform roles played by teachers and instructors; and (4) multimodal communication through drawing tools, rich text, and video changes the "face" of mathematics. The virtual, non-human objects that are part of collaborative collectives of humans-with-media are not tools that we simply use for predetermined purposes. Humans-media interactions, which are quickly evolving with changes in the online world, are organic, reorganizing and restructuring our understanding of what it means for practising mathematics teachers to collaborate in a virtual environment.

INTRODUCTION

Since the mid 1990s, as the WWW became available in the virtual world, there has been resurgence and a *redefinition* of the idea of *distance education*. This modality of education is of course much older and used regular mail and television as the main means of communication between students and teacher. The main characteristic of this kind of education is that, while ideas were transmitted, students and teachers did not share the same space, and until the 1990s, the interaction was limited to teacher-to-students dialogue and did not include student-to-student dialogue. The Internet introduced the possibility of online collaboration among teachers in "distance education" settings, using synchronous (occurring at the same time) and asynchronous interaction with different modes of

K. Krainer and T. Wood (eds.), Participants in Mathematics Teacher Education, 181–206.

communication such as chat rooms, forums, wikis, videoconferences and multimodal ones in which text, pictures, video and voice are combined in different ways.

Distance education with the strong use of the Internet has been renamed online education. This modality of education has been used in undergraduate courses, as reported by Engelbrecht and Harding (2005), mainly with the independent learning model, which stresses the download of didactical material by learners. In such a model, the emphasis is on posting "instructional material on the web". Expressions such as "self-learning" and others that negate the role of the teacher are associated with this model of online education.

Interestingly, parallel to the growth of online learning in mathematics teacher education and in teacher education in general, there has been a growing interest in the collaboration of teachers. Krainer (2003), for example, notes that "Increasingly, papers in teacher education refer to some kind of 'communities' among teachers" (p. 94). There is also growing evidence that collaboration among teachers is a key ingredient for their professional development (e.g., Krainer, 2001; Peter-Koop, Santos-Wagner, Breen, & Begg, 2003). In trying to understand teacher professional development, many distinctions have been made among terms such as cooperation, collaboration, collegiality, teams, networks, and communities to address issues of power, conflict, conflict resolution and reflection (Begg, 2003; Krainer, 2003; Santos-Wagner, 2003; Lave & Wenger, 1991). Because of the recent availability of online collaborative tools, it is not surprising that the role of technology has not been addressed in most of the work on teacher collaboration.

However, some exceptions can be found in the last few years. Literature that addresses issues of teacher collaboration in online and face-to-face settings identifies a variety of methods for creating a collaborative focus: using multimedia cases (McGraw, Lynch, Koc, Budak, & Brown, 2007; Llinares & Olivero, this volume), identifying pedagogical issues of common interest (Arbaugh, 2003; Groth, 2007), using student work as a focus of reflection and discussion (Kazemi & Franke, 2004), and mathematical content (Lachance & Confrey, 2003; Davis & Simmt, 2006). A gap in the literature on the collaboration of practising mathematics teachers, and the focus of our chapter, is the role of virtual environments and tools both as factors *mediating teacher collaboration* and as *co-actors in the collaborative process*.

Our work on online teacher collaboration is based on a perspective that knowledge is constructed in interactions with others, what has been labelled as a Vygostikyan, sociocultural approach. By "others" we also refer to digital tools that permeate our new media culture. Borba and Villarreal (2005) see *humans-with-media* as actors in the production of knowledge and they note that humans-with-media form a collective where new media also serve to disrupt and reorganize human thinking. They base their view in authors such as Lévy (1997), who suggests that technology itself is an actor in the collaborative process. Lévy sees technology not simply as a tool used for human intentions, but rather as an integral component of the cognitive ecology that forms when humans collaborate in a technology immersive environment.

In our research (Borba & Penteado, 2001; Gracias, 2003; Borba, 2005; Borba & Villarreal, 2005; Gadanidis & Namukasa, 2005; Santos, 2006; Gadanidis, Namukasa, & Moghaddam, in review) we have used online education models that value the interaction among teacher educators and prospective or practising teachers by using synchronous and asynchronous interactions. Another characteristic of models we used in our courses and of the research that we developed involves exploration of what is new in computer technology. The medium used is considered in a deep way as a co-actor, that is an active, modifying agent that transforms the collaborative process, in the same way that writing is seen as being modified by the medium used, be it paper and pencil, or computer word processing. Other authors in this area, such as McGraw et al. (2007) and Rey, Penalva, and Llinares (2007) do not seem to take into consideration that the effect of media is important; they assume writing in online environments to be "neutral", as far as media is concerned, in their analysis of the way mathematicians, mathematics teachers, prospective educators and practising teachers interact. It is too early to try to draw strong conclusions regarding the role of the Internet in mathematics teacher education as there is little research on media as a co-actor in online education. Therefore, in this chapter, we would like to provide examples to inspire those concerned with teacher education to think about this issue which, as recently as 2005, was not a major topic in the ICMI study that took place in Brazil (http://stwww.weizmann.ac.il/G-math/ICMI/log_in.html), although studies such as Pateman, Dougherty, and Zilliox (2003), and Hoines and Fuglestad (2004) began to appear at conferences such as the Psychology of Mathematics Education (PME). We will first give examples that come from both Brazil[1] and Canada separately and then a final one that involved collaboration between both research teams. In these examples, we will show that, although we have experienced different kinds of online courses and used different types of interfaces, there is a common underlying goal of providing tools for interaction and supporting a collaborative culture among participants and among teachers and researchers. We will also show how a given tool shapes the nature of interaction, stressing, therefore, the role of media in the way teachers collaborate and the way knowledge is produced among participants.

EXPERIENCES IN USING ONLINE MATHEMATICS EDUCATION IN BRAZIL

Brazilian mathematics education has organized itself, among other means, in research groups. This type of organization has helped us to focus our efforts in conducting research. For instance, the first author of this paper participates in GPIMEM, a fifteen-year-old research group, registered in our national research group database. Since 1993, we have studied the role of different software in mathematics education, and how pedagogical approaches that involve students in choosing problems to be solved are in resonance with the use of information

---

[1] Some of the examples presented in this chapter from the Brazilian side have been presented since 2004 at PME conferences. See for example Borba (2005); Borba and Zulatto (2006); Borba (2007).

technology, including the Internet. Since the late 1990s, we have been involved with online education, specifically. First, we started studying the scarce literature available then in a search for one model of online courses to guide our work. Since 2000, we offered online courses as a means of experiencing distance education, as we continued to study the increasing number of studies and descriptions of online distance education. Courses such as these are of paramount importance in Brazil due to the size of the country and the concentration of knowledge production in the southeastern region, where the states of São Paulo and Rio de Janeiro are located. Internet-based courses are one way of connecting research centres such as São Paulo State University (UNESP) with people in remote locations, where the closest university may be more than several hundred kilometres away. This kind of practice and research illustrate how online education can be a path for social equity.

To present the way GPIMEM views online education, we will briefly depict the way we conceptualise technology in mathematics education as a result of our experience with software we used in the classroom. We have developed the theoretical notion of *humans-with-media* (Borba & Vilarreal, 2005) as a means of stressing the idea that knowledge is constructed by collectives which involve humans and different technologies of intelligence (Lévy, 1993), such as orality, paper-and-pencil, and information and communication technology (ICT). Different humans, or different technologies, result in different kinds of knowledge production. Knowledge production involves humans and some medium. This notion has provided important insights as we examined how different interfaces, such as graphing calculators, function software, or dynamic geometry software, affected knowledge production (Borba, 2004). We, as a group, illustrated how different media shape the way mathematics is produced. For example, students-with-graphing-calculators are more likely to raise conjectures and discuss mathematical ideas related to them (see e.g., Borba & Villarreal, 2005) than students working without such mathematical modelling and representation tools; also, collectives of humans-with-geometry-software-paper-and-pencil have integrated simulation and demonstration, as shown by Santos (2006). We were curious to know whether the Internet would also be equally as active in the way mathematics is done as we have argued that geometry and function software have been.

Based on research developed by GPIMEM we discuss the following issues: (1) our view about the role of technology in knowing; (2) our model of online courses based on interactions; (3) the importance of synchronous relationships; and (4) the active role of different internet interfaces on the construction of mathematical knowledge by teachers. We elaborate on each of these below and discuss them in the context of teacher collaboration.

Chat as the Main Interface for Online Courses

In order to learn how to teach online and to develop research, some members of our group have been researching how collectives formed of humans-with-Internet construct knowledge. For this purpose, among others, we offered several online courses for mathematics practising teachers. These courses were based on our previous experience with technology, which led us to believe that real-time interaction with the teacher is paramount when one works with technology. This is why, in most of our courses, we emphasized that at least one part of the course be synchronous, either through chat or videoconference. We have offered online courses such as *Trends in Mathematics Education*. These courses have fostered the development of communities that discuss issues related to the topics presented: teaching and learning of functions and geometry using software, ethnomathematics, modelling, adult education in mathematics, critical mathematics education, and so on. Eight versions of the "Trends course" have been offered, all of them with updated literature discussions along with adopting different virtual environments and evolving changes in the model adopted.

Each course brings together approximately 20 practising teachers online at regularly scheduled times over a period of about three months. The first author of this chapter and a collaborator taught all the eight courses offered until 2007. Almost every week, chat sessions of about three-hours long were scheduled. The teachers who took the course each time were, for the most part high school teachers, but university level teachers, teacher educators and others, such as curriculum developers, also took part in a group that could thus be labelled as heterogeneous. It was common in these chat sessions to have simultaneous dialogues, since different teachers would pursue different aspects of a given problem, or would pose a different problem, or talk about something that happened recently in their classroom. Courses were, therefore, designed in such a way that interaction was the key word. In 2003 and 2004, we used a free online environment, Teleduc[2], which requires a Linux server, but can be accessed by computers that use different platforms. Chat rooms became the principal means of synchronous interaction in the course. Preparation for a session would be done through asynchronous interactions, mainly e-mail and regular mail. For example, prior to a session on ethnomathematics, participants were mailed a book by D'Ambrosio (2001), the major proponent of ethnomathematics. All participants were expected to have read the book before the session, and two of them would be responsible for raising questions to generate discussion. After the class, a third teacher would generate a summary for the class that would be published in the virtual environment of the course and be made accessible to all participants.

However, when the objective of the class involved doing mathematics a different kind of preparation was required. Problems involving the use of function, for example, were sent beforehand to the teachers, and they attempted to solve them before the class; during the chat session, different solutions were discussed. When we decided to include problem solving sessions, as part of our online course, we also started to investigate how mathematics produced via chat might be shaped

---

[2] TelEduc is a free plataform for online courses developed by Nied and the "Instituto de Computação da Unicamp", chaired by Dr. Heloísa Vieira da Rocha. It is available for download at: http://hera.nied.unicamp.br/teleduc.

by this particular medium, and this became an important research question for us as mentioned before.

The problems that we posed to the teachers taking the online courses were designed to be solved with the use of plotters such as Winplot,[3] or a geometry software, Geometricks (Sadolin, 2000). Prior to a chat meeting, teachers could send their solutions to the virtual environment used in a given course, which might then be posted, for example, in a tool called portfolio. However, it was not possible to simultaneously share a figure with the other course participants. Such a situation generated discomfort for some participants. In the 2003 class, prior to a scheduled chat meeting with all 20 teachers participating in one of the courses, a problem was posed to them regarding Euclidean geometry. Different solutions and questions were raised by all participants, but one teacher's reflections caught our special attention; during the discussion, Eliane,[4] said: "I confess that, for the first time, I felt the need for a face-to-face meeting right away [...] it lacks eye-to-eye contact." She then followed up, explaining that discussing geometry made her want to see people and to share a common blackboard. In this case, there was no follow-up discussion to clarify what she meant. From her comment, we started to think about an initial answer to our question regarding the transformation of mathematics in online courses: the clash between Euclidean geometry, a symbol of space in our culture, and virtual space, a symbol of the beginning of the 21st Century, may permeate things such as doing mathematics. Some of the teachers did feel a need to share a screen during the synchronous interactions. Just seeing a solution in a portfolio, and commenting on it in another part of the virtual environment was not enough. As we will see later in this chapter, there are interfaces in the virtual world that can overcome part of this discomfort. For our research, it meant that the possibilities of the tool, of the virtual environment, shaped the way teachers were producing mathematics collectively.

A more detailed example will show a different facet of the way chat may transform the way mathematics is displayed, and in our view, this signifies changes in mathematics.

In the 2004 class, we posed the following problem[5] to the teachers who participated in the course, which is based on a true story that happened in a face-to-face classroom, taught by the first author of this chapter:

> Biology students at UNESP, São Paulo State University, take an introductory course in pre-calculus/calculus. The teacher of this course asks the students to explore, using a graphing calculator, what happens when the values 'a', 'b' and 'c' in $y = ax^2 + bx + c$ are changed. Students have to report on their findings. One of them [Renata] stated: "When b is greater than zero, the

---

[3] http://www.gregosetroianos.mat.br/softwinplot.asp

[4] Eliane Matesco Cristovão, High School teacher, from the 2003 class.

[5] Translation of this problem and of the excerpt from Portuguese into English was done by the author and Anne Kepple.

increasing part of the parabola will cross the y-axis [...]. When b is less than zero, the decreasing part of the parabola will cross the y-axis." What do you think of this statement? Justify your response.

The mathematics involved in the conjecture, and its accuracy according to academic mathematics, is developed in detail in Borba and Villarreal (2005). But it is interesting to see how the teachers, participants of this online course, dealt with it. Some aspects of it were eliminated since they were seen as irrelevant to the understanding of the dialogue, or because they were part of a conversation that was not associated with the solution of the problem.

Carlos, a high school teacher, started the debate at 19:49:07 (these numbers indicate the hour, minutes and seconds when the message reached the on-line course), reporting on what one of his students, in a face-to-face class, had said: "When a is negative, or b is positive, the parabola goes more to the right, but when a is negative and b is also negative, the parabola goes more to the left." He challenged the group to see if the student's sentence could lead them to solve the problem. Since the debate was not gaining momentum, the professor of the course, the first author of this chapter, tried to bring the group back to what Carlos had said:

(19:53:15) *Marcelo Borba*: The solution that Carlos' student presented regarding 'a' and 'b'. Does anyone have an algebraic explanation for it?

(19:54:53) *Taís*: It has something to do with the x coordinate of the vertex of the parabola.

(19:55:30) *Carlos*: after a few attempts (constructing many graphs changing the value of 'a', 'b', and 'c') the students concluded that what was proposed by Renata [the Biology student who first stated the conjecture in one of Borba's face-to face-classes] is really true.

The issues at stake are distinct. Carlos tried to do what the professor proposed to the group, but Taís raised a new issue, the vertex idea. As can be observed on the excerpt below, the two issues also have intersections:

(19:57:07) *Taís*: $Xv = -b / 2a$ [...] if 'a' and 'b' have different signs, Xv is positive.

(19:59:16) *Norma*: I constructed many graphs and I checked that it is correct, afterwards I analyzed the coordinates of the parabola vertex $Xv = -b / 2a$, and developed an analysis of the 'b' sign as a function of 'a' being positive or negative, then I verified the sign of the vertex crossing. [...] with the concavity upwards or downwards, and checked if it was increasing or decreasing. [...] did I make myself clear?

Norma presented her ideas, which according to the interpretation developed, are similar to the one made by Taís, and can be labelled the vertex solution. After further discussion about this, the professor presents another solution based on the derivative of y, $y' = 2ax + b$:

(20:07:03) *Marcelo Borba*: Sandra, [...] I just saw it a little differently. I saw it [...] I calculated $y'(0) = b$. [...] and therefore when 'b' is positive the parabola will be increasing and analogously [...].

Since a few people said they did not understand this comment, the educator went back to explain his solution.

(20:10:59) *Marcelo Borba*: [...] as I calculate the value of y', $y' > 0$, then the function is increasing, and therefore I consider $y'(0)$, which is equivalent to the point at which y crosses the y-axis, and $y'(0) = b$, and therefore 'b' decides the whole thing!!!! Got it?

(20:29:24) *Badin*: The parabola always intercepts the y-axis at the point where the x coordinate is zero. In order for this point to belong to the increasing "half" of the parabola ($a > 0$), it should be left of the x_v, this means x_v should be less than zero. Therefore, $-b / 2a < 0$ is equivalent to $-b < 0$ (remember, $a > 0$). But $-b < 0$ is equivalent to $b > 0$. In other words, if $b > 0$, the point where the graph crosses the y-axis is in the increasing part of the parabola. The demonstration for $a < 0$ is analogous.

At this point, some of the teachers had been discussing the problem and both solutions – the vertex and the derivative – for 40 minutes. The large spaces shown by the clock between the different citations from course participants indicate the size and number of sections that were eliminated in this paper, as there were about four messages per minute. For 10 more minutes, additional refinement and shared understanding of the solutions were presented. More examples of people's writing about their understanding in the chat are available in the naturally recorded data. Educational issues regarding the use of Winplot to explore the problem and generate conjectures were discussed. But what is new about the Internet in this case?

Before going further, the reader should be aware that some sentences were omitted to make it easier to follow the interaction, and that the translation from Portuguese into English suppressed most of the informality and typos that normally occur in this kind of environment. There were other actors involved in the discussion and refinement of the solutions of the problem, but for the purpose of clarity, only a few are included here. When we compare the solution presented by the teachers – the vertex one – to the original situation that took place in a normal classroom situation in 1997, there are similarities and differences. Students used graphing calculators to generate many conjectures for the problem relating coefficients of parabolas of the type $y = ax^2 + bx + c$ to different graphs. Similarly, the teachers used Winplot (or other software, in some examples) to investigate the problem just described, and later the problem related to Renata's conjecture. In the face-to-face classroom, the professor (author) led the discussion, and eventually presented the vertex solution (as he did not know the answer either, at first). The students never wrote the explanation for the conjecture. In an on-line learning environment based on chat, writing is natural, and everyone involved had to express themselves in writing (see also Llinares & Olivero, this volume). Although we know that some aspects of writing in a chat situation are different compared to writing with paper and pencil, there is a fair amount of research showing the benefits of writing for learning (see e.g., Sterret, 1990). However, the data presented here is insufficient, and the design of the study is inappropriate, to support arguments about "benefits". Still it can be argued that chats transform the mathematics that is produced by the participants of the course. The chat tool, together with human beings, generate a kind of written mathematics that is different from that developed in the face-to-face classroom, where gestures and looks form part of the communication as well. We have been building evidence, with other examples, of how collectives of humans-with-Internet-software generate different kinds of knowledge, which does not mean that the mathematical results were different. But if the process is considered, most of us at GPIMEM believe that we may be on the way to discovering a qualitatively different medium that, like the "click and drag" tool of the dynamic geometry, offers a new way of doing mathematics that has the potential to change the mathematics produced, because writing in non-mathematical language becomes a part of doing mathematics. At this point, it is too early to confirm this, but we believe that this "working hypothesis" (Lincoln & Guba, 1985) regarding the transformation of mathematics by the Internet is one that we have been pursuing in research developed within virtual environments like the ones described, but also in different ones, such as the ones we present below.

In virtual collaboration, the participants that influence the nature and the focus of the collaborative process are not only the human participants, but also the technological tools and the collaboration affordances and constraints that they introduce. In Borba and Penteado (2001), and Gracias (2003), we show that "multialogues" – understood as simultaneous dialogues – are a characteristic of interaction in chat rooms. Unlike in a regular class, when more than one person talks at the same time only when there is group work, in chat, theoretically all can "talk" at the same time. In a videoconference environment, new kinds of collaboration emerge. Interaction and collaboration, two key words of our model of online courses we have, can also be supported drawing on the literature on teacher education, where authors such as Hargreaves (1998), Larraín and Hernández (2003), Fiorentini (2004), and Llinares and Krainer (2006) claim that collaboration and sharing are powerful actions that generate new knowledge. If we bring these ideas to online courses, we have a strong argument for generating courses that emphasize interaction not only with the leader of the course, but among participants. In a cyclic model, we researched different types of courses offered, chose one that emphasizes collaboration, and investigated how different platform interfaces for such courses shape the knowledge that is produced, or in other words, how different collectives of humans-with-media produce different kinds of mathematics and collaboration. As we will see next, different interfaces mean different possibilities of online education.

Video Conference as the Main Interface for Online Courses

A course, entitled *"Geometry with Geometricks"*, was developed in response to a demand from mathematics teachers from a network of schools sponsored by the Bradesco Foundation spread throughout all the Brazilian states. The teachers from these 40 schools, which include some in the Amazon rainforest, have access to different kinds of activities, such as courses that are administered at a pedagogical centre located in the greater São Paulo area. Following the improvement of Internet connections in Brazil, the administrators of the school network realized that online courses could become a good option, since sending teachers from different parts of Brazil (which is larger in area than the continental US) to a single location to take courses was neither cost nor pedagogically effective. Lerman and Zehetmeier (this volume) point to cost as an important factor for programmes that involve practising teachers when goals include encouraging teachers to reflect on their practice outside the classroom. The cost factor is related to the size of the country, and the pedagogical consideration is related to the fact that teachers would usually participate in the courses for a short period of time, with little or no chance of implementing new ideas while still taking the course. Our model, based on online interaction and applications in their face-to-face classes in middle and high school, gained respect gradually within this institution.

The pedagogical headquarters of this network of schools approached us, asking for a course about how to teach geometry using Geometricks, dynamic geometry software originally published in Danish and translated into Portuguese. It has most of the basic commands of other software such as Cabri II and Geometer Sketchpad, and it was designed for plane geometry. As we know from previous research on the interaction of information technology and mathematics education, just having a piece of software available, and a well-equipped laboratory with 50 microcomputers, as is the case of these schools, is not enough to guarantee their successful use, even if the teachers are paid above average compared to their colleagues from other schools.

In our research group, we designed a course using an exploratory problem solving approach similar to that discussed by Schoenfeld (2005); it was divided into four themes within geometry (basic activities, similarity, symmetry and analytic geometry). Problems usually had more than one way of being solved, and they could be incorporated at different grade levels of the curriculum according to the degree of requirements for a solution, and according to the preference of the teacher. Both intuitive and formal solutions were recognized as being important, and the articulation of trial-and-error and geometrical arguments were encouraged. We "met" online for two hours on eight Saturday mornings over a period of approximately three months. Besides this synchronous activity, there was a fair amount of e-mail exchanged during the week for clarification regarding the problems proposed and technical issues regarding the software; in addition, also

190

pedagogical issues regarding the use of computer software in the classroom were raised, for example: should we introduce a concept in the regular classroom and then take the students to the laboratory, or the other way around? Pedagogical themes were also discussed during the online meetings, in particular in one session in which, instead of the students working on problems during the week, they had to read a short book about the use of computers in mathematics education (Borba & Penteado, 2001). We encouraged teachers to solve problems together in face-to-face or online fashion.

The Bradesco Foundation had already purchased an online platform that allowed participants to have access to chat, forum, e-mail, and video conference that allowed the download of activities, as well. In our course, participants could download problems, and they could also post their solutions if they wanted to, or they could send them privately to one of the leaders of the course (the authors of this paper). The platform allowed the screen of any of the participants to be shared with everyone else. For example, we could start showing a screen of Geometricks on our computer, and everyone else could see the dragging that we were performing on a given geometrical construction. A special feature, which is important for the purpose of this paper, was the capability to "pass the pen" to another participant who could then add to what we had done on a Geometricks file. In this case technological possibilities transformed the way collaboration could happen. Different teachers, who were taking the online course, could lead a problem solving activity. As it will be described, there were times when one teacher would have the pen, and another would be commenting or giving instructions on how to proceed with a given problem.

This example can illustrate how the convergence of different ideas generates the collective construction of knowledge about geometry (content knowledge) about use of a given geometry software in the classroom (pedagogical content knowledge), and about use of the geometry software itself (technological knowledge). This problem involved symmetry. A Geometricks file had already been given to them with the figure MNOPQ, presented below (Figure 1). Teachers were asked to find the symmetric figure, in relation to axis "q". Teachers were reminded in the text that the symmetric figure had to remain symmetric even after being dragged.

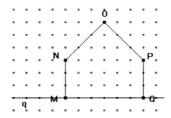

Figure 1. Picture of the file given to teachers.

191

As mentioned earlier, teachers were given each problem before the synchronous sessions and could interact with one of the teachers of the course by e-mail or other means. This allowed us to sometimes choose issues to start the debate and, at the same time, we could also limit undesired exposure of some errors. For this problem, the vast majority of solutions used a "count dot approach" in which they counted how many dots a given vertex was distant from "q". The result is visualized in Figure 2. We invited a volunteer to make a construction. We passed the pen to one participant who offered to do so, who in turn was helped by another who was acting like a sports narrator. After the construction was done, we asked questions such as: is MVWZQ symmetric to MNOPQ? The "argument" was quite intense, and the participants were divided. The issue about dragging emerged, and we came to the conclusion that if the dragging of a vertex is considered to be essential, that solution would not generate a symmetric figure (see Figure 3).

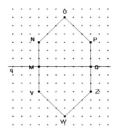

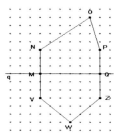

Figure 2. The first solution of the teachers.

Figure 3. Dragging and passes the test of dragging.

Different solutions were developed by different actors who took over the pen and/or whose voices emerged, including the one presented in Figure 4 – where circumferences are used playing the role of a compass in dynamic geometry – that would still be symmetric after dragging since, as we pull a point away from the axis, for example, the symmetric point will do the same, since it is part of the circumference. This issue is relevant, and for authors such as Laborde (1998) and Arzarello, Micheletti, Olivero, and Robutti (1998), a straight quadrilateral with four equal sides and four angles is only considered a square in a dynamic geometry software if it passes the "test of dragging", which means, in this case, that it is still a square after different kinds of manipulation are performed. For these authors, if the resulting figure is no longer a square, we did not have a construction of a square but just a drawing. We agree with these authors that this is an important issue, even though in our course, we also emphasized the relevant role of "drawing solutions" depending on the grade level, the complexity of the problem, or as a path for more complex solutions. Other examples such as these were developed during this course. Teachers were overwhelmingly positive about the idea of collective problem solving during the synchronous videoconference sessions, especially when they compared the experience with others in which just we, the leaders, would present our solution or present one of their solutions in a more expository manner of teaching. Our own assessment, as leaders, was that this virtual collaboration created a bonding among teachers that was not experienced when we did not use this technical feature. The issue about drawing versus construction is not new in the literature; what we believe to be original in the episode reported is the fact that it came from an online course, and that it resulted from collaboration among teachers. In such collaboration, they learned from each other, which is considered important by authors such as Lin and Ponte (this volume).

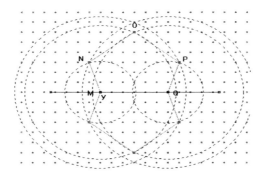

Figure 4. The second solution.

Hargreaves (2001) proposed that teaching is a *paradoxical profession*. On the one hand, everyone expects from teachers, even in developing Third World countries, efforts to help the construction of learning communities in the new "knowledge society". Even though most teachers were not educated in a time when microcomputers were extensively available, they are required to teach using computers and software in the classroom. On the other hand, there is discourse in governments and segments of society that claims we should have a "shrinking" of the state due to the needs of this knowledge society, and teachers become one of their first victims with funding cuts for sectors such as education. Teachers should enhance the knowledge society, even though they are some of their first victims. Whether teachers are aware of this dilemma or not, they feel the need, and there is institutional pressure, to constantly be working on their professional development. Integrating software into the face-to-face classroom is still a challenge as teachers enter a risk zone (Penteado, 2001) in which the students sometimes know better how to manipulate computers and often come up with original solutions to a given problem, or even create new problems which are not easy to handle. Soon the demand to incorporate the Internet in the classroom should rise as it seems like we are moving towards a "blended" learning approach, in which virtual and face-to-face interaction will happen "in" the classroom.

It makes sense, therefore, that teachers experience online courses, in particular if one considers the cost factor, as in the case described above. Reimann (2005), in his plenary at PME 29, emphasized the need to build artefacts on the Internet that could foster collaboration. We agree and believe that we are helping to construct collaborative practices within online continuing education courses offered to mathematics teachers. This type of collaboration was possible due to a design in the platform that allowed us to do so. Of course, having the possibility is just one step, and a pedagogical approach that enhanced participation should always be pursued. But we want to emphasize that we should also be creating demands for technical developments in online platforms, and this is an area in which our research group, GPIMEM, has started working in the last few years.

We would like to say that once design features are incorporated either into software, such as dragging, or into online platforms, like the "pass the pen" option, participants become co-actors in the process of creating and recreating knowledge. Different media, different people, imply different perspectives in the knowledge constructed. That is why we believe that using the construct of humans-with-media is useful to analyse educational practices that use technology, since they foster the search for specific uses of an available interface. "Pass the pen" was a unique characteristic of this platform that made possible the co-construction of mathematical knowledge in an online course.

Engelbrecht and Harding (2005) have presented a study that shows that many courses offered are based on independent learning with very little interaction among participants. Those who take courses like these are expected to download material and learn by themselves, and they are then assessed through some kind of standardized test. Many teachers can be enrolled in courses like these, thus generating profit for the organizers, and they dismiss the role of interaction in teachers' professional development. At the other end of the spectrum are courses that use the Internet as a means of generating quick feedback among participants. For example, forum is used for asynchronous relations so that participants express their ideas and doubts and post solutions to problems. Synchronous relationships that employ chats, videoconference, and other tools, make it possible to share ideas in real time, even if people do not share the same space. Courses such as these are based on the idea that media should not be domesticated, which means that we, as mathematics educators, should try to design curricula that fully explore the possibilities of new media or interfaces. In the examples presented, we emphasized how mathematics gains different characteristics, and teachers collaborate in different ways, depending on the interface used. At GPIMEM, we are in the process of learning from these experiences to shed light on face-to-face mathematics education, as we are more knowledgeable about the role of different media in the production of knowledge. As the reader will see, there are commonalities and particularities as we learn some from the Canadian experience.

THE CASE OF ONLINE PRACTISING MATHEMATICS TEACHER EDUCATION IN
ONTARIO, CANADA: ISSUES AFFECTING TEACHER COLLABORATION

Our experience, in the Canadian case, based on online education courses offered to
practising teachers at the Faculty of Education, University of Western Ontario, in
Canada, points to the following issues: (1) online courses versus face-to-face
courses; (2) asynchronous versus synchronous online course communication; (3)
text-based versus multimodal communication; and (4) read-only versus read/write
communication. We elaborate on each of these below and discuss them in the
context of teacher collaboration.

Context

Our Faculty of Education has three teacher education programmes: a teacher
education programme, a continuing teacher education programme, and a graduate
programme (masters and PhD). Our continuing teacher education programme
offers over 150 online courses to Ontario teachers, with approximately 5,000
teachers taking our courses annually. To support the development of community
and collaboration, the number of participants in each of the courses we offer is
capped at 25 teachers. These courses are part of a provincially mandated and
certified regimen of additional qualifications which lead to teacher professional
development and in some cases to salary increases. Six of these courses are
specifically for mathematics teachers. In addition, we offer three mathematics-for-
teachers courses which are not part of the provincial regimen of courses. Our
graduate programme offers a fully certified online Master of Education degree in
addition to its traditional face-to-face masters and PhD degree programmes (where
some courses are also offered either fully or partially online). Our prospective
teacher education programme offers some components of its mathematics and
language arts programme online, where we replaced large group lectures with
online content and discussion (Gadanidis & Rich, 2003).

Face-to-Face Versus Online Classrooms

In the case of courses for practising teachers, our experience indicates that most of
them prefer online as opposed to face-to-face courses. Over ten years ago, our
continuing teacher education programme was fully face-to-face, and we offered our
courses in the evenings, at weekends and during the summer break. We offered
courses on campus as well as in remote areas, with approximately 2,700 teachers
taking our courses annually. However, once we started offering courses online,
teachers opted for these rather than the face-to-face courses. Currently, our
continuing teacher education programme is approximately 95 percent online. It is
important to note that we do still offer the face-to-face courses, however teachers
choose not to take them. It is also important to note that there are other providers
offering the same courses, both face-to-face and online, and they have experienced
a similar trend. The main reason for this shift from face-to-face to online, based on

surveys we conduct on a regular basis, is that teachers lead busy lives, in and out of school, and having to attend classes at set times is a scheduling burden.

Asynchronous Versus Synchronous Classrooms

Teachers also tell us that the asynchronous nature of our online program makes it appealing. Rather than having to schedule their lives around an arbitrarily scheduled class, they can choose to participate during a time in the day or night that is most convenient for them. The indication we have from teacher feedback is that if our online courses used a synchronous mode, many teachers would either opt to take online courses from another provider that used an asynchronous mode or they would take a face-to-face course. It is important to note that we have a significant number of Ontario teachers that teach overseas in countries such as the Middle East and Singapore and it would not be possible for them to participate in synchronous discussions because of time zone differences. The fact that most of our practising teachers choose our online rather than our face-to-face courses, and indicate that they prefer asynchronous rather than synchronous online discussion environments, does not necessarily mean that one mode is educationally better than another, or that it is a simple either-or choice between modes (as hybrid environments can and do exist). However, it is interesting to consider some of the differences between these modes and how the differences may impact on teacher online collaboration.

Face-to-face and synchronous online discussions are temporal experiences. They occur in real time and they have a linear quality. In the Brazilian case we noted that online synchronous chat is different to face-to-face synchronous communication because the former allows for more than one discussion theme to be conducted simultaneously, with chat postings woven into a complex tapestry of ideas being discussed simultaneously. This would be analogous to the (impossible) face-to-face situation where teachers work in small groups but somehow everyone can hear what everyone else is saying without the dialogues overlapping. The tapestry of multi-theme postings in an online synchronous chat may cause some confusion or disorientation. However, as we noted in the Brazilian case, this multi-linear, multi-tasking environment can provide a novel, complex and rich experience of collaboration.

In the Ontario case, a chat tool does exist in the e-learning platform we employ. However, the chat tool is rarely used. The asynchronous online discussion used in our courses introduces some interesting affordances for collaboration. Unlike typical synchronous discussions (especially when the synchronous communication is oral rather than textual), where it is possible for a small number of people to dominate the discussion, asynchronous discussion makes it possible for everyone to contribute to every discussion theme. In fact, this is an expectation in our online courses. A significant part of the assessment (typically about 30%) focuses on the discussion component, and teacher participation is assessed based on its frequency, regularity and quality. Another difference is that in an asynchronous environment, teachers can take more time to think about the ideas of others and to craft their own responses before posting in the online discussion.

Textual Versus Multimodal Communication

Until the end of 2004, our online courses used a platform where communication was primarily textual. However, in 2004, we made a decision to offer some of our mathematics course for elementary teachers in an online setting. This created a challenge because of the lack of an ability to communicate visual aspects of mathematics, like diagrams. Consequently, late in 2004, we developed a new online platform (Gadanidis, 2007) that offered multimodal communication by allowing users to embed the following within discussion postings: rich text (using a text editor that is similar to those found in a word processor); diagrams (using a built-in draw tool); video or audio (using a built-in tool that allowed the capture of video or audio from a web cam); as well as multimedia content, such as JPEG images and Flash interactive content. The immediate difference this made to online discussion was the visual appeal. Opening a discussion thread the reader was faced with postings where text was bolded, coloured and formatted, and accompanied with colourful mathematical drawings and images. Figure 5 shows a drawing created by an elementary teacher to illustrate her conception of what parallel lines may be transformed onto a sphere, a flat piece of paper and a rolled piece of paper.

Figure 5. An elementary teacher uses the Draw Tool to show three representations of "parallel" lines.

Figure 6 shows the diagram an elementary teacher created to explain to another teacher how slope is calculated. Does this type of communication make a difference? Kress (2003) and Kress and van Leeuwen (1996, p. 111) suggest that in a digital environment "meaning is made in many different ways, always, in the many different modes and media which are co-present in a communicational ensemble". In terms of mathematics meaning making, being able to communicate via images and user-created diagrams adds layers of meaning and elaboration that enhance how ideas are expressed and understood. In addition, the ability to add video in the discussion postings (using a web cam) makes the online discussion feel personal. For example, prior to a face-to-face graduate seminar in Brazil, video postings were used to introduce the Canadian instructors and the Brazilian students to one another and to introduce ideas to be discussed in the seminar. Also, the ability to add video allows for embodied communication of mathematics, through gestures and the use of physical materials. Figure 7 shows how elementary school students in Brazil used the video capture tool to illustrate how L patterns can be used to physically represent odd numbers and their sums as square patterns. With the steady growth of bandwidth, the mode of online interaction and the content generated are increasingly multimodal. It makes sense that online discussion and collaboration among mathematics teachers would use the multimodal communication tools available.

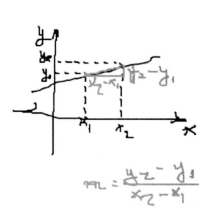

Figure 6. An elementary teacher's explanation of slope.

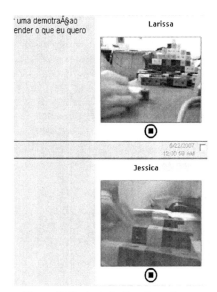

Figure 7. Students in Brazil posting videos of physical patterns.

It should be noted that because the "Mathematics-for-Teachers" courses developed in the Ontario case were aimed at elementary teachers, the drawing tool was sufficient for most needs to communicate visual aspects of mathematical ideas. If this platform was used for discussing more complex mathematics, this could be accommodated by embedding Flash applets in discussion postings that allow teachers to explore more complex ideas using graph plotters, probability simulations, etc.

Read-Only Versus Read/Write Communication

The Web is today in the process of transforming itself from a read-only to a read/write environment. In terms of online education, this transformation is perhaps best reflected through the use of wikis. A wiki is a collaborative website that can be edited by anyone who has access to it. When in late 2004 we created a platform that allowed for the multimodal communication discussed above, we also created the ability to use wiki discussion postings. When someone creates a discussion posting, they have the option of making it a wiki posting. This means that everyone else in the discussion can edit that posting.

The wiki feature has been used in a graduate course called the "Analysis of Teaching" to create collaborative tasks that focus on mathematics pedagogy. For example, we have used the transcript of a typical grade 8 US mathematics lesson as depicted in the 1995 TIMSS Video Study (see excerpt below), by posting this transcript in a wiki posting and then asking teachers to collaboratively edit the transcript in ways that would improve the quality of the lesson. This is an interesting and rather complex collaborative writing experience in that as teachers start editing the transcript, other teachers have to adapt their own ideas to fit with the edits made up to that point. This does not mean that they cannot edit the edits of other students, but rather that they have to keep the changing flow of the lesson in mind as they make edits: they cannot simply make an edit to one section without taking into account the edits that precede and follow. That is, students need to understand the edits of other students – seeing the lesson through the pedagogical lenses of others – and then negotiate a synthesis of their edits with existing edits. Thus the final edited lesson is the result of sophisticated collaborative editing process.

Teacher: Here we have vertical angles and supplementary angles. [...]. Angle A is vertical to which angle?
Students: 70.
Teacher: Therefore, angle A must be [...].
Students: 70.
Teacher: 70, right. Go from there. Now you have supplementary angles. Don't you? [...]. Now, what angle is supplementary to angle B, I mean, I'm sorry, Angle A?
Students: B.
Teacher: [...] and so is [...]?
Students: C.
Teacher: Supplementary angles add up to what number?
Student: 180.

The TIMSS Video Study (Stiegler, 1999) activity is one of the first collaborative writing activities we use in the "Analysis-of-Teaching" course, to get teachers comfortable with writing collaboratively and editing the ideas of others. Because they are editing a transcript that is not their own, it is easier for them to make edits without feeling that they might hurt someone's feelings. Later on in the course, students post transcripts from their own teaching, and discuss these in wiki postings. Our experience at the graduate level is that teachers are very hesitant to edit the ideas of others or to have their own ideas edited. One other thing that we do to help shift their perspective is to discuss how the peer review process works for scholarly writing. For example, when we submit a paper for possible publication in a scholarly journal, we receive feedback from the reviewers about edits that we could make to improve the paper. Sometimes, these edits are written on a separate piece of paper, sometimes they are written in the margins, and sometimes there are suggested edits in the text of the paper. This is typically a tremendous learning process, both for the reviewer and for the author. We thus try to emphasise that peer review and peer editing is a natural and rewarding scholarly experience. Nonetheless, some students never fully engage in the process, and instead make superficial edits or react negatively to edits of their own work. It takes more than a couple of collaborative writing activities to shift some students' view of graduate work as personal and private and of the instructor as the only person who has the right to give feedback and make editing suggestions.

A LOOK TO THE FUTURE

Borba and Villarreal (2005) have argued how different software interfaces interact with our cognition and reorganize our thinking. Our thinking about online education has been disrupted and reorganized as we have used and thought *with* emerging online affordances like multimodal and read/write communication. For example, using a wiki in our online teaching is a very different experience than teaching in a physical classroom. It is also very different from using simple text-based discussion platforms with read-only discussion postings. Using a wiki does not only disrupt and reorganize our thinking about how we structure classroom interaction, it also becomes a lens that changes how we see other aspects of our online teaching, such as course content, evaluation practices, our role as instructors, and generally what constitutes knowledge and how it is or should be constructed collaboratively in an online environment. The emerging multimodal and collaborative tools of online teaching and learning environments are not simply tools that we use for predetermined purposes. Rather, they can be seen as co-actors in the cognitive ecology of online environments, existing in a complex, organic relationship between humans and technology (Gadanidis & Borba, 2008).

Collaborating without Geographical Boundaries

From the examples presented in the Brazilian cases and in the Canadian cases, the reader may be led to believe that online education is a solution for many of the problems of teaching education, and that it brings no problems. In the Canadian case, for example, where teachers have the option of choosing an online or a face-to-face version of a course, they overwhelmingly opt for the online version. In the Brazilian case there has been very positive assessment of the online courses made not only by the teachers who participated in the courses, but also by administrators of the private schools who paid for the courses attended by their teachers, as reported by Borba (2007). On the other hand, in other courses, in which there was a fair number of teachers dropping out, members of the research group based in Brazil attempted to know the reasons why teachers left the course, but they could not, since there were not enough respondents. In addition, in the Brazilian case, a few problems have already been identified, such as the lack of a common geometric figure to share synchronously in some environments, but at the same time we have also shown how different interface such as videoconferencing can solve such a limitation. But in other papers we have pointed out limitations such as technical difficulties to deal with a given platform or even inability to type fast enough in order to participate in a session (Borba, Malheiros, & Zulatto, 2007). Other authors such as Ponte and Santos (2005) and Ponte, Oliveira, Varandas, Oliveira, and Fonseca (2007) have shown how different teachers live this experience in different ways. They report that although some teachers are positive about the online experience, there are others who are far from that, for reasons which include the fact that once you "say/write" something it is recorded electronically and accessible for everyone to read. So we can say that the modality of online courses for teachers is still open for debate and for research. Moreover, we need to investigate whether styles of learning are connected to the medium used. It may be the case that some teachers prefer online and others like face-to-face-courses.

One aspect of teachers' online learning that is brought to light by the two cases from Brazil and Canada is that *collaboration* can happen in very different ways and using very different tools and methods. For example, if you read only the Brazilian case, you might appreciate the value of synchronous communication as a tool for online collaboration. On the other hand, if you read only the Canadian case, you might appreciate the value of asynchronous communication as a tool for online collaboration. Another aspect that is brought to light by both cases is that the online world is changing at a rapid pace. In both cases, the technological tools used changed dramatically over short periods of time. The reason for this is the rapid development of new online technologies coupled with the rapid growth of Internet access and bandwidth. The text-based, read-only online world of a few years ago is rapidly evolving into a multimodal, read/write social networking environment (Sprague, Maddux, Ferdig, & Albion, 2007). This is bound to have an impact on the virtual collaboration of practising mathematics teachers. The question is how widespread will this impact be? In a review of online education, Sprague et al. (2007, p. 158) suggest "that so-called 'early-adopters' of technology may have made up the majority of faculty and students who have so far been involved in the online education phenomenon". It will be interesting to look back five or ten years from now and see whether the use of the new collaborative affordances of the WWW is also limited mostly to the "early-adopters" or whether their use pervades online mathematics teacher education. In the same direction, it should be interesting to confirm whether, in fact, the online world has been "an actor" in transforming mathematics. This has been proposed by Borba and Villarreal (2005) in the case of the introduction of given software, and in the way we are proposing for online mathematics teacher education.

Given the ongoing development of the WWW as a social/collaborative environment, we believe that a promising path for research is the one that investigates the synergy between the virtual tools used and the collaborative nature of the online education/professional development of practising mathematics teachers. Moreover, the virtual tools that are part of collaborative collectives of *humans-with-media* are not tools that we simply use for predetermined purposes: they are *active "participants"* in the collaborative process. Human-media interactions, which are quickly evolving with changes in the online world, are organic, reorganizing and restructuring our understanding of what it means for practising mathematics teachers to collaborate in a virtual environment. For example, we have seen in the Brazilian case how online technology tools can transform abstract mathematics objects like polygons into tangible objects of communal attention and action. What changes mathematically and what changes in terms of the collaborative process when mathematical objects become communal objects? We have also seen in the Canadian case how *multimodal communication* through drawing tools, rich text, and video changes the "face" of mathematics. How does mathematics change when it is expressed in multimodal forms? How does a media-rich environment affect the collaborative process?

In typical online teacher education settings, the mode of communication is textual. Texts on chats and forums are changing the way mathematics is expressed. Bringing everyday language to the forefront of mathematics communication is already transforming mathematics that is constructed in online mathematics education. In the cases presented, communication also involved diagrams, pictures, video and interactive content. These modes of communication are increasingly *changing the mathematics* that is constructed in such online environments. We believe that these are examples of how non-human authors become co-actors in the production of mathematical knowledge.

In the Brazilian case we can see the "passing the pen" tool transforming collaboration as teachers can collectively and synchronously solve a problem in a natural way. In the Canadian case, we can see teachers learning to have communal production, which can be also seen as being shaped by the possibilities that the wiki-like environment they used for asynchronous communication. We believe that the examples presented in this chapter illustrate how *tools become co-actors* in the way teachers collaborate and construct knowledge. Design of online tools is a topic we should be interested as these non-human objects can become parts of collectives of humans-with-media that produce knowledge. To study the role of online tools on the role of collaboration in teacher education seems to be a promising path for research, as the examples presented are not sufficient for us to assure that online tools shape mathematics and collaboration. At this point, it seems that we have to see virtual tools as co-actors in the collaboration of practising teachers as a working hypothesis to be confirmed, rejected or re-elaborated in the future.

Also, since the social nature of the WWW appears to be permeating our society (with the emergence of social networking sites such as MySpace and YouTube), it might be worth exploring less formal or perhaps emergent collaborative relationships among mathematics teachers. It might also be worth exploring the effect of the pervasive nature of WWW on equity of access, as both the Brazilian and the Canadian cases involve both urban as well as geographically remote areas.

ACKNOWLEDGEMENTS

Although they are not responsible for the content of this chapter, the authors would like to thank Ricardo Scucuglia, Marcus Maltempi, Silvana Santos, Sandra Barbosa, Ana Paula Malheiros, Regina Franchi and Rubia Zulatto, members of GPIMEM, UNESP, for their comments on earlier versions of this chapter. We would also like to thank CNPq, FAPESP and SSHRC, funding agencies of the Brazilian and Canadian government for partially funding research presented in this chapter. Finally we would like to thank the editors of this book for the review of this chapter.

REFERENCES

Arbaugh, F. (2003). Study groups as a form of professional development for secondary mathematics teachers. *Journal of Mathematics Teacher Education, 6*, 139–163.

Arzarello, F., Micheletti, C., Olivero, F., & Robutti, O. (1998). Dragging in Cabri and modalities of transition from conjectures to proofs in geometry. *Proceedings of 22nd Conference of the International Group for the Psychology of Mathematics Education* (Vol. 2, pp. 32–39). Stellenbosch, South Africa: University of Stellenbosch.

Begg, A. (2003). More than collaboration: Concern, connection, community and curriculum. In A. Peter-Koop, V. Santos-Wagner, C. Breen, & A. Begg (Eds.), *Collaboration in teacher education: Examples from the context of mathematics education* (pp. 253–266). Dordrecht, the Netherlands: Kluwer.

Borba, M. C. (2004). Dimensões da educação matemática a distância [Dimensions of the distance mathematics education]. In M. A. V. Bicudo & M. Borba (Eds.), *Educação matemática: pesquisa em movimento* [Mathematics Education: research in action]. (pp. 296–317). São Paulo: Cortez.

Borba, M. C. (2005). The transformation of mathematics in on-line courses. In H. Chick & J. Vincent (Eds.), *Proceedings of the 29th Conference of the International Group for the Psychology of Mathematics Education* (Vol. 2, pp. 169–176). Melbourne, Australia: University of Melbourne.

Borba, M. C. (2007). Integrating virtual and face-to-face practice: A model for continuing teacher education. In J. Woo, H. Lew, K. Park, & D. Seo (Eds.), *Proceedings of the 31st Conference of the International Group for the Psychology of Mathematics Education* (Vol. 1, pp. 128–131). Seoul, Korea: Seoul National University.

Borba, M. C., Malheiros, A. P. S., & Zulatto, R. B. A. (2007). *Educação a distância online* [Online distance education]. Belo Horizonte, Brazil: Autêntica.

Borba, M. C., & Penteado, M. (2001). *Informática e educação matemática* [Computers and mathematics education]. Belo Horizonte, Brazil: Autêntica.

Borba, M. C., & Villarreal, M. E. (2005). *Humans-with-media and the reorganization of mathematical thinking: Information and communication technologies, modeling, visualization and experimentation.* New York: Education Library, Springer.

Borba, M. C., & Zullato, R. (2006). Different media, different types of collective work in online continuing teacher education: Would you pass the pen, please? In J. Navotná, H. Maraová, M. Krátká, & N. Stehliková (Eds.), *Proceedings of the 30th Conference of the International Group for the Psychology of Mathematics Education* (Vol. 2, pp. 201–208). Prague, Czech Republic: Charles University.

D'Ambrosio, U. (2001). *Etnomatemática – elo entre as tradições e a modernidade* [Etnomathematics – link between traditions and modernity]. Belo Horizonte, Brazil: Autêntica.

Davis, B., & Simmt, E. (2006). Mathematics-for-teaching: An ongoing investigation of the mathematics that teachers (need to) know. *Educational Studies in Mathematics, 61,* 293–319.

Engelbrecht, J., & Harding, A. (2005). Teaching undergraduate mathematics on the internet 1: Technologies and taxonomy. *Educational Studies in Mathematics, 58,* 235–252.

Fiorentini, D. (2004). Pesquisar práticas colaborativas ou pesquisar colaborativamente? [Should we research about collaboration or should we develop collaborative research?]. In M. C. Borba & J. L. Araújo (Eds.), *Pesquisa qualitativa em educação matemática* [Qualitative research in mathematics education]. Belo Horizonte, Brazil: Autêntica.

Gadanidis, G. (2007). Designing an online learning platform from scratch. In L. Cantoni & C. McLoughlin (Eds.), *Proceedings of Ed-Media 2004, World Conference on Educational Multimedia, Hypermedia and Telecommunications* (Vol. 1, pp. 1642–1647). Chesapeake, Vancouver, Canada: Association for the Advancement of Computing in Education.

Gadanidis, G., & Borba, M. (2008). Our lives as performance mathematicians. *For the Learning of Mathematics, 28*(1), 44–51.

Gadanidis, G., & Namukasa, I. (2005). Math therapy. *The Fifteenth ICMI Study: The Professional Education and Development of Teachers of Mathematics.* State University of Sao Paulo at Rio Claro, Brazil, 15–21 May 2005. Retrieved October 15, 2007, from http://stwww.weizmann.ac.il/G-math/ICMI/log_in.html

Gadanidis, G., Namukasa, I., & Moghaddam, A. (in review). Mathematics-for-teachers online: Facilitating conceptual shifts in elementary teachers' views of mathematics. *Bolema.*

Gadanidis, G., & Rich, S. (2003). From large lectures to online modules and discussion: Issues in the development of online teacher education. *The Technology Source.* Retrieved October 15, 2007, http://technologysource.org/article/from_large_lectures_to_online_modules_and_discussion/

Gracias, T. A. S. (2003). *A reorganização do pensamento em um curso a distância sobre tendências em educação matemática* [The reorganization of thinking in a distance course on trends in mathematics education]. Doctoral Thesis in Mathematics Education. Instituto de Geociências e Ciências Exatas, Universidade Estadual Paulista, Rio Claro, Sao Paulo, Brazil.

Groth, R. E. (2007). Case studies of mathematics teachers' learning in an online study group. *Contemporary Issues in Technology and Teacher Education, 7*(1), 490–520.

Hargreaves, A. (1998). *Os professores em tempos de mudança. O trabalho e a cultura dos professores na Idade Pós-Moderna* [Changing teachers, changing times: Teachers work and culture in the postmodern age]. Lisboa, Portugal: McGraw-Hill.

Hargreaves, A. (2001). Emotional geographies of teaching. *Teachers College Record, 103*(6), 1056–1080.

Hoines, M. J., & Fuglestad, A. B. (Eds.). (2004). *Proceedings of the 28th Conference of the International Group for the Psychology of Mathematics Education.* Bergen, Norway: Bergen University College.

Kazemi, E., & Franke, M. L. (2004). Teacher learning in mathematics. Using student work to promote collective inquiry. *Journal of Mathematics Teacher Education, 7,* 203–235.

Kress, G. (2003). *Literacy in the new media age.* London: Routledge.

Kress, G., & Van Leeuwen, T. (1996). *Reading images: The grammar of visual design.* London: Routledge.

Krainer, K. (2001). Teachers' growth is more than the growth of individual teachers: The case of Gisela. In F.-L. Lin & T. J. Cooney (Eds.), *Making sense of mathematics teacher education* (pp. 271–294). Dordrecht, the Netherlands: Kluwer Academic Publishers.

Krainer, K. (2003). Teams, communities & networks. *Journal of Mathematics Teacher Education, 6*, 93–105.

Laborde, C. (1998). Relationships between the spatial and theoretical in geometry: The role of computer dynamic representations in problem solving. In D. Insley & D. C. Johnson (Eds.), *Information and communications technologies in school mathematics* (pp. 183–195). Grenoble, France: Chapman and Hall.

Lachance, A., & Confrey, J. (2003). Interconnecting content and community: A qualitative study of secondary mathematics teachers. *Journal of Mathematics Teacher Education, 6*, 107–137.

Larraín, V., & Hernández, F. (2003). O desafio do trabalho multidiciplinar na construção de significados compartilhados [The challenge of multi-disciplinary projects in the construction of shared meanings]. *Pátio, 7*(26), 45–47.

Lave, J., & Wenger, E. (1991). *Situated learning: Legitimate peripheral participation.* New York: Cambridge University Press.

Lévy, P. (1993). *As tecnologias da inteligência: o futuro do pensamento na era da informática* [Technologies of intelligence. The future of thought in the computer age]. Rio de Janeiro: Editora 34.

Lévy, P. (1997). *Collective intelligence: Mankind's emerging world in cyberspace.* New York: Plenum Press.

Lincoln, Y. S., & Guba, E. G. (1985). *Naturalistic inquiry.* Beverly Hills, CA: Sage Publication, Inc.

Llinares, S., & Krainer, K. (2006). Mathematics (student) teachers and teacher education as learners. In A. Gutiérrez & P. Boero (Eds.), *Handbook of research on the psychology of mathematics education: past, present and future* (pp. 429–460). Rotterdam, the Netherlands: Sense Publishers.

McGraw, R., Lynch, K., Koc, Y, Budak, A., & Brown, K. (2007). The multimedia case as a tool for professional development: an analysis of online and face-to-face interaction among mathematics pre-service teachers, in-service teachers, mathematicians, and mathematics teacher educators. *Journal of Mathematics Teacher Education, 10*, 95–121.

Pateman, N. A., Dougherty, B. J., & Zillox, J. (Eds.). (2003). *Proceedings of the 27th Conference of the International Group for the Psychology of Mathematics Education held jointly with the 25th conference of PME-NA.* College of Education. Honolulu, HI: University of Hawai'i.

Penteado, M. G. (2001). Computer-based learning environments: Risks and uncertainties for teacher. *Ways of Knowing Journal, 1*(2), 23–35.

Peter-Koop, A., Santos-Wagner, V., Breen, C., & Begg, A. (Eds.). (2003). *Collaboration in teacher education. Examples from the context of mathematics education.* Dordrecht, the Netherlands: Kluwer Academic Publishers.

Ponte, J. P., Oliveira, P., Varandas, J. M., Oliveira, H., & Fonseca, H. (2007). Using ICT to support reflection in pre-service mathematics teacher education. *Interactive Educational Multimedia, 10* (14), 79–89.

Ponte, J. P., & Santos, L. (2005). A distance in-service teacher education setting focused on mathematics investigations: The role of reflection and collaboration. *Interactive Educational Multimedia, 11*, 104–126.

Reimann, P. (2005). Co-constructing artefacts and knowledge in net-based teams: Implications for the design of collaborative learning environments. *Proceedings of the 29th Conference of the International Group for the Psychology of Mathematics Education* (Vol. 1, pp. 53–68). University of Melbourne, Australia.

Rey, C., Penalva, C., & Llinares, S. (2007). *Aprendizaje colaborativo y formación de asesores em matemáticas: Análisis de un caso* [Collaborative learning and training consultant in mathematics: Analysis of a case]. Manuscript Universidad de Alicante, Spain.

Sadolin, V. (2000). *Geometricks: Software de geometria dinâmica com fractais* [Geometricks: Dynamic geometry software with fractals]. Translation into Portuguese: M. G. Penteado, M. C. Borba, & R. Amaral. Sao Paulo, Brazil: UNESP.

Santos, S. C. (2006). *A produção matemática em um ambiente virtual de aprendizagem: O caso da geometria euclidiana especial* [The mathematical production in a virtual environment for learning:

The case of spatial Euclidian geometry space]. Master Thesis in Mathematics Education. Instituto de Geociências e Ciências Exatas, Universidade Estadual Paulista, Rio Claro, Sao Paulo, Brazil.

Santos-Wagner, V. (2003). The role of collaboration for developing teacher-researchers. In A. Peter-Koop, V. Santos-Wagner, C. Breen, & A. Begg (Eds.), *Collaboration in teacher education. Examples from the context of mathematics education* (pp. 99–112). Dordrecht, the Netherlands: Kluwer Academic Publishers.

Schoenfeld, A. (2005). *Curriculum development, teaching, and assessment*. International meeting in honour of Paulo Abrantes. Lisboa, Portugal: Lisbon University.

Sprague, D., Maddux, C., Ferdig, R., & Albion, P. (2007). Online education: Issues and research questions. *Journal of Technology and Teacher Education 15*(2), 157–166.

Sterret, A. (Ed.). (1990). Using writing to teach mathematics. *Mathematical Association of America (MAA) Notes, 16*.

Stigler, J. W., Gonzales, P., Kawanaka, T., Knoll, S., & Serrano, A. (1999). *The TIMSS 1995 Videotape Classroom Study: Methods and findings from an exploratory research project on eighth-grade mathematics instruction in Germany, Japan, and the United States. NCES (1999-074)*. US Department of Education. Washington, DC: National Center for Education Statistics.

Marcelo C. Borba
Department of Mathematics
Graduate Program in Mathematics Education
Sao Paulo State University
Brazil

George Gadanidis
Faculty of Education
University of Western Ontario
Canada

SECTION 4

SCHOOLS, REGIONS AND NATIONS AS MATHEMATICS LEARNERS

ELHAM KAZEMI

9. SCHOOL DEVELOPMENT AS A MEANS OF IMPROVING MATHEMATICS TEACHING AND LEARNING

Towards Multidirectional Analyses of Learning across Contexts

This chapter focuses on supporting the teaching and learning of mathematics through school development. School development entails organizational learning and the use of social, structural and material resources to support teaching and learning: how are schools or mathematics departments organized to support the teaching and learning of mathematics? I begin by reviewing why and how researchers have conceptualized the school as a productive setting for supporting and improving the teaching and learning of mathematics. I draw on literature from organizational learning and professional communities to show how recent studies theorize improving instruction and student learning. Much of the literature emphasizes mechanisms for such improvement to be highly dependent on how schools employ resources and how they are organized to support teachers' collective learning together outside of the classroom. The chapter ends by proposing new directions for research on professional inquiry and its relation to the improvement of teaching and learning mathematics and school development.

INTRODUCTION

In this chapter, I take up the issue of how schools cultivate organizational supports for teaching that aims to successfully engage all kinds of learners in complex mathematical learning. In particular, I hold a view of mathematical learning that respects students' intellectual integrity and considers schools to be places for vibrant intellectual engagement in which students and teachers develop sophisticated understanding of mathematics, identities as mathematical thinkers, and are engaged in ongoing inquiry. My interest in school development is to understand what allows the school community to continually strive to improve mathematics instruction in order to strengthen student learning. Much of the literature on school development naturally focuses on supporting teacher learning and building teacher capacity (see e.g., Borko, Wolf, Simone, & Uchiyama, 2003; Lerman & Zehetmeier, this volume; Nickerson, this volume). Thus, a large portion of this chapter is devoted to research focused on cultivating professional communities where teachers are the major players. In considering school development, I view membership in a school's professional community to include teachers, instructional leaders (e.g., coaches), and administrative leaders. A school

K. Krainer and T. Wood (eds.), Participants in Mathematics Teacher Education, 209–230.

development perspective emphasizes the interdependence of professionals in the school community – how schools carve out time and space and employ social, intellectual, and material resources to support joint inquiry among teachers, instructional leaders and administrators (Collinson, in press; Lampert, Boerst, & Graziani, under review). I review how researchers have conceptualized and described this joint inquiry and propose directions for future research.

DEVELOPING A SCHOOL'S ABILITY TO SUPPORT MATHEMATICAL LEARNING

What Is Organizational Learning?

One of the strengths of the mathematics education literature has been our careful attention to supporting teachers to improve their instruction. My goal in this chapter is to harness our understandings of supporting individual teachers to think about school-wide professional learning (see also Knapp, 1997; Krainer, 2006; Oliveira & Hannula, this volume; Perrin-Glorian, DeBlois, & Robert, this volume). One clear area of growth for mathematics education research on school development is to develop a framework for explaining how activities engaged by teachers and other professionals at the school level achieve organizational purposes and affect student learning outcomes (Boreham & Morgan, 2004). Collinson and Cook (2007) define *organizational learning* as "the deliberate use of individual, group, and system learning to embed new thinking and practices that continuously renew and transform the organization in ways that support shared aims" (p. 8). According to Boreham and Morgan (2004), when organizations learn, "co-workers transcend the boundaries which separate them from colleagues, establish a common (and expanded) understanding of the object of their joint activity and make a collective decision on how to achieve it" (p. 313). In recent work, Lampert et al. (under review, p. 35) have been examining how organizational assets – material, intellectual, and social – become resources to support successful teaching of complex learning; they explain this view in the following way:

> Assets are effective in supporting the common practice of ambitious instruction when they are widely used as tools for solving common instructional problems. When common use is enabled by the organization of practice, assets can shape the culture of teaching and learning. For this reason, our analysis has focused not only on the nature of material, social, and intellectual assets, but also on how instruction at the school is organized so that assets can become resources that are routinely drawn upon to support a challenging approach to teaching and learning across the school.

Lampert et al.'s views echo other researchers who suggest that we need to move beyond making direct causal links between resources available at a school level (such as adequate funding, leadership, highly qualified teachers, curricular materials, release time for teachers) to student achievement. Instead, the argument is to examine how such resources are used to support instruction, which mediates student achievement (see also Cohen, Raudenbush, & Ball, 2003).

Professional Inquiry as a Key Resource in Supporting School Development

The existence of robust professional inquiry at the school level has received a considerable amount of attention as one of the key resources in supporting school development. Promoting collective professional inquiry within a school emerged in part as a response to a large body of organizational and classroom research that documented the successes and failures of teachers' attempts at implementing reform practices designed to change classroom instruction. Changing daily routines inside classrooms, the goals and purposes of mathematics instruction, and dominant discourse patterns and relationships between teachers and students have proven difficult. Significantly impacting classroom instruction is challenging because of what organizational researchers have labelled the *loose coupling* between traditional school structures, management, and teachers' everyday decision-making. While teachers may enjoy considerable autonomy, this loose coupling in traditional organizational structures creates barriers for instructional reform (Weick, 1976). More recent work on teachers' responses to reform initiatives suggests that the congruence, intensity, pervasiveness and voluntariness of the reforms themselves have an effect on how teachers change their classroom practices (Coburn, 2004). Decoupling may be one of many responses teachers have to reform initiatives. Others include rejecting reform visions, assimilating, accommodating, or developing parallel structures to reform practices.

To counter forces that keep teachers isolated and encourage idiosyncratic responses to instructional initiatives, researchers have attempted to build models that are built into the regular workday, arguing they have more promise of being maintained, sustained and integrated into teachers' practice than an occasional weekend or summer institute (see also Jaworski, this volume; Lerman & Zehetmeier, this volume). A focus on schools as a unit of change means that a collective intellectual culture needs to be cultivated among key professionals (administrators, instructional leaders, and teachers) who work within the organization. Basing professional inquiry within the workplace can allow school professionals to work together to make sense of demanding mathematics teaching and coordinate their efforts across grade levels. Importantly, collective inquiry serves to break down the dominant *"egg crate model"* of schooling – teachers housed together in a school yet working individually in their own classrooms with little coordination and collaboration with colleagues in the same building. The dominant cellular model has promoted isolation and norms of privacy (Lortie, 1975). That said, it is important to note, as many researchers have pointed out, that simply bringing teachers and leaders together in regular meetings does not mean they will be able to critique and learn from their practice. How learning opportunities are structured and enacted make all the difference in teacher learning.

To the extent that we have conducted cross-national comparisons of teaching, we know that variation does exist in what counts as "doing" school mathematics. The case could be made that a view of mathematics as a static body of procedures to memorize and apply with fidelity is a vision that many mathematics educators in the US try to move away from in their professional development work with teachers. Much of the literature about supporting instructional improvement is aimed toward helping teachers learn to treat mathematics as a sense-making enterprise that involves argumentation, reasoning, and justification at its core (see also Seago, this volume). Cross-national comparisons have helped us see that expository teaching approaches are not necessarily universal. In elementary classrooms in Japan, for example, significant time is spent on justifying and connecting mathematical ideas (Hiebert, Stigler, Jacobs, Givvin, & Garnier, 2005). It may be fair to say that a procedural approach to teaching and learning mathematics is nonetheless ubiquitous (Givvin, Hiebert, Jacobs, Hollingsworth, & Gallimore, 2005). Although some variation exists internationally in cultural scripts for teaching (Clarke, Emanuelsson, Jablonka, & Mok, 2006; Clarke, Keitel, & Shimizu, 2006), static notions of learners, especially durable notions of ability and competence may be more pervasive across the globe. Schooling institutions are typically organized to classify, sort, and promote students with higher mathematical ability and higher achievement (e.g., Spade, Columba, & Vanfossen, 1997). Schooling practices can embody a view of ability that often takes intelligence as an inherent and stable trait (Boaler, 2002; Horn, 2007). Reforming mathematics instruction at a school level is often coupled with trying to upend static views of students' ability and intelligence in order to subvert tracking, grouping, and classification systems that keep students in ability bins (e.g., Boaler, 2002; Horn, 2007; Oakes, 1985; Rousseau, 2004; Sfard & Prusak, 2005). This view sees schools and classrooms as "necessarily cultural and social spaces that can perpetuate social inequities by positioning multiple forms of learning and knowing as 'having clout'" (DIME, 2007, p. 407). Promoting school development has the potential to enable school professionals to interrogate how they view students in relation to instruction and how their actions and policies privilege certain students over others.

Visions of Ambitious Teaching, Teacher Learning and the Meaning of Inquiry

Current research on teaching and learning puts forth a vision of teaching mathematics that has been labelled a number of different ways: teaching for understanding, reform-oriented teaching, standards-based instruction, problem-centred instruction, inquiry-oriented teaching. These terms have been used to convey both a level of intellectual rigor, and the nature of the classroom community needed to achieve that rigor. Lampert and colleagues (under review) use the term *ambitious teaching* to mean, "adjusting teaching to what particular students are able to do (or not)" (p. 2) in order to engage all kinds of students in complex problem solving activity, mathematical reasoning, and justification; they identify the challenges of ambitious teaching to include (p. 35):
− Teachers need to move around flexibly in the multiple dimensions of subject matter in relation to student performance, adjusting teaching to learning.
− Teachers need to create an environment where students are willing and motivated to take the risks that intellectual performance entails.

– Teachers need to take what students can do as an integrated indication of what they know and what they need to learn rather than breaking subject matter into meaningless bits of information.

To meet such challenges, it seems reasonable to argue that teachers must have access to substantive learning opportunities for themselves. The literature on teacher learning is replete with uses of the term inquiry. Richardson (1994) distinguishes formal educational research from teachers' own *practical inquiry* by describing how practical inquiry aims to help teachers change their instructional practice or increase understanding by studying their own contexts, practices, or students. When conducted with colleagues, practical inquiry can develop a local sense of shared norms and local standards of practice. Cochran-Smith and Lytle (1999, p. 288) describe inquiry as *stance:*

> Teachers and student teachers who take an inquiry stance work within inquiry communities generate local knowledge, envision and theorize their practice, and interpret and interrogate the theory and research of others. Fundamental to this notion is the idea that the work of inquiry communities is both social and political; that is, it involves making problematic the current arrangements of schooling; the ways knowledge is constructed, evaluated, and used; and teachers' individual and collective roles in bringing about change.

The critical perspective reflective in Cochran-Smith and Lytle's view of inquiry as stance is reflected in other views of professional inquiry designed to help teachers not only develop new knowledge and skills but interrogate their views and question and critique the political nature of schooling as it relates to students learning mathematics (e.g., Gutiérrez, 2007; Horn, 2005; King, 2002). This more critical stance of inquiry is an attempt to support teachers to consider how schools and learning opportunities affect access and equity in students' academic identities and trajectories in successfully learning mathematics and pursuing mathematics as they continue through schools.

Viewing schools as *sites for teacher learning* rather than as places where teachers simply work is well supported by sociocultural theories of learning. Drawing from the notion that knowledge and meaning are constructed through practice, Franke, Carpenter, Fennema, Ansell, and Behrend (1998, p. 68) argue for supporting learning that is self-sustaining and generative; they claim that teachers' supported efforts to engage in classroom practices guided by student learning can serve as a basis for their own continued growth and problem solving of classroom dilemmas:

> It is in developing an understanding of their practices in relation to their students' learning that teachers develop the understanding necessary to generate new ideas. If a teacher struggles to understand why the students are successful, how they are solving problems, how their thinking develops, and how instruction might help students to build on their current conceptions, connections are made, understanding develops, and the potential for more

connections becomes possible. Thus, there exists a basis for the teacher to learn and continue to grow.

Through Franke and colleagues' work, we have learned how teachers can use their own practices to make sense of student learning. However, we need to understand further how teachers' classroom practices and broader school-based professional communities can provide the basis for teachers to continue to develop their practice. In their work, Franke and colleagues argued that teachers who are generative develop detailed understanding of their own students' thinking, organize that knowledge and view it as their own to create, adapt, and change. These teachers learn from interacting with their students; they are focused in the ways they listen to, interpret, and make use of their students' thinking. In this chapter on school development, I consider how teachers' participation in multiple and potentially overlapping communities of practice shapes and re-shapes their identities and constitutive skills and knowledge as teachers of mathematics.

THEORIZING ABOUT PROFESSIONAL COMMUNITY

The main mechanism for supporting teachers' generative learning for ambitious teaching has been through building and sustaining *professional communities* of teachers. Theorizing teacher learning through participation in professional community draws on sociocultural theories of learning which take participation as a key construct (see also Jaworski, this volume). Lave and Wenger (1991) define a *community of practice* as "a set of relations among persons, activity and world, over time and in relation with other tangential and overlapping communities of practice" (p. 98). A community of practice can be defined through *mutual engagement* in a *joint enterprise* which develops *shared repertoire*s of practice (Wenger, 1998). Lave (1996) describes learning as "changing participation in changing 'communities of practice'" (p. 150). Learning is not a process of acquiring or transmitting knowledge. Rather learning is apparent in the way participation transforms within a community of practice (Rogoff, 1997). The shifts in participation do not merely mark a change in a participant's activity or behaviour; a shift in participation also involves a transformation of roles and the crafting of a new *identity*, one that is linked to but not completely determined by new knowledge and skills (Lave, 1996; Lave & Wenger, 1991; Rogoff, 1994, 1997; Wenger, 1998). Lave (1996, p. 157) states, "crafting identities is a social process, and becoming more knowledgeably skilled is an aspect of participation in a social practice. By this reasoning, who you are becoming shapes crucially and fundamentally what you 'know'." Knowledge and the development of skill are clearly important in understanding learning. Developing skill and knowledge is in service of changing participation in a particular community.

Lave and Wenger (1991) describe *transforming participation* in terms of movement from legitimate peripheral to full participation. As a legitimate participant, one is connected and belongs to the community of practice in question, but as a peripheral participant, one engages less fully in the community. The peripheral participant has access and can move towards full participation, thus developing an identity of full participation. Full participation entails "developing an identity as a member of a community and becoming knowledgeably skillful" (Lave, 1991, p. 65). Analysis of learning focuses on the structuring of the community's work practices and learning resources; learning is detectable in members' participation in the work of the community.

What Does Professional Community Mean for Mathematics Teaching and Learning?

As mathematics education researchers have drawn on the community of practice theory, they have identified key features of professional community, the strength of which inspires instructional innovation and commitment to students. Several reviews exist which compare these features and common to all these communities is a shared sense of purpose and collective and coordinated collaborative activity with a commitment to students (e.g., Dean & McClain, 2006; Sowder, 2007). Dean and McClain (2006, pp. 13–14) define these as:

A shared purpose or enterprise such as: ensuring that students come to understand central mathematical ideas while simultaneously performing more than adequately on high stakes assessments of mathematics achievement.

A shared repertoire of ways of reasoning with tools and artefacts that is specific to the community and the shared purpose including normative ways of reasoning with instructional materials and other resources when planning for instruction or using tasks and other resources to make students' mathematical reasoning visible.

Norms of mutual engagement encompassing both general norms of participation as well as norms specific to mathematics teaching such as the standards to which the members of the community hold each other accountable when they justify pedagogical decisions and judgments.

Gutiérrez (1996) calls high school mathematics departments with strong professional communities as "*organized for advancement*" because their collective activity makes a difference in advancing student learning and achievement. In addition, several researchers emphasize teachers' ability to wield influence and control over important decisions that affect a school's activities, policies, and curriculum (Erickson, Brandes, Mitchell, & Mitchell, 2005; King, 2002; Little, 1999; Secada & Adajian, 1997).

Cultivating Professional Inquiry at the School Level

This chapter underscores the idea that school development necessarily involves learning. Boreham and Morgan (2004) argue that organizations learn because members of the community are able to coordinate their perspectives and actions

215

towards achievement of common goals. They found that organizations learn by developing *relational practices,* "the kind of practice[s] by which people connect with other people in their world, and which direct them to interact in particular ways" (p. 315). These relational practices include:
- opening space for creation of shared meaning
- reconstituting power relations
- providing cultural tools to mediate learning.

Those relational practices can be connected to developing social and intellectual resources (opening space for creation of shared meaning and reconstituting power relations) and material resources (providing cultural tools to mediate learning). In what follows, I draw on the professional community and inquiry literature to identify the following dimensions that make possible these relational practices.
- Activating school leaders
- Navigating fault lines, dealing with micropolitical issues among teachers
- Developing and sustaining a focus
- Engaging parents as intellectual and social resources

Activating school leaders. When the school is the centre of change, theories of action for supporting professional learning communities (PLCs) among mathematics teachers necessitate contention with school cultures and institutional realities. Gamoran and colleagues (2003) contend that PLCs need access to resources – material, human, and social – if they are to remain viable. Here the role of school leaders in facilitating the availability and use of such resources can be critical. School leaders refer not only to school principals or heads but also to curriculum leaders, mathematics coaches, teacher mentors, or faculty coordinators. There is variance documented in the literature as to how much direct involvement in a professional community principals have versus other mathematics leaders (Burch & Spillane, 2003; King, 2002; Krainer & Peter-Koop, 2003; Wolf, Borko, Elliott, & McIver, 2000). In some cases, principals participate in teacher meetings in order to learn alongside teachers and spend time in classrooms. In others, the principal is supportive by allocating school level resources in providing space and time and by making goals of teacher interactions congruent with school and district level goals (Coburn & Russell, in press). Whether and how leadership strategies interact with supporting professional development in a PLC at the school level in mathematics, is a burgeoning area of research. Findings underscore the situated way in which leadership strategies interact with local conditions.

Halverson (2007) documented the way school leaders make use of certain structures to enable the building of a professional community. Key to Halverson's (2007) analysis is that a professional community is a "form of organizational trust" (p. 94) resulting from the kinds of interactions teachers have to consider in using alternative instructional strategies to improve student learning. His analysis of the role of school leaders in supporting a professional community focuses in part on *leaders' use of artefacts,* such as role positions, daily schedules, meetings and meeting agendas. Moreover, he found that school leaders sequence the use of these artefacts in different ways to initiate interactions, facilitate development of mutual obligations, and provide feedback about how those obligations are being met at a systemic level. One of the key material resources in supporting teachers' ability to work together is *time and space* and to do so in the rushed pace of the normal work week. Halverson found that leaders strategically made use of local contingencies in order to carve out space and time for teachers to initiate and legitimate time to talk about instruction – in one case through Breakfast Club meetings and in two others through grant-writing projects to respond to a new accountability mandate. Examples abound in the literature of other means that school leaders employ to initiate conversations, including such things as analysis of student work (e.g., Kazemi & Franke, 2004), implementing common units of lessons (e.g., Borasi, Fonzi, Smith, & Rose, 1999), study groups (e.g., Arbaugh, 2003), and regular department meetings (e.g., Horn, 2005). Coburn and Russell's (in press) use of *social network analysis* also supports the importance of school leaders in allocating human resources such as coaching expertise in collective professional interaction. They found that the allocation of coaches affected depth of interactions in PLCs.

Navigating fault lines. Establishing professional communities is not just a matter of decreeing that one exists. There is nothing neither positive nor harmonious inherent in the term community, and if we consider the countless times researchers have characterized the work of teaching and school reform as complex, we should expect that forming inquiry communities within schools should not be a trivial matter. Research on PLC and school-based reform has highlighted how managing tensions and conflicts are critical for the viability of the PLC (Rousseau, 2004). Grossman, Wineburg, and Woolworth (2001) identified the navigation of *fault lines* as one of the central concerns of building a supportive teacher community. These fault lines are not necessarily interpersonal conflicts among teachers but may be tensions regarding disciplinary goals and views of teaching and learning mathematics that exist in the school or department (e.g., Rousseau, 2004). Because participating in a PLC is about *changing school cultures* and *breaking norms of privacy* while at the same time *building norms of critical colleagueship*, researchers have also attended to the ways such participation affects transformations in *teacher identity* (e.g., Drake, 2006; Kelchtermans, 2005; Battey & Franke, in press). Researchers argue that teachers' individual reactions to a PLC's demands are mediated by social and cultural contexts as well as teachers' working dynamic identities. "Teachers' identities carry personal histories, emotion, values, and knowledge and they shape how teachers participate in professional development and their classrooms" (Battey & Franke, in press, p. 27).

Research has discussed the paradoxes and conflicts that are bound up in cultivating PLCs. Many researchers have noted that in order for teacher inquiry to have a school-wide effect, it must move beyond individual teachers. But mandating participation in teacher inquiry at the school-level can also backfire. Here leadership must be strategic in inviting a critical mass of participation that can have a pronounced affect on school culture (Berger, Boles, & Troen, 2005; Krainer,

2001). The role of key school leaders (whether principals, school facilitators, or coaches), again becomes critical in creating a press for teacher inquiry *and* in developing collective ownership (Berger et al., 2005; Nickerson & Moriarty, 2005).

Developing and sustaining a focus. If schools are successful in carving out time and space for teachers to meet together, in managing conflicts and tensions, the next dimension I wish to highlight is how researchers describe the importance of developing and sustaining a focus on students. Because time and space are precious resources in schools, collegial interactions need to be focused in order to be productive. Some studies indicate that material resources such as curriculum units or lessons, student work, videotaped lessons can be leveraged successfully in order to achieve this focus (e.g., Borasi et al., 1999; Kazemi & Franke, 2004; Seago, this volume; Sherin, 2004). Lin's (2002) study is illustrative. The school-based professional inquiry she described focused on grade-level collaborations. First-grade teachers met to develop, observe, and reflect on lessons from the Taiwanese mandated learner-oriented reform curriculum. To provide sufficient focus for their collective inquiry, the first-grade teachers selected a common lesson to plan and observe in each other's classrooms. They used these common lessons and observations to write classroom cases that in effect focused and deepened their conversations, beyond what observation alone would have accomplished. Three types of cases emerged from this collaborative inquiry: (1) analysis of students' varied solutions and strategies; (2) students' interpretations of other students' thinking; and (3) comparisons of two different instructional approaches to teaching the same topic. Cases were developed in several phases; each successive phase refined and elaborated the teaching context and the questions for discussions. The creation of teaching cases situated in teachers' own classrooms when all teachers were able to teach the same lesson enabled the teachers to very carefully analyse the effect of task design and sequencing on students' mathematical thinking; students' ability to use symbolic and pictorial representations to solve problems; and for teachers to compare and think deeply about how their instructional choices (e.g., "Is binding straws important for students' ability to count by tens?") impacted student performance. This was dependent, of course, on teachers' willingness to examine their own practice and to raise questions for one another. This kind of inquiry is dependent on cultivating norms of inquiry, navigating fault lines, and developing resources for time to meet.

Engaging parents as intellectual and social resources. The *role of parents* in school development has received much less attention than the work of teachers, administrators, and leaders. This makes sense given the amount of attention of coordinating professionals who work at the school itself. Nonetheless, recent work on parents has illuminated a number of issues related to parents' engagement, raising possible considerations for parents' role in supporting school development.

Improving mathematics instruction involves a dramatic transformation from viewing mathematics as a fixed body of procedures to memorize and apply with fidelity to a discipline that is fundamentally about complex problem solving, justification, and argumentation. Studies investigating parents' views have revealed that parents can feel disempowered in relation to reform-oriented mathematics (Martin, 2006; Remillard & Jackson, 2006). At the same time, interventions that have aimed to work with families around mathematics as a complex problem solving discipline have reported significant increases in families' feelings of empowerment (Civil & Bernier, 2006). Reports of building school capacity may include events such as *parent nights* designed to mitigate these anxieties by beginning dialogue with families about goals of ambitious mathematics teaching and learning (e.g., Kramer & Keller, 2008). We have much more to learn about how engagement with families can support school development efforts, in what kinds of social and political contexts, and to what ends. Might leadership, for example, leverage family views, practices and questions to catapult teacher inquiry (e.g., Anderson, 2006) or could family practices undercut professional community?

Studying the Practices of School-Based Professional Communities

Cultivating a viable professional community naturally begs questions about how members of the school community actually interact with one another as they discuss teaching practice. What might it look like for teachers and leaders to engage in *critical colleagueship* (Lord, 1994) oriented to improving mathematics teaching and learning? I find the work of Little and Horn (2007) to be particularly instructive in thinking about the practices of a professional community. They are developing a conceptual scheme to examine what actually happens in collective professional learning communities. How do participants actually work together? What do they say and do? How do they interact with one another around artefacts of practice and how do they talk about classroom instruction? Little (2002) offers two central questions for examining interactions within teacher communities:

1. What faces of practice are made visible through talk and with what degree of transparency?
2. How does interaction open up or close down opportunities to learn?

The *face* of practice refers to "those parts of practice that come to be described, demonstrated, or otherwise rendered in public exchanges among teachers" (Little, 2002, p. 934), which may include artefacts such as student work. *Transparency* of practice conveys "how fully, completely, and specifically various parts of practice are made visible or transparent in the interaction" (Little, 2002, p. 934). These two questions seem central to us in order to understand what views of practice are made available to teachers through their collective inquiry. As I describe below, I contend that the understanding of the inner workings of school-based professional development communities should be then related to teachers' participation in and out of the group setting. This relational view can help us understand who teachers are becoming through this process (Battey & Franke, in press; Enyedy, Goldberg,

& Welsh, 2006), and how they are enacting their developing identities, skills, and knowledge with their students in the classroom.

Little and Horn (2007; see also Horn, 2005) have documented in detail how the rendering of classroom interactions in professional conversations shape opportunities for teacher learning. By contrasting informal conversations in mathematics department meetings in two different high schools, they compare how teachers use *replays* and *rehearsals* to reason publicly about their instructional practice and to consider alternative interpretations and re-formulations of pedagogical dilemmas and problems in ways that propel their teaching forward. During replays, teachers recount "blow-by-blow accounts of classroom events, often acting out both the teacher and students' roles" (Horn, 2005, p. 225). Through rehearsals, teachers act out classroom interactions that might occur in the future, anticipating what they might say and how students might respond. In careful analysis of teacher-to-teacher talk, Horn documents how teachers move in and out of these modes as they reconsider their pedagogical choices and ready themselves for continued experimentation. However, the presence of replays and rehearsals during collegial interactions is not sufficient for such experimentation. How such replays and rehearsals function in framing pedagogical issues, questions, dilemmas and frustrations is what matters.

Prior work by Kazemi and Franke (2004; see also Franke & Kazemi, 2001; Franke, Kazemi, Shih, Biagetti, & Battey, 2005) documented detailed images of the evolution of collective inquiry among elementary teachers analysing their students' mathematical work in monthly school-based meetings in which each teacher had posed a similar mathematical problem (focused on number and operations) to his or her class. The analysis of the teacher talk revealed that the workgroup conversations evolved as teachers learned to talk about their work. Salient developments included the following:

- Teachers first had to learn to *attend to the details of their students' thinking.* Even though meetings were structured from the very beginning to detail students' strategies, teachers did not come to the first meeting prepared to do so. Instead, many teachers assumed that the pieces of paper themselves would tell the story. It was further evident in the way they posed the problems that many assumed that conversations with students about their solutions were not necessary. Maintaining the structure of the workgroup promoted an emphasis on documenting the details of student thinking. Kazemi and Franke (2004) intentionally facilitated the discussions so that teachers would return to the idea of noticing how students were learning to break apart and put together numbers using their knowledge of the base ten structure of the number system. In order for teachers to interpret their students' reasoning, they began to use the student work as a trace rather than a complete record of their students' reasoning. Without such a mathematical focus, meetings may not encourage teachers to follow a particular course of experimentation in their classrooms.
- Teachers' close consideration of student reasoning opened up *opportunities to deliberate mathematical and pedagogical questions.* Examining student work, as structured in this professional development, allowed teachers to surface their

confusions and uncertainties, not just about student reasoning but also about mathematics and classroom practice. The discussions opened up opportunities for teachers to notice the mathematical ideas students were using. This led to the group's engagement with sophisticated computational strategies they were noticing in their classrooms. The use of student work provided an entry point for teachers to explore mathematical ideas and have opportunities to make sense of efficient student-generated algorithms. Pedagogical issues related to helping children develop more sophisticated strategies also surfaced once the group saw students in teachers' own classrooms using such strategies.

– *Diversity in teachers' experimentation served as a resource for learning.* Teachers differed in how they reported on their engagement with students in their classrooms. Not all the teachers experimented with these ideas in the same way. Because the group had multiple ways of relating the professional development discussions to their classroom practices, the experiences of some teachers generated new conjectures about what to try in the classroom. The frustrations teachers shared in the group also underscored the challenges they faced in helping children articulate and build their ideas. This diversity became a resource for teachers to compare and question each other's practices.

Understanding how teachers' interact with one another in PLCs and how those interactions evolve and develop learning opportunities for teachers is vital for research and development work in fostering collective inquiry at the school level. In the next subchapter, I argue for relating this evolving research base to the well-known research on teachers' classroom instruction.

CONNECTING PROFESSIONAL LEARNING COMMUNITIES WITH CLASSROOM TEACHING AND LEARNING

Earlier in this chapter, I proposed the view that school development deals with the development of organizational supports for ambitious mathematics teaching and learning. Much of the literature emphasizes mechanisms for such improvement to be highly dependent on how schools employ resources and how they are organized to support teachers' collective learning together outside of the classroom. What I would like to offer in the remainder of this chapter is a proposal for attending to one aspect of the relationship between *joint inquiry* at the school level and classroom instruction. My discussion is not meant to be comprehensive; it identifies one shortcoming of how we have typically thought about the impact of teachers' and leaders' joint inquiry on mathematics instruction and student learning. Some of our current research base is limited in scope to a unidirectional view of the impact of cultivating professional inquiry at the school level to teachers' classroom practice. I propose that what needs to be addressed and developed are ways to characterize and document the *multi-directional influence between participation in joint inquiry and the individuality of classroom practice.* In this last subchapter, I outline the rationale for this approach and describe some of the necessary theoretical and empirical work that lies ahead.

Teachers are simultaneously involved in multiple activity settings, including their own classroom, school, and district. When they are involved in sustained inquiry with colleagues and leaders at the school, this constitutes another important mediating context. I use the construct of *activity settings* to focus on the boundaries and relationships between the classroom, school and district (see also Cobb & Smith, this volume). Activity settings overlap; that is, they do not exist as insular social contexts but rather as sets of relationships that coexist with others (Engeström, 2001). Activity settings can have temporal, conceptual, and physical boundaries (Grossman, Smagorinsky, & Valencia, 1999). It is this *dynamism across activity settings* and how that shapes teacher learning that I am concerned with in this chapter. To develop these ideas further and specify a way of talking about learning, I draw on Cook and Brown's (1999) distinction between *knowledge* and *knowing*. Knowledge, in their view, is something that we "possess". We "deploy" this knowledge in our actions. In their words, "Knowing refers to the epistemic work that is done as part of action or practice, like that done in actual riding of a bicycle or the actual making of a medical diagnosis" (p. 387). Knowledge, then, can be seen a tool of action because individuals or groups can use knowledge (whether tacit or explicit) to discipline their interactions with the world. This distinction seems both relevant and important in thinking about teacher learning. Much has been written about the kinds of specialized knowledge that teachers need, among them, knowledge of the discipline, their students, and instructional strategies (Ball & Bass, 2000; Shulman, 1986). Professional inquiry clearly needs to develop teachers' knowledge, and we have been rightfully concerned with figuring out what kinds of knowledge teachers gain through inquiry.

Cook and Brown (1999) would agree that knowledge is essential for practice but it is not sufficient for explaining what it takes to be good at what you do: "An accomplished engineer may possess a great deal of sophisticated knowledge; but there are plenty of people who possess such knowledge yet do not excel as engineers" (p. 387). In addition to all the kinds of knowledge that teachers need, they also have *to be able to teach*. For me, this means that we have to attend to the *interplay between knowledge and knowing* in the professional community and in teachers' classroom context. In addition, we need to attend to the interplay between teachers' development of knowledge and ways of knowing in the professional development and classroom contexts over time. We need to link the knowledge and ways of knowing that teachers develop together with what happens as teachers try to use the knowledge and ways of knowing they gain in joint inquiry in the context of their classroom teaching. Teachers may develop similar ways of examining and talking about students' mathematical thinking through inquiry with colleagues in their school but we clearly need to concern ourselves with how they are drawing on that knowledge when they interact with students, or in Cook and Brown's terms, how knowledge is deployed in the service of disciplining action (knowing). Moreover, I argue that researchers should examine what teachers are learning during and after conversations with colleagues, looking at the *coevolution* of participation between classroom practice and professional inquiry. I claim that this coevolution between the contexts of professional collaboration and classrooms should itself be a key unit of analysis as we try to explicate the mechanisms by which teachers learn in and through professional inquiry. By seeing how teachers' participation across these contexts co-evolves, we will have better views of the relationship between joint professional inquiry, learning and instruction, and school development.

The Implications of a Multidirectional Analysis for Studying and Designing Collective Inquiry

A multidirectional analysis of professional learning across contexts where teachers and leaders work together and the classroom leads us to the following implications for the study and design of these efforts. We should: (1) understand and elicit the diversity of teachers' experimentation and the effect of depictions of that work in joint inquiry and (2) examine the situated nature of primary artefacts.

Understanding the diversity of teachers' experimentation. In order to understand the relationship between the contexts of joint inquiry and the classroom, and how teachers' and leaders' participation across these settings co-evolves, we must understand individual teachers' classroom experimentation, and how this influences their collaboration with colleagues. How do teachers deploy their knowledge in the classroom? What ways of knowing do they demonstrate in their instructional practice? What do teachers bring to the collective as a result of their experimentation? In addition to documenting the diversity of individual teachers' classroom experimentation, we also need to document and study what actually happens when teachers and leaders come together and their collective learning trajectories as they participate in this context. It is essential that we document the diversity of teachers' classroom experimentation and study the nature of how this experimentation relates to their experiences over time with their colleagues and to their developing identities – what kinds of teachers do they want to become? What ways of knowing are developed over time? How and what knowledge do teachers develop of subject matter, students' thinking, and practice as they engage in collective analysis around common objects of inquiry?

While the argument here is about research on teachers' joint learning, there are also implications for the design of *collective inquiry* (see also Jaworski, this volume; Seago, this volume). I argue not only that teachers' experimentation should be studied but that leaders of teachers' joint inquiry should incorporate *depictions* of teachers' classroom experimentation in collaborative engagement. Depictions of practice are images or stories that seek to capture the events in the classroom as they played out, earlier referenced as replays and rehearsals. They are created intentionally to support the analysis of teaching. Written cases and video-cases are perhaps the most visible example of depictions available in the literature. But there are other examples: replays and rehearsals (Horn, 2005) are depictions that are created through teachers' talk; teachers' journals can also serve as a depiction.

If professional educators sought openings to elicit teachers' experimentation in a principled way, collective inquiry could serve as a place to pursue questions and dilemmas teachers encounter as they engage in transforming their practice. While it is easy to advocate that we incorporate depictions of practice and discuss teachers' classroom experimentation in the context of collective inquiry more extensively, I recognize that sharing episodes from the classroom can easily and unproductively spiral into a show-and-tell. Leaders of collective inquiry will need to become more knowledgeable and skilled about how to use teachers' classroom experiences. For example, how can the dilemmas teachers face about modifying tasks, managing pacing, and orchestrating classroom discourse be usefully depicted and used as a springboard for discussion? How can leaders utilize one teacher's experiences to support another to develop more focused and reflective attempts to experiment in the classroom? Many researchers have written extensively about the intentional use of records of practice (e.g., Sherin, 2004; Lampert & Ball, 1998; Little, 2004), arguing that we must attend not only to the careful selection of representations but also how they are negotiated in practice.

Examining the situated nature of primary artefacts. *Primary artefacts* are objects that originate (or are produced for use) in instructional practice. In the case of teaching, primary artefacts include copies of student work, lesson plans, mathematical tasks, and curriculum materials. They can travel across boundaries, into contexts where teachers and leaders collaborate, but they are not created solely for the purpose of collectively analysing teaching. Primary artefacts allow particular components of teaching to be extracted from the context of instructional practice, lessening the complexity by narrowing teachers' focus.

Primary artefacts are produced and used in practice, and so ways of knowing include the use and production of primary artefacts. If we are concerned with teachers developing new ways of knowing in their classroom practice, then we should attend to the relationship between ways of knowing in professional development and in the classroom. And if we are going to use primary artefacts as a tool in professional development, we must attend to how they are situated in particular activities, and how this affects their meaning. For example, student work is a primary artefact commonly used in collective work of teachers. The way student work is situated in collective inquiry may look very different from its use in the classroom. Teachers and leaders may sit together to analyse a collection of pre-selected student work to illustrate the range of solution strategies students used in their classroom. They may spend extended time debating what students understand, generating questions they might ask to better understand the students' thinking, or considering which strategies they would choose to highlight in a whole class discussion. In contrast, in their classrooms, teachers may only have a few minutes to survey students' written work in order to make assessments and instructional decisions. The teacher typically engages in this work alone, in the midst of a lesson, while students are working on the task. While collective inquiry may certainly help teachers gain knowledge they can deploy in this classroom situation, it may not help them develop the ways of knowing they need to monitor students in the moment and to interact with them in ways that assess and advance students' mathematical thinking. Researchers and leaders must attend to the meaning teacher's make of primary artefacts across contexts as these artefacts are situated in different activities. We need to better understand how the ways of knowing involved in these activities differ, and how they influence one another.

CONCLUSION

Writing about school development is necessarily a synthetic enterprise. In this chapter, I conceptualized school development as a school's efforts to support ambitious teaching and learning. Specifically, I took a learning perspective on school development. This perspective highlights how schools support professional learning. Collinson (in press, p. 7) states:

Vibrant, innovative organizations work at developing their organizational capacity by establishing an environment in which members, and thereby the organization, can continuously learn and improve. Developing members, along with careful recruiting and hiring of fresh talent, ensures innovation and renewal.

The way we understand and study professional learning in schools has significant implications for the way we structure and support teachers' collective learning opportunities, the goals we create for inquiry, and as researchers and educators, the ways we collaborate with schools to improve mathematics teaching and learning. To understand teacher collective learning within the context of school-based professional development, I have argued that we need to develop conceptual frameworks to take into account both the dynamics of individual teacher learning and vulnerabilities to developing their instructional practices as well as the resources and settings that support learning.

One noteworthy aspect of writing this chapter on school development was the opportunity to review research that draws on both classroom level research and organizational and policy implementation research. New collaborations forged between classroom researchers and policy or organizational researchers (e.g., Cobb & Smith, 2007; Cobb & Smith, this volume; Gamoran et al., 2003; Little & Horn, 2007) can enrich our view of designing for a tighter coupling between teacher learning and whole school development that would ultimately benefit professional culture within the school and students' mathematical learning. That said – here are a number of issues that remain to be incorporated into our studies of and designs for school development.

- We need to explicate significant differences between working with schools at the primary and secondary level and how those impact the ways schools support ambitious teaching and learning. There seem to be different challenges with respect to teachers' skills and identities as mathematics teachers, tracking or grouping practices, testing practices and their consequences, curriculum

organization, and relationships among teachers, school leaders, and parents (e.g., Lee, Smith, & Croninger, 1997; Spade, Columba, & Vanfossen, 1997).
– As was evident in this chapter, the research literature on school development attends predominantly to the role of teachers and school leaders. How parents and families figure into school development and supporting ambitious teaching remains underdeveloped and undertheorized.
– Our understanding of school development can be strengthened through further study of how prospective and novice teachers are involved in collective inquiry as a way to recruit and continue to develop practices of the school community (see Leikin, this volume).

Our field's ability to address these issues and others over the next decade will advance our understanding of school development and inform the next generation of interventions aimed at supporting ambitious teaching.

ACKNOWLEDGMENTS

I would like to thank Allison Hintz for her invaluable assistance identifying research used in the literature review. Work with Megan Franke, Amanda Hubbard, and Magdalene Lampert has been instrumental in developing some of the theoretical ideas. I am grateful for the helpful comments of Paul Cobb, Gilah Leder, Heinz Steinbring, and Terry Wood on previous versions of this chapter. I am especially indebted to Konrad Krainer for his help in formulating the focus of this chapter.

REFERENCES

Anderson, D. D. (2006). Home to school: Numeracy practices and mathematical identities. *Mathematical Thinking and Learning, 8,* 261–286.
Arbaugh, F. (2003). Study groups as a form of professional development for secondary mathematics teachers. *Journal of Mathematics Teacher Education, 6,* 139–163.
Ball, D. L., & Bass, H. (2000). Interweaving content and pedagogy in teaching and learning to teach: Knowing and using mathematics. In J. Boaler (Ed.), *Multiple perspectives on mathematics teaching and learning* (pp. 83–104). Westport, CT: Ablex.
Battey, D., & Franke, M. L. (in press). Transforming identities: Understanding teachers across professional development and classroom practice. *Teacher Education Quarterly.*
Berger, J. G., Boles, K. C., & Troen, V. (2005). Teacher research and school change: Paradoxes, problems, and possibilities. *Teaching and Teacher Education, 21,* 93–105.
Boaler, J. (2002). *Experiencing school mathematics: Traditional and reform approaches to teaching and their impact on student learning.* Mahwah, NJ: Lawrence Erlbaum Associates.
Borasi, R., Fonzi, J., Smith, C. F., & Rose, B. J. (1999). Beginning the process of rethinking mathematics instruction: A professional development program. *Journal of Mathematics Teacher Education, 2,* 49–78.
Boreham, N., & Morgan, C. (2004). A sociocultural analysis of organisational learning. *Oxford Review of Education, 30,* 307–325.
Borko, H., Wolf, S. A., Simone, G., & Uchiyama, K. P. (2003). Schools in transition: Reform efforts and school capacity in Washington State. *Educational Evaluation and Policy Analysis, 25,* 171–202.
Burch, P., & Spillane, J. P. (2003). Elementary school leadership strategies and subject matter: Reforming mathematics and literacy instruction. *Elementary School Journal, 103,* 519–535.

Civil, M., & Bernier, E. (2006). Exploring images of parental participation in mathematics education: Challenges and possibilities. *Mathematical Thinking and Learning, 8,* 309–330.

Clarke, D. J., Emanuelsson, J., Jablonka, E., & Mok, I. A. C. (Eds.). (2006). *Making connections: Comparing mathematics classrooms around the world.* Rotterdam, the Netherlands: Sense.

Clarke, D. J., Keitel, C., & Shimizu, Y. (Eds.). (2006). *Mathematics classrooms in twelve countries: The insider's perspective.* Rotterdam, the Netherlands: Sense.

Cobb, P., & Smith, T. (2007, October). *The challenge of scale: Designing schools and districts as learning organizations for instructional improvement in mathematics.* Invited plenary at the North American Chapter of the International Group for the Psychology of Mathematics Education, Lake Tahoe, NV.

Coburn, C. E. (2004). Beyond decoupling: Rethinking the relationship between institutional environment and the classroom. *Sociology of Education, 77,* 211–244.

Coburn, C. E., & Russell, J. L. (in press). District policy and teachers' social networks. *Educational Evaluation and Policy Analysis.*

Cochran-Smith, M., & Lytle, S. L. (1999). Relationships of knowledge and practice: Teacher learning in communities. In A. Iran-Nejad & C. D. Pearson (Eds.), *Review of research in education* (Vol. 24, pp. 249–305). Washington, DC: American Educational Research Association.

Cohen, D. K., Raudenbush, S. W., & Ball, D. L. (2003). Resources, instruction, and research. *Educational Evaluation and Policy Analysis, 25,* 119–142.

Collinson, V. (in press). Leading by learning: New directions in the 21st century. *Journal of Educational Administration.*

Collinson, V., & Cook, T. F. (2007). *Organizational learning: Improving learning, teaching, and leading in school systems.* Thousand Oaks, CA: Sage.

Cook, S., & Brown, J. S. (1999). Bridging epistemologies: The generative dance between organizational knowledge and organizational knowing. *Organization Science, 10,* 381–400.

Dean, C., & McClain, K. (2006, April). *Situating the emergence of a professional teaching community within the institutional context.* Paper presented at the annual meeting of the American Educational Research Association, Chicago.

Diversity in Mathematics Education Center for Learning and Teaching (DIME). (2007). Culture, race, power, and mathematics education. In F. K. Lester (Ed.), *Second handbook of research in mathematics teaching and learning* (pp. 405–433). Greenwich, CT: Information Age Publishers.

Drake, C. (2006). Turning points: Using teachers' mathematics life stories to understand the implementation of mathematics education reform. *Journal of Mathematics Teacher Education, 9,* 579–608.

Engeström, Y. (2001). Expansive learning at work. *Journal of Education and Work, 14,* 133–156.

Enyedy, N., Goldberg, J., & Welsh, K. M. (2006). Complex dilemmas of identity and practice. *Science Education, 90,* 68–93.

Erickson, G., Brandes, G. M., Mitchell, I., & Mitchell, J. (2005). Collaborative teacher learning: Findings from two professional development projects. *Teaching and Teacher Education, 21,* 787–798.

Franke, M. L., Carpenter, T., Fennema, E., Ansell, E., & Behrend, J. (1998). Understanding teachers' self-sustaining, generative change in the context of professional development. *Teaching and Teacher Education, 14,* 67–80.

Franke, M. L., & Kazemi, E. (2001). Learning to teach mathematics: Developing a focus on students' mathematical thinking. *Theory into Practice, 40,* 102–109.

Franke, M. L., Kazemi, E., Shih, J., Biagetti, S., & Battey, D. (2005). Changing teachers' professional work in mathematics: One school's journey. In T. A. Romberg, T. P. Carpenter, & F. Dremock (Eds.), *Understanding mathematics and science matters* (pp. 209–230). Mahwah, NJ: Lawrence Erlbaum Associates.

Gamoran, A., Anderson, C. W., Quiroz, P. A., Secada, W. G., Williams, T., & Ashmann, S. (2003). *Transforming teaching in math and science: How schools and districts can support change.* New York: Teachers College Press.

Givvin, K. B., Hiebert, J., Jacobs, J. K., Hollingsworth, H., & Gallimore, R. (2005). Are there national patterns of teaching? Evidence from the TIMSS 1999 video study. *Comparative Education Review, 49*, 311–343.

Grossman, P. L., Smagorinsky, P., & Valencia, S. (1999). Appropriating tools for teaching English: A theoretical framework for research on learning to teach. *American Journal of Education, 108*, 1–29.

Grossman, P., Wineburg, S., & Woolworth, S. (2001). Toward a theory of community. *Teachers College Record, 103*, 942–1012.

Gutiérrez, R. (1996). Practices, beliefs, and cultures of high school mathematics departments: Understanding their influence on student advancement. *Journal of Curriculum Studies, 28*, 495–529.

Gutiérrez, R. (2007, October). *Context matters: Equity, success, and the future of mathematics education*. Invited plenary at the North American Chapter of the International Group for the Psychology of Mathematics Education, Lake Tahoe, NV.

Halverson, R. (2007). How leaders use artifacts to structure professional community in schools. In L. Stoll & K. S. Louis (Eds.), *Professional learning communities: Divergence, depth, and dilemmas* (pp. 93–105). Berkshire, UK: Open University Press.

Hiebert, J., Stigler, J. W., Jacobs, J. K., Givvin, K. B., & Garnier, H. (2005). Mathematics teaching in the United States today (and tomorrow): Results from the TIMSS 1999 video study. *Educational Evaluation and Policy Analysis, 27*, 111–132.

Horn, I. S. (2005). Learning on the job: A situated account of teacher learning in high school mathematics departments. *Cognition and Instruction, 23*, 207–236.

Horn, I. S. (2007). Fast kids, slow kids, lazy kids: Framing the mismatch problem in mathematics teachers' conversations. *Journal of Learning Sciences, 16*, 37–79.

Kazemi, E., & Franke, M. L. (2004). Teacher learning in mathematics: Using student work to promote collective inquiry. *Journal of Mathematics Teacher Education, 7*, 203–235.

Kelchtermans, G. (2005). Teachers' emotions in educational reforms: Self-understanding, vulnerable commitment and micropolitical literacy. *Teaching and Teacher Education, 21*, 995–1006.

King, M. B. (2002). Professional development to promote schoolwide inquiry. *International Journal of Teaching and Teacher Education, 18*, 243–257.

Knapp, M. (1997). Between systemic reforms and the mathematics and science classroom: The dynamics of innovation, implementation, and professional learning. *Review of Educational Research, 67*, 227–266.

Krainer, K. (2001). Teachers' growth is more than the growth of the individual teachers: The case of Gisela. In F.-L. Lin & T. J. Cooney (Eds.), *Making sense of mathematics teacher education* (pp. 271–293). Dordrecht, the Netherlands: Kluwer.

Krainer, K. (2006). How can schools put mathematics in their centre? Improvement=content+ community+context. In J. Novotná, H. Moraová, M. Krátká, & N. Stehliková (Eds.), *Proceedings of the 30th International Group for the Psychology of Mathematics Education* (Vol. 1. pp. 84–89). Prague, Czech Republic: Charles University.

Krainer, K., & Peter-Koop, A. (2003). The role of the principal in mathematics teacher development: Bridging the dichotomy between leadership and collaboration. In A. Peter-Koop, A. Begg, C. Breen, & V. Santos-Wagner (Eds.), *Collaboration in teacher education: Examples from the context of mathematics education* (pp. 169–190). Dordrecht, the Netherlands: Kluwer.

Kramer, S. L., & Keller, R. (2008). An existence proof: Successful joint implementation of the IMP curriculum and a 4 x 4 block schedule at a suburban U.S. high school. *Journal for Research in Mathematics Education, 39*, 2–8.

Lampert, M., & Ball, D. L. (1998). *Teaching, multimedia, and mathematics: Investigations of real practice*. New York: Teachers College Press.

Lampert, M., Boerst, T., & Graziani, F. (under review). Using organizational assets in the service of ambitious teaching practice.

Lave, J. (1991). Situating learning in communities of practice. In L. B. Resnick, J. M. Levine, & S. D. Teasley (Eds.), *Perspectives on socially shared cognition* (pp. 63–82). Washington, DC: American Psychological Association.

Lave, J. (1996). Teaching, as learning, in practice. *Mind, Culture, and Activity, 3*, 149–164.

Lave, J., & Wenger, E. (1991). *Situated learning: Legitimate peripheral participation.* Cambridge, UK: Cambridge University Press.

Lee, V. E., Smith, J. B., & Croninger, R. G. (1997). How high school organization influences the equitable distribution of learning in mathematics and science. *Sociology of Education, 70*, 128–150.

Lin, P. (2002). On enhancing teachers' knowledge by constructing cases in classrooms. *Journal of Mathematics Teacher Education, 5*, 317–349.

Little, J. W. (1999). Organizing schools for teacher learning. In L. Darling-Hammond & G. Sykes (Eds.), *Teaching as the learning profession: Handbook of policy and practice* (pp. 233–262). San Francisco: Jossey-Bass.

Little, J. W. (2002). Locating learning in teachers' community of practice: opening up problems of analysis in records of everyday work. *Teaching and Teacher Education, 18*, 917–946.

Little, J. W. (2004). "Looking at student work" in the United States: Competing impulses in professional development. In C. Day & J. Sachs (Eds.), *International handbook on the continuing professional development of teachers* (pp. 94–118). Buckingham, UK: Open University Press.

Little, J. W., & Horn, I. S. (2007). 'Normalizing' problems of practice: Converting routine conversation into a resource for learning in professional communities. In L. Stoll & K. S. Louis (Eds.), *Professional learning communities: Divergence, depth, and dilemmas* (pp. 79–92). Berkshire, UK: Open University Press.

Lord, B. (1994). Teachers' professional development: Critical colleagueship and the roles of professional communities. In N. Cobb (Ed.), *The future of education: Perspectives on national standards in America* (pp. 175–204). New York: The College Board.

Lortie, D. (1975). *Schoolteacher: A sociological study.* Chicago: University of Chicago Press.

Martin, D. (2006). Mathematics learning and participation as racialized forms of experience: African American parents speak on the struggle for mathematics literacy. *Mathematical Thinking and Learning, 8*, 197–229.

Nickerson, S. M., & Moriarty, G. (2005). Professional communities in the context of teachers' professional lives: A case of mathematics specialists. *Journal of Mathematics Teacher Education, 8*, 113–140.

Oakes, J. (1985). *Keeping track: How schools structure inequality.* New Haven, CT: Yale University Press.

Remillard, J. T., & Jackson, K. (2006). Old math, new math: Parents' experiences with standards-based reform. *Mathematical Thinking and Learning, 8*, 231–259.

Richardson, V. (1994). Conducting research on practice. *Educational Researcher, 23*(5), 5–10.

Rogoff, B. (1994). Developing understanding of the idea of communities of learners. *Mind, Culture, & Activity, 1*, 209–229.

Rogoff, B. (1997). Evaluating development in the process of participation: Theory, methods, and practice build on each other. In E. Amsel & A. Renninger (Eds.), *Change and development* (pp. 265–285). Hillsdale, NJ: Lawrence Erlbaum Associates.

Rousseau, C. K. (2004). Shared beliefs, conflict, and a retreat from reform: The story of a professional community of high school mathematics teachers. *Teaching and Teacher Education, 20*, 783–796.

Secada, W. G., & Adajian, L. B. (1997). Mathematics teachers' change in the context of their professional communities. In E. Fennema & B. S. Nelson (Eds.), *Mathematics teachers in transition* (pp. 193–219). Mahwah, NJ: Lawrence Erlbaum Associates.

Sfard, A., & Prusak, A. (2005). Telling identities: In search of an analytic tool for investigating learning as a culturally shaped activity. *Educational Researcher, 34*, 14–22.

Sherin, M. G. (2004). New perspectives on the role of video in teacher education. In J. Brophy (Ed.), *Using video in teacher education* (pp. 1–27). New York: Elsevier Science.

Shulman, L. S. (1986). Those who understand teach: Knowledge growth in teaching. *Educational Researcher, 57*, 1–22.

Sowder, J. (2007). The mathematical education and development of teachers. In T. A. Romberg, T. P. Carpenter, & F. Dremock (Eds.), *Understanding mathematics and science matters* (pp. 157–223). Mahwah, NJ: Lawrence Erlbaum Associates.

Spade, J. Z., Columba, L., & Vanfossen, B. E. (1997). Tracking in mathematics and science: Courses and course-selection procedures. *Sociology of Education, 70,* 108–127.

Weick, K. E. (1976). Educational organizations as loosely coupled systems. *Administrative Science Quarterly, 21,* 1–19.

Wenger, E. (1998). *Communities of practice: Learning, meaning, and identity.* Cambridge, UK: Cambridge University Press.

Wolf, S. A., Borko, H., Elliott, R. L., McIver, M. C. (2000). "That dog won't hunt!": Exemplary school change efforts within the Kentucky reform. *American Educational Research Journal, 37,* 349–393.

Elham Kazemi
College of Education
University of Washington
USA

PAUL COBB AND THOMAS SMITH

10. DISTRICT DEVELOPMENT AS A MEANS OF IMPROVING MATHEMATICS TEACHING AND LEARNING AT SCALE[1]

This chapter focuses on research that can inform the improvement of mathematics teaching and learning at scale. In educational contexts, improvement at scale refers to the process of taking an instructional innovation that has proved effective in supporting students' learning in a small number of classrooms and reproducing that success in a large number of classrooms. We first argue that such research should view mathematics teachers' instructional practices as situated in the institutional settings of the schools and broader administrative jurisdictions in which they work. We then discuss a series of hypotheses about structures that might support teachers' ongoing improvement of their classroom practices. These support structures range from teacher networks whose activities focus on instructional issues to relations of assistance and accountability between teachers, school leaders, and leaders of broader administrative jurisdictions. In describing support structures, we also attend to equity in students' access to high quality instruction by considering both the tracking or grouping of students in terms of current achievement and the category systems that teachers and administrators use for classifying students. In the latter part of the chapter, we outline an analytic approach for documenting the institutional setting of mathematics teaching that can feed back to inform instructional improvement efforts at scale.

INTRODUCTION

In educational contexts, improvement at scale refers to the process of taking an instructional innovation that has proved effective in supporting students' learning in a small number of classrooms and reproducing that success in a large number of classrooms. In countries with centralized educational systems, it might be feasible to propose taking an instructional innovation to scale at the national level. However, proposals for instructional improvement at the national level are usually impractical in countries with decentralized education systems because the infrastructure that would be needed to support coordinated improvement at the national level does not exist. The case of instructional improvement at scale that we consider in this chapter is located in a country with a decentralized education

[1] The analysis reported in this chapter was supported by the National Science Foundation under grant No. ESI 0554535. The opinions expressed do not necessarily reflect the views of the Foundation. The hypotheses that we discuss in this chapter were developed in collaboration with Sarah Green, Erin Henrick, Chuck Munter, John Murphy, Jana Visnovska, and Qing Zhao. We are grateful to Kara Jackson for her constructive comments on a previous draft of this chapter.

K. Krainer and T. Wood (eds.), Participants in Mathematics Teacher Education, 231–253.

system, the US, in which there is a long history of local control of schooling. Each US state is divided into a number of independent school districts. In rural areas, districts might serve less than 1,000 students whereas a number of urban districts serve more than 100,000 students. In the context of the US educational system, when we speak of scale we have in mind the improvement of mathematics teaching and learning in urban districts as they are the largest jurisdictions in which it is feasible to design for improvement in the quality of instruction (Supovitz, 2006). In this chapter, we speak of instructional improvement at the level of the school and the district with the understanding that the appropriate organizational unit or administrative jurisdiction beyond the school needs to be adjusted depending on the structure of the educational system in a particular country.

The central problem that we address in this chapter is how mathematics education research can generate knowledge that contributes to the ongoing improvement of mathematics teaching and learning at scale. The daunting nature of "the problem of scale" is indicated by the well-documented finding that prior large-scale improvement efforts in mathematics and other subject matter areas have rarely produced lasting changes in either teachers' instructional practices or the organization of schools (Elmore, 2004; Gamoran, Anderson, Quiroz, Secada, Williams, & Ashman, 2003). Schools frequently experience external pressure to change, a condition that Hesse (1999) has termed policy churn. However, in most countries, classroom teaching and learning processes have proven to be remarkably stable amidst the flux. Cuban (1988), a historian of education, likened the situation to that of an ocean tossed by a storm in which all is calm on the sea floor even as the tempest whips up waves at the surface.

Researchers who work closely with teachers to support and understand their learning will probably not be surprised by Elmore's (1996) succinct synopsis of the results of educational policy research on large-scale reform: the closer that an instructional innovation gets to the core of what takes place between teachers and students in classrooms, the less likely it is that it will implemented and sustained on a large scale. This policy research emphasizes that although research-based curricula and high-quality teacher professional development are necessary, they are not sufficient to support the improvement of mathematics instruction at scale. Instructional improvement at scale also has to be framed as a problem of organizational learning for schools and larger administrative jurisdictions such as districts (Blumenfeld, Fishman, Krajcik, Marx, & Soloway, 2000; Coburn, 2003; McLaughlin & Mitra, 2004; Stein, 2004; Tyack & Tobin, 1995). This in turn implies that in addition to developing new approaches for supporting students' and teachers' learning, reformers also need to view themselves as institution-changing agents who seek to influence the institutional settings in which teachers develop and refine their instructional practices (Elmore, 1996; Stein, 2004). We capitalize on this insight in our chapter by emphasizing the importance of coming to view mathematics teachers' instructional practices as situated within the institutional setting of the school and larger jurisdictions such as districts. This perspective implies that supporting teachers' improvement of their instructional practices requires changing these settings in fundamental ways.

In the US context, the institutional setting of mathematics teaching, as we conceptualize it, encompasses *district and school policies* for instruction in mathematics. It therefore includes both the adoption of curriculum materials and guidelines for the use of those materials (e.g., pacing guides that specify a timeline for completing instructional units) (Ferrini-Mundy & Floden, 2007; Remillard, 2005; Stein & Kim, 2006). The *institutional setting* also includes the people to whom teachers are accountable and what they are held accountable for (e.g., expectations for the structure of lessons, the nature of students' engagement, and assessed progress of students' learning) (Cobb & McClain, 2006; Elmore, 2004). In addition, the institutional setting includes social supports that give teachers access to new tools and forms of knowledge (e.g., opportunities to participate in formal professional development activities and in informal professional networks, assistance from a school-based mathematics coach or a principal who is an effective instructional leader) (Bryk & Schneider, 2002; Coburn, 2001; Cohen & Hill, 2000; Horn, 2005; Nelson & Sassi, 2005), as well as incentives for teachers to take advantage of these social supports.

The findings of a substantial and growing number of studies document that teachers' instructional practices are partially constituted by the materials and resources that they use in their classroom practice, the institutional constraints that they attempt to satisfy, and the formal and informal sources of assistance on which they draw (Cobb, McClain, Lamberg, & Dean, 2003; Coburn, 2005; Spillane, 2005; Stein & Spillane, 2005). The findings of these studies call into question an implicit assumption that underpins many reform efforts, that teachers are autonomous agents in their classrooms who are unaffected by what takes place outside the classroom door (e.g., Krainer, 2005). In making this assumption, reformers are, in a very real sense, flying blind with little if any knowledge of how to adjust to the settings in which they are working as they collaborate with teachers to support their learning. In contrast, the empirical finding that teachers' instructional practices are partially constituted by the settings in which they work orients us to anticipate and plan for the school support structures that need to be developed to support and sustain teachers' ongoing learning.

INVESTIGATING INSTRUCTIONAL IMPROVEMENT AT SCALE

One of the primary goals of our current research, which is still in its early stages, is to generate knowledge that can inform the ongoing improvement of mathematics teaching and learning at scale. To this end, we are collaborating with four large, urban districts that have formulated and are implementing comprehensive initiatives for improving the teaching and learning of middle-school mathematics. We will follow 30 middle-school mathematics teachers and approximately 17 instructional leaders in each of the four districts for four years to understand how the districts' instructional improvement initiatives are playing out in practice. In doing so, we will conduct one round of data collection and analysis in each district each year for four years to document: 1) the institutional setting of mathematics teaching, including formal and informal leaders' instructional leadership practices,

2) the quality of the professional development activities in which the teachers participate, 3) the teachers' instructional practices and mathematical knowledge for teaching, and 4) student mathematics achievement. The resulting longitudinal data on 120 teachers and approximately 68 school and district leaders in 24 schools in four districts will enable us to test a series of hypotheses that we have developed about school and district support structures that might enhance the effectiveness of mathematics professional development. We will outline these hypothesized support structures later in the next section of this chapter.

In addition to formally testing our initial hypotheses, we will share our analysis of each annual round of data with the districts to provide them with feedback about the institutional settings in which mathematics teachers are developing and revising their instructional practices, and we will collaborate with them to identify any adjustments that might make the districts' improvement designs for middle-school mathematics more effective. We will then document the consequences of these adjustments in subsequent rounds of data collection. In addition, we will attempt to augment our hypotheses in the course of the repeated cycles of analysis and design[2] by identifying additional support structures and by specifying the conditions under which particular support structures are important. In doing so, we seek to address a pressing issue identified by Stein (2004): the proactive design of school and district institutional settings for mathematics teachers' ongoing learning.

In the remainder of this chapter, we focus on two types of conceptual tools that, we contend, are central to the improvement of mathematics teaching and learning at scale. The first is a *theory of action*[3] for designing schools and larger administrative jurisdictions as learning organizations for instructional improvement in mathematics. The second is an *analytic approach* for documenting the institutional setting of mathematics teaching that can produce analyses that inform the ongoing improvement effort.[4]

DESIGNING FOR INSTRUCTIONAL IMPROVEMENT IN MATHEMATICS

In preparing for our collaboration with the four urban school districts, we formulated a series of hypotheses about school and district support structures that we conjecture will be associated with improvement in middle-school mathematics teachers' instructional practices and student learning. In developing these hypotheses, we assumed that a school or district has adopted a research-based instructional programme for middle-school mathematics and that the programme was aligned with district standards and assessments. In addition, we assume that mathematics teachers have opportunities to participate in sustained professional

---

[2] In engaging in these repeated cycles of analysis and design, we will, in effect, attempt to conduct a design experiment at the level of the school and district.

[3] The term theory of action was coined by Argyris and Schön (1974, 1978) and is central to most current perspectives on organizational learning. A theory of action establishes the rationale for an improvement design and consists of conjectures about both a trajectory of organizational improvement and the specific means of supporting the envisioned improvement process.

[4] These two types of conceptual tools serve to ground the two aspects of the design research cycle, namely design and analysis (e.g., Cobb, Confrey, diSessa, Lehrer, & Schauble, 2003; Design-Based Research Collaborative, 2003).

development that is organized around the instructional materials they use with students. The proposed support structures, which are summarized in Table 1, therefore fall outside mathematics educators' traditional focus on designing high-quality curricula and teacher professional development. To the extent that the hypotheses prove viable, they specify the types of institutional structures that a school or district organizational design might aim to engender as it attempts to improve the quality of mathematics teaching across the organization.

As background for non-US readers, we should clarify that large school districts such as those with which we are collaborating have a central office whose staff are responsible for selecting curricula and for providing teacher professional development in various subject matter areas including mathematics. In this chapter, we use the designation *district leaders* to refer to members of the central office staff whose responsibilities focus on instruction. We speak of *district mathematics leaders* to refer to central office staff whose responsibilities focus specifically on the teaching and learning of mathematics.

Table 1. The proposed support structures

Primary Support Structure	Facilitating Support Structure	Hypothesized Consequence
Teacher Networks	Time for collaboration Access to expertise	Social support for development of ambitious instructional practices
Shared Instructional Vision	Brokers Negotiation of the meaning of key boundary objects	Coherent instructional improvement effort
Accountability Relations and Relations of Assistance	Leadership content knowledge	Effective instructional leadership practices
De-tracked instructional Programme	Category system for classifying students	Equity in students' learning opportunities

Teacher Networks

We developed our hypotheses about potential support structures by taking as our starting point forms of classroom instructional practice that are consistent with current research on mathematics learning and teaching (Kilpatrick, Martin, & Schifter, 2003). Teachers who have developed high quality instructional practices of this type attempt to achieve a significant mathematical agenda by building on students' current mathematical reasoning. To this end, they engage students in mathematically challenging tasks, maintain the level of challenge as tasks are enacted in the classroom (Stein & Lane, 1996; Stein, Smith, Henningsen, & Silver, 2000), and support students' efforts to communicate their mathematical thinking in classroom discussions (Cobb, Boufi, McClain, & Whitenack, 1997; Hiebert et al.,

1997; Lampert, 2001).[5] These forms of instructional practice are complex, demanding, uncertain, and not reducible to predictable routines (Ball & Cohen, 1999; Lampert, 2001; McClain, 2002; Schifter, 1995; Smith, 1996). The findings of a number of investigations indicate that *strong professional networks* (see also Lerman & Zehetmeier, and Borba & Gadanidis, this volume) in which teachers participate voluntarily can be a crucial resource as they attempt to develop instructional practices in which they place students' reasoning at the centre of their instructional decision making (Cobb & McClain, 2001; Franke & Kazemi, 2001b; Gamoran, Secada, & Marrett, 2000; Kazemi & Franke, 2004; Little, 2002; Stein, Silver, & Smith, 1998).

There is abundant evidence that the mere presence of collegial support is not by itself sufficient: both the focus and the depth of teachers' interactions matter. With regard to *focus*, it is clearly important that activities and exchanges in teacher networks centre on issues central to classroom instructional practice (Marks & Louis, 1997). Furthermore, the findings of Coburn and Russell's (in press) recent investigation indicate that the *depth* of interactions around classroom practice make a difference in terms of the support for teachers' improvement of their classroom practices. Coburn and Russell clarify that interactions of greater depth involve discerning the mathematical intent of instructional tasks and identifying the relative sophistication of student reasoning strategies, whereas interactions of less depth involve determining how to use instructional materials and mapping the curriculum to district or state standards.

Teacher networks that focus on issues relevant to classroom instruction constitute our first hypothesized support structure. In addition, we anticipate that networks in which interactions of greater depth predominate will be more supportive social contexts for teachers' development of ambitious instructional practices than those in which interactions are primarily of limited depth (Franke, Kazemi, Shih, Biagetti, & Battey, in press; Stein et al., 1998).

Access of Teacher Networks to Key Resources

Mathematics teacher networks do not emerge in an institutional vacuum. Gamoran et al.'s (2003) analysis reveals that to remain viable, teacher networks and communities need access to resources. The second and third hypothesized support structures concern two specific types of resources that facilitate the emergence and development of teacher networks (see Table 1).

Time for collaboration. The first resource is time built into the school schedule for mathematics teachers to collaborate. As Gamoran et al. (2003) make clear, time for collaboration is a necessary but not sufficient condition for the emergence of teacher networks. Although institutional arrangements such as teachers' schedules do not directly determine interactions, they can enable and constrain the social

---

[5] The research base for these broad recommendations is presented in a research companion volume to the National Council of Mathematics' (2000) Principles and Standards for School Mathematics edited by Kilpatrick, Martin, and Schifter (2003).

relations that emerge between teachers (and between teachers and instructional leaders) (Smylie & Evans, 2006; Spillane, Reiser, & Gomez, 2006).

Access to expertise. The second resource for supporting the emergence of teacher networks of sufficient depth is access to colleagues who are already relatively accomplished in using the adopted instructional programme to support students' mathematical learning. In the absence of this resource, it is difficult to envision how interactions within a teacher network will be of sufficient depth to support teachers' development of ambitious instructional practices. In this regard, Penuel, Frank, and Krause (2006) found that improvement in mathematics teachers' instructional practices was associated with access to mentors, mathematics coaches[6], and colleagues who were already expert in the reform initiative. Their results indicate that accomplished fellow teachers and coaches can share exemplars of instructional practice that are tangible to their less experienced colleagues, thus supporting their efforts to improve their instructional practices.

Shared Instructional Vision

In considering additional support structures, we step back to locate teacher networks first within the institutional context of the school, and then within the context of the broader administrative jurisdiction. At the school level, it seems reasonable to speculate that teacher networks will be more likely to emerge and sustain if the vision of high quality mathematics instruction that they promote is consistent with the instructional vision of formal or positional school leaders. Research in the field of educational leadership indicates that this intuition is well founded. The results of a number of studies reveal that professional development, collaboration between teachers, and collegiality between teachers and formal school leaders are rarely effective unless they are tied to a shared vision of high quality instruction that gives them meaning and purpose (Elmore, Peterson, & McCarthey, 1996; Newman & Associates, 1996; Rosenholtz, 1985, 1989; Rowan, 1990). In the case of US schools, formal school leaders might include the school principal, an assistant principal with responsibility for curriculum and instruction, a mathematics department head, and possibly a school-based mathematics coach. The notion of a shared instructional vision encompasses agreement on instructional goals and thus on what it is important for students to know and be able to do mathematically,[7] and on how students' development of these forms of mathematical knowledgeability can be effectively supported.

---

[6] Mathematics coaches are teachers who have been released from some or all of their instructional responsibilities in order to assist the mathematics teachers in a school in improving the quality of their instruction. Ideally, coaches should be selected on the basis of their competence as mathematics teachers and should receive professional development that focuses on both mathematics teaching and on supporting other teachers' learning.

[7] A focus on instructional goals takes us onto the slippery terrain of mathematical values (Hiebert, 1999). It is important to note that values are not a matter of mere subjective whim or taste but are instead subject to justification and debate (Rorty, 1982).

Our argument for the importance of a shared instructional vision is not restricted to the school but also extends to broader administrative jurisdictions. We illustrate this point by taking the relevant administrative jurisdiction in the US context, the school district, as an example. As is the case for the relevant jurisdiction in most countries, there are typically a number of distinct departments or units within the administration of large districts whose work has direct consequences for the teaching and learning of mathematics. For example, one unit is typically responsible for selecting instructional materials in various subject matter areas including mathematics, and for providing teacher professional development. A separate unit is typically responsible for hiring and providing professional development for school leaders. The unit responsible for assessment and evaluation would also appear critical given the importance of the types of data that are collected to assess school, teacher, and student learning. In addition, depending on the district, the unit responsible for special education might also be influential to the extent that it focuses on how mainstream instruction serves groups of students identified as potentially at-risk. Spillane et al.'s (2006) findings indicate that staff in different administrative units whose work contributes to the district's initiative to improve the quality of mathematics teaching and learning frequently understand district-wide initiatives differently. In such cases, the policies and practices of the various units are fragmented and often in conflict with each other. This has consequences both for the coherence of the district's instructional improvement effort and for the degree to which the institutional settings of mathematics teaching support teachers' ongoing improvement of their instructional practices. Our fourth hypothesized support structure therefore concerns the development of a shared *instructional vision* between participants in teacher networks, formal school leaders, and district leaders. We anticipate that mathematics teachers' improvement of their instructional practices will be greater in schools and broader jurisdictions in which a shared instructional vision consistent with current reform recommendations has been established.

Brokers

The development of a shared instructional vision of high quality mathematics instruction in a school and a broader jurisdiction such as a district is a non-trivial accomplishment. This becomes apparent when we note that mathematics teachers, principals, and district curriculum specialists, and so forth constitute distinct occupational groups that have different charges, engage in different forms of practice, and have different professional affiliations (Spillane et al., 2006). The fifth support structure concerns the *presence of brokers* who can facilitate the development of a shared instructional vision by bridging between perspectives and agendas of different role groups (see Table 1). Brokers are people who participate at least peripherally in the activities of two or more groups, and thus have access to the perspectives and meanings of each group (Wenger, 1998). For example, a principal who participates in professional development with mathematics teachers might be able to act as a broker between school leaders and mathematics teachers in the district, thereby facilitating the alignment of perspectives on mathematics teaching and learning across these two groups (e.g., Wenger, 1998). Extending our focus beyond the school, we anticipate that brokers who can bridge between school and district leaders and between units of the district central office will also be critical in supporting the development of a shared instructional vision across the district. Brokers who can help bring coherence to the reform effort in a relatively large jurisdiction such as an urban district by grounding it in a shared instructional vision constitute our fifth support structure.

Negotiating the Meaning of Key Boundary Objects

The sixth hypothesized support structure also facilitates the development of a shared instructional vision (see Table 1). Mathematics teachers and instructional leaders use a range of *tools* as an integral aspect of their practices. Star and Griesemer (1989) call tools that are used by members of two or more groups boundary objects. For example, mathematics teachers and instructional leaders in most US schools use state mathematics standards and test scores, thereby constituting them as *boundary objects*. Tools that are produced within a school or district might also be constituted as boundary objects. For example, the district leaders in one of the districts in which we are working are developing detailed curriculum frameworks for middle-school mathematics teachers to use as well as a simplified version for school leaders. It is important to note that boundary objects such as state and district standards, test scores, and curriculum frameworks can be and are frequently used differently and come to have different meanings as members of different groups such as teachers and school leaders incorporate them into their practices (Star & Griesemer, 1989; Wenger, 1998). Boundary objects do not therefore carry meanings across group boundaries. However, they can serve as important focal points for the negotiation of meaning and thus the development of a shared instructional vision. The value of boundary objects in this regard stems from the fact that they are integral to the practices of different groups and are therefore directly relevant to the concerns and interests of the members of the groups. From the point of view of organizational design, this observation points to the importance of developing venues in which members of different role groups engage together in activities that relate directly to teaching and instructional leadership in mathematics.

Our sixth hypothesis is therefore that a shared vision of high quality mathematics instruction will emerge more readily in schools and districts in which members of various groups explicitly negotiate the meaning and use of key boundary objects. In speaking of *key* boundary objects, we are referring to tools that are used when developing an agenda for mathematics instruction (e.g., curriculum frameworks) and when making mathematics teaching and learning visible (e.g., formative assessments, student work), as well as tools that are used while actually teaching.

Accountability Relations between Teachers, School leaders, and District Leaders

The picture that emerges from the support structures we have discussed thus far is that of a coherent reform effort grounded in a shared instructional vision, in which networks characterized by relatively deep interactions support teachers' ongoing learning. Although the activities of teachers as well as of school and district leaders are aligned in this picture, we have not specified the relationships between members of these different role groups. The next two potential support structures address this issue.

The seventh hypothesized support structure concerns *accountability relations* between teachers, school leaders, and district leaders. At the classroom level, instruction that supports students' understanding of central mathematical ideas involves what Kazemi and Stipek (2001) term a high press for conceptual thinking. Kazemi and Stipek clarify that teachers maintain a high conceptual press by 1) holding students accountable for developing explanations that consist of a mathematical argument rather than simply a procedural description, 2) attempting to understand relations among multiple solution strategies, and 3) using errors as opportunities to reconceptualize a problem, explore contradictions in solutions, and pursue alternative strategies. Analogously, we hypothesize that the following accountability relations will contribute to instructional improvement:

– Formal school instructional leaders (e.g., principals, assistant principals, mathematics coaches) hold mathematics teachers accountable for maintaining conceptual press for students and, more generally, for developing ambitious instructional practices.
– District leaders hold school leaders accountable for assisting mathematics teachers in improving their instructional practices.

We anticipate that the potential of these accountability relations to support instructional improvement will both depend on and contribute to the development of a shared instructional vision. In the absence of a shared vision, different school leaders might well hold teachers accountable to different criteria, some of which are at odds with the intent of the district's instructional improvement effort (Coburn & Russell, in press).

Relations of Assistance between Teachers, School Leaders, and District Leaders

Elmore (2000, 2004) argues, correctly in our view, that it is unethical to hold people accountable for developing particular forms of practice unless their learning of those practices is adequately supported. We would, for example, question a teacher who holds students accountable for producing mathematical arguments to explain their thinking but does little to support the students' development of mathematical argumentation. In Elmore's terms, the teacher has violated the principle of *mutual accountability*, wherein leaders are accountable to support the learning of those who they hold accountable. The eighth hypothesized support structure comprises the following *relations of support and assistance*:

- Formal school instructional leaders (e.g., principals, assistant principals, mathematics coaches) are accountable to teachers for assisting them in understanding the mathematical intent of the curriculum, in maintaining conceptual press for students and, more generally, in developing ambitious instructional practices.
- District leaders are accountable to school leaders to provide the material resources needed to facilitate high quality mathematics instruction, and to support school leaders' development as instructional leaders.

Leadership Content Knowledge

The ninth hypothesized support structure follows directly from the relations of accountability and assistance that we have outlined and concerns the *leadership content knowledge* of school and district leaders (see Table 1). Leadership content knowledge encompasses leaders' understanding of the mathematical intent of the adopted instructional materials, the challenges that teachers face in using these materials effectively, and the challenges in supporting teachers' reorganization of their instructional practices (Stein & Nelson, 2003). Ball, Bass, Hill, and colleagues have demonstrated convincingly that ambitious instructional practices involve the enactment of a specific type of mathematical knowledge that enables teachers to address effectively the problems, questions, and decisions that arise in the course of teaching (Ball & Bass, 2000; Hill & Ball, 2004; Hill, Rowan, & Ball, 2005). Analogously, Stein and Nelson (2003) argue that effective school and district instructional leadership in mathematics involves the enactment of a subject-matter-specific type of mathematical knowledge, leadership content knowledge, that enables instructional leaders to recognize high-quality mathematics instruction when they see it, support its development, and organize the conditions for continuous learning among school and district staff. Stein and Nelson go on to argue that the leadership content knowledge that principals require to be effective instructional leaders in mathematics includes a relatively deep understanding of mathematical knowledge for teaching, of what is known about how to teach mathematics effectively, and of how students learn mathematics, as well as "knowing something about teachers-as-learners and about effective ways of teaching teachers" (p. 416). They extend this line of reasoning by proposing that district leaders who provide professional development for principals should know everything that principals need to know and should also have knowledge of how principals learn.

We see considerable merit in Stein and Nelson's arguments about the value of leadership content knowledge in mathematics. However, the demands on principals seem overwhelming if they are to develop deep leadership content knowledge in all core subject matter areas including mathematics. This is particularly the case for principals of middle and high schools. We therefore suggest that it might be more productive to conceptualize this type of expertise as being distributed across formal and informal school leaders rather than residing exclusively with the principal. In other words, we suggest that the depth of leadership content knowledge that

241

principals require is situational and depends in large measure on the expertise of others in the school. In cases where principals can capitalize on the expertise of a core group of relatively accomplished mathematics teachers or an effective school-based mathematics coach, for example, the extent of principals' leadership content knowledge in mathematics might not need to be particularly extensive. In such cases, it might suffice for principals to understand the *characteristics of high quality instruction* that hold across core subject matter areas provided they also understand the overall mathematical intent of the instructional programme and appreciate that using the programme effectively is a non-trivial accomplishment that requires ongoing support for an extended period of time. We speculate that this limited knowledge might enable principals to collaborate effectively with accomplished teachers and possibly school-based coaches. Stein and Nelson (2003, p. 444) acknowledge the viability of this approach when they observe that

> where individual administrators do not have the requisite knowledge for the task at hand they can count on the knowledge of others, if teams or task groups are composed with the recognition that such knowledge will be requisite and someone, or some combination of people and supportive materials, will need to have it.

The ninth support structure is therefore leadership content knowledge in mathematics that is distributed across the principal, teachers, and the coach. This hypothesized support structure implies that it will be important for principal professional development to attend explicitly to the issue of leveraging teachers' and coaches' expertise effectively.

Equity in Students' Access to Ambitious Instructional Practices

The student population is becoming increasingly diverse racially and ethnically in most industrialized countries and in a number of developing countries. An established research base indicates that access to ambitious instructional practices for students who are members of historically under-served populations (e.g., students of colour, students from low-income backgrounds, students who are not native language speakers, students with special needs) is rarely achieved (see Darling-Hammond, 2007). In addition, a small but growing body of research that suggests that ambitious instructional practices are not enough to support all students' mathematical learning unless they also take account of the social and cultural differences and needs of historically marginalized groups of students (see Nasir & Cobb, 2007). This work indicates the importance of professional development for teachers and instructional leaders in mathematics that focuses squarely on meeting the *needs of underserved groups* of students. In addition, it has implications for the establishment of institutional support structures that are likely to result in access to appropriate instructional practices for historically marginalized groups of students. The final two support structures that we discuss concern *equity* in students' learning opportunities.

De-tracked instructional programme. Tracking, or the grouping of students according to current achievement, often prevails in schools that serve students from marginalized groups. However, current research indicates that "tracking does not substantially benefit high achievers and tends to put low achievers at a serious disadvantage" (Darling-Hammond, 2007, p. 324; see also Gamoran, Nystrand, Berends, & LePore, 1995; Horn, 2007; Oakes, Wells, Jones, & Datnow, 1997). The tenth support structure is therefore a rigorously de-tracked instructional programme in mathematics.

Category system for classifying students. The final support structure concerns the categories of mathematics students that are integral to teachers' and instructional leaders' practices. Horn's (2007) analysis of the contrasting systems for classifying students constructed by the mathematics teachers in two US high schools is relevant in this regard because it indicates that these classification systems were related to the two groups of teachers' views about whether mathematics should be tracked (see Table 1). Significantly, Horn's analysis also indicates that the contrasting classification systems also reflected differing views of mathematics as a school subject. The teachers in one of the schools differentiated between formal and informal solution methods, and viewed the latter as illegitimate. They also took a sequential view of school mathematics and assumed that students had to first master prior topics if they were to make adequate progress. This conception of school mathematics was reflected in the teachers' classification of students as more or less motivated to master mathematical formalisms, and as faster and slower in doing so. The teachers' classification of students in terms of stable levels of motivation and ability grounded their perceived need for separate mathematics courses for different types of students.

In sharp contrast, the mathematics teachers at the second school that Horn (2007) studied tended to take a non-sequential view of school mathematics and conceptualized it as a web of ideas rather than an accumulation of formal procedures. These teachers also rejected the categorization of students as fast or slow because it emphasized task completion at the expense of considering multiple strategies. In addition, the teachers in this school viewed it as their responsibility to support students' engagement both by selecting appropriate tasks and by influencing students' learning agendas. Thus, these teachers addressed the challenge of teaching mathematics to all their students in the context of a rigorously de-tracked mathematics programme by focusing primarily on their instructional practices rather than on perceived mismatches between students and the curriculum. In doing so, they constructed categories for classifying students that characterized them in relation to their current instructional practices rather than in terms of stable traits. Building on Horn's analysis, the eleventh support structure is a category system that classifies students in relation to current instructional practices rather than in terms of seemingly stable traits.

Reflection

We developed the proposed support structures summarized in Table 1 by mapping backwards from the classroom and, in particular, from a research-based view of high quality mathematics instruction. In doing so, we have limited our focus to the establishment of institutional settings that support school and district staff's ongoing improvement of their practices. This backward mapping process could be extended to develop conjectures that are directly related to the traditional concerns of policy researchers. For example, several of the hypothesized support structures involve conjectures about the role of mathematics coaches and school leaders. These conjectures have implications for district hiring and retention policies. In addition, the hypotheses imply that the allocation of frequently scarce material resources should be weighted towards what Elmore (2006) terms the bottom of the system (see also Gamoran et al., 2003). As the notion of *distributed leadership* is currently fashionable,[8] it is worth noting that the hypotheses do not treat the distribution of instructional leadership as a necessary good. In the absence of a common discourse about mathematics, learning, and teaching, the distribution of leadership can result in a lack of coordination and alignment (Elmore, 2000). As Elmore (2006) observes, effective schools and districts do not merely distribute leadership. They also support *people's development of leadership capabilities*, in part by structuring settings in which they learn and enact leadership. As the proposed support structures indicate, important outcomes of an initiative to improve the quality of mathematics learning and teaching include "the system capacity developed to sustain, extend, and deepen a successful initiative" (Elmore, 2006, p. 219).

DOCUMENTING THE INSTITUTIONAL SETTING OF MATHEMATICS TEACHING

The hypothesized support structures that we have discussed constitute a *theory of action* for designing schools and larger administrative jurisdictions such as school districts as learning organizations for instructional improvement in mathematics. We now consider a second conceptual tool that is central to the improvement of mathematics teaching and learning at scale, an analytic approach for documenting the institutional setting of mathematics teaching. In addition to formally testing our hypotheses about potential support structures, we will share our analysis of the data collected each year with the four districts and collaborate with them to identify any adjustments that might make the districts' improvement designs for middle-school mathematics more effective. To accomplish this, we require an analytic approach for documenting the institutional setting of mathematics teaching that can feed back to inform the districts' ongoing improvement efforts.

---

[8] Spillane and colleagues (Spillane, 2005; Spillane, Halverson, & Diamond, 2001, 2004) proposed distributed leadership as an analytic perspective that focuses on how the functions of leadership are accomplished rather than on the characteristics and actions of individual positional leaders. However, as so often happens in education, the basic tenets of this analytic approach have been translated into prescriptions for practitioners' actions. In our view, this is a fundamental category error that, if past experience is any guide, might well have unfortunate consequences (e.g., Cobb, 1994, 2002).

The analytic approach that we will take makes a fundamental distinction between schools and districts viewed as *designed organizations* and as *lived organizations*. A school or district viewed as a designed organization consists of formally designated roles and divisions of labour together with official policies, procedures, routines, management systems, and the like. Wenger (1998) uses the term designed organization to indicate that its various elements were designed to carry out specific tasks or to perform particular functions. In contrast, a school or school district viewed as a lived organization comprises the groups within which work is actually accomplished together with the interconnections between them. As Brown and Duguid (1991, 2000) clarify, people frequently adjust prescribed organizational routines and procedures to the exigencies of their circumstances (see also Kawatoko, 2000; Ueno, 2000; Wenger, 1998). In doing so, they often develop collaborative relationships that do not correspond to formally appointed groups, committees, task forces, and teams (e.g., Krainer, 2003). Instead, the groups within which work is actually organized are sometimes non-canonical and not officially recognized. These non-canonical groups are important elements of a school or district viewed as a lived organization.

Given the goals of our research, we find it essential to document the districts in which we are working as both designed organizations and as lived organizations. One of our first steps has been to document the districts as designed organizations by interviewing district leaders about their plans or designs for supporting the improvement of mathematics teaching and learning. In analysing these interviews, we have teased out the suppositions and assumptions and have framed them as testable conjectures. The process of testing these conjectures requires that we document how the districts' improvement designs are playing out in practice, thereby documenting the schools and districts in which we are working as lived organizations.

Methodologically, we will use what Hornby and Symon (1994) and Spillane (2000) refer to as a snowballing strategy and Talbert and McLaughlin (1999) term a bottom-up strategy to identify groups within the schools and districts whose agendas are concerned with the teaching and learning of mathematics. The first step in this process involves conducting audio-recorded semi-structured interviews with the participating 30 middle-school mathematics teachers in each district to identify people within the district who influence how the teachers teach mathematics in some significant way. The issues that we will address in these interviews include the professional development activities in which the teachers have participated, their understanding of the district's policies for mathematics instruction, the people to whom they are accountable, their informal professional networks, and the official sources of assistance on which they draw.

The second step in this bottom-up or snowballing process involves interviewing the formal and informal instructional leaders identified in the teacher interviews as influencing their classroom practices. The purpose of these interviews is to understand formal and informal leaders' agendas as they relate to mathematics instruction and the means by which they attempt to achieve those agendas. We will then continue this snowballing process by interviewing people identified in the second round of interviews as influencing instruction and instructional leadership in the district. In terms familiar to policy researchers, this bottom-up methodology focuses squarely on the activity of what Weatherley and Lipsky (1977) term street-level bureaucrats whose roles in interpreting and responding to district efforts to improve mathematics instruction are as important as those of district leaders who designed the improvement initiative. The methodology therefore operationalizes the view that what ultimately matters is how district initiatives are enacted in schools and classrooms (e.g., McLaughlin, 2006).

In addition to identifying the groups in which the work of instructional improvement is accomplished and documenting aspects of each group's practices, our analysis of the schools and districts as lived organizations will also involve documenting the interconnections between the groups. To do so, we will focus on *three types of interconnections*, two of which we introduced when describing potential support structures. Interconnections of the first type are constituted by the activities of *brokers* who are at least peripheral members of two or more groups. As we noted, brokers can bridge between the perspectives of different groups, thereby facilitating the alignment of their agendas. As our hypotheses indicate, our analysis of brokers will be relatively comprehensive and will seek to clarify whether there are brokers between various groups in the school (e.g., mathematics teachers and school leaders), between school leaders and district leaders, and between key units of the district central office. *Boundary objects* that members of two or more groups use routinely as integral aspects of their practices constitute interconnections of the second type. As we have noted, there is the very real possibility that members of different groups will used boundary objects differently and imbue them with different meanings (Wenger, 1998). Our analysis will therefore seek to identify boundary objects and to document whether members of different groups used them in compatible ways.

The third type of interconnection is constituted by *boundary encounters* in which members of two or more groups engage in activities together as a routine part of their respective practices. Three of the hypothesized support structures focus explicitly on boundary encounters: the explicit negotiation of the meaning of boundary objects, relations of accountability, and relations of assistance. In addition to documenting the frequency of boundary encounters between members of different groups, our analysis will focus on the nature of their interactions.

A recent finding reported by Coburn and Russell (in press) indicates the importance of pushing for this level of detail. They studied the implementation of elementary mathematics curricula designed to support ambitious instruction in two school districts. As part of their instructional improvement efforts, both districts hired and provided professional development for a cadre of school-based mathematics coaches (see also Nickerson, this volume). Coburn and Russell found that there were significant differences in the depth of the interactions between the coaches and the professional development facilitators in the two districts. In the first district, interactions were relatively deep and focused on issues such as discerning the mathematical intent of instructional tasks and on identifying and building on student reasoning strategies. In the second district, interactions were typically of limited depth and focused primarily on how to use instructional materials and on mapping the curriculum to district or state standards. Coburn and Russell also documented the nature of interactions between coaches and teachers in the two districts. They found that teacher-coach interactions increased in depth to a far greater extent in the first district than in the second district. In addition, interactions between teachers when a coach was not present also increased in depth in the first but not the second district. In other words, the contrasting routines of interaction in coach professional development sessions became important features of interactions in teacher networks in the two districts.

In our view, Coburn and Russell's analysis represents a significant advance in research on instructional improvement at scale. To this point, policy researchers have tended to frame social networks as conduits for information about instructional and instructional leadership practices. However, research in mathematics education makes it abundantly clear that information about ambitious instructional practices is, by itself, insufficient to support teachers' development of this form of practice. Coburn and Russell's analysis focuses more broadly on interactions across groups as well as within social networks, and highlights the importance of co-participation in collective activities. In addition, their findings demonstrate that the depth of co-participation matters. Their analysis therefore establishes a valuable point of contact between research on policy implementation and research on mathematics teachers' learning. This latter body of work documents that teachers' co-participation in activities of sufficient depth with an accomplished colleague or instructional leader is a critical source of support for teachers' development of ambitious practices (e.g., Borko, 2004; Fennema et al., 1996; Franke & Kazemi, 2001a; Goldsmith & Shifter, 1997; Kazemi & Franke, 2004; Wilson & Berne, 1999). We anticipate that Coburn and Russell's (in press) notion of routines of interaction will prove to be a useful analytic tool as we seek to understand whether the nature of the boundary encounters in which school and district staff engage in activities together influences how they subsequently interact with others in different settings.

PROVIDING FEEDBACK TO INFORM INSTRUCTIONAL IMPROVEMENT

In the approach that we have outlined, the analysis of a school or district as a lived organization involves identifying the groups in which the work of instructional improvement is actually accomplished and documenting interconnections between these groups. An analysis of the lived organization therefore focuses on what people actually do and the consequences for teachers' instructional practices and students' mathematical learning. In contrast, an analysis of a school or district as a designed organization involves documenting the school or district plan or design for supporting instructional improvement in mathematics. This design specifies organizational units and positional roles as well as organizational routines, and involves conjectures about how the enactment of the design will result in the improvement of teachers' instructional practices and student learning. An analysis of the designed organization documents both this design and the tools and activities that will be employed to realize the design by enabling people to improve their practices. In giving feedback to the four collaborating districts to inform their improvement efforts, we will necessarily draw on our analyses of the districts as both designed and lived organizations.

To develop this feedback, we will identify gaps between the districts' designs for instructional improvement and the ways in which those designs are actually playing out in practice by comparing our analyses of each district as a designed organization and as a lived organization. This approach will enable us to differentiate cases in which a theory of action proposed by a district is not enacted in practice from cases in which the enactment of the theory of action does not lead to the anticipated improvements in the quality of teachers' instructional practices (Supovitz & Weathers, 2004). As an illustration, one of the districts with which we are collaborating is investing some of its limited resources in mathematics coaches with half-time release from teaching for each middle school. The district's theory of action specifies that the coaches' primary responsibilities are to facilitate teacher collaboration and to support individual teachers' learning by co-teaching with them and by observing their instruction and providing constructive feedback. Suppose that the district's investment in mathematics coaches does not result in a noticeable improvement in teachers' instructional practices. It could be the case that the theory of action of the district has not been enacted. For example, the coaches might be tutoring individual students or preparing instructional materials for the mathematics teachers in their schools rather than working with teachers in their classrooms. In attempting to understand why this is occurring, we would initially focus on coaches' and school leaders' understanding of the coaches' role in supporting teachers' improvement of their instructional practices. Alternatively, it could be the case that the coaches are working with teachers in their classrooms, but their efforts to support instructional improvement are not effective. In this case, we would initially seek to understand how, specifically, the coaches are attempting to support teachers' learning and would take account of the process by which the coaches were selected and the quality of the professional development in which they participated.

As this illustration indicates, our goal when giving feedback is not merely to assess whether the district's design is being implemented with fidelity, although our analysis will necessarily address this issue. We also seek to understand why the district's theory of action is playing out in a particular way in practice by taking seriously the perspectives and practices of street-level bureaucrats such as teachers, coaches, and school leaders. In doing so, we will draw on both an analysis of the district design as a potential resource for action and an analysis of the district as a lived organization that foregrounds people's agency as they develop their practices within the context of others' institutionally situated actions (e.g., Feldman & Pentland, 2003).

DISCUSSION

In this chapter, we have focused on the question of how mathematics education research might contribute to the improvement of mathematics teaching and learning at scale. We addressed this question by first clarifying the value of viewing mathematics teachers' instructional practices as situated in the institutional settings of the schools and districts in which they work. Against this background, we presented a series of hypotheses about school and district structures that might support teachers' ongoing improvement of their classroom practices. We then went on to outline an analytic approach for documenting the institutional settings of mathematics teaching established in particular schools and districts that can feed back to inform the instructional improvement effort.

We conclude this chapter by returning to the *relation between research in educational policy and leadership and in mathematics education*. To this point, researchers in these fields have conducted largely independent lines of work on the improvement of teaching and learning (e.g., Engeström, 1998; Franke, Carpenter, Levi, & Fennema, 2001). Research in educational policy and leadership tends to focus on the designed structural features of schools and how changes in these structures can result in changes in classroom instructional practices. In contrast, research in mathematics education tends to focus on the role of curriculum and professional development in supporting teachers' improvement of their instructional practices and their views of themselves as learners. In this chapter, we have argued that mathematics education research that seeks to contribute to the improvement of teaching and learning at scale will have to transcend this dichotomy by drawing on analyses of schools and districts viewed both as designed organizations and as lived organizations. In the interventionist genre of research that we favour, organizational design is at the service of large-scale improvement in the quality of teachers' instructional practices. In research of this type, the attempt to contribute to improvement efforts in particular schools and administrative jurisdictions constitutes the context for the generation of useful knowledge about the relations between the institutional settings in which teachers' work, the instructional practices they develop in those settings, and their students' mathematical learning. This genre of research therefore reflects de Corte, Greer, and Verschaffel's (1996) adage that if you want to understand something try to change it, and if you want to change something try to understand it.

REFERENCES

Argyris, C., & Schön, D. (1974). *Theory of practice*. San Francisco: Jossey-Bass.

Argyris, C., & Schön, D. (1978). *Organizational learning: A theory of action perspective*. Reading, MA: Addison Wesley.

Ball, D. L., & Bass, H. (2000). Interweaving content and pedagogy in teaching and learning to teach: Knowing and using mathematics. In J. Boaler (Ed.), *Multiple perspectives on mathematics teaching and learning* (pp. 83–106). Stamford, CT: Ablex.

Ball, D. L., & Cohen, D. K. (1999). Developing practice, developing practitioners: Towards a practice-based theory of professional education. In G. Sykes & L. Darling-Hammond (Eds.), *Teaching as the learning profession: Handbook of policy and practice* (pp. 3–32). San Francisco: Jossey-Bass.

Blumenfeld, P., Fishman, B. J., Krajcik, J. S., Marx, R., & Soloway, E. (2000). Creating usable innovations in systemic reform: Scaling-up technology – Embedded project-based science in urban schools. *Educational Psychologist, 35*, 149–164.

Borko, H. (2004). Professional development and teacher learning: Mapping the terrain. *Educational Researcher, 33*(8), 3–15.

249

Brown, J. S., & Duguid, P. (1991). Organizational learning and communities-of-practice: Towards a unified view of working, learning, and innovation. *Organizational Science, 2*, 40–57.

Brown, J. S., & Duguid, P. (2000). *The social life of information.* Boston: Harvard Business School Press.

Bryk, A. S., & Schneider, B. (2002). *Trust in schools: A core resource for improvement.* New York: Russell Sage Foundation.

Cobb, P. (1994). Constructivism in mathematics and science education. *Educational Researcher, 23*(7), 4.

Cobb, P. (2002). Theories of knowledge and instructional design: A response to Colliver. *Teaching and Learning in Medicine, 14*, 52–55.

Cobb, P., Boufi, A., McClain, K., & Whitenack, J. W. (1997). Reflective discourse and collective reflection. *Journal for Research in Mathematics Education, 28*, 258–277.

Cobb, P., Confrey, J., diSessa, A. A., Lehrer, R., & Schauble, L. (2003). Design experiments in education research. *Educational Researcher, 32*(1), 9–13.

Cobb, P., & McClain, K. (2001). An approach for supporting teachers' learning in social context. In F.-L. Lin & T. Cooney (Eds.), *Making sense of mathematics teacher education* (pp. 207–232). Dordrecht, the Netherlands: Kluwer Academic Publishers.

Cobb, P., & McClain, K. (2006). The collective mediation of a high stakes accountability program: Communities and networks of practice. *Mind, Culture, and Activity, 13*, 80–100.

Cobb, P., McClain, K., Lamberg, T., & Dean, C. (2003). Situating teachers' instructional practices in the institutional setting of the school and school district. *Educational Researcher, 32*(6), 13–24.

Coburn, C. E. (2001). Collective sensemaking about reading: How teachers mediate reading policy in their professional communities. *Educational Evaluation and Policy Analysis, 23*, 145–170.

Coburn, C. E. (2003). Rethinking scale: Moving beyond numbers to deep and lasting change. *Educational Researcher, 32*(6), 3–12.

Coburn, C. E. (2005). Shaping teacher sensemaking: School leaders and the enactment of reading policy. *Educational Policy, 19*, 476–509.

Coburn, C. E., & Russell, J. L. (in press). District policy and teachers' social networks. *Educational Evaluation and Policy Analysis.*

Cohen, D. K., & Hill, H. C. (2000). Instructional policy and classroom performance: The mathematics reform in California. *Teachers College Record, 102*, 294–343.

Cuban, L. (1988). *The managerial imperative and the practice of leadership in schools.* Albany, NY: State University of New York Press.

Darling-Hammond, L. (2007). The flat earth and education: How America's commitment to equity will determine our future. *Educational Researcher, 36*, 318–334.

De Corte, E., Greer, B., & Verschaffel, L. (1996). Mathematics learning and teaching. In D. Berliner & R. Calfee (Eds.), *Handbook of educational psychology* (pp. 491–549). New York: Macmillan.

Design-Based Research Collaborative (2003). Design-based research: An emerging paradigm for educational inquiry. *Educational Researcher, 32*(1), 5–8.

Elmore, R. F. (1996). Getting to scale with good educational practice. *Harvard Educational Review, 66*, 1–26.

Elmore, R. F. (2000). *Building a new structure for school leadership.* Washington, DC: Albert Shanker Institute.

Elmore, R. F. (2004). *School reform from the inside out.* Cambridge, MA: Harvard Education Press.

Elmore, R. F. (2006, June). *Leadership as the practice of improvement.* Paper presented at the OECD International Conference on Perspectives on Leadership for Systemic Improvement, London.

Elmore, R. F., Peterson, P. L., & McCarthey, S. J. (1996). *Restructuring in the classroom: Teaching, learning, and school organization.* San Francisco: Jossey Bass.

Engeström, Y. (1998). Reorganizing the motivational sphere of classroom culture: An activity – theoretical analysis of planning in a teacher team. In F. Seeger, J. Voigt, & U. Waschescio (Eds.), *The culture of the mathematics classroom* (pp. 76–103). New York: Cambridge University Press.

Feldman, M. S., & Pentland, B. T. (2003). Reconceptualizing organizational routines as a source of flexibility and change. *Administrative Science Quarterly, 48*, 94–118.

Fennema, E., Carpenter, T. P., Franke, M. L., Levi, L., Jacobs, V. R., & Empson, S. B. (1996). A longitudinal study of learning to use children's thinking in mathematics instruction. *Journal for Research in Mathematics Education, 27*, 403–434.

Ferrini-Mundy, J., & Floden, R. E. (2007). Educational policy research and mathematics education. In F. Lester (Ed.), *Second handbook of research on mathematics teaching and learning* (Vol. 2, pp. 1247–1279). Greenwich, CT: Information Age Publishing.

Franke, M. L., Carpenter, T. P., Levi, L., & Fennema, E. (2001). Capturing teachers' generative change: A follow-up study of teachers' professional development in mathematics. *American Educational Research Journal, 38*, 653–689.

Franke, M. L., & Kazemi, E. (2001a). Learning to teach mathematics: Developing a focus on students' mathematical thinking. *Theory Into Practice, 40*, 102–109.

Franke, M. L., & Kazemi, E. (2001b). Teaching as learning within a community of practice: Characterizing generative growth. In T. Wood, B. S. Nelson, & J. Warfield (Eds.), *Beyond classical pedagogy in elementary mathematics: The nature of facilitative teaching* (pp. 47–74). Mahwah, NJ: Lawrence Erlbaum Associates.

Franke, M. L., Kazemi, E., Shih, J., Biagetti, S., & Battey, D. (in press). Changing teachers' professional work in mathematics: One school's journey. *Understanding mathematics and science matters.*

Gamoran, A., Anderson, C. W., Quiroz, P. A., Secada, W. G., Williams, T., & Ashman, S. (2003). *Transforming teaching in math and science: How schools and districts can support change.* New York: Teachers College Press.

Gamoran, A., Nystrand, M., Berends, M., & LePore, P. C. (1995). An organizational analysis of the effects of ability grouping. *American Educational Research Journal, 32*, 687–715.

Gamoran, A., Secada, W. G., & Marrett, C. B. (2000). The organizational context of teaching and learning: Changing theoretical perspectives. In M. T. Hallinan (Ed.), *Handbook of sociology of education* (pp. 37–63). New York: Kluwer Academic/Plenum Publishers.

Goldsmith, L. T., & Shifter, D. (1997). Understanding teachers in transition: Characteristics of a model for the development of mathematics teaching. In E. Fennema & B. S. Nelson (Eds.), *Mathematics teachers in transition* (pp. 19–54). Mahwah, NJ: Lawrence Erlbaum Associates.

Hesse, F. M. (1999). *Spinning wheels: The politics of urban school reform.* Washington, DC: The Brookings Institute.

Hiebert, J. I. (1999). Relationships between research and the NCTM Standards. *Journal for Research in Mathematics Education, 30*, 3–19.

Hiebert, J. I., Carpenter, T. P., Fennema, E., Fuson, K. C., Wearne, D., Murray, H., Olivier, A., & Human, P. (1997). *Making sense: Teaching and learning mathematics with understanding.* Portsmouth, NH: Heinemann.

Hill, H. C., & Ball, D. L. (2004). Learning mathematics for teaching: Results from California's mathematics professional development institutes. *Journal for Research in Mathematics Education, 35*, 330–351.

Hill, H. C., Rowan, B., & Ball, D. L. (2005). Effects of teachers' mathematical knowledge on teaching for student achievement. *American Educational Research Journal, 42*, 371–406.

Horn, I. S. (2005). Learning on the job: A situated account of teacher learning in high school mathematics departments. *Cognition and Instruction, 23*, 207–236.

Horn, I. S. (2007). Fast kids, slow kids, lazy kids: Classification of students and conceptions of subject matter in math teachers' conversations. *Journal of the Learning Sciences, 16*, 37–79.

Hornby, P., & Symon, G. (1994). Tracer studies. In C. Cassell & G. Symon (Eds.), *Qualitative methods in organizational research: A practical guide* (pp. 167–186). London: Sage Publications.

Kawatoko, Y. (2000). Organizing multiple vision. *Mind, Culture, and Activity, 7*, 37–58.

Kazemi, E., & Franke, M. L. (2004). Teacher learning in mathematics: Using student work to promote collective inquiry. *Journal of Mathematics Teacher Education, 7*, 203–225.

251

Kazemi, E., & Stipek, D. (2001). Promoting conceptual thinking in four upper-elementary mathematics classrooms. *Elementary School Journal, 102*, 59–80.

Kilpatrick, J., Martin, W. G., & Schifter, D. (Eds.). (2003). *A research companion to principles and standards for school mathematics.* Reston, VA: National Council of Teachers of Mathematics.

Krainer, K. (2003). Editorial: Teams, communities, and networks. *Journal of Mathematics Teacher Education, 6*, 93–105.

Krainer, K. (2005). Pupils, teachers and schools as mathematics learners. In C. Kynigos (Ed.), *Mathematics education as a field of research in the knowledge society. Proceedings of the First GARME Conference* (pp. 34–51). Athens, Greece: Hellenic Letters.

Lampert, M. (2001). *Teaching problems and the problems of teaching.* New Haven, CT: Yale University Press.

Little, J. W. (2002). Locating learning in teachers' communities of practice: Opening up problems of analysis in records of everyday work. *Teaching and Teacher Education, 18*, 917–946.

Marks, H. M., & Louis, K. S. (1997). Does teacher empowerment affect the classroom? The implications of teacher empowerment for instructional practice and student academic performance. *Educational Evaluation and Policy Analysis, 19*, 245–275.

McClain, K. (2002). Teacher's and students' understanding: The role of tool use in communication. *Journal of the Learning Sciences, 11*, 217–249.

McLaughlin, M. W. (2006). Implementation research in education: Lessons learned, lingering questions, and new opportunities. In M. I. Honig (Ed.), *New directions in educational policy implementation* (pp. 209–228). Albany, NY: State University of New York Press.

McLaughlin, M. W., & Mitra, D. (2004, April). *The cycle of inquiry as the engine of school reform: Lessons from the Bay Area School Reform Collaborative.* Paper presented at the annual meeting of the American Educational Research Association, San Diego, CA.

Nasir, N. S., & Cobb, P. (Eds.). (2007). *Improving access to mathematics: Diversity and equity in the classroom.* New York: Teachers College Press.

Nelson, B. S., & Sassi, A. (2005). *The effective principal: Instructional leadership for high-quality learning.* New York: Teachers College Press.

Newman, F. M., & Associates. (1996). *Authentic achievement: Restructuring schools for intellectual quality.* San Francisco: Jossey-Bass.

Oakes, J., Wells, A. S., Jones, M., & Datnow, A. (1997). Detracking: The social construction of ability, cultural politics, and resistance to reform. *Teachers College Record, 98*, 482–510.

Penuel, W. R., Frank, K. A., & Krause, A. (2006, June). *The distribution of resources and expertise and the implementation of schoolwide reform initiatives.* Paper presented at the Seventh International Conference of the Learning Sciences, Bloomington, IN.

Remillard, J. (2005). Examining key concepts in research on teachers' use of mathematics curricula. *Review of Educational Research, 75*, 211–246.

Rorty, R. (1982). *Consequence of pragmatism.* Minneapolis, MN: University of Minnesota Press.

Rosenholtz, S. J. (1985). Effective schools: Interpreting the evidence. *American Journal of Education, 93*, 352–388.

Rosenholtz, S. J. (1989). *Teacher's workplace.* New York: Longman.

Rowan, B. (1990). Commitment and control: Alternative strategies for the organizational design of schools. In C. Cazden (Ed.), *Review of Educational Research* (Vol. 16, pp. 353–389). Washington, DC: American Educational Research Association.

Schifter, D. (1995). Teachers' changing conceptions of the nature of mathematics: Enactment in the classroom. In B. S. Nelson (Ed.), *Inquiry and the development of teaching: Issues in the transformation of mathematics teaching* (pp. 17–25). Newton, MA: Center for the Development of Teaching, Education Development Center.

Smith, J. P. (1996). Efficacy and teaching mathematics by telling: A challenge for reform. *Journal for Research in Mathematics Education, 27*, 387–402.

Smylie, M. A., & Evans, P. J. (2006). Social capital and the problem of implementation. In M. I. Honig (Ed.), *New directions in educational policy implementation* (pp. 187–208). Albany, NY: State University of New York Press.

Spillane, J. P. (2000). Cognition and policy implementation: District policy-makers and the reform of mathematics education. *Cognition and Instruction, 18*, 141–179.

Spillane, J. P. (2005). *Distributed leadership.* San Francisco: Jossey Bass.

Spillane, J. P., Halverson, R., & Diamond, J. B. (2001). Towards a theory of leadership practice: Implications of a distributed perspective. *Educational Researcher, 30*(3), 23–30.

Spillane, J. P., Halverson, R., & Diamond, J. B. (2004). Distributed leadership: Towards a theory of school leadership practice. *Journal of Curriculum Studies, 36*, 3–34.

Spillane, J. P., Reiser, B., & Gomez, L. M. (2006). Policy implementation and cognition: The role of human, social, and distributed cognition in framing policy implementation. In M. I. Honig (Ed.), *New directions in educational policy implementation* (pp. 47–64). Albany, NY: State University of New York Press.

Star, S. L., & Griesemer, J. R. (1989). Institutional ecology, "Translations" and boundary objects: Amateurs and professionals in Berkeley's Museum of Vertebrate Zoology. *Social Studies of Science, 19*, 387–420.

Stein, M. K. (2004). Studying the influence and impact of standards: The role of districts in teacher capacity. In J. Ferrini-Mundy & F. K. Lester, Jr. (Eds.), *Proceedings of the National Council of Teachers of Mathematics Research Catalyst Conference* (pp. 83–98). Reston, VA: National Council of Teachers of Mathematics.

Stein, M. K., & Kim, G. (2006, April). *The role of mathematics curriculum in large-scale urban reform: An analysis of demands and opportunities for teacher learning.* Paper presented at the annual meeting of the American Educational Research Association, San Francisco.

Stein, M. K., & Lane, S. (1996). Instructional tasks and the development of student capacity to think and reason: An analysis of the relationship between teaching and learning in a reform mathematics project. *Educational Research and Evaluation, 2*, 50–80.

Stein, M. K., & Nelson, B. S. (2003). Leadership content knowledge. *Educational Evaluation and Policy Analysis, 25*, 423–448.

Stein, M. K., Silver, E. A., & Smith, M. S. (1998). Mathematics reform and teacher development: A community of practice perspective. In J. G. Greeno & S. V. Goldman (Eds.), *Thinking practices in mathematics and science learning* (pp. 17–52). Mahwah, NJ: Lawerence Erlbaum Associates.

Stein, M. K., Smith, M. S., Henningsen, M. A., & Silver, E. A. (2000). *Implementing standards-based mathematics instruction: A casebook for professional development.* New York: Teachers College Press.

Stein, M. K., & Spillane, J. P. (2005). Research on teaching and research on educational administration: Building a bridge. In B. Firestone & C. Riehl (Eds.), *Developing an agenda for research on educational leadership* (pp. 28–45). Thousand Oaks, CA: Sage Publications.

Supovitz, J. A. (2006). *The case for district-based reform.* Cambridge, MA: Harvard University Press.

Supovitz, J. A., & Weathers, J. (2004). *Dashboard lights: Monitoring implementation of district instructional reform strategies.* Unpublished manuscript, University of Pennsylvania, Consortium for Policy Research in Education.

Talbert, J. E., & McLaughlin, M. W. (1999). Assessing the school environment: Embedded contexts and bottom-up research strategy. In S. L. Friedman & T. D. Wachs (Eds.), *Measuring environment across the life span* (pp. 197–226). Washington, DC: American Psychological Association.

Tyack, D., & Tobin, W. (1995). The "Grammar" of schooling: Why has it been so hard to change? *American Educational Research Journal, 31*, 453–479.

Ueno, N. (2000). Ecologies of inscription: Technologies of making the social organization of work and the mass production of machine parts visible in collaborative activity. *Mind, Culture, and Activity, 7*, 59–80.

Weatherley, R., & Lipsky, M. (1977). Street-level bureaucrats and institutional innovation: Implementing special education reform. *Harvard Educational Review, 47*, 171–197.

Wenger, E. (1998). *Communities of practice*. New York: Cambridge University Press.

Wilson, S. M., & Berne, J. (1999). Teacher learning and the acquisition of professional knowledge: An examination of research on contemporary professional development. In A. Iran-Nejad & P. D. Pearson (Eds.), *Review of research in education* (Vol. 24, pp. 173–209). Washington, DC: American Educational Research Association.

Paul Cobb
Vanderbilt University
USA

Thomas Smith
Vanderbilt University
USA

JOHN PEGG AND KONRAD KRAINER

11. STUDIES ON REGIONAL AND NATIONAL REFORM INITIATIVES AS A MEANS TO IMPROVE MATHEMATICS TEACHING AND LEARNING AT SCALE

The chapter considers four examples of large-scale projects involving national reform initiatives in mathematics drawn from four continents – Europe, North America, Australia and Asia. Poor student performance on international and/or national assessment programmes was, in part, a catalyst for each programme. The underlying issue driving each of these studies was the perceived importance of improved student learning outcomes in mathematics and science in these countries. All the projects focus on initiating purposeful pedagogic change through involving teachers in rich professional learning experiences. The primary purpose of this chapter is two-fold. First, a brief description is provided of each project in order to give an insight into different countries' efforts to improve teaching and learning at scale. Second, an analysis and discussion of common features are undertaken leading to lessons learned.

INTRODUCTION AND BACKGROUND

All over the world, countries face challenges in terms of supporting students to achieve their potential in the important area of mathematics. As we move into the 21st century, we find new meaning to calls about the *importance of mathematics* knowledge and know-how to economic growth.

Glenn (2000, p. 7) writing for a US readership, identified four important and enduring reasons for the need for students to achieve to their potential in mathematics and science. These were:
- The rapid pace of change in both the increasingly interdependent global economy and in the American workplace demands widespread mathematics- and science-related knowledge and abilities;
- Our citizens need both mathematics and science for their everyday decision-making;
- Mathematics and science are inextricably linked to the nation's security interests; and
- The deeper, intrinsic value of mathematical and scientific knowledge shape and define our common life, history, and culture. Mathematics and science are primary sources of lifelong learning and the progress of our civilization.

These or similar sentiments have prompted education authorities around the world to look at better ways of (i) increasing the mathematics skills of students, (ii)

K. Krainer and T. Wood (eds.), Participants in Mathematics Teacher Education, 255–280.

developing more effective programmes to support teachers meet the demands of modern classrooms, and (iii) increasing the attraction and retention of qualified mathematics teachers by improving the education of prospective teachers as well as addressing the professional needs of practising teachers.

Any student who experiences ongoing failure in school faces a myriad of difficulties in achieving *long-term employment*, and useful and fulfilling occupations. Those who exhibit consistent weaknesses in basic skills in mathematics are particularly vulnerable. Test data provide a compelling case for the need to develop programmes and approaches that improve mathematics outcomes for all students and particularly for those who are performing at or below the international or national benchmarks. Equally important is the need of mathematics instruction to address affective aspects of learning. It is a great challenge to raise all students' interest in and joy of mathematics, to let them experience the benefit and beauty of this subject and to decrease their fears and feelings of failing, in particular taking into account gender and diversity issues. Cognitive and affective factors are closely interconnected.

International data point out that the *life chances* of students to acquire mathematics competencies are not uniform across a nation. Some students approach education (and the learning of mathematics) with advantages that are not found throughout the population. In particular, those who live in poverty, in rural locations or belong to at-risk minorities often have less chance of success than others. Hence, driving many reform initiatives is the principle of equity of educational opportunity regardless of current life opportunities as well as an expectation of achievement regardless of the current ability level.

The central question for most nations is where best to direct efforts so that meaningful and *sustainable change* can be managed in a cost-effective way. While the problems each nation faces are complex and unique, much can be gained by analysing different approaches. The large-scale projects described in this text, highlight how four countries have, in part, attempted to address education issues. While their programmes are sophisticated in design and implementation, they have a central, common theme, namely, they are directed at the professional learning of prospective and practising teachers.

This focus on teachers' learning is not arbitrary: it is evident that reform programmes must access students through their teachers. However, how large is teachers' impact on students' learning? Over the past few years, a consistent theme has begun to emerge concerning the variance identified in the *analysis of student learning* over many large-scale projects. Identified factors that contribute to major sources of variation in student performance (Hattie, 2003) include student (50%), home (5-10%), schools (5-10%), principals (mainly accounted for in schools), peer effects (5-10%), and teachers (30%). This research implies that genuine improvement in learning can be achieved by improving the beliefs, emotions, knowledge, and practice of teachers. The picture is consistent; it is what *mathematics teachers* believe, feel, know, and do, that is a powerful determinant in student learning.

In the following, *four large-scale projects* involving significant national reform initiatives from four continents are described. Given the complexity and authors' deeper knowledge of their own initiatives in Austria and Australia, a slightly more extensive focus is placed on these two cases. The four countries vary greatly in size (and distances to be travelled), spread of the population, importance of teacher shortages, and the educational disadvantage experienced by minorities. The first two projects can be traced back to the results of student assessments in Austria (Europe) and the state of Ohio (US, North America). The remaining two initiatives address in different ways the under-achievement of students in rural and regional areas in comparison to their metropolitan peers. One is from Australia and the other is from South Korea (Asia).

Hence, as we consider the different initiatives outlined we identify two underpinning tenets. First, more than at any time in our history, more citizens than ever need to achieve their mathematically potential if they are to have active and fulfilling occupations. Second, if we are to bring about sustainable change then money and effort needs to be directed to encouraging and supporting quality teaching.

In order to facilitate comparison across the four projects, a common structure has been employed in the next section. Each description considers:
- Impulse for the initiative and challenge
- Goals and intervention strategy
- Implementation and communication
- Evaluation and impact
- Challenges and further steps

AUSTRIA: IMST – INNOVATIONS IN MATHEMATICS, SCIENCE AND TECHNOLOGY TEACHING

Austria participated in all three cohorts (primary, middle and high school) of the 1995 TIMSS achievement study. Whereas the results for the primary and the middle school were rather promising, the results of the Austrian high school students (grades 9 to 12 or 13), particularly with regard to the TIMSS advanced mathematics and physics achievement test, shocked the public (Mullis et al., 1998). These data were a catalyst for the government and education community to re-evaluate the status of mathematics and science education and saw the responsible federal ministry launch the IMST – *Innovations in Mathematics and Science Teaching* – research project (1998-1999). The purpose of this nation-wide programme was to address an identified *complex picture of diverse problematic influences* on the status and quality of mathematics and science teaching.

Impulse for the Initiative and Challenge

In addition to the disappointing performance of Austria's high school students on TIMSS, Austria was among those nations with the highest achievement differences between boys and girls. Also, students showed poor results with regard to items

257

that referred to higher levels of thinking, and less than a third of Austrian students felt that they were involved in reasoning tasks in most or every mathematics lesson(s).

In seeking to explain these results and findings, Austrian researchers were convinced that there were manifold causes. For example, the answers to a written questionnaire by Austrian teachers, teacher educators and representatives of the education authorities showed that teachers were predominantly seen as dedicated and as having a lot of pedagogical and didactic autonomy. On the one hand, there were many creative initiatives being carried out by individuals, groups or institutions; on the other hand, many of these initiatives were carried out in isolation, and a networking structure was missing.

Mathematics education and related research was seen as poorly anchored at Austrian teacher education institutions. Subject experts dominate university teacher education, other teacher education institutions show a lack of research in mathematics education; the collaboration with educational sciences and schools is – with exception of a few cases – underdeveloped. A competence centre like those found in many other countries was not existent. Also, the overall structure (including two institutions for the education of prospective teachers that are mostly unconnected, a variety of different kinds of schools with corresponding administrative bodies in the ministry and in the institutions for the education of practising teachers, etc.) showed a picture of a "fragmentary educational system" of lone fighters with a high level of (individual) autonomy and action, however, there was little evidence of reflection and networking (Krainer, 2001).

Goals and Intervention Strategy

The analyses led to the four year project IMST^2 (2000-2004) – now called *Innovations in Mathematics, Science and Technology Teaching*: the addition of "Technology" in the project title was to express the fundamental importance of technologies for mathematics and science teaching. The project (Krainer, Dörfler, Jungwirth, Kühnelt, Rauch, & Stern, 2002) focused solely on the upper secondary school level and involved the subjects, biology, chemistry, mathematics and physics. IMST^2 was financed by the responsible federal ministry and the Austrian Council of Research and Technology Development. In order to take systemic steps to overcome the "fragmentary educational system", the approach of a "learning system" (Krainer, 2005a) was taken. It adopted enhanced *reflection* and *networking* as the basic intervention strategy. The theoretical framework builds on the ideas of action research (Altrichter, Posch, & Somekh, 1993), constructivism (von Glasersfeld, 1991) and systemic approaches to educational change and system theory (Fullan, 1993; Willke, 1999).

Besides stressing the dimensions of reflection and networking, "innovation" and "work with teams" were two additional features. Innovations were not regarded as singular events that replace an ineffective practice but as continuous processes leading to a natural further development of practice. Teachers and schools defined their own starting point for innovations and were individually supported by researchers and expert teachers. The IMST² intervention built on teachers' strengths and aimed at making their work visible (e.g., by publishing teachers' reports on the website). Thus teachers and schools retained ownership of their innovations. Another important feature of IMST² was the emphasis on supporting teams of teachers from a school.

The two major tasks of IMST² were

– The initiation, promotion, dissemination, networking and analysis of innovations in schools (and to some extent also in teacher education at university); and

– Recommendations for a support system for the quality development of mathematics, science and technology teaching.

The second task led to a plan for a sustainable support system (Krainer, 2005b). Consequently, IMST² was followed by the project IMST3 (2004-2007) which included all secondary schools and later by the project IMST3 Plus (2007-2009) which broadened the support of schools to the primary level.

In IMST3 and IMST3 Plus about three times more schools were supported and also the participation in regional networks was fostered. It was intended to build up a network of practitioners, researchers and administrative staff that to help to support the schools. Another task was to contribute to the implementation of a better infrastructure for mathematics and science education. The improved infrastructure was considered a basis and precondition for implementing a sustainable network of persons and institutions. Therefore, for example, the IMST project team designed a plan on how to establish competence centres for mathematics, science and technology education.

Implementation and Communication

The operative implementation of most parts of IMST has been entrusted to the Institute of Instructional and School Development at the University of Klagenfurt. Though having this university institute as a key player in the whole process, the whole project was understood as an initiative, and influenced by a wide network of people and institutions in order to improve mathematics and science teaching and learning in Austria.

In the years 2000-2004, IMST supported about 50 innovation projects at Austrian upper secondary schools (and partially at other organisations, e.g., teacher education institutions) in each school-year. The participation was voluntary and gave teachers and schools a choice among four priority programmes (Basic education; School development; Teaching and learning processes; Practice-oriented research: Students' independent learning) according to the challenges sifted out in the above mentioned research project. In general, teachers in all four priority programmes – and also later in a specific programme on gender sensitivity and gender mainstreaming – were supported by staff members of IMST. The priority programmes can be regarded as small professional communities that not only supported each participant to proceed with his or her own project but also generated a deeper understanding of the critical reflection of one's own teaching, of formulating research questions, of looking for evidence based on viable data, and on methods that help to gather that data.

Since 2004, the direct support of about 150 innovative projects is organized within an IMST fund. Whereas the fund aims primarily at reaching experienced teachers who are able to disseminate their experiences and results to other teachers (at their school, in their district or nation-wide), the formation of regional networks in each federal state aims at reaching a greater number of teachers. In addition, a gender network and a project "examination culture" have been established in order to offer advice and professional development activities for teachers. All these four measures of IMST3 (fund, regional networks, gender network and examination culture) were continued in the phase of IMST3 Plus. Step by step these measures are opened to teachers at the primary level.

Throughout all phases of IMST, the project is accompanied by a website, an annual conference and a quarterly newsletter.

Evaluation and Impact

Evaluation was an integral part of IMST since its start (Krainer, 2007). The *self-evaluation* comprised forms of a *process-oriented evaluation* (generating steering knowledge for the project management and the project teams), an *outcome-oriented evaluation* (working out the impact of the project at different levels of the educational system), and a *knowledge-oriented evaluation* (generating new theoretical and practical knowledge about the interconnection between the project's interventions and its impact). In many cases, this self-evaluation included data gathering and feedback by external experts. In addition, several *independent evaluations* were commissioned looking at the impact of the project or parts of it. For example, three international experts evaluated IMST² (2000-2004) and IMST3 (2004-2006) at the end of these periods of the project and wrote corresponding reports. Also parts of IMST3 (e.g., the priority programmes or the networks) were externally evaluated.

The self-evaluation of IMST was done at different levels, in particular at the school, classroom and individual teachers' level, and at the Austrian educational system level. The *teachers* used different forms of action research methods. In some cases, they were supported by their mentoring teams by means of external evaluation (interviews, questionnaires, analyses of videos). Overall, the reports indicated significant gains of students' and teachers' affective and cognitive growth.

Specht (2004) reported that IMST² is seen as an important, useful and effective support for instructional and school development in mathematics and science. He (p. 51) identified concrete changes in teachers' orientations to actions, in particular concerning their readiness for innovations in teaching, their increased ability to reflect and self-evaluate, their higher care in choosing teaching contents and their more intensive collaboration with colleagues.

With the start of IMST3 in 2004, efforts to investigate the impact of the programme were increased. In particular, student questionnaires and more systematic analyses of teachers' reports were introduced. Answers to the teacher questionnaire demonstrated a high level of satisfaction with the programme. Teachers were highly motivated even though the additional workload of the programme could be substantial. IMST students were generally more interested in their subjects (in comparison to students in the Austrian PISA sample), and reported less anxiety. However, this may be due to their teachers, who show a high level of motivation already before they entered the IMST programmes.

A longitudinal study (Müller, Andreitz, Hanfstingl, & Krainer, 2007) based on the self-determination theory of Deci and Ryan (2002) was performed in all classes taking part. The study showed that teachers who experience support from their colleagues and principal assess their students as being more motivated. Their students felt more intrinsically motivated than students from less supported teachers. However, if teachers felt pressure from colleagues and the principal, teachers' and students' intrinsic motivation decreased. Overall, the study showed that teachers trying to improve their practice should not be isolated.

An external evaluation of the regional networks of IMST[2], on the basis of a questionnaire directed at principals and superintendents (Heffeter, 2006, p. 47), found that this particular measure promotes the communication and change of experiences among teachers. The study also suggested that the IMST process has the potential to break up thinking patterns that have become entrenched in the Austrian educational system.

The external evaluations of IMST[2] and IMST3 by international experts (Prenzel, Schratz, & Messner, 2007) regarded the project as a national and international remarkable and successful development programme. Suggestions focused to a large extent on an increasing emphasis on generating new scientific knowledge that coincides with the main strategy of IMST.

Challenges and Further Steps

In the remaining time of IMST3 Plus (2007-2009), four major challenges are to be taken into consideration. Firstly, the work with primary schools has to be started. This is connected with intensive collaborations with the new established teacher education institutions (Pädagogische Hochschulen) in Austria. Secondly, the recent formation of IMST networks at the district level (e.g., the VIA_MATH project) generates new questions of adequate support and evaluation. Here, a good interplay between the IMST fund and the regional networks seems necessary as well as collaborations with the regional school boards and the teacher education institutions. Thirdly, the ongoing discussion on the plan for the time after 2009 has to be finalized. Fourthly, steps towards improving the opportunities for research in mathematics education at the primary school level have to be taken. It should be mentioned that Austria has so far no professor for mathematics education at the primary school level that means that research in that area is rather underdeveloped. Recently, IMST promotes the establishment of regional centres for mathematics and science education where teacher educators and researchers working at the primary and the secondary level are expected to collaborate.

UNITED STATES, OHIO: SYSTEMIC REFORM OF SCIENCE AND MATHEMATICS EDUCATION

Traditionally, education in the US was a matter for local communities to control and fund. The publication of "A Nation at Risk" (NCEE, 1983) initiated a US-wide desire to move schools towards universal standards for accountability in mathematics and science teaching and learning. The standards-movement led to the fact that today both state and federal governments play a much larger role in US education. While federal documents contained recommendations for improving teaching practices and student learning for all, the specific means for achieving theses goals were left to individual states. As part of this pattern, Ohio established a model curriculum for science, established outcomes to be measured, and recently developed content standards. Ohio was one of the first states in the US to receive federal funds under the State Systemic Initiative of the National Science Foundation (NSF). Ohio's Systemic Initiative, Project Discovery, was initially funded from 1991-1996 (more info can be found at http://www.units.muohio.edu/discovery/). The following description is based largely on Wagner and Meiring (2004) and Beeth, McCollum, and Tafel (submitted).

Impulse for the Initiative and Challenge

In addition to the federal concerns about mathematics and science learning, there was also a specific concern in Ohio: despite the fact that this state ranked high (sixth) in science and technology based industry in the United States, Ohio's schools ranked only in the mid-twenties in those subjects. Public media reports on student learning brought attention to the need for reform of educational practices.

Ohio's Department of Education issued standards that asked for a more problem solving and inquiry based approach to classroom instruction. The Discovery Project Summer Institutes offered teachers a place to work on their professional competence.

Goals and Intervention Strategy

The overall goal of Discovery was to improve mathematical and scientific knowledge of middle school students, and to achieve equity between students of different ethnic groups as well as gender equity through inquiry based instruction. At the time of conception, national standards were not yet developed, thus Discovery preceded the later move to achieve national coherence in the conception of mathematics and science teaching.

Unlike other approaches to educational reform, the Discovery project did not simply standardise a curriculum, but addressed the methods in which science and mathematics are taught. The project's principal goal was to educate the educators and produce a cadre of teachers capable of implementing inquiry based instruction in the classroom. In particular, Discovery focused on increasing teachers' content knowledge.

The Discovery project went on to emphasize *partnerships* between teachers and parents in mathematics and science education and incorporated methods to address learning gaps between demographic groups.

Implementation and Communication

Discovery installed six-week professional development courses for in-service teachers, which taught research based inquiry methods for individual middle-school teachers. These courses were taught by university researchers and science educators as well as master teachers throughout Ohio. The inquiry based method focused on interaction and communication between students, discussion of alternative methods of problem solving, supporting claims with data and less emphasis on traditional rote memorization. Participants observed and discussed each other's teaching of classes targeted at inquiry learning. After the course, participants met several times during the following year working on a portfolio and to exchange their experiences.

After the initial funding period, Discovery institutes have been continuing to offer courses, albeit to a lesser extent. The initiative expanded to include teachers at all grade levels and to include some site-based and other administrators, as well.

Evaluation and Impact

Evaluation of the programme occurred at three levels. Firstly, the scientific and mathematical knowledge of students participating in the Discovery project was compared with that of students not participating in the programme. Students in the programme fared an average of 7% better on standardized tests. Secondly, gender and ethnicity based performance gaps were assessed over time; and the programme was shown to decrease the gap in achievement for these groups of learners.

Finally, passing rates of students for different schools were compared. This comparison showed improvements in passing grades for schools with higher percentages of Discovery trained teachers. An outgrowth of Discovery has been the establishment of multiple professional development initiatives and networks of K-16 institutions through a variety of state and national funding mechanisms.

Challenges and Further Steps

The activities leading to the most remarkable improvements in the study were considered too expensive to implement at a state-wide level. To mitigate some of the programme costs the state focused its efforts on the 9th and 10th grades, and distributed Discovery training materials to schools capable of implementing the programme. In 1995, the state of Ohio initiated the SUSTAIN project to maintain the results already achieved by the federally funded project Discovery.

SUSTAIN's primary focus is in creating a *partnership* between state universities and state schools by providing inquiry based education methods to its education students. SUSTAIN was also designed to foster collaboration among Ohio's higher education institutions and with public school districts through regional professional development centres named Centres of Excellence in Mathematics and Science.

At present, considerable investment is directed towards technology based, K-16, educational and professional development support structures delivered through both virtual and clinical learning experiences.

AUSTRALIA: SIMERR NATIONAL CENTRE

In 2004, the National Centre of Science, Information and Communication Technology, and Mathematics Education for Rural and Regional Australia (SiMERR National Centre) received an establishment grant from the Australian Federal Government. This remains one of the largest education grants awarded in Australia and indicates the importance attached to issues concerning rural and regional education.

SiMERR was established at the University of New England (UNE) in Armidale, a rural centre, utilising a collaborative model involving groups of academics in each state (referred to as state Hubs). SiMERR carries out research and professional development activities with a focus on improving the learning outcomes of all Australian students, especially those studying in rural and regional Australia.

Impulse for Initiative and Challenge

The rationale for the SiMERR National Centre was based on compelling evidence from many sources (e.g., Programme for International Assessment (PISA), Thomson, Cresswell, & De Bortoli, 2004; Thomson & De Bortoli, 2007; the Trends in International Mathematics and Science Study (TIMSS), Zammit, Routitsky, & Greenwood, 2002; and national basic skills test information, MCEETYA, 2006) concerning the performance of students in rural and regional Australia, about a third of the Australian student population.

These data quantified the extent of inequities for rural students in learning outcomes in science and mathematics education and underscore the most significant challenge currently facing education in Australia – equity of educational opportunity for all school students regardless of location (e.g., Lyons, Cooksey, Panizzon, Parnell, & Pegg, 2006; Roberts, 2005; Vinson, 2002).

Table 1 illustrates one example of data currently available. Here the columns illustrate PISA summary data for Australia in 2003 and 2006 considered in terms of location. There are significant differences in achievement between students in each of these location groups.

Table 1. PISA 2003/2006 Mathematics achievement (mean scores) by location (Thomson, Cresswell, & De Bortoli, 2004; Thomson & De Bortoli, 2007)

Average Score	2003	2006
Australia Overall	524	520
OECD countries	500	498
Metropolitan Australia	528	526
Provincial Australia	515	508
Remote Australia	493	468

Goals and Intervention Strategy

SiMERR was established to carry out strategic and applied research, and work with rural communities to achieve improved educational outcomes for students.

The *vision* of the work of SiMERR is formulated in three can-do-statements:
- Parents can send their children to rural or regional schools knowing they will experience equal opportunities for a quality education;
- Students can attend rural or regional schools realising their academic potential in Science, ICT and Mathematics; and
- Teachers can work in rural or regional schools and be professionally connected and supported.

To achieve this mission, SiMERR programmes identify and address important educational issues of (i) specific concern to education in rural Australia, and (ii) national concern in mathematics, science and ICT education across Australia by working in rural schools.

Implementation and Communication

SiMERR members are involved in approximately 120 projects. While some involve small numbers of schools (often in remote areas), teachers, and students, other projects span across regions or state jurisdictions.

Many projects have national relevance, not only for rural areas but also more broadly for all Australian students. It has become clear that in working to address the needs of rural students, the findings and solutions that are emerging offer ways of enhancing student-learning outcomes in metropolitan areas as well. In an exemplary way, this is sketched below in brief descriptions of five large-scale projects.

1. National Survey of Issues in Teaching and Learning Science, ICT and Mathematics in Rural and Regional Australia (Lyons et al., 2006).
This project involved extensive questionnaire surveys of teachers and parents of students from primary and secondary schools across Australia. Every provincial and remote school, and a sample of metropolitan schools, in Australia were invited to participate in the survey. Focus group interviews were conducted with a

representative sample of teachers, parents and students from rural schools in each state.

The survey data provided critical information about key themes that are considered to be limiting student outcomes in mathematics for rural and regional Australia as well as offering some practical ways of addressing these issues. The recommendations focus on several key areas including:

- Staffing issues such as attraction and retention of teachers;
- Teacher training and qualifications;
- Professional development needs of teachers;
- Resource material needs of teachers;
- Learning opportunities and experiences of students.

2. Identifying and Analysing Processes of Groups of Teachers Producing Outstanding Educational Outcomes in Mathematics (Pegg, Lynch, & Panizzon, 2007)

This project explored factors leading to outstanding mathematics outcomes in junior secondary education for students across the ability spectrum. The focus was on the characteristics of and processes used by groups of teachers. Mathematics faculties achieving outstanding student-learning outcomes were identified by drawing upon extensive quantitative and qualitative data-bases. The study involved intensive case studies to identify faculty-level factors. Seven common themes are reported and these are the strong sense of team, staff qualifications and experience, teaching style, time on task, assessment practices, expectations of students, and teachers caring for students.

The research highlighted a number of potential important issues for schooling into the future around the needs:

- To provide opportunities to help teachers develop the knowledge and skills necessary to exercise effective leadership in the role of faculty leader;
- For early career teachers to work with and learn from experienced mid and later career teachers;
- To facilitate strong group interaction within faculties;
- For relevant school-based professional development;
- For high subject-knowledge standards for new and current teachers;
- To create a culture in which teaching and learning, rather than behaviour management, dominates all classrooms; and
- To develop common goals among teachers, students and the local community.

3. QuickSmart intervention programme for middle-school students performing at or below National Numeracy Benchmarks (Pegg & Graham, 2005, 2007)

This research programme is referred to by the generic title *QuickSmart* because it teaches students how to become *quick* (and accurate) in response speed and *smart* in strategy use. This teaching programme sought to improve automaticity, operationalised by students' fluency and facility with basic mathematics facts for those students in their middle years of schooling below national benchmarks. The programme refers to intensive focused instruction associated with the students being withdrawn in pairs from class for three periods a week over a 30-week time-frame.

The results found that improving automaticity in basic skills frees up working memory processing, enabling students to undertake more advanced tasks that were not specifically focused on during the intervention programme and these positive effects are still in play years after the intervention.

4. Maths: Why Not? Unpacking reasons for students' decisions concerning higher-level mathematics in the senior secondary years (McPhan, Morony, Pegg, Cooksey, & Lynch, 2008)

The project considers why many capable students are not choosing to take higher-level mathematics in the senior years of schooling. This lack of numbers runs counter to the national need for a highly skilled workforce to remain competitive in the global knowledge economy. Australia is facing a multi-faceted skills shortage just when there is a need for more students to leave school with a sound grounding in higher mathematics.

The results provide an important "toehold" to a number of critical issues underpinning the learning and teaching of senior mathematics in Australia. More importantly, it offers a means of connecting the learning and teaching of mathematics from the perspective of current and projected skills shortages. The project offers new insights into the problem and a platform for constructive national action.

5. Collaborative innovations in rural and regional secondary schools: Enhancing student learning in mathematics and science (Panizzon & Pegg, 2008)

This project created networks of rural teachers to form learning communities in science and mathematics. Each team of teachers in a particular school identified an important issue they believe was impeding student learning within their own school. This issue became the focus of the professional learning.

Teachers were supported at an optimum time with help varying from school to school depending on the needs of the staff and students. Support was provided by (i) consultants with expertise in curriculum, assessment, and quality pedagogy visiting and working with the teachers at key points during the eighteen months of the project, and (ii) teams of teachers met on a few occasions to share their experiences with other teachers involved in the project. These meetings were crucial because they facilitated opportunities for teachers geographically isolated to meet collectively and communicate their ideas, challenges and successes. The model of professional learning used was seen to be highly relevant and cost-effective for schools that were widely separated by distance.

Evaluation and Impact

Evaluation of SiMERR occurs through two separated but related processes. The first concerns sets of agreed milestones concerning progress on a six-monthly basis. These targets were mutually agreed to, and offer a broad context within which SiMERR attempts to address its mission. The second process is related to individual projects undertaken by academics associated with SiMERR, including those internally financed through targeted funds within the Centre or from successful contracts with funding bodies outside of SiMERR.

Tying down "impact" in such a diverse area is fraught with problems. At the heart of the work of SiMERR is building a network where teachers, educators, universities, education authorities, and communities can reflect and initiate actions on improving the current situation in rural areas for teachers and students.

There are important signs that projects are having an influence. A critical purpose of these approaches is to have an evidential basis from which informed policy decisions can be made on how funding and actions might best target the real learning needs of different groups of students. In terms of the five projects outlined above there are now:

- Recommendations to advise Federal policy as it relates to addressing inequity in rural students learning outcomes as a result of the SiMERR National Survey;
- Published books identifying characteristics of faculty departments achieving outstanding educational student learning outcomes across the student ability spectrum;
- Recommendations to guide Federal Government policy on ways to encourage and facilitate more senior secondary students to undertake high-level mathematics courses;
- Solid evidence that students (including Indigenous students) who have been performing at or below national benchmarks in numeracy for many years can be supported and show considerable improvement in basic mathematical skills and understanding;
- Evidence of the nature of the successes for rural schools in solving issues relevant to them in teaching mathematics and how this professional learning can be encouraged and sustained.

As a result of SiMERR activities there is now: a large number of research activities that have been awarded to academic groups (SiMERR Hubs) to support rural schools, teachers and students; a stronger national awareness and a higher media presence about rural concerns in education; and stronger support for professional teaching associations to provide more targeted professional support for teachers in rural locations.

Challenges and Further Steps

SiMERR has sought to influence positively the educational outcomes of rural students whose educational opportunities do not match those of their metropolitan counterparts, and to reduce the professional isolation of teachers. This has been pursued through targeted research programmes to inform education policy, teaching practice and pedagogy, professional development programmes, and teaching and learning interventions for teachers and students.

Engendering and maintaining a climate of collaboration and trust among universities and their staff, education jurisdictions and their schools, teachers and communities around the country is critical to the success of the SiMERR operation. The capacity to engage schools to participate in activities is built on networking with teachers, education authorities and professional education organizations. These fruitful connections are important in building trust and rapport between schools and researchers, and they also facilitate discussion and collegiality. They are also critical players in attempts to move the findings of research to scale (see Cobb and Smith, this volume).

The model of collaboration developed by SiMERR is in contrast to the highly competitive practices of universities in other fields of endeavour within Australia. It is recognised as important for the long-term that individual universities are supported to maintain and celebrate their own integrity, identity and successes as well as those achievements of the collective.

SOUTH KOREA: NURI – NEW UNIVERSITY FOR RURAL INNOVATION

South Korea has achieved extremely strong national growth that has resulted in rapid economic development since the 1950s. However, Kitawaga (2006, p. 15) pointed out that although dramatic, the post-war revival in South Korea was more about the developments in Seoul rather than more broadly across the nation. A recent consequence of this imbalance has seen the Government launch major decentralisation reforms with strong regional development policies.

In order to address this issue in 2004, the South Korean government allocated over one billion US-dollars and embarked on a series of projects referred to as the New University for Rural Innovation (NURI) initiative. At the Kongju National University NURI funds were allocated to address rural education issues. In particular, the focus was on the development of a new programme as part of the Bachelor of Education programme for prospective secondary teachers.

Impulse for the Initiative and Challenge

In the PISA results of 2003, South Korean fifteen year olds were in the top group of countries in science, mathematics and problem solving, placing them second overall (OECD, 2006). However, the same PISA data show that there is a low level of satisfaction towards schooling, and parents have their children undertake extensive learning activities out of school time. It is estimated that 73% of students in primary and secondary education receive private tutoring after school hours with an additional 2.2% of GDP (Gross Domestic Product) allocated to private tutoring. Private outlays for education in South Korea are the highest of any OECD country (OECD, 2006, p. 29).

Also of concern was the achievement gap between students enrolled in rural schools as compared to those in urban areas. While the average score in mathematics for South Korean students was 542 compared to the OECD average of 500, those students who lived in communities of 3,000 or less had an average score of 447. This score compared unfavourably with the OECD average for small communities of 477. These data in mathematics were further confirmed (Im, 2007a, p. 99) when an effect size gap between rural and regional students of 0.62 was identified.

Goals and Intervention Strategy

The NURI project includes:
- A programme for developing ICT pedagogical skills, involving effective ways of using computers in education as well as the establishment and management of teaching and learning systems for e-learning.
- A programme for developing understanding of rural societies and rural schools by exploring issues of rural education more explicitly.
- A programme to help prospective teachers adjust to rural schools and rural life by volunteering for service in rural communities. This involves voluntary work in educational contexts, practicum in rural schools, inviting rural school students to university campus, development of a practicum manual for classroom teaching in rural schools.
- A programme for enhancing pedagogical skills in classroom teaching built around microteaching and the establishment of two laboratories for analysis of classroom behaviours.
- A programme for learning foreign language, improving teaching school subjects in English, visiting rural schools in foreign countries.
- A programme for enhancing teacher knowledge and enhancing success rates for securing teaching positions.

Implementation and Communication

This programme was developed as the education part of the four-year NURI project and was based on NURI-TEIC (Teacher Education Innovation Centre) team's meta-analysis (Im, Lee, & Kwon, 2007) of previous studies with Korean participants on the educational gap between rural and urban areas in Korea. The programme designed built on the current programme for prospective teachers with an additional emphasis on developing teachers' classroom skills, involving learning and practising ICT, and learning to understand rural societies and schools in a deeper way.

Findings from the implementation program are discussed regularly with representatives of the seven Departments at Kongju University as well as colleagues at other universities who are interested in or who have made contributions to the initiative. Also the NURI-TEIC team maintains strong cooperative relationships with over 80 community schools, the Chungnam Provincial Office of Education, and the Kongju city office.

Evaluation and Impact

There are numerous ways in which the initiative is being evaluated (Im, 2007b). Most important is that the number of prospective teachers who are passing tertiary examinations is increasing over the rate in years prior to the advent of the programmes. There has also been a commensurate increase in the number of other certificates of attainment, such as ICT competencies, than in the past.

As part of the evaluation of the impact of the NURI project, the prospective teachers and secondary students have undertaken surveys. In both cases, the results of the surveys have identified improvements in perceptions. Prospective teachers have responded positively to the changes in the course finding it more useful and relevant than in the past. Secondary students reported that the prospective teachers were more knowledgeable about them and their communities and they were more appreciative of the efforts of the prospective teachers than in the past.

Challenges and Further Steps

The NURI project at Kongju National University is set to finish during 2008. However, plans are in place to apply for a further 5-year (2009-2014) post-NURI grant to the South Korean government. The strength of this new application is on the track record evidence accumulated. Clearly, many of the benefits of the current funding in terms of course structures, resources and data on prospective teachers' development will still be available. However, it remains to be seen at this stage whether all the initiatives currently being undertaken can be maintained in the absence of such funding.

One of the great challenges lies with the evaluation of the initiative. Firstly, it takes time for the full effect of a programme, such as described, to be felt. Secondly, outcomes in complex areas such as addressing issues associated with poor student learning in rural education are subject to many competing and complex interactions. These often fall outside of the education focus of the intervention and have much to do with the socio-economic viability of the particular rural area. Hence, attributing success of a program or otherwise is difficult. These issues increase the complexity of providing justifications for the spending allocated and proof that tax-payer money is not wasted.

COMPARATIVE ANALYSIS, IMPLICATIONS, SYNTHESIS

The motivation for the initiatives described in this chapter was a perceived deficiency in mathematics (and science) skills of particular groups of students, following large-scale international surveys or state-wide surveys revealing regional inequalities.

The surveys also revealed some structural problems with the overall education system. In Austria, it was mostly the system's fragmentary nature and lack of researchers in science education. In Ohio, they identified a lack of overt standards of education upon which to make judgements. In Australia, there was no specific national research body or a comprehensive national agenda dedicated to improve the learning outcomes of rural students. For South Korea, it was the difficulty of attracting and retaining teachers in rural areas.

In all four cases, a government intervention followed. Improving the teaching and learning of mathematics and science became a matter of national policy and funds were allocated to begin to address the situation. National or regional centres were established and initiatives to improve standards or to address inequities commenced.

Participants and Their Roles

The relevant environments and participants in these initiatives were the federal and state government bodies (which financed and oversaw these initiatives), education experts from selected universities and (in the case of Australia) professional teaching organisations, and targeted schools (their teachers and students, partially also parents and community groups). Significantly, all initiatives build on forming regional and district structures incorporating local stakeholders (see also Cobb & Smith, this volume).

In three countries, a particular university was given the role to set up a centre, which coordinated the entire initiative. In the Australian and the Austrian case, the leading university linked, through a tender process, to the involvement of academic staff from several other universities and other institutions throughout the country.

Initial participation in all four countries involved only particular schools and particular segments of the student population. In Austria, initially it was upper secondary schools and later extended to all secondary schools, and finally also to primary schools, in Ohio students of middle-school years, in Australia samples of rural and regional schools and teachers were chosen for different initiatives, and in South Korea secondary schools were involved.

Goals and Intervention Strategy

In all four countries, the overall goal was to improve the teaching and learning in mathematics and science by improving the teachers' skills, establishing teacher networks through which teachers could communicate with each other and with education experts and, in some cases, establishing a nation-wide support system (Austria) or state-wide standards (Ohio).

In Austria, the major goals were: the initiation, promotion, dissemination, networking and analysis of innovations in schools (and to some extent also in teacher education institutes) and recommendations for a support system for the quality development of mathematics, science and technology teaching. Innovation was the key word; participation was voluntary. Teachers and schools defined their own starting points and goals and were then supported by researchers and expert teachers. The emphasis was on supporting teams of teachers from one school rather than individual teachers. The teachers and schools retained ownership of their innovations. Another important aim of the Austrian initiative was networking.

In Ohio, the overall goal was to improve the mathematical and scientific knowledge of students, and to achieve equity among students of different ethnic groups as well as gender equity through inquiry-based instruction. The Discovery project also aimed to develop state-wide standards for mathematics and science teaching. This involved developing shared methods of teaching science and mathematics rather than standardising a curriculum. A particular focus was on educating the teachers (through Summer Institutes) in how to implement inquiry-based instruction in the classroom.

In Australia, the goal was to enhance teacher growth in rural and regional areas and to maximise high levels of teaching competence and student learning outcomes in the critical subject areas of mathematics, science and ICT. An additional goal was to set up teacher networks to help address professional isolation. The focus on science and ICT in addition to mathematics gave teachers a greater chance of interacting with a critical mass of teachers.

The South Korean initiative aimed to enhance pedagogic skills of prospective teachers. Focus was primarily on improving their e-learning skills, their understanding of rural societies and rural schools, and enhancing their microteaching skills.

The theoretical frameworks used differed among these countries. However, all these programmes built on the assumption that teachers play a key role in the intended change; thus they (as well as their students) were seen as active constructors of their knowledge. In Austria, the theoretical framework built on the ideas of action research and systemic approaches to educational change and system theory. In Ohio, it revolved around inquiry-based instruction. In Australia, it involved implementation of teaching methods and approaches supported by empirical evidence through ongoing research into teaching mathematics and helping move these activities to scale. In South Korea, various programmes to enhance teacher knowledge and microteaching skills, as well as their sociological understanding of rural schools and communities drawn from empirically based information from the research literature.

The four countries used various intervention strategies to achieve their goals. The broader the goal the more strategies were used. Thus in Austria the primary strategy was to support teams of teachers from a particular school through different programmes. The broader focus was on promoting innovation, dissemination of knowledge, networking, carrying out analyses of innovations, and building a sustainable support system. In Ohio, the primary strategy was to involve teachers in Summer Institute programmes to improve their competence and content knowledge. An additional focus was on developing standards. In Australia, the intervention strategy involved collaboration with communities, educational authorities, professional associations and industry groups with the aim to develop solutions to problems faced by teachers, particularly those who are professionally isolated. In South Korea, the main strategy comprised programmes of pre-service education to complement and extend the traditional mathematics preparation programme and programmes to help prospective teachers adjust to rural schools and rural life. The latter involved practice-teaching periods in rural schools, inviting rural school students to university campus, and development of practice-teaching manuals for classroom teaching in rural schools.

Collaboration, Communication, Partnership as Central Notions

In all four countries, there was a strong emphasis on *collaboration* and *communication* between various social agents during all stages of the initiative. Long-term collaboration was seen as an essential basis for reform and sustainability of any reforms. By comparison, working on short-term professional learning activities was implicitly understood as being ineffective and highly unlikely to result in sustained improvements and teacher growth.

Collaboration in Austria took the form of a wide network of people and institutions involved in the initiative. Staff and members of IMST supported large numbers of teachers over several years. To facilitate communication between teachers they also worked out inter-disciplinary connected concepts for basic education at the upper secondary level for four subjects. There was collaboration among teachers and staff members from the first meeting during which goals and research questions were established to guide later analyses of the effectiveness of new teaching methods. Teachers also helped each other as "critical friends". The various programmes operated as small professional communities that supported each participant. Furthermore, regional networks were established through which experienced teachers were able to disseminate their knowledge to other teachers. Communication was also facilitated by the IMST website which includes all documents written by staff members and teachers, by an annual conference, and by a quarterly newsletter.

In Ohio, the collaboration brought together in-service teachers and university researchers and science educators who constructed professional development courses and taught in those courses. The teachers participating in the programme observed each other teaching classes and providing feedback to each other. After the course they met several times during the following year and exchanged their experiences. The emphasis on collaboration and communication also extended to classroom practice where inquiry-based methods encouraged interaction and communication between students. The collaboration also involved the partnerships between teachers and parents in science education. Finally, the Discovery project also led to the establishment of multiple professional development initiatives and networks of K-16 institutions through a variety of state and national funding mechanisms.

In Australia, the emphasis on collaboration led to the formation of a National Centre at the University of New England and the nation-wide network of "hubs" located at several universities. The hub members communicated with each other and regularly met to share ideas. Each hub has its own website with hyperlinks to other websites and to SiMERR website. Hub coordinators, disciplinary groups and project teams also regularly conducted video meetings. In 2005 and 2007, the Hub members and relevant stakeholder organizations met at National Summits. Other meetings of members across Hubs coincided with disciplinary-based conferences or workshops. The collaboration and communication between various stakeholders was also stimulated by a higher media profile of issues of rural and regional education.

Collaboration and communication is also an important issue in the South Korean initiative. It involves the relevant branches of the South Korean government, education experts at Kongju National University, educators with common interests from other universities, province education authorities, Kongju city office, and teachers. The purpose of the work with these groups is to inject different perspectives into the development and implementation of the program as well as ownership of ideas across a broad base helping ensure greater flexibility and cooperation at all levels of society.

In all cases, the *exchange of experiences* played a predominant role among teachers, among university staff, as well as between teachers and university staff.

Evaluation and Impact

Evaluations were an *integral part* of each initiative and these evaluations revealed positive outcomes. In Austria, evaluation processes were a central part of IMST from its inception. The focus was on process-oriented, outcome-oriented, and knowledge-oriented evaluation. It involved both self-evaluation and evaluation by external experts. Independent international experts also assessed the overall effectiveness of IMST. The results of these evaluations indicated that the intended goals were achieved in the most part as well as possible improvements for the continuation of the project. Answers to teachers' questionnaires indicated a high level of satisfaction with the programme. Recently, more research on students' and teachers' beliefs and growth is being carried out.

In Ohio, the evaluation of the programme centred on the test results of students in the Discovery Project as compared with students/classes who were not involved. Students in the programme performed better. Further, when school cohorts were compared, schools with a higher percentage of Discovery trained teachers also performed better than those schools that had fewer trained teachers in the programme.

In Australia, members of SiMERR have been involved in approximately 120 projects throughout Australia across the four discipline areas. The results so far indicate that projects are beginning to have a major influence on teacher professional learning resulting in improved student-learning outcomes with increased effect-size measures. Interestingly, in a number of cases, data are showing that the policy announcements, programmes and the solutions developed for rural areas are also having an impact when implemented on student-learning outcomes in urban areas.

The evaluations of the NURI project in South Korea show an increasing number of prospective teachers who are passing tertiary examinations. Surveys of both prospective teachers and students indicate high levels of satisfaction. Teachers find the courses relevant and secondary students report that the teachers are more knowledgeable of them and their communities. The midterm report of the NURI project received strong endorsement from the Ministry of Education of South Korea.

All projects delivered positive results that demonstrated growth for participant teachers and their students. These data appear to have had a three-fold impact, on policy, institutions, and the way teachers fundamentally work. These examples make the point that when programmes are well developed and involve collaboration, communication and learning partnerships, real changes can be expected. However, crucially they still depend on continuing government support and in most cases the allocation of funds.

The experiences documented above indicate that the presence of an intensive evaluation not only allows stakeholders to react to the results of the evaluation during a project (in the sense of a formative evaluation) but also – partly related with the former aspect – increases the likelihood that a programme (or parts of it) is prolonged or enlarged, or implemented in the system in one form or another.

CONCLUSION

What are the lessons learned from comparing these four cases? Although, challenges arose from similar sources of data (e.g., studies like TIMSS, PISA, or national tests), each country has its own genuine context and specific strengths and weaknesses. Also, those people charged with leading changes in these countries bring different skills, and knowledge and belief sets to each enterprise. Thus projects invariably evolve to take different forms, emphases and directions. However, in all programmes, *collaboration, communication*, and *partnerships* were seen to have played a major role, not only between teachers and university staff members of the programme but also within these groups.

Close *collaboration* was an important aspect among stakeholder groups formed by the *ministry* (policy, funding), the *school practice* (teachers), and the *scientific community* (teacher educators, researchers). An intensive kind of evaluation yielding relevant data to all parties concerned and the discussion about the results seems to enrich the quality of the project and contributes to its further support by helping to shape policy decisions.

Communication occurred in: oral forms (e.g., workshops, seminars, conferences, and network meetings); written forms (e.g., newsletters, reflective papers by teachers, other publications); and electronic forms (e.g., materials on a website, chat-rooms, emails, etc). This open approach is supported by research on "successful" schools showing that such schools are more likely to have teachers who have continual substantive interactions (Little, 1982) or that inter-staff relations are seen as an important dimension of school quality (Pegg, Lynch, & Panizzon, 2007; Reynolds et al., 2002). Similar results can be found in other national programmes (e.g., in Germany, Prenzel, & Ostermeier, 2006).

A very important issue concerned the insight of the significance of *partnerships*. Teachers were not only seen as "participants" of teacher education but as crucial "change agents" of the education system, regarded as collaborators and experts. Consequently, they were expected and encouraged to take an active role in their professional growth. Teachers were critical stakeholders who were themselves learners in the process of bringing about improved learning environments for students. Teachers needed to be sensitively supported by teacher educators through research-based advice and evaluation that gave meaningful feedback to teachers and generated new scientific knowledge.

Specific *recommendations* are not easy to make since conditions and contexts in these countries are very different. However, it seems worthwhile that in any major intervention the following questions are considered: What kind of active role do national programmes ascribe to their teachers as change agents? How can exchange of experiences among teachers and researchers be promoted? How can communication (e.g., using stakeholder networks) and infrastructure (e.g., national centres) be established and further developed? How can evaluation contribute both to the improvement of the projects' process and their impacts as well as to the generation of scientific knowledge (which in turn contributes to the improvement of interventions)? How can the collaboration between different stakeholders of nations' educational change, above all, policy makers, teachers, and researchers be designed in a way that all parties – including the students and parents – feel empowered by national initiatives? How does the involvement in such (mostly) larger intervention projects change the role of researchers? What form should evidence take to provide reliable feedback about the success or otherwise of the initiative? How can the sustainability of innovations be supported and evaluated (see also Lerman & Zehetmeier, this volume)? We believe that mathematics educators need to be active participants in the discussion of these kinds of questions.

REFERENCES

Altrichter, H., Posch P., & Somekh, B. (1993). *Teachers investigate their work. An introduction to the methods of action research*. London: Routledge.

Beeth, M. E., McCollum, T. L., & Tafel, J. (submitted). Systemic reform of science and mathematics education in Ohio (US). In R. Duit & R. Tytler (Eds.), *Quality development projects in science education. Special issue of the International Journal of Science Education* (planned for 2008).

Deci, E. L., & Ryan, M. R. (Eds.). (2002). *Handbook of self-determination research*. Rochester: University Press.

Fullan, M. (1993). *Change forces. Probing the depths of educational reform*. London: Falmer Press.

Glenn, J. (Chair). (2000). *Before it's too late:* A Report to the Nation from the National Commission on Mathematics and Science Teaching for the 21st Century. Education Publications Center, US Department of Education.

Hattie, J. A. (2003). *Teachers make a difference: What is the research evidence?* Australian Council for Educational Research Annual Conference on: Building Teacher Quality.

Heffeter, B. (2006). *Regionale Netzwerke. Eine zentrale Maßnahme zu IMST3. Ergebnisbericht zur externen fokussierten Evaluation. Ein Projekt im Auftrag des BMBWK* [Regional networks. A main measure of IMST3. Report on the results of the external focused evaluation]. Vienna: BMBWK.

Im, Y.-K. (2007a). *Issues and tasks of rural education in Korea*. Paper presented at the International Symposium on Issues and Tasks of Rural Education in Korea and Australia, Kongju National University, November.

Im, Y.-K. (2007b). *New University for Regional Innovation (NURI), Teacher Education Innovation Centre (TEIC) project: Midterm report.* Report prepared for the Korea Research Foundation, NURI-TEIC at Kongju National University, South Korea.

Im, Y.-K., Lee, T.-S., & Kwon, D.-T. (2007). *Analysis of the educational gap between rural and urban areas.* Kongju, Korea: Kongju National University, New University for Regional Innovation – Teacher Education Innovation Centre (NURI-TEIC).

Kitawaga, F. (2006). Using the region to win globally: Japanese and South Korean innovations. *PASCAL Observatory, November.*

Krainer, K. (2001). Teachers' growth is more than the growth of individual teachers: The case of Gisela. In F.-L. Lin & T. Cooney (Eds.), *Making sense of mathematics teacher education* (pp. 271–293). Dordrecht, the Netherlands: Kluwer.

Krainer, K. (2005a). Pupils, teachers and schools as mathematics learners. In C. Kynigos (Ed.), *Mathematics education as a field of research in the knowledge society. Proceedings of the First GARME Conference* (pp. 34–51). Athens, Greece: Hellenic Letters (Pubs).

Krainer, K. (2005b). IMST3 – Ein nachhaltiges Unterstützungssystem [IMST3 – A Sustainable Support System]. *Austrian Education News (Ed. BMBWK), 44,* December 2005, 8–14. (Internet: http://www.bmukk.gv.at/enfr/school/aen.xml (last search: Jan. 7, 2008).

Krainer, K. (2007). Die Programme IMST und SINUS: Reflexionen über Ansatz, Wirkungen und Weiterentwicklungen [The programmes IMST and SINUS: Reflections on approach, impacts and further developments]. In D. Höttecke (Ed.), *Naturwissenschaftliche Bildung im internationalen Vergleich. Gesellschaft für Didaktik der Chemie und Physik. Tagungsband der Jahrestagung 2006 in Bern* [Scienctic literacy in international comparison. Society of didactics of chemistry and physics. Proceedings of the annual conference 2006 in Bern] (pp. 20–48). Münster, Germany: LIT-Verlag.

Krainer, K., Dörfler, W., Jungwirth, H., Kühnelt, H., Rauch, F., & Stern, T. (Eds.). (2002). *Lernen im Aufbruch: Mathematik und Naturwissenschaften. Pilotprojekt IMST²* [Changing learning: Mathematics and science. The project IMST²]. Innsbruck, Austria: Studienverlag.

Little, J. W. (1982). Norms of collegiality and experimentation: Workplace conditions of school success. *American Educational Research Journal, 19,* 325–340.

Lyons, T., Cooksey, R., Panizzon, D., Parnell, A., & Pegg, J. (2006). *Science, ICT and mathematics education in rural and regional Australia:* Report from the SiMERR National Survey. Canberra: Department of Education, Science and Training.

MCEETYA (2006). *National Report on Schooling in Australia 2006, Preliminary paper.* Retrieved September 2007, from http://www.mceetya.edu.au/mceetya/anr/

McPhan, G., Morony, W., Pegg, J., Cooksey, R., & Lynch, T. (2008). *Maths? Why not?* Final Report prepared for the Department of Education, Employment and Workplace Relations (DEEWR), March. Available at: http://www.aamt.edu.au/AAMT-in-action/Projects/Maths-Why-Not

Müller, F. H., Andreitz, I., Hanfstingl, B., & Krainer, K. (2007). *Effects of the Austrian IMST Fund of instructional and school development. Some results from the school year 2006/2007 focusing on teacher and student motivation.* European Association for Research on Learning and Instruction (EARLI): 12th Biennial Meeting Conference, Budapest, Hungary, August 28–September 1, 2007.

Mullis, I. V. S., Martin, M. O., Beaton, A. E., Gonzalez, E. J., Kelly, D. J., & Smith, T. A. (1998). *Mathematics and science achievement in the final year of secondary school: IEA's Third International Mathematics and Science Study.* Boston: Center for the Study of Testing, Evaluation, and Educational Policy, Boston College.

NCEE – National Commission on Excellence in Education (1983). *A nation at risk* [On-line]. Available: http://www.ed.gov/pubs/NatAtRisk/title.html

OECD (2006). *Sustaining high growth through innovation: Reforming the R7D and education systems in Korea.* Economic Department Working Papers no. 470, Paris: OECD.

Panizzon, D., & Pegg, J. (2008). *Collaborative innovations in rural and regional secondary schools: Enhancing student learning in Science, Mathematics and ICT.* Report submitted ASISTM Curriculum Corporation. Podcasts of Teacher comments available at http://www.une.edu.au/simerr/Science/index.html

Pegg, J., & Graham, L. (2005). The effect of improved automaticity and retrieval of basic number skills on persistently low-achieving students. In H. L. Chick & J. L. Vincent (Eds.), *Proceedings of the 29th Conference of the International Group for the Psychology of Mathematics Education* (Vol. 4, pp. 49–56). Melbourne, Australia: University of Melbourne.

Pegg, J., & Graham, L. (2007). Addressing the needs of low-achieving mathematics students: Helping students 'trust their heads'. Invited Key Note Address to the 21st Biennial Conference of the Australian Association of Mathematics Teachers. In K. Milton, H. Reeves, & T. Spencer (Eds.), *Mathematics: Essential for earning, essential for life* (pp. 33–46). Hobart: AAMT.

Pegg, J., Lynch, T., & Panizzon, D. (2007). *An exceptional schooling outcomes project: Mathematics.* Brisbane, Australia: Post Press.

Prenzel, M., & Ostermeier, C. (2006). Improving mathematics and science instruction: A program for the professional development of teachers. In F. Oser, F. Achtenhagen, & U. Renold (Eds.), *Competence oriented teacher training. Old research demands and new pathways* (pp. 79–96). Rotterdam, the Netherlands: Sense Publishers.

Prenzel, M., Schratz, M., & Messner, R. (2007). *Externe Evaluation von IMST3. Bericht an das Bundesministerium für Unterricht, Kunst und Kultur* [External evaluation of IMST3. Report to the Federal Ministry for Education, the Arts and Culture]. Vienna: BMUKK.

Reynolds, D., Creemers, B., Stringfield, S., Teddlie, C., & Schaffer, G. (Eds.). (2002). *World class schools. International perspectives on school effectiveness.* London: Routledge.

Roberts, P. (2005). *Staffing an empty schoolhouse: Attracting and retaining teachers in rural, remote and isolated communities.* Sydney: NSW Teachers Federation.

Specht, W. (2004). Die Entwicklungsinitiative IMST²: Erwartungen, Bewertungen und Wirkungen aus der Sicht der Schulen [The development programme IMST²: Expectations, experiences and results seen from the perspective of schools]. *ZSE Report 68.* Graz, Austria: Zentrum für Schulentwicklung.

Thomson, S., & De Bortoli, L. (2007). The *PISA 2006 survey of students' scientific, reading and mathematical literacy skills Exploring Scientific Literacy: How Australia measures up.* Melbourne: Australian Council for Educational Research.

Thomson, S., Cresswell, J., & De Bortoli, L. (2004). *Facing the future: A focus on mathematical literacy among Australian 15-year-old students in PISA.* Camberwell, Melbourne: Australian Council for Educational Research.

Vinson, A. (2002). *Inquiry into public education in New South Wales Second Report September 2002.* Retrieved August 2005, from www.pub-edinquiry.org/reports/final_reports/03/

von Glasersfeld, E. (Ed.). (1991). *Radical constructivism in mathematics education.* Dordrecht, the Netherlands: Kluwer.

Wagner, S., & Meiring, S. P. (Eds.). (2004). *The story of SUSTAIN: Models of reform in mathematics and science teacher education.* Columbus, Ohio: Ohio Resource Center for Mathematics, Science, and Reading.

Willke, H. (1999). *Systemtheorie II: Interventionstheorie* [System theory II: Intervention theory]. 3rd ed. Stuttgart, Germany: Lucius & Lucius UTB.

Zammit, S., Routitsky, A., & Greenwood L. (2002). *Mathematics and science achievement of junior secondary school students in Australia.* TIMSS Australia Monograph No. 4, Melbourne: Australian Council for Educational Research.

John Pegg
National Centre for Science, ICT and
Mathematics Education for Rural and Regional Australia
University of New England
Australia

JOHN PEGG AND KONRAD KRAINER

Konrad Krainer
Institut für Unterrichts- und Schulentwicklung
University of Klagenfurt
Austria

SECTION 5

TEACHERS AND TEACHER EDUCATORS AS KEY PLAYERS IN THE FURTHER DEVELOPMENT OF THE MATHEMATICS TEACHING PROFESSION

GERTRAUD BENKE, ALENA HOŠPESOVÁ, AND MARIE TICHÁ

12. THE USE OF ACTION RESEARCH IN TEACHER EDUCATION

In recent years, action research has found its way in teacher education and mathematics teacher development in particular. In this article, we introduce action research in its various conceptions. We go on to present studies on the way action research is used in prospective and practising teacher development. The article addresses issues educational researchers have to attend to, when supporting teachers in engaging in action research projects, and discusses what accounts of action research should attend to enable future meta-analysis on the impact of action research. The article includes two examples of a support system of action research, one from Austria, detailing an organizational structure to enable many teachers at different schools to engage in action research, one from the Czech Republic, presenting the results of a project of close collaboration of teachers with researchers, engaging in joint reflection.

INTRODUCTION

In the last two decades *action research* has seen a revival in the educational community at large (see e.g., Adler, Ball, Krainer, Fou-Lai, & Novotná, 2005; Krainer, 2006).[1] With new research on educational change small and large, the important *role of the participants* in enabling, shaping and maintaining change processes has become more and more recognized (Fullan, 2001; Wagner, 1997). For example, the Czech psychologist, Helus (2001, p. 37) emphasized: "A successful effort to change the school is only possible if the teacher becomes its leading agent". Seeing the practitioners at each system level as the pivotal figures of change processes, it is not surprising that action research is seen as one lever to better practices in education. Action research promises to support the change of the most important change agents, to ground changes locally where change is necessary, and to bring about personal growth that affords the retention of the pursued changes.

In this chapter, we will explore the use of action research in professional development generally and then specifically in mathematics education. To that end, we will first introduce action research and then discuss the educational context of

---

[1] For example, in their presentation of the discussions of a thematic group on teacher education of the European Research in Mathematics Education conference (ERME), Krainer and Goffree conclude that they see an "[I]ncreased importance of action research as the systematic reflection of practitioners into their own practice" (Krainer & Goffree, 1999, p. 230).

K. Krainer and T. Wood (eds.), Participants in Mathematics Teacher Education, 283–307.

action research: What are the problems action research is meant to solve, what is the context of action research? Next, we will elaborate on different conceptions and core elements of action research, to provide a framework for the subsequent discussion of action research in mathematics education and in the professional development of mathematics teachers. The examination will be completed by the presentation and discussion of two programmes or projects that use action research for (practising) teacher training in Austria and the Czech Republic. Finally, we will raise concerns and issues about using action research in teacher development in mathematics education.

CHARACTERISTICS AND ASPECTS OF ACTION RESEARCH

Action research is most frequently traced back to the work of the sociologist Kurt Lewin (1948), who constructed a theory of action research in the 1940s, although elements of the theory can be found earlier the writings of John Dewey (for a discussion of pre-cursors see Masters, 2000). Lewin incorporated key elements of today's action theory. He pointed out the importance of the *participation of practitioners in all phases of the research process*, and saw action research as a cyclical process of planning, action, and evaluation giving way to further planning, action and evaluation. Action research in education in particular is typically traced back to the teacher-researcher movement of Stenhouse (1975) who envisioned teachers taking an active role in curriculum development. Yet, action research – under the guidance of researchers – was already used in the field of curriculum studies in the late 1940s and early 1950s. Since then, action research in general (and in various forms, see below) has formed its own specialized community within educational research, with heterogeneous strands, since local (national) developments are strongly influenced by nationally prevalent theories (e.g., the approach of "Handlungsforschung" in Germany). Altrichter (1990) presents an account of the way action research fits into the framework of academic research in general. As of today, there is no unanimous definition of action research, Adler (1997, p. 99) even argues that there is a "war of definition" being waged. Given the different perspectives and associated claims and value judgments (see below), she and others (e.g., Jaworski, 1998) make the case that other terms like "practical inquiry" are more appropriate.

However, action research conceptions share a number of *characteristics*, even though they may differ in the importance of the adherence to any of them. Other *aspects* are notable in that they are contested or changing. In the following, we will present such characteristics and aspects.

(1) In any conception, action research is practical in the sense that it is a form of *localized problem solving*. Something in the local setting is meant to be understood and if needed, changed for the better. Closely tied with this general goal is the participation of the actors of the specific social system. This has a twofold background that may gain different emphases. On the one hand, there is the social theoretical stance, that participants have a unique access and

knowledge about their local system, and are thus in a position to generate a more in depth-insight into their system (Cochran-Smith & Lytle, 1990, 1999). On the other hand, there is the theoretical and practical insight gained from organizational studies (Fullan, 2001; Weick, 1995), that successful change processes are dependent on the support of the agents of a social system. Engaging agents in action research not only generates different kinds of knowledge, but also transfers ownership of the resulting recommendations for change to these agents and increases the likelihood that positive change will happen. Thus, action research can be framed as libratory (Braz Dias, 1999; Gutiérrez, 2002).[2]

(2) In practice, action research conceptions differ in how much *responsibility* is conferred to the practitioners, in our case the teachers. Different terminologies have been used to differentiate different conceptions of the interaction between for example, university based researchers and school based teachers. One extreme conception of action research portrays a more traditional relationship between researcher and practitioner in which the researchers pose a problem, "do the research" (in communication with the practitioner) and ask the practitioners to validate the results and implement suggested changes. Another form of relationship sees the researchers and the practitioners as true collaborators who are constantly in a process of a joint construction of meaning about the situation at hand, its problems and possible solutions. This position entails that the localized working theories of action of the practitioners are just as valued as established academic theories. Both practitioner and researcher are seen as having different ways of seeing the world, with the practitioners' perspective being validated by their histories of action. The quality of proposals for change are validated by the emergent practice (or falsified by the failure of the system to respond as expected). Finally, action research can also be understood as practitioner research without the necessary and continuous involvement of any academic researcher. Instead, researchers may be consulted at all phases of the action research process, but the ownership of the overall enterprise rests firmly with the practitioners. Of course, one may envision many forms of cooperation and collaboration in between these extremes.

Accounts of actual action research usually show the teacher to be more active than in the first conception; teachers are at least thinking or reflecting on their own practices. But theoretical discussions on the breath of action research may frame almost any valued aspect of teacher participation in a research project under the heading of action research. In all these cases, the practitioners are called on to help to approach local problems with locally suited solutions.

(3) A further important element of any conception of action research is the notion of *reflection* (Fendler, 2003), which can also be traced back to Dewey.

---

[2] For an early discussion of action research striving for a liberating education see Carr and Kemmis (1986).

Elliott's definition of action research frames it as teachers' systematic reflection of professional situations aiming on their further development (Elliott, 1981, p. 1). Despite the importance of this concept, there is little theoretical and philosophical exploration to be found about what exactly "reflection" is supposed to mean. Instead "reflection" is generally taken to be a self-evident expression, which stands in a critical juxtaposition to action. Theoretical explorations frequently take up Schön's (1983) notion of *reflection in action*, *reflection on action* and *reflection for action* as well as *reflection on reflection in action*. With these notions Schön explores the relationship between "knowing" and "doing", touching on many of the issues, which were later discussed by Suchman (1987) and others exploring situated cognition. We always know more about a situation than we can express. At the same time, we never know everything. When a situation surprises us, and we are able to attune our plans or unfolding practice to address surprising or new insights into a situation, Schön is talking about "reflection in action". Reflection on action and reflection for action both take place outside the pressures of having to act at the (extended) moment of reflection. The first (reflection on action) is looking backwards, thinking about what happened. Reflection for action is looking forward, carefully considering plans for action (instead of just reacting). Finally, reflection on reflection in action captures the careful consideration of what happened in reflection-in-action. Why did something surprise us, what elements of our (automatic) practice made us not expect something, how did we deal with it, what made it (un)successful? An example: If one is planning a unit taking into consideration what may happen, one is reflecting for action. If the unit took place, and one ponders about reasons for unexpected student answers, one is reflecting on action. If a usually engaged student becomes disruptive in class, and one manages to think about why and take immediate action based on the assumed cause that she was frustrated due to a misunderstanding (rather than responding with some routine reaction to disruptive students), one is reflecting in action. If one later on reflects why one would come to the conclusion that she was frustrated, and whether the chosen strategy was effective, one is reflecting on reflection in action.

One further important element of Schön's account of a reflective practitioner was his conception of a *reflective practice* as a practice in which a practitioner is engaged in a constant conversation with his or her problem situation. Reflection on action and reflection for action may lead to promising plans for action. But in practice, life will always surprise us; thus expert performance requires being able to adjust, to be flexible, to reflect in action – and to learn from our adjustments to situations by reflecting on reflections in action (Doerr & Tinto, 2000). The complexity of practice portrayed by Schön is a beautiful rendering of the situation teachers face in their daily lives, in which complex social systems with multiple actors make the outcome (or the process) of most plans quite unpredictable.

(4) The *content*, action research is concerned with, varies greatly. In terms of subject area, action research projects were originally more prevalent in the humanities (especially concerned with literacy), but now many action research projects are also found in mathematics and the sciences. Nevertheless, if one looks into articles published in the journal *Educational Action Research*, one will frequently find no indication of the subject considered in an action research project in the abstract, and sometimes not in the entire article.[3] We believe that the omission of the subject area is not accidental. Action research as classroom teacher research will usually problematise some aspects of classroom practice. This puts the interaction between student(s) and teacher or just between students into focus. Thus, action research projects frequently set out with pedagogical issues of classroom management and organization, or the projects trial some previously conceived classroom innovation and seek to confirm or disabuse the beliefs inherent in the conception (e.g., Watling, Catton, Hignett, & Moore, 2000). Ball (2000) points out that it takes time, experience, and self-confidence to see classroom problems as possible problems of subject didactics and/or ultimately as problems of a lack of subject knowledge.

(5) The notion of reflection and action is also closely tied in with the conception of the place of *beliefs* in a theory of change. In general, action research projects follow explicitly or implicitly the assumption that – when considering the relationship between beliefs and practice – practice takes precedence. In other words, it is assumed that a change in beliefs will not necessarily bring about a change in (teaching) practices, but changes or difficulties in teaching practices may change beliefs about a situation (or lead to a quest for understanding and a new formation of beliefs) (Fullan, 2001). Thus, action research projects do in general not set out to teach someone available expert knowledge on any particular problematic issue. If teachers are collaborating with or guided by researchers, expert knowledge might take the form of already synthesized and contextually sensitive contributions or advice, the breath of possibly available information is usually not made explicit; and reports of action research projects frequently do not present a survey of available literature on the issue the action research project was concerned with. Knowledge imported concerns foremost methodological issues about the action research itself. How does one plan an action research project, how does one collect evidence and arrive at an interpretation? The theoretical section of action research projects frequently addresses this theoretical and methodological frame of "an" action research project in terms of its process characteristics.

(6) Conceptions of action research differ also in the significance they assign to *peer support* and *collaboration*. Early reports of action research and reports of action research in mathematics teacher education in the Journal of Mathematics

---

[3] We have made a data-base keyword search for mathematics in the last ten volumes of *EAR*; the results show only 6 articles from 1997-2006.

Teacher Education (e.g., Halai, 1998) present action research projects of individual teachers. In recent years, more and more reports are about collaborative action research, like action research projects of groups of teachers, and some conceptions consider such a cooperation as a necessary element of an action research project. No person lives for him- or herself, no practice can be transformed in a social vacuum. Sustainable change needs a community. While those conceptions do not refute outright that action research could be done by individuals, the emphasis on (peer) feedback and discussion with peers as a structural prerequisite for an honest self-appraisal, for example, for self-reflection, render solitary projects as less potential and hence less desirable.

(7) A notion not frequently used or reflected upon in articles on action research in mathematics education, but which we deem as an important conceptual contribution is Elliott's notion of *first and second order action research*. With this distinction, Elliott (1991) makes the point that doing action research is different than facilitating practitioners in their efforts. Thus, researchers collaborating with teachers on action research project have a different job, and need to reflect on different issues than the teachers engaged in action research (Losito, Pozzo, & Somekh, 1998).

In the last decades, we have seen the call for and implementation of *"reforms of education"* in many educational systems around the world. Fullan (2001, p. 37) argued that many of these reforms failed and that "change will always fail until we find some way of developing infrastructures and processes that engage teachers in developing new understandings". Furthermore, "[c]hange as a change in practice entails changing (1) materials, (2) teaching approaches, (3) beliefs" (Fullan, 2001, p. 70). "To change beliefs, people need at least some experience of new behavio[u]ral practices they can discuss and reflect on" (Fullan, 2001, p. 45). Action research offers a way to address this need. What is it about action research, which lets some researchers see so much promise to change education practice, while others set their stakes somewhere else?

A strength of action research is that the "action" it is concerned with is the (behavioural) situation and the behaviour of the teacher engaged in improving the situation at the same time. Action research provides a voice for teachers to share an emic view of their experiences with other teachers and the research community at large. The sharing of experiences has raised a number of methodological questions. What is the nature of the story being shared, what makes a story worthwhile being shared? "When does a self-study become research?" (Bullough & Pinnegar, 2001) Is this research at all? And if it is to count as research proper, what does this entail (Altrichter, 1990; Melrose, 2001)?

In general, from the point of view of some researchers, questions raised about self-studies (Feldman, 2003) – and thus about action research, which can be seen as a specific form of self-study[4] – are the same as those being raised about case studies, with the key question of "What is this a case for?", addressing generalizability. A related issue is the ability to particularize the general (case) to a particular context or particular issues.[5] Where one community of researchers may ask the question: "What is this a case for?", another may ask: "Does this research present enough details about a situation, to tell us something worthwhile about the context we are concerned about (e.g., mathematics teaching)?"

All of this, of course, presupposes the stance of the educational researcher or the research community asking for contributions of teacher research to comply with the standards of research in general, and thus it asks for a high level of (research) proficiency of the members of this discourse community. If teachers enter into the education research community, if they raise their own voice within this community, they have to adhere. Considering the place of teacher in the educational system, this asks for a lot of competence of any one individual.

Educators who do not want to charge teachers with following all the prescriptions for doing "good, valid research" will frequently argue for substituting "action research" with less loaded expressions like "teacher inquiry" (Feldman & Minstrell, 2000). On the one hand, this will lighten expectation about "action research projects": They can be conceived as "good worthwhile projects" without falling short of standards of research at universities. Teachers engaged in such projects do not need to feel lacking. On the other hand, there are reports of many other teachers who feel self-empowered by doing research themselves on par with academic educational research. Educators who do not see action research projects necessarily as doing "research proper" usually value action research projects for their local problem solving and the professional learning happening within the course of such action research projects. Thus, they see action research more as a means to professional development than as a means to produce general and generalizable knowledge into teaching and learning.

Cochran-Smith and Lytle (1990) hold that teacher research is a different game, which follows different rules and standards of quality; it is a genre all by itself and should not be judged by time-honoured standards of educational research.

A different approach, which we turn to now, does not see teacher research as (foremost) providing new insights into teaching and learning – even though those contributions are valued – but regards teacher inquiry as a way to foster professional development. In this perspective, teacher research is not an end in itself, but the means to accomplish something else, and debates on the validity and generalizability of teacher research miss the point. The question is not about the quality of the products of teacher research, but the changes doing teacher research brings about in practitioners and their practices.

---

[4] Strictly speaking, this is not entirely true but depends on the conception of action research as discussed above. If teachers are investigating their own practice, they are engaged in self-study. This does not imply that they want to change their practice. But if self-study is instrumental in a developmental process, it turns into action research.

[5] We are grateful to Konrad Krainer for bringing up this point.

On a theoretical level, some conceptions of professional development (Bruner, 1996; Climent & Carrillo, 2001; Helus, 2001; Jaworski, 2003; Krainer, 1996) integrate the important concept of reflection into the theoretical conception of what is required of a competent teacher – for example, they include the "competence of reflection" as a further core dimension of teacher competence theories (e.g., of Bromme, 1994; Harel & Kien, 2004).

Action Research as a Means for Professional Development in Mathematics Education

Judged from the number of articles on research methods in action research and teacher inquiry which appeared in the *Educational Researcher*, action research and teacher inquiry has encountered a growing interest in the last. As for mathematics, the *Journal of Mathematics Teacher Education* devoted an entire issue to action research and teacher inquiry in 2006 (JMTE 9.3); and action research and teacher inquiry features prominently in the *European Society for Research in Mathematics Education* (ERME), for example, in a special volume of the first CERME-proceedings (see e.g., Krainer & Goffree, 1999) and the continuous special interest group on teacher education at its conferences. Nevertheless, most papers on action research that encourage professional development of practising teachers are not presented as such. Instead, the papers focus on the problems and gains of the action research project itself, with changing practices, beliefs and understanding of the teachers being only part of the parcel. On further reflection, this mode of presentation is not surprising: Presenting action research projects as professional development enterprises objectifies teachers, and portrays them as in need of change. Putting the teacher as the learner into the centre, creating a story of learning might promote a story of a previously lacking individual's development. Given the entire philosophy of action research, such a move would counter the very approach, which rests on an appreciation of the knowledge in practice, and the practitioner as a professional. Nevertheless, papers on action research do generally report on changes of belief and practice, even though reports may vary on how elaborate those accounts are. While we have not found a systematic survey on the outcome of action research for professional development, a recent series of surveys on continuing professional development published by the EPPI-Centre (Evidence for Policy and Practice Information and Co-ordinating Centre) in London sheds light onto possible outcomes of action research.

Action research is prominent in studies on collaborative *Continuing Professional Development* (CPD). In their review of the literature on the impact of collaborative continuing professional development for teachers K-9, the CPD Review Group (Cordingley, Bell, Rundell, & Evans, 2003, p. 32)[6] reported that 26% of all the surveyed studies employed action research. In this report, action research as a method to foster collaborative continuing professional development,

---

[6] The review is not particular to mathematics, but twelve of the 30 studies with a curriculum focus on mathematics; of the 17 studies selected for an in-depth review, six concern mathematics.

is only second to Peer Coaching (30.5%) closely followed by Workshops (25%) and Coaching (25%).[7] The report (Cordingley et al., 2003, p. 4) finds that "the collaborative CPD was linked with improvements in both teaching and learning; many of these improvements were substantial". The authors report benefits to teachers with respect to self-confidence as teachers, a heightened belief in their self-efficacy as teachers, an increase in the motivation for collaborative work, and an increase in the willingness to change their practice. Likewise, students demonstrated higher motivation, better performance, and more positive attitude to specific subjects as well as more active participation. The authors also point out some important features that seem to have been *conducive* to the attainment of the positive results (and studies lacking elements were less effective):

➢ the use of external expertise linked to school-based activity;
➢ observation [e.g., teachers visiting and observing each others classroom, or researchers videotaping a lesson as a basis for further – joint – reflection];
➢ feedback (usually based on observation);
➢ an emphasis on peer support rather than leadership by supervisors;
➢ scope for teacher participants to identify their own CPD focus;
➢ processes to encourage, extend and structure professional dialogue;
➢ processes for sustaining the CPD over time to enable teachers to embed the practices in their own classroom setting"

(Cordingley et al., 2003, p. 5)

The report also highlights the importance of expert input, including subject input, if "an intervention [is] intended to achieve subject specific changes" (Cordingley et al., 2003, p. 6). Furthermore, it stresses the importance that teachers are in a position to work on their own expressed learning needs, which also entails the adoption of differentiation strategies (such that each teacher can truly work on his or her individual concerns), that the collaboration is sustained and that teachers find a place where it is save to admit needs (and report problems and possible mistakes).

While this review is very positive on collaborative continuing professional development arriving at recommendations which square with principles of action research, another review (Gough, Kiwan, Sutcliffe, Simpson, & Houghton, 2003) finds that "while student attainment and learning styles profit from reflection, self-directed learning, planned action and similar approaches, there is no clear evidence on whether these approaches influence or change the learner's identity, reflective capacity or their attitudes about learning" (Gough et al., 2003, p. 64). Yet, (changes in) identity and reflective capacity are constructs which are difficult to capture; generally reflection is still a much valued element of action research and teacher inquiry projects, more recent case studies on the use of reflection in professional development programmes are positive (Even, 2005; Scherer & Steinbring, 2006; Tichá & Hošpesová, 2006).

---

[7] Note that any study may make use of more than one type of invention.

In his review of models of professional development, Foreman-Peck (2005, p. 9) states: "Practitioner inquiry and research is a strong element in professional development courses for teachers, [and] an important part of teachers' personal professional development". The above mentioned report (Gough et al., 2003) also finds that 56% of the surveyed studies which featured professional development planning (PDP) reported on activities which occurred as part of some coursework (e.g., an action research project done as a requirement in a teacher education programme). The authors raise the question "whether the emphasis on course-specific outcomes in any way restricts the reflection that takes place as part of such interventions" (Gough et al., 2003, p. 45).

In the following, we want to discuss and problematize different aspects and dimensions of action research that feature in the literature on mathematics teacher education.[8]

(1) *Choice of a topic and temporal dimension.* The choice of the topic of action research is closely tied in with the question of where the incentive is coming from to do action research. If action research starts with the teacher, issues focus on localized, specific questions. Sometimes (e.g., Watson & De Geest, 2005) papers report that researchers defining an agenda were looking for volunteers. In general, little is said about processes and negotiations leading up to the collaboration. The same is true for the last case, when action research is done as part of some course requirement. From our own experience, we know that defining the problem such that it is "workable", that it becomes clear what issues one needs to consider, what evidence one should attend to and collect can be a difficult and time-consuming process. Additionally, questions and the corresponding action research programme may change in the process. At the same time, we found few reports on aspects addressing these issues. One notable exception is Feldman and Minstrell (2000, p. 448) who state that this first phase may take up to one year. Ball (2000) also observes that simply finding a topic may take a long time. These are important elements. We need to know more about reasonable time-spans, the time more and less experienced teachers need to become comfortable with action research or self-directed inquiry.

(2) *Authorship and theorizing the area of investigation.* As discussed above, theories on action research stress the unique characteristic of knowledge

---

[8] For the review, we systematically screened all volumes of the *Journal of Mathematics Teacher Education* (JMTE); we looked at all articles for the last 10 years of *Educational Action Research* (EAR), which were returned by a data-base search for "mathematics" (6 articles, 2 book reviews); we included the major articles which were returned by a keyword search for mathematics and "action research" in the JSTOR-database (in June 2007); we looked at articles keyworded for 'action research' in the *Proceedings of the Psychology of Mathematics Education* (PME), 2007 (none!) and the appropriate sections of CERME). This was complemented by various – but not systematically collected – articles from the handbooks of teacher education, discussions on various aspects of teacher inquiry in the *Educational Researcher* and additional information, which is grounded in our local research contexts.

generated through action research and that doing this type of research requires a different approach, which gives precedence to insights gained by a grounded or "bottom-up" perspective of a situation, clearly rejecting preconceived notions as might be engrained in theories brought in from the outside. Yet, as educational researchers, we still hope to "bridge the gap" (see also Jaworski, 2006; Scherer & Steinbring, 2006), and that those implicit theories which guide the perception and interpretation of the action researchers become explicit and thus enable, on the one hand, a communication between insights generated in the situation, and understandings found through traditional avenues and, on the other hand, a deeper understanding of possible points of view of engaged and reflective practitioners.

A theoretical-terminological framework strives to capture the different *modes of cooperation* between teachers and researchers, and thus which logic and aims was given precedence (the logic of a certain practice in a field, or the logic of research). Thus one may talk about *participatory research* (with teachers/practitioners taking part in a research project), about *cooperative research* (with teachers/practitioners cooperating, such that each may reach their individual goals) and *collaborative research* (in which both try to learn from each other and both strive to achieve their shared, negotiated goals). All conceptions have clear consequences for authorship, decision processes and the status of academic and practitioner theories. Theorizing what research does to a field this way, also highlights how issues of authorship, aims of the enterprise and considered knowledge are interwoven.

Most papers written in peer reviewed journals end up being written by the researchers collaborating with teachers.[9] Thus, even if action research (depending on the definition) may strive for an emic perspective, reports on action research are usually presented "from the outside". This does not imply a second-order action research perspective, since only a minority of articles focuses on the particular practice of the researcher in enabling and supporting action research projects. Rather, most projects are still reported from an "objective", almost outside point of view. There are some exceptions (see e.g., the report of a teachers' book project in Ponte, Serrazina, Sousa, & Fonseca, 2003), but generally we found that those people, who report about their own development, came into the process as a teacher being engaged with their own practice, and ended up becoming at least part-time educational researchers (as e.g., in the case of Deborah Ball, John Mason, and Jim Minstrell). Minstrell (in Feldman & Minstrell, 2000) states in a by-line, that he became so interested that he earned a Ph.D. What does this imply about action research as a professional development incentive? And what (kind of) people will be attracted to action research? With respect to those questions, teacher inquiry required by some programme provides an interesting context, since this is one

---

[9] See also Adler, Ball, Krainer, Lin, F.-L., & Novotná (2005, p. 371) who found, that "Most teacher education research is conducted by teacher educators studying the teachers with whom they are working".

avenue in which teachers may not have chosen to pursue by themselves. This is one group which did not necessarily self-select for the substantial involvement required when questioning and researching ones own practice. Yet, so far we lack reports which attend to the more reluctant participants,[10] as well as reports which describe failures in going through an entire cycle of doing action research (a notable exception is Nickerson & Moriarty, 2005). How does one have to design a setting which encourages people not already perceiving a need to take up action research, and supports them while they struggle through the processes? What makes them drop out? (Christenson et al., 2002) When does someone become disenfranchised?

The *theoretical grounding* is quite heterogeneous. However, apart from a general grounding in core concepts of teacher education – like Shulman's (1986, 1987) account of teacher competences – there are two concepts which seem prominent: Schön's (1983) account of reflection, and Wenger's (1998) notion of communities of practice. As noted by (Cordingley, Bell, Thomason, & Firth, 2005), most action research projects are done in a collaborative context. If the action research itself is not performed by a community of inquiry (García, Sánchez, Escudero, & Llinares, 2006; Jaworski, 2006), it studies the impact of the action researcher on a community (of learners). In both cases, peripheral members of some learning community are learning to become full members of a (reflective, self-directed) community of practitioners. If – in the education context – the communities of practice (Lave & Wenger, 1991) is conceived as a community of inquiry (Jaworski, 2006), one can see action research becoming subsumed in a more encompassing concept which integrates the stances of action research with a social learning and social community point of view. Elliott (1991) has maintained that action research is a group effort. However, given the above mentioned "war of definition", with the resulting uncertainty what someone means when they speak of action research, as well as the critique ventured again the notions of "action" and "research" in "action research", we may see a (terminological) *move to "communities of inquiry"* which at the same time stresses the importance of having communities support change, and avoids the problems of using a contested notion. However, it remains to be seen how such a conception will deal (or exclude) the individual teacher doing research (or inquiry) on their own classroom without being embedded in a community.

(3) *Mathematical content.* In the articles we found reporting on action research in mathematics teacher education, mathematics and mathematical concepts form an undercurrent, a background, which is frequently not elaborated on. Mathematical concepts turn up in discussed classroom transcripts, to explore teachers' thinking and practice (and to ground teachers' joint reflection, see e.g., Goodell, 2006) and to discuss missed and taken up opportunities to learn. Nickerson and Moriarty (2005) discuss the importance of subject matter

---

[10] Ross and colleagues discuss that low self-efficacy of teachers leads them to avoid engaging in action researcher (Ross, Rolheiser, & Hogaboam-Gray, 1999).

knowledge for the practice of their teachers. In their report, they talk about Habor View teachers, who had a comparably high level of subject knowledge at the beginning of the project, and the Palm teachers, who did not (Nickerson & Moriarty, 2005, p. 133):

> Our analysis suggests that teachers' knowledge of mathematics affected their collective control over decisions related to the mathematics program. Habor View teachers felt empowered to alter the curriculum. Palm teachers did not feel that they could. Increased mathematical knowledge supported teachers' recognition of the need for assistance.

While this claim seems plausible, one has to consider that teacher training differs vastly across the world. What are the necessary thresholds to empower teachers to feel comfortable to make the "right choices"? How much knowledge is "enough"? And how can we support teachers to become aware that they (may) have "enough" (in their context!) – despite recognizing that there is still more to be learnt?

(4) *Success and failure stories.* In mathematics teacher education, action research projects are usually presented by a number of case studies which demonstrate *successes* (with examples focusing on subject didactical elements). Studies focus on "what happens" during the action research projects, and the resulting changes. To enable future systematic meta-analyses, reports should be more detailed about contextual elements like processes leading up to the action research projects (subject selection, negotiation of topics, relationship between researcher-teacher, kind and extent of external support) as well as elements of the unfolding processes (time-spans). So far, we know little about "drop-outs", possible particular characteristics about or histories of those teachers who volunteer to undertake action research projects, and of what happens "after". Not knowing about the necessary time investment for different groups of teachers (stratified by experience, attitude and other possible factors) as well as the related outcome, we cannot gauge the relative impact of different conceptions of action research or other similar approaches (e.g., self-study) as professional development. In particular, it is still an open question as to how much (little) input and direction one needs to provide, in order to reach the reported positive benefits.

TWO EXAMPLES OF ACTION RESEARCH PROJECTS

The following two examples present first a case from Austria of a support system for teachers to engage in action research projects of their own choosing. The second case is taken from the Czech Republic, and presents a project, in which teachers were supported to collaboratively reflect and further develop their mathematics teaching. Thus, both cases can be seen as being at very different ends of a continuum (or continuous space): in the Austrian case, teachers (individuals or teams of teachers) choose topics of their own interest to work on. Their reports are rarely concerned with questions of didactics of mathematics; much more common are action research projects which trial the use of some teaching method (e.g., group work, or self-directed learning environments). In the Czech case, practitioners were invited to work on several topics (application, grasping of situation, problem posing, and geometry) and teachers then decided to focus on part-whole relation and fractions. Thus, it was much more oriented towards a common topic, while supporting teachers in their work and individual development. And it was naturally more concerned with didactics of mathematics.

Austria: The IMST Project[11]

In order to promote teacher development in mathematics and the natural sciences, the Austrian ministry of education launched the IMST3 project (Innovations in Mathematics, Science and Technology Teaching, 2004-2009; Krainer, 2007) which provides as one measure a fund for teacher research. This fund succeeded the IMST² project (2000-2004), which already supported teachers doing action research (Altricher, Posch, & Somekh, 1993) of their classrooms, schools or educational aspects concerning an entire region (Krainer et al., 2002). In both phases, the IMST project invited teachers, and teams of teachers (of the same or different schools) to submit project proposals for a one year project (with the option to submit a proposal to continue or extend already running projects). With the IMST3 project (and a growth in size of participants), the application to the fund makes use of an already highly structured online submission form, which asks, for example, how gender issues are attended to, and how people intend to evaluate the results of their changes or the state of affairs. Project proposal workshops across the country offer advice for teachers who find the required definition of their projects difficult. Moreover, since 2006 it is possible to participate as a teacher or team with the purpose of developing a project (proposal) to be submitted the following year.

Taking in account the primary area of expertise of the involved teacher educators, at the beginning the fund set out to support teachers of college-bound high school students and to a lesser degree 9th to 13th grade students in general. In 2004, the call was extended to lower secondary schools. In 2007 elementary school teachers were included for the first time. Thus, in 2007, the call for projects became open to mathematics and science teachers at all grade levels.

The project proposals are evaluated by educators and mentor teachers; projects may be accepted with recommendations for further explication or changes. Each year about 150 projects are accepted. The contract with the teachers provides them with a budget for project expenses (as defined in the project proposal) and a small monetary compensation. It requires them to participate in two workshops and to submit a project report at the end of the year. Teachers are invited to a start-up-day, in which they are introduced to their advising teams, a specific advisor teacher (one

---

[11] Note that the article of Lerman and Zehetmeier (this volume) also reports on the IMST project. However, their presentation does not address the details of the fund presented here.

for about seven projects) and two other team members. These advisor teachers are experienced teachers at schools or teacher education institutes. Within this year, they attend two project workshops of their choosing out of, for example, an orientation workshop, a writing-workshop, an evaluation workshop, or a gender workshop. Throughout the year, they are asked to hand in an "action plan" (including their evaluation), which is discussed with their specific advising teacher. Likewise, the project report at the end of the year may be commented on and be revised before it is accepted by the advising teachers, and eventually be published in the internet. Thus, the fund provides some direction while clearly setting out the requirement to have teams of teachers work on issues of their own choosing. The support of the advising teacher focuses mostly on running the project: stating clear goals, working out a plan to proceed, planning the evaluation, and writing up the experience. Above and beyond teachers can consult experts to work on additional questions.

In the four years of running the fund, we encountered many of the same issues and concerns noted in the literature above:

- Action research requires a lot of time and energy from teachers. Thus, asking teachers to volunteer undertaking an action research project usually leads to a self-selection of already engaged and enthusiastic teachers.
- In schools in which principals supported teachers and they were embedded in a community of like-minded teachers, teachers were able to effect substantial changes, for example, introducing a new student-centred feedback culture in the school, or introducing observations of each others teaching. In other schools, changes were restricted to the respective classroom.
- In a series of interviews (Benke, Erlacher, & Zehetmeier, 2006), we found that experienced teachers, who had tended to self-critically question their own teaching, reported a heightened sense of self-confidence due to the project. They felt more assured that they were on the right track, which also allowed them to be more assertive in discussions with colleagues.
- We did not observe Fullan's or Elmore's problem, but it is certainly something to keep in mind: "It is a mistake for principals to go only with like-minded innovators. As Elmore (1995) puts it: '[S]mall groups of self-selected reformers apparently seldom influence their peers.' (p. 20). They just create an even greater gap between themselves and others that eventually becomes impossible to bridge" (Fullan, 2001, pp. 99-100 and 148).
- As has been found elsewhere, the projects dealt more with pedagogical questions than with content-related ones (as e.g., mathematics). In one case, in which a mathematics teacher educator invited teachers to use materials he had developed explicating core conceptual elements, many teachers stopped posing their own questions, they "executed" the materials without realizing that the materials did not require "standard" pedagogical or didactical approaches. In other words, starting with "teacher problems" affords side-stepping mathematical didactical issues.

- In the IMST-fund projects, many teachers started out with a vision what they wanted to work on. Yet, in order to afford a systematic, data-driven exploration for the required evaluation, most of them still needed to further explicate "the problem" to make it concrete enough to be able to look for evidence for some claim. Other teachers – who had less experience with a research point of view, before becoming interested in submitting a project proposal – needed substantial support to turn a vague interest in "working on their teaching" into a concrete project idea which they could state in a project proposal.

- The very contextual and locally grounded nature of the projects led to a flower garden of initiatives. Teachers enjoyed sharing their experiences, but working on different sites and starting with different problems made joint efforts for evaluation across contexts almost impossible. Thus, in most schools local teams designed their own instruments for assessment addressing their very specific goals. In general, that led to a multitude of small, locally significant findings, which addressed different aspects of enjoying, learning and doing mathematics across different age levels and school types. Taken together with the national context, which does not require state wide centralized tests at any time during schooling (which could for example measure achievement gain scores), it was not possible to make coherent statements on the overall impact on learning of the fund without a further massive intervention into those classrooms. Instead IMST had to content itself with measures of attitude, self-confidence, and subject-related anxiety. In these measures, IMST classes on average performed significantly better than the average Austria mathematics class (of that age group and school type; Andreitz, Hanfstingl, & Müller, 2007). However, the participating teachers usually demonstrated high levels of job motivation and interest already when entering the projects, thus the good results may be due to the special self-selected group of teachers.

- Each project had to hand in a report at the end of the year. Reports can have various purposes, which might at times conflict with each other. The report should present the project to the public, at the same time, writing is a means to engage in reflection. In general, teachers reported that this is the most difficult step of the entire project. Teachers (in Austria) are not used to write, reflective accounts of their classroom practices or projects. Retrospectively, teachers uniformly valued the experience as a vital piece of their learning from the project (see also Schuster, 2008).

- Benke (2004) found a marked difference between those project reports (of the precursor of the IMST project, IMST[2]) which were written by individuals and those which were written by teams – the latter included almost no reflective elements; teams tended to report on the results of reflection, but did not mirror the process of reflecting in writing. Moreover, the project reports of teachers reflect the value judgements and judgements of relevance of the writing teachers. These may at time be quite at odds with judgements of relevance of researchers or educators.

298

- An open issue is the further use of the project reports. The reports are all published on the webpage for all projects. Teachers and their school enjoy having the project reports for internal and external communication purposes. Yet teachers are not prone to look up, what someone else has done or to learn about another project. IMST is presently working on a strategy to better disseminate the project reports to interested teachers – which is incidentally an issue action research, as a strategy for professional teacher development still needs to take up. Even if problems are locally grounded, and each community of inquiry needs to find their own answers to their own problems, the answers of the others make us richer, and we need to learn from them as well.

Czech Republic: A Comenius Project on Understanding of Mathematics Classroom Culture

The intervention into professional teacher education reported here was developed within the scope of a more encompassing international project on "Understanding of mathematics classroom culture in different countries". Within this project, it was decided to collect video records of teaching episodes. Although originally not intended, these episodes became core elements of joint reflection and development of the participating teachers in the national and international meetings. Instead of videotaping a "regular classroom teacher", the project team began to carefully discuss and then plan individual lessons which covered the required curriculum. Thus, lessons turned into "teaching experiments" for all participants. The topic that was selected jointly for such an inquiry approach was one of the most difficult concepts in mathematics education at primary school level – the concept of fractions.[12] Thus, the Czech team agreed that the experimental teaching should focus on: (a) the creation of the notion of the part and the whole, and (b) the continuous enrichment of various modes of representation and interpretation.

The cooperation in the Czech team gradually settled roughly on the following routines:

- Preparation of the teaching experiments usually began at a joint meeting of the Czech team of teachers and researchers. The group discussed the topic of the upcoming experiment, the potentialities of the use of various methods and techniques, and the mathematical content in greater detail if necessary. The topic of the experiment usually addressed the needs of the teacher who would then conduct the experiment in his or her class.
- The teaching experiment was usually realized by one teacher in her class. If two of the teachers were teaching the same grade, the experiment was carried out by both of them. After the joint session, the preparation and lesson planning of the teachers was individual.

---

[12] Many teachers tend to use a schematic approach and so they focus on drills of numerical operations with fractions, and students usually master these operations relatively quickly. But, if we investigate the level of students' conceptions of fractions, we often find out that it is very low (Tichá, 2003).

- The experimental teaching was video recorded by one researcher using a camcorder. During the project, the researchers made 25 video recordings of lessons (or parts of it). The intrusion into the course of the lesson was minimal as the students became accustomed to being video recorded.
- The teacher who had taught the recorded lesson was the first to watch the recording and to select interesting segments which to discuss with colleagues. She consulted with the researcher who made the video recording about her choice of episodes before sharing with her colleagues.
- The selected video episodes were (sometimes repeatedly) watched as a group but reflected upon individually by all members of the team. Therefore, all the members of the team were prepared for subsequent joint reflection.
- The selected video episodes formed the basis for joint reflection of the whole team. These teacher discussions were usually recorded by the researchers, which enabled them to conduct a follow-up analysis of the joint reflection.
- Several episodes were also jointly reflected by the international team.

Throughout the project, the teachers, who taught at different grades levels, gradually began to change their perspective on the meaning and essence of mathematics education; in addition the researchers found their own understanding of the school practice was also changing. In joint reflections on these short video episodes, the teachers and researchers discussed, for example, possible approaches to teaching a certain topic and sources of various beliefs. After some time of close cooperation, the teachers began to recognize their different teaching styles and philosophies of school mathematics, didactical approaches, subject matter knowledge and so on (Bromme, 1994) as fundamental sources of differences; and they used these insights when reflecting on their different professional orientation and undergraduate training. The discussion usually centred on two areas: (i) students' work, and (ii) teachers' opinions on how to approach a specific topic. What was surprising to the researchers was that the whole discussion was penetrated by considerations on the essence and meaning of mathematics education and also by considerations on the sense of joint reflections. They concluded that joint reflection should be used in particular for: (a) cultivation of the teachers' behaviour and actions, (b) formation of more perceptive teachers' approaches to students' ways of thinking and the ability to utilize them in teaching, and (c) becoming more conscious of moments valuable from the point of view of students' cognitive processes. However, teachers still needed some guidance on how to reflect on pedagogical situations (Scherer, Söbeke, & Steinbring, 2004). The project team recommends that prospective teachers should be systematically prepared for reflections on teaching and should be familiar with the relevant literature. Practising teachers (participating in the project) themselves admitted that they would appreciate some instruction and guidelines that they could follow in order to have more productive reflections. However, they would not like them to be too binding and admitted they were not really sure they would make use of these instructions.

Using video recordings made it possible to create and cultivate skills in assessment of students' answers, to diagnose students' mistakes and their sources. Given the support of joint reflection, participants learned to exert deeper insight into the content taught and into how content was grasped by the students. Although the aim of the project was not to support professional development of the participating teachers, significant changes in their perception of teaching of mathematics could be observed, as well as changes of the teachers' reflections (Tichá & Hošpesová, 2006), and the teaching itself. We have to stress that the changes of the teachers differed depending on their personalities, education, experience, age and so on. We illustrate this idea with the following brief accounts of the change made by *two teachers* participating in the project, Anna and Cecily:

Anna was entering the project with the stated intention to change her teaching of mathematics. The video recordings of her lessons taken at the beginning, reveal her considerable mastery of methodology and her effort to prepare for students such problems that they would be able to solve them without greater difficulties. However, she always tried to ensure that her students would also understand the process of numerical operations that they were taught.

After a few meetings of our team, Anna stopped looking for merely effective methodological approaches. In her lessons, she began to create problem situations for which the solution would promote understanding and lead to building of concepts. For example, she found her inspiration in German textbooks and prepared the teaching experiment for her second grade students dealing with nonstandard procedures of subtraction. She asked her students to decide which of a set of given calculations were correct and also to explain why. As for the justifications of the students, she was not satisfied merely with calculation of the result. She insisted that the explanation should be comprehensible to all other students. The goal of teaching in the second grade is usually a practice of addition and subtraction of numbers up to 100. It is by no means usual to ask the students to develop their own procedures or to explain unusual procedures. In the discussion on the issue she stressed that she wanted to promote understanding of the counting procedures and realized how her students would cope with the problem. In the joint reflection, she stressed that she had no experience with such a type of problem; and her satisfaction with the students' performance was visible; the lesson is analysed in greater detail in Tichá and Hošpesová (2006). After that experience, Anna returned to the problem several times, modified it and followed her pupil's development. Her action research served her actual practical needs.

Our second example tells of *Cecily*, who entered the project as a regular teacher with a solid knowledge about teaching and mathematics and who was interested in learning more about different approaches and representations and in further developing of her own abilities. For her, participation in discussions was a stimulus for further studies. Gradually, her interest moved from the effort to "show something", to a search for problems, misunderstandings and their sources and causes. She started to propose content and methods of investigations, sometimes to suggest modifications of the conditions of performed research. For example, she carried out her own instruction experiment with an entire class. Immediately after the lesson, she suggested a repetition of this experiment with a group of six students, which allowed studying individual processes. Another time, she suggested a modification of the research performed with teachers for her students. After a reflection of this teaching episode, she suggested to jointly reflect on the same episode with other participants (Tichá & Hošpesová, 2006). During the cooperation, Cecily entered her PhD study.

Cecily constitutes an example for the claim that those teachers who are strongly invested in action research or reflective inquiry are prone to go on for further study to become a "true researcher" – in which they might leave the non-academic teaching profession (this has not happened in this case – yet). For this teacher, the participation and collaboration in the Comenius team meant a great challenge for her further education (Tichá & Hošpesová, 2006). This is also attested in her written self-reflections.

After the first year of the project, Cecily wrote:

> Before starting the project I didn't know what to expect at all. I just knew that it was something about mathematics. I wasn't able to imagine the reason or the aim of the project. I told myself that I would see.

After three years, she commented:

> [...] for me it was very interesting to meet teachers from other countries and compare our teaching experiences and opinions. I started to think about what we should have to prepare for our presentation. [...]. I found that it was very useful to see myself as another person during discussions with my colleagues because it is one of the ways of improving my work and thinking about myself differently.

And after beginning her doctoral degree programme, she reflected:

> When watching the video, it is not easy to separate the outer and inner view of my activity during the lesson (compare this with the above). I think that it is impossible to see oneself as another person. When watching the recorded lesson, I relive the whole lesson step by step again and again. I can see what I could not see during the lesson itself, I can find out why the students misunderstood, but sometimes, despite all my effort, I do not know why something happened the way it happened and why some misunderstandings both of the students and myself could not be solved. I am not sure whether my conjecture is correct; it seems probable to me. It is really useful in this position to have a view of another person who can see the matter in a different way, and the subsequent discussion can lead to finding the solution. When analysing our own lessons and behaviour, we can discover many things. At certain moments, I might think that there is nothing more to analyse, but the view of other people and the discussion with them shows that there are matters that I haven't noticed.

SUMMARY – THE CONTRIBUTIONS OF ACTION RESEARCH AND OUR EXPERIENCE

Looking back, we find ourselves still very much at the beginning. Practitioners and educational researchers working with action research are generally positive about their experiences, even though the objectives of researchers and teachers seemingly so similar – to improve teaching and achieve higher standard of education – are vastly different. In general, researchers look for answers to theoretical questions while teachers deal with practical problems. For *teachers* doing action research, it brings about a change of understanding and assessing of (a) their own role, (b) what is essential for their work, (c) their own professional knowledge, and it brings about (d) a new way of reflecting their own practice. To *researchers*, it means (a) a deepening of understanding of processes, which take place at mathematics teaching, (b) improvement of quality of teacher competence assessment (from intuition to junior researcher), (c) possibility to influence teacher competences, and (d) improvement of didactic research.

But as reflected above, the strong and theoretically well supported tenet to work with problems located at the chosen sites, precludes any easy systematic evaluation of the overall impact of action research and the differential contribution of specific implementations. Moreover, the practice-theory problem, that is the question of how to communicate insights from practice and insights from educational research at large – in particular the community of mathematics didactitians – between the communities of practitioners and researchers, is very much at the heart of effective action research.

In brief, action research remains a promising strand of professional development and education research, which still has to prove itself. However, regardless of the specific contributions of action research to professional development, engaging in action research forces the educational researcher to consider many questions very much at the heart of educational research for teacher development and learning in general; for example: How can we examine changes in teachers' beliefs and knowledge? How can university people support teachers to reflect more deeply? What criteria are characteristic for a "reflective teacher"? A teacher has different tensions and priorities than a researcher. How does a teacher-researcher balance these tensions? How can we examine the benefit of joint reflection? And ultimately following Dewey's vision: How can we support teachers' growth to become truer to themselves as teachers and persons?

REFERENCES

Adler, J. (1997). Professionalism in process: mathematics teacher as researcher from a South African perspective. *Educational Action Research, 5*, 87–103.

Adler, J., Ball, D., Krainer, K., Lin, F.-L., & Novotná, J. (2005). Reflections on an emerging field: Researching mathematics teacher education. *Educational Studies in Mathematics, 60*, 359–381.

Altrichter, H. (1990). *Ist das noch Wissenschaft? Darstellung und wissenschaftstheoretische Diskussion einer von Lehrern betriebenen Aktionsforschung* [Is that still science? Presentation and scientific discussion of action research done by teachers]. München, Germany: Profil Verlag.

Altrichter H., Posch P., & Somekh B. (1993). *Teachers investigate their work. An introduction to the methods of action research.* London: Routledge.

Andreitz, I., Hanfstingl, B., & Müller, F. H. (2007). *Projektbericht. Begleitforschung des IMST-Fonds der Schuljahre 2004/05 und 2005/06* [Project report. Results of the research on the IMST-Fond of the years 2004/05 and 2005/06]. Institut für Unterrichts- und Schulentwicklung, Universität Klagenfurt.

Ball, D. L. (2000). Working on the inside: Using one's own practice as a site for studying mathematics teaching and learning. In E. Kelly & R. Lesh (Eds.), *Handbook of research design in mathematics and science education* (pp. 365–402). Mahwah, NJ: Lawrence Erlbaum Associates.

Benke, G., Erlacher, W., & Zehetmeier, S. (2006). *Anhang zum Projekt IMST3 2004/05. Miniaturen zu IMST²* [appendix to the project report IMST3 2004/05. Miniatures on IMST²]. Klagenfurt: Institut für Unterrichts- und Schulentwicklung, Universität Klagenfurt.

Benke, G. (2004). Dokumentenanalyse der Innovationen der Schwerpunktprogramme S1-S4 im Projektjahr 2001-02 [Analysis of the reports of the projects of the programmes S1-S4 in 2001/02]. In K. Krainer (Ed.), *Ergebnisbericht zum Projekt IMST² 2002/03* (pp. 371-398). Klagenfurt, Austria: Universität Klagenfurt, Fakultät für Interdisziplinäre Forschung und Fortbildung, Abteilung "Schule und gesellschaftliches Lernen".

Braz Dias, A. L. (1999). Becoming critical mathematics educators through action research. *Educational Action Research, 7,* 15–34.

Bromme, R. (1994). Beyond subject matter: A psychological topology of Ts' professional knowledge. In R. e. a. Biehler (Ed.), *Didactics of mathematics as a scientific discipline* (pp. 73 –88). Dordrecht, the Netherlands: Kluwer Academic Publishers.

Bruner, J. (1996). *The culture of education.* Cambridge, MA: Harvard University Press.

Bullough, R. V. J., & Pinnegar, S. (2001). Guidelines for quality in autobiographical forms of self-study research. *Educational Researcher, 30*(3), 13–21.

Christenson, M., Slutsky, R., Bendau, S., Covert, J., Dyer, J., Risko, G., & Johnston, M. (2002). The rocky road of teachers becoming action researchers. *Teaching and Teacher Education, 18,* 259–272.

Climent, N., & Carrillo, J. (2001). Developing and researching professional knowledge with primary teachers. In J. Novotná (Ed.), *CERME 2. European research in mathematics education II, Part 1* (pp. 269–280). Prague, Czech Republic: Charles University, Faculty of Education.

Cochran-Smith, M., & Lytle, S. L. (1990). Research on teaching and teacher research: The issues that divide. *Educational Researcher, 19*(2), 2–11.

Cochran-Smith, M., & Lytle, S. L. (1999). Relationships of knowledge and practice: Teacher learning in communities. In A. Iran Nejad & C. D. Pearson (Eds.), *Review of research in education* (Vol. 24, pp. 249–305). Washington, DC: AERA.

Cordingley, P., Bell, M., Rundell, B., & Evans, D. (2003). The impact of collaborative CPD on classroom teaching and learning. In *Research evidence in education library. Version 1.1.* London: EPPI-Centre, Social Science Research Unit, Institute of Education.

Cordingley, P., Bell, M., Thomason, S., & Firth, A. (2005). The impact of collaborative continuing professional development (CPD) on classroom teaching and learning. Review: How do collaborative and sustained CPD and sustained but not collaborative CPD affect teaching and learning? In *Research Evidence in Education Library.* London: EPPI-Centre, Social Science Research Unit, Institute of Education, University of London.

Doerr, H. M., & Tinto, P. P. (2000). Paradigms for teacher-centered, classroom-based research. In E. Kelly & R. Lesh (Eds.), *Handbook of research design in mathematics and science education* (pp. 403–427). Mahwah, NJ: Lawrence Erlbaum Associates.

Elliott, J. (1991). *Action research for educational change.* Milton, Keynes: Open University Press.

Even, R. (2005). Integrating knowledge and practice at MANOR in the development of providers of professional development for teachers. *Journal of Mathematics Teacher Education, 8,* 343–357.

Feldman, A. (2003). Validity and quality in self-study. *Educational Researcher, 32*(3), 26–28.

Feldman, A., & Minstrell, J. (2000). Action research as a research methodology for the study of the teaching and learning of science. In E. Kelly & R. Lesh (Eds.), *Handbook of research design in mathematics and science education* (pp. 429–435). Mahwah, NJ: Lawrence Erlbaum Associates.

Fendler, L. (2003). Teacher reflection in a hall of mirrors: Historical influences and political reverberations. *Educational Researcher, 32*(3), 16–25.

Foreman-Peck, L. (2005). *A review of existing models of practitioner research. A review undertaken for The National Academy of Gifted and Talented Youth.* Coventry, UK: Warwick University.

Fullan, M. (2001). *The new meaning of educational change* (3 ed.). New York: Teachers College Press, Columbia University.

García, M., Sánchez, V., Escudero, I., & Llinares, S. (2006). The dialectic relationship between research and practice in mathematics teacher education. *Journal of Mathematics Teacher Education, 9*, 109–128.

Goodell, J. E. (2006). Using critical incident reflections: A self-study as a mathematics teacher educator. *Journal of Mathematics Teacher Education, 9*, 221–248.

Gough, D., Kiwan, D., Sutcliffe, K., Simpson, D., & Houghton, N. (2003). *A systematic map and synthesis review of the effectiveness of personal development planning for improving student learning.* London: EPPI-Centre, Social Science Research Unit.

Gutiérrez, R. (2002). Enabling the practice of mathematics teachers in context: Toward a mew equity research agenda. *Mathematical Thinking and Learning 4*(2&3), 145–187.

Halai, A. (1998). Mentor, mentee, and mathematics: A story of professional development. *Journal of Mathematics Teacher Education, 1*, 295–315.

Harel, G., & Kien, H. L. (2004). Mathematics Ts′ knowledge base: Preliminary results. In M. J. Høines & A. B. Fuglestad (Eds.), *Proceedings of the 28th Conference of the International Group for the Psychology of Mathematics Education* (Vol. 3, pp. 25–32). Bergen, Norway: Bergen University College.

Helus, Z. (2001). Čtyři teze k tématu „změna školy" [Four theses on school reform]. *Pedagogika, 51*(1), 25–41.

Jaworski, B. (1998). Mathematics teacher research: Process, practice and the development of teaching. *Journal of Mathematics Teacher Education, 1*, 3–31.

Jaworski, B. (2003). Research practice into/influencing mathematics teaching and learning development: Towards a theoretical framework based on co-learning partnerships. *Educational Studies in Mathematics, 54*, 249–282.

Jaworski, B. (2006). Theory and practice in mathematics teaching development: Critical inquiry as a mode of learning and teaching. *Journal of Mathematics Teacher Education, 9*, 187–211.

Krainer, K. (1996). Some considerations on problems and perspectives of in service mathematics teacher education. In C. Alsina (Ed.), *8th International congress on Mathematics Education: Selected Lectures* (pp. 303–321). Sevilla, Spain: SAEM Thales.

Krainer, K. (2006). Action research and mathematics teacher education. Editorial. *Journal of Mathematics Teacher Education, 9*, 213–219.

Krainer, K. (2007). Die Programme IMST und SINUS: Reflektionen über Ansatz, Wirkungen und Weiterentwicklungen [The programmes IMST and SINUS: reflection on the approach, the effects and further developments]. In D. Höttecke (Ed.), *Naturwissenschaftliche Bildung im internationalen Vergleich. Gesellschaft für Didaktik der Chemie und Physik. Tagungsband der Jahrestagung 2006 in Bern* (pp. 20–48). Münster, Germany: Lit Verlag.

Krainer, K., Dörfler, W., Jungwirth, H., Kühnelt, H., Rauch, F., & Stern, T. (2002). *Lernen im Aufbruch: Mathematik und Naturwissenschaften. Pilotprojekt IMST²* [Learning in the making: Mathematics and the natural sciences. Pilotproject IMST²]. Innsbruck, Austria: Studienverlag.

Krainer, K., & Goffree, F. (1999). Investigations into teacher education: Trends, future research and collaboration. In K. Krainer, F. Goffree, & P. Berger (Eds.), *European research in mathematics education I.III. On research in mathematics teacher education* (pp. 223–242). Osnabrück, Germany: Forschungsinstitut für Mathematikdidaktik.

Lave, J., & Wenger, E. (1991). *Situated learning. Legitimate peripheral participation*. Cambridge, UK: Cambridge University Press.

Lewin, K. (1948). Action research and minority problems. In G. W. Lewin (Ed.), *Resolving social conflicts* (pp. 201–216). New York: Harper & Brothers.

Losito, B., Pozzo, G., & Somekh, B. (1998). Exploring the labyrinth of first and second order inquiry in action research. *Educational Action Research, 6*, 219–240.

Masters, J. (2000). The History of action research [Electronic version]. *Action Research E-Reports*. Retrieved 21.08.2007.

Melrose, M. J. (2001). Maximizing the rigor of action research: Why would you want to? How could you? *Field Methods, 13*(2), 160–180.

Nickerson, S. D., & Moriarty, G. (2005). Professional communities in the context of teachers' professional lives: A case of mathematics specialists. *Journal of Mathematics Teacher Education, 8*, 113–140.

Ponte, J. P., Serrazina, L., Sousa, O., & Fonseca, H. (2003). *Professionals investigate their own practice*. Paper presented at the CERME III. European Congress of Mathematics Education.

Ross, J. A., Rolheiser, C., & Hogaboam-Gray, A. (1999). Effects of collaborative action research on the knowledge of five Canadian teacher-researchers. *The Elementary School Journal, 99*, 255–274.

Scherer, P., Söbeke, E., & Steinbring, H. (2004). *Praxisleitfaden zur kooperativen Reflexion des eigenen Mathematikunterrichts* [A practitioners guide to cooperative reflection of ones' own mathematics classroom teaching]. Unpublished manuscript, Universitäten Bielefeld, & Dortmund.

Scherer, P., & Steinbring, H. (2006). Noticing children's learning processes – Teachers jointly reflect on their own classroom interaction for improving mathematics teaching. *Journal of Mathematics Teacher Education, 9*, 157–185.

Schön, D. A. (1983). *The reflective practitioner. How professionals think in action*. New York: Basic Books.

Schuster, A. (2008). *Warum Lehrerinnen und Lehrer schreiben* [Why teachers write]. Doctoral thesis. Klagenfurt, Austria: University of Klagenfurt.

Shulman, L. S. (1986). Those who understand: Knowledge growth in teaching, *Educational Researcher, 15*, 4–14.

Shulman, L. S. (1987). Knowledge and teaching: Foundations of the new reform, *Harvard Educational Review, 57*(1), 1–22.

Stenhouse, L. (1975). *An introduction to curriculum research and development*. London: Heinemann.

Suchman, L. (1987). *Plans and situated actions: The problem of human machine communication*. Cambridge, UK: Cambridge University Press.

Tichá, M. (2003). Following the path discovering fractions. In J. Novotná (Ed.), *International Symposium Elementary Mathematics Teaching (SEMT 05) Proceedings* (pp. 17–26). Prague, Czech Republic: Charles University, Faculty of Education.

Tichá, M., & Hošpesová, A. (2006). Qualified pedagogical reflection as a way to improve mathematics education. *Journal of Mathematics Teacher Education, 9*, 129–156.

Wagner, J. (1997). The unavoidable intervention of educational research: A framework for reconsidering researcher-practitioner cooperation. *Educational Researcher, 26*(7), 13–22.

Watling, R., Catton, T., Hignett, C., & Moore, A. (2000). Critical reflection by correspondence: perspectives on a junior school 'media, mathematics and the environment' workshop. *Educational Action Research, 8*, 419–434.

Watson, A., & De Geest, E. (2005). Principled teaching for deep progress: Improving mathematical learning beyond methods and materials. *Educational Studies in Mathematics, 58*, 209–234.

Weick, K. E. (1995). *Sensemaking in organizations*. Thousand Oaks, CA: Sage.

Wenger, E. (1998). *Communities of practice*. New York: Cambridge University Press.

Gertraud Benke
Institute of Instructional and School Development
University of Klagenfurt
Austria

Alena Hošpesová
Faculty of Education
University of South Bohemia České Budějovice
Czech Republic

Marie Tichá
Institute of Mathematics, v. v. i.
Academy of Sciences of the Czech Republic
Czech Republic

BARBARA JAWORSKI

13. BUILDING AND SUSTAINING INQUIRY COMMUNITIES IN MATHEMATICS TEACHING DEVELOPMENT

Teachers and Didacticians in Collaboration

Teachers and didacticians both bring areas of expertise, forms of knowing and relevant experience to collaboration in mathematics teaching development. The notion of inquiry community, provides a theoretical and practical foundation for development. Within an inquiry community all participants are researchers (taking a broad definition). With reference to a research and development project in Norway (Learning Communities in Mathematics – LCM) this chapter explains the theoretical notions, discusses how one community was conceived and emerged in practice and addresses the issues contingent on emergence and sustaining of inquiry practices. In doing so it provides examples of collaborative activity and the reciprocal forms of expertise, knowing and experience that have contributed to community building. It illuminates issues and tensions that have been central to the developmental process and shows how an activity theory analysis can help to navigate the complexity in characterizing development.

INTRODUCTION

This chapter focuses on *co-learning inquiry*, a mode of developmental research in which knowledge and practice develop through the inquiry activity of the people engaged (Jaworski, 2004a, 2006). This involves the creation of *inquiry communities between didacticians and teachers* to explore ways of improving learning environments for students in mathematics classrooms. Research both charts the developmental process and is a tool for development. The chapter draws on a research and development project in Norway,[1] *Learning Communities in Mathematics* (LCM), for which co-learning inquiry and communities of practice have formed a theoretical basis. The nature of inquiry, development and research in the project is used as a basis for extracting more general principles and issues.

The LCM project focused on how learners of mathematics at any level of schooling can develop conceptual understanding of mathematics that is reflected in nationally and internationally measured success. The project was rooted in

---

[1] The LCM project was funded by the Research Council of Norway (RCN) in their advertised programme Kunnskap, Utdanning og Laering (Knowledge, Education and Learning – KUL): Project number 157949/S20.

established systems and communities in which education is formalised and mathematics learning and teaching take place.[2]

The chapter weaves theory and practice to address meanings and roots of co-learning inquiry and inquiry community and issues in creating and sustaining inquiry communities for development of learning and teaching mathematics.

THEORETICAL BACKGROUND

Knowledge in Sociocultural Settings

Knowledge is seen to be both brought by people engaged in the educational process and embedded in the practices and ways of being of these people – students in classrooms, teachers of mathematics in schools, and mathematics didacticians in a university.

According to Lave and Wenger (1991), knowledge is in participation in the practice or activity, and not in the individual consciousness of the participants. "The unit of analysis is thus not the individual, nor the environment, but a relation between the two" (Nardi, 1996, p. 71). So, the practice, or activity, in which participants engage is crucial to a situated (social practice theory) perspective. Wenger (1998) talks of *belonging* to a community of practice involving engagement, imagination and alignment. The terms *participation, belonging, engagement* and *alignment* all point towards the situatedness of activity and the growth of knowledge in practice.

Within the communities of our project we recognize both *individuals* and *groups*: that is we ascribe *identity* to both. Holland, Lachicotte, Skinner, and Cain (1998, p. 5) write, "Identity is a concept that figuratively combines the intimate or personal world with the collective space of cultural forms and social relations". Identity refers to ways of being (Holland et al., 1998). We talk about ways of being in the LCM project community and in the other various communities of which project members are a part, leading to a concept of *inquiry as a way of being* (Jaworski, 2004a). Inquiry is first of all a tool used by participants in a community of practice in consideration and development of the practice, that of mathematics learning and teaching in classrooms. Inquiry mediates between the activity of the classroom and the developmental goals of participants. Participants engage in action that involves inquiry and learn from the outcomes of their action relative to established ways of being. Relationships between individuals and the communities in which they are participants are complex with respect to the forms of knowledge they encompass and growth of knowledge within the communities.

Wertsch (1991, p. 12) emphasises that "the relationship between action and mediational means is so fundamental that it is more appropriate, when referring to the agent involved, to speak of 'individual(s)-acting-with-mediational-means' than

---

[2] A copy of the project proposal can be obtained from the author by direct communication.

to speak simply of 'individual(s)'". Wertsch refers to Vygotsky's (1978, p. 57; emphasis in original) well known law of cultural development which states:

> Every function of a child's cultural development appears twice: first, on the social level, and later, on the individual level; first *between* people (*interpsychological*), and then *inside* the child (*intrapsychological*). This applies equally to voluntary attention, to logical memory, and to the formation of concepts. All the higher functions originate as actual relations between human individuals.

Such a perspective sees learning as *participation* in social practice or activity. As we participate we "take part" in the practices or activities involved, grow into those practices or activities, and learn through our doing and acting. We *engage* mentally and physically, and communicate with those around us. We use the language, words or gestures, of the practice or activity to engage and communicate. Different social groups use language in different ways and within any group we speak or learn to speak the group language.

Leont'ev (1979, pp. 47–48) writes,

> in a society, humans do not simply find external conditions to which they must adapt their activity. Rather these social conditions bear with them the motives and goals of their activity, its means and modes. In a word, society produces the activity of the individuals it forms.

Thus, activity is necessarily motivated; actions have explicit goals, and individuals engage in activity with goal-directed action leading to integral formation of "the intramental plane". Mediation is central to this formation, with the mediational means (tools, signs or other) a key focus in activity theory (Leont'ev, 1979; Wertsch, 1991).

Thus, starting from identity as meaning belonging in practice, with knowledge firmly rooted in practice (Wenger, 1998), we move to identity as the mediational formation of the intramental plane through goal-directed action (Wertsch, 1991). This extension of belonging through goal-directed action offers a theoretical grounding for the extension of alignment to critical alignment through processes of inquiry. I shall return to this below.

Co-Learning Inquiry

Co-learning inquiry means people learning together through inquiry; inquiry being a mediational tool as indicated above. The term "co-learning" comes from Wagner (1997, p. 16) who writes

> In a co-learning agreement, researchers and practitioners are both participants in processes of education and systems of schooling. Both are engaged in action and reflection. By working together, each might learn something about the world of the other. Of equal importance, however, each may learn

something more about his or her own world and its connections to institutions and schooling.

An aim of the LCM project was that didacticians from the university and teachers from schools would work together to explore and develop mathematics learning and teaching in classrooms. In such collaboration, both groups are practitioners and, since both engage in exploration and inquiry, both are researchers. We thus adapted slightly the words from Wagner (1997, p. 16) to read: "teachers and didacticians are both practitioners and researchers in processes of education and systems of schooling". The simple aim, that didacticians and teachers would work together as both practitioners and researchers, was both a guiding force for LCM and a source of tension in relation to power and hierarchy. Didacticians conceptualized the project, gained the funding, invited participation from schools, and set up the basic project design. Given such clear "ownership" of the project, could it be possible to redress the obvious hierarchy and create some kind of sharing of power and responsibility? This question will be addressed throughout the chapter with relation to the developmental project (LCM) and the theoretical perspectives outlined above.

Inquiry Community

Inquiry community was part of didacticians' vision for the LCM project; a theoretical concept rooted in wide previous experience and a number of key sources. According to Chambers Dictionary, inquiry means to ask a question; to make an investigation; to acquire information; to search for knowledge. Wells (1999, p. 122) speaks of "dialogic inquiry" as "a willingness to wonder, to ask questions, and to seek to understand by collaborating with others in the attempt to make answers to them". He emphasizes the importance of *dialogue* to the inquiry process in which questioning, exploring, investigating, and researching are key activities or roles of teachers and didacticians (and ultimately students). These activities can be discerned through the analysis of dialogue in interactions within the community.

Didacticians had distinguished between use of inquiry *as a tool* in teaching and learning, and developing inquiry as *a way of being*, so that the identity of an individual or group within an inquiry community would be rooted in inquiry (Jaworski, 2004a). Developing inquiry as a way of being involves *becoming, or taking the role of,* an inquirer; becoming a person who questions, explores, investigates and researches within everyday, normal practice. The vision has much in common with what Cochran-Smith and Lytle (1999) speak of as "inquiry as stance" – the stance of teachers who engage in an inquiry way of being. Participants in a community of inquiry aspire to develop an inquiry way of being, an inquiry identity, in engagement in practice. A focus of the LCM project was to explore what inquiry could mean in mathematics classrooms and in the activity of teachers and didacticians trying to explore development of mathematics teaching and learning.

These words suggest that we do not necessarily have inquiry ways of being in "normal" practice. Brown and McIntyre (1993), researching teaching in classrooms from observation of classroom activity and interviews with teachers, suggested that teaching and learning in classrooms develops "normal desirable states". Teachers and students find ways of working together that fit as well as possible with expectations of educational and social systems and groups and allow a workable environment. The workable environment comes from an implicit agreement between teachers and students about what is expected, and what is acceptable in classroom activity – a sort of didactic contract (Brousseau, 1984). Such ways of working and being in classrooms might be characterized as *communities of practice*[3] (Lave & Wenger, 1991), in which participants align themselves with the normal desirable state. However, the normal desirable state does not necessarily foster the kinds of mathematical achievement didacticians, and society more broadly, would like to see.[4]

In terms of Wenger's (1998) theory, that *belonging to a community of practice* involves *engagement, imagination* and *alignment*, we might see the normal desirable state as *engaging* students and teachers in forms of practice and ways of being in practice with which they *align* their actions and conform to expectations. *Imagination* ensures comfortable existence within the broader social expectations and acceptable or desirable patterns of activity.

One of the reasons for introducing inquiry as a tool – for example, in designing inquiry tasks to stimulate inquiry in the classroom – is to challenge the normal (desirable) state and question what it is achieving. For example, if students are learning mathematics through text book exercises, in which the goal is to practise skills and become fluent with operations, we might ask questions about the degree of conceptual understanding that is afforded by this practice. If the normal desirable state is to be sure that students can *do* what is required, and not to worry too much about understanding, then it could be that we are denying students an important opportunity – to understand the mathematics they are learning, and to relate particular ideas more widely, both in mathematics and in real world applications. So, we might ask, what can we do in classrooms to enable students to understand better the mathematics they meet in text book exercises? This is a developmental question. As soon as we strive to address such a question, we enter an inquiry or a research process.

In an inquiry community, we are not satisfied with the normal (desirable) state, but we approach our practice with a questioning attitude, not to change everything overnight, but to start to explore what else is possible; to wonder, to ask questions,

---

[3] The *practice* is that of engaging in classroom activity according to the norms and expectations of the particular setting in which activity takes place. Such practice is often referred to as mathematics teaching and/or learning.

[4] The TIMSS and PISA studies provide ample evidence of this, for Norway and for many other countries. See, for example, Kjærnsli, Lie, Olsen, and Turmo, 2004; Grønmo, Bergem, Kjærnsli, Lie, and Turmo (2004); Mullis, Martin, Gonzalez, and Chrostowski (2004); Mullis, Martin, Beaton, Gonzalez, Kelly, and Smith (1998).

and to seek to understand by collaborating with others in the attempt to provide answers to them (Wells, 1999). In this activity, if our questioning is systematic and we set out purposefully to inquire into our practices, we become researchers.

The community of the LCM project, set up to generate a community of inquiry, had to learn, to grow into, to come to know what it could mean to work in inquiry ways, to develop questioning attitudes, to design inquiry tasks and to foster students' own inquiry. Thus the community of inquiry was an *emergent* rather than an *established* form of practice. Inquiry practices in schools bring new elements to established practices. Thus, in order to move from a community of practice to a community of inquiry, participants will engage in existing practices, aligning to some extent with those practices, but in a questioning or inquiry mode. This has been termed *"critical alignment"* (Jaworski, 2006). It involves a recognition that within existing practices, alignment (in Wenger's terms) is essential, but if we bring a critical attitude to alignment – that is we question, we explore, we seek alternatives while engaging – then we have possibilities to develop and change the normal states.

Activity Theory as an Analytical Tool

The theoretical ideas outlined above have allowed us to conceptualise the roots of inquiry communities; we have found, however, that they do not go far enough in allowing us to analyse the various forms of data we have generated in order to cut through complexities in the various communities in which the LCM project has been embedded. For this reason we have turned to activity theory which has allowed us to inter-relate concepts of community, inquiry and critical alignment in seeking to explain issues and tensions in the project and emergent growth of knowledge.

We start here from transitions between intermental and intramental planes (Vygotsky, 1978; Wertsch, 1991) and the roles of didacticians and teachers in promoting development in mathematics classrooms. As I shall explain below, practices within the LCM project, although goal-directed, were not pre-designated. It is one thing to propose creation of a community of inquiry and quite another to realize it. A major part of our developmental activity and associated research involved exploring the creation and nature of an inquiry community. The inquiry community was emergent in the project as were the knowledge and learning associated with it. As the people of the project engaged with the activity of the project within the project community, also working simultaneously in other communities of practice (schools or university), people learned and knowledge grew. From knowledge and activity within existing communities of practice, and activity within the project, new understandings, and new ways of being and acting, emerged. In Wertsch's (1991) terms, people acting with mediational means within their respective communities, with goals relating to developing mathematics learning and teaching in classrooms, form, as part of their communicative interaction, their *inter*mental plane. We see the intermental plane to be the learning and knowing that occurs within the community as a whole, with the formation of *intra*mental planes as individuals participate in mediated action. Leont'ev's (1979) concepts of motivated activity and goal-directed action have been employed in analysis of data to chart learning in LCM (Goodchild & Jaworski, 2005; Jaworski & Goodchild, 2006), along with Engeström's (1999) *mediational triangle* and concept of *expansive learning* (see below).

CREATING AN INQUIRY COMMUNITY

Starting Points: From Motives to Goal-Directed Action

The term "community" designates a group of people identifiable by who they are in terms of how they relate to each other, their common activities and ways of thinking, beliefs and values. Activities are likely to be explicit, whereas ways of thinking, beliefs and values are more implicit. Wenger (1998, p. 5) describes community as "a way of talking about the social configurations in which our enterprises are defined as worth pursuing and our participation is recognisable as competence".

According to Rogoff, Matusov, and White (1996, p. 388), in a *learning community*, "learning involves transformation of participation in collaborative endeavour". The idea of *inquiry* community makes the nature of transformation more explicit: didacticians and teachers (and ultimately students) will engage together *in inquiry activity*. What such activity should or could consist of, and how it should or could relate to activity in existing communities of practice, the classrooms, schools and university settings was a focus of research in LCM.

LCM was motivated by developmental aims from which project activity was designed. In submitting a proposal to seek funding, didacticians proposed certain forms of action which would give shape to the project. These included workshops for teachers and didacticians in university settings, design of tasks for workshops and classrooms, teacher teams in schools for design of classroom activity, and collection of data from all activity. Thus, realization, or operationalization of the project required activity in which this design was implemented into project practice. We proposed engagement in an *inquiry cycle* (plan, act & observe, reflect and analyse, feedback) in the design process as the basis for our practical realization of a developmental research paradigm – more of this below.

The *nature* of the inquiry cycle was something that emerged in project activity. The proposed practices set out in the initial design were what engaged us initially along with the philosophy of co-learning inquiry. We (didacticians) wished to collaborate with teachers as *partners* in developing and researching mathematics teaching in classrooms (Jaworski, 1999). We wanted to try to avoid positions of offering teachers models of practice and supporting their implementation, or of bringing teachers into developmental practice after the design stage and including them only then in the action (Jaworski, 2004b). Nevertheless, the project had been conceived by didacticians: the philosophical basis of the project (in co-learning inquiry) was not negotiable but was clearly open to interpretation; the more practical aspects of project design could be negotiated but award of funding brought with it a responsibility for didacticians to achieve what had been set out, so at some levels it was not possible to start to (re)negotiate the ground with teachers. So, the initial position was that motivation for the project was in place together with some designated action and goals. A major developmental question at this stage was how to bring teachers into the project.

Action and Inquiry

In creating an inquiry community, the participants have to come together in goal-directed action. Establishing goals within a community is itself a developmental task, and goes with initial action. In their invitation to schools and teachers to participate, didacticians set out the principles of the project and outlined its operation based on workshops at the university and innovation in schools and classrooms. Schools were recruited for two years, with the possibility of a third year.[5]

So, with regard to action and goals some things were taken as basic (e.g., workshops and co-learning inquiry) and (many) others were open to negotiation and experimentation in project activity. The motivating principle on which we all agreed (didacticians and teachers) was our desire to develop better learning environments for students in mathematics at the levels of schooling with which we were associated. Unsurprisingly, the ways of thinking about this principle were deeply related to the communities of practice from which we came, and these varied across the schools and between schools and university. The knowledge we brought to the project initially was also deeply embedded in our established communities with sociohistorical precedents and cultural practices forming identities in the project.[6]

Two examples from LCM illustrate the initial position. Didacticians' planning for workshops was rooted in their philosophy for the project and their knowledge of educational literature and research relating to teacher education and developmental practice in mathematics classrooms. Some had pioneered small group problem solving in mathematics teaching at the university (Borgersen, 1994) and all believed strongly in investigative approaches to teaching mathematics at any educational level. This embedded knowledge was highly motivational in the activity that didacticians planned for workshops. Teachers came from an educational system in which initial teacher education was provided in a university with practice in schools, and continuing teacher education was provided through workshops and seminars led by teachers from the university. There was expectation by at least some teachers that didacticians would lead the way in proposing developmental activity. A quotation from a teacher Agnes, in a focus

---

[5] Eight schools from early primary to upper secondary joined the project and 40 teachers participated during three years. Some funding was given to schools to support teachers in attending workshops in school time. Further details can be found in Jaworski (2005).

[6] Norwegian culture and society along with educational values and systems were in common for most project participants (teachers and didacticians).

group interview at the end of two years of classroom activity indicates that she struggled in the beginning because didacticians did not seem to show teachers what to do.

> Agnes: [...] in the beginning I struggled, had a bit of a problem with this because then I thought very much about you should come and tell us how we should run the mathematics teaching. This was how I thought, you are the great teachers [...] (FG_060313. Translated from the Norwegian by Espen Daland)

Thus teachers found it difficult in the initial stages to initiate innovative activity in their schools because it had not been their custom to think of doing so and they expected a clear lead from didacticians. There were other barriers as well, which I shall come to.

In LCM, particularly in the first year, it was the workshops which led the way in bringing participants together to build community and create an inquiry approach to thinking about mathematics, teaching and learning. Didacticians planned tasks to stimulate thinking and action: these were increasingly influenced over three years by teachers' comments, suggestions and requests for particular forms of activity. In any workshop, teachers and didacticians worked side by side on tasks, usually in small groups, in a mode intended to create genuine collaboration in doing mathematics and talking about associated classroom issues. Groups were organized sometimes to cross school levels, at other times to align with levels more or less finely. Plenary sessions allowed input on relevant topics, presentations from school activity (often using video recordings from classrooms), and feedback from group activity and discussion.

In all workshops, mathematical tasks were chosen or designed carefully (mainly by didacticians – discussed further below) for their mathematical or didactical appropriateness for the stage of the project. In the first workshops, problems were chosen which had rich potential for stimulating mathematical thinking and which were accessible to people with widely different mathematical experience. Later, problems or tasks were designed related to curriculum topics. All work on tasks led to discussions, in both small group and plenary, around the didactics and pedagogy of creating tasks for classrooms and the associated issues.[7]

The workshops were spaced throughout the school year so that, between workshops, school activity and innovation could take place. Two forms of activity in school emerged from this opportunity. In some cases, teachers took tasks from the workshops and, with suitable modification, used them in their classrooms with students. Frequently, reporting at a workshop included presentations from such student activity. In other cases, the teacher team in a school designed a task or set of tasks to bring an inquiry approach to a curriculum topic. Varying degrees of collaboration between teachers and didacticians were involved in designing and

---

[7] A special issue of the Journal of Mathematics Teacher Education (JMTE 4-6, 2007) is devoted to research into the design and use of mathematical related tasks in teacher education.

planning such tasks. Didacticians often recorded classroom activity on video when such innovation took place, and video became an important medium in the project for sharing experience of task design and use in schools. We see here clear examples of mediation between inter- and intra-mental planes.

Thus early action took place in workshops in the university and in school activity stimulated by the workshops. Inquiry was evident in the planning process, in ways in which teachers took workshop ideas back to schools and tried out ideas in classrooms and in the developing relationships between the participants as activity progressed. I shall talk later about the outcomes of such activity in terms of participants' learning and issues and tensions which arose.

An Inquiry Cycle in the Design Process

From the beginning of the projects, *design* was a central factor in creating workshop or classroom activity and innovation. Didacticians followed loosely a *design research* approach to creating activity in workshops (Kelly, 2003; Wood & Berry, 2003). The approach was inquiry-based and iterative (plan, act and observe, reflect and analyse, feedback to planning) and was in Kelly's terms "generative and transformative" (2003, p. 3). Typically, following an initial planning meeting, a small team of didacticians took on the design of tasks according to agreed criteria for the coming workshop: for example, tasks relating to algebra at a range of levels including opportunities for generalization and justification of conjectures. The small team circulated the outcomes of their design process and these were discussed in a subsequent meeting. After the workshop, one meeting of didacticians was dedicated to reflecting on the workshop activity including outcomes from the use of tasks; these reflections feeding into subsequent decision making and planning. This inquiry process was centrally important in sharing knowledge and expertise among didacticians, stimulating creativity, generating a group outcome in terms of tasks for a workshop, and building new knowledge within the didactician community.

Didacticians envisaged a similar process for school teams planning for the classroom. Unsurprisingly, the outcomes were very variable, and related to particular school circumstances. While, in at least one school, the design cycle, in planning and implementing tasks and reflecting on their use by students, was exemplary (Fuglestad, Goodchild, & Jaworski, 2006; Hundeland, Erfjord, Grevholm, & Breiteig, 2007) in other schools planning was more ad hoc, often individual and relating to one class only (Daland, 2007). The most common practice observed was teachers' use of workshop tasks, modified for classrooms. Teachers reported in subsequent workshops from their classroom activity and the engagement of their students, and video extracts showed evidence of classroom innovation. The words of Agnes, continuing from the quotation above, testify to teacher growth through this process:

[…] but now I see that my view has gradually changed because I see that you are participants in this as much as we are even though it is you that organise.

Nevertheless I experience that you are participating and are just as interested as we are to solve the tasks on our level and find possibilities, find tasks, that may be appropriate for the students, and that I think is very nice. So I have changed my view during this time. (FG_060313. Translated from the Norwegian by Espen Daland)

Project activity in schools proved a major learning experience for didacticians as I discuss below.

A Developmental Research Paradigm

The central use of *design*, as in *design of tasks* and activity for workshops and classrooms suggested a design research approach to the project. Didacticians would design for workshops, albeit taking into account strongly the views and suggestions of teachers. Teachers would design for the classroom, drawing on experiences in workshops and inviting didacticians' contributions as appropriate. However, the theory of design research (see Wood & Berry, 2003) proved too "clinical". The design cycle, even in the activity of didacticians, was rarely conceived "up front", and emerged largely from human interactivity around the aims of the project. In schools, it was often hard to recognize clearly the elements of a cycle, intertwined as they were with the multitude of factors that make up teachers' lives.

Here we recognize the developmental nature of the projects – activity emerged from engagement. *Action, observation, reflection* and *analysis* in the inquiry/design cycle led to growing awareness of the nature of co-learning in the projects. This inquiry cycle was overtly a learning process for all participants who acted as insider researchers, inquiring into their own practices and feeding back what they learned into future action (Bassey, 1995; Jaworski, 2004b; Goodchild, 2007). The systematic nature of such inquiry varied considerably across the project.

From the beginning, didacticians collected data as far as possible from all activity – all meetings at which didacticians were present were recorded on audio, all workshop activity on video or audio, photographs were taken and documents carefully stored. Some school meetings were audio recorded and some classroom activity video recorded. A large data bank was organized to which all didacticians had access. These data were not related to particular research questions; rather research questions evolved through activity and data was used according to need. As didacticians followed up initial research questions in analysis of data and writing of papers, more refined questions emerged which then fed into future activity and further research. In this way, the emergent nature of research in the project became centrally visible, and it was possible to trace links between research activity and developmental progress.[8]

---

[8] See Gravemeijer (1994) and Goodchild (Volume 4 of this Handbook) for related and extended accounts of developmental research.

INQUIRY COMMUNITY AND OUTCOMES IN THE LCM PROJECT

The essence of an inquiry community is that, through goal-directed action in communities of practice, participants explore, inquire into, their own practice with the motive of learning how to improve the practice (see also Benke, Hošpesová, & Tichá, this volume). All participants engaged in the project community, but they were also a part of other communities which made demands on their work and lives, and the inquiry process resulted in a more critical scrutiny of the range of practices and possibilities they afforded. Thus, didacticians and teachers, in their respective established communities both aligned with the practices of those communities and looked critically at their engagement. Teachers participated in the day to day life of their schools and, integrally, explored the use of inquiry-based tasks in their classrooms and observed their students' mathematical activity and learning. Didacticians collected and analysed data and wrote research papers, as expected of university academics and, integrally, explored the design of tasks for workshops and their work with teachers in school environments to support teachers in their project activity. Activity in the project community emerged from action. Action in the form of task design led to action in a workshop, which led in its turn to action in schools, each of these feeding back to inform succeeding stages of activity. The inquiry community of the project could not be separated from the established communities of which project members were a part. Interaction between established communities, their joint enterprise, mutual engagement and shared repertoire (Eriksen 2007; Wenger, 1998), and the emerging project community led to recognition of a complexity of inter-relations, issues and tensions as the project progressed. As indicated earlier, didacticians used activity theory to try to make sense of the complexity and address issues and tensions.

Mediated Action and Engeström's Triangle

Relating to Vygotsky's (1978) law of cultural development and ideas from Leont'ev (1979) and Wertsch (1991), expressed above, a simple triangle (see Figure 1) expresses the mediational process as individuals or groups (the subject of activity) engage in action to achieve goals (the object of activity).

In all cases, according to the theory, activity is mediated: for example, activity in workshops is mediated by the tasks in which teachers and didacticians engage; activity in schools is mediated by the ideas teachers' bring from workshops related to tasks for the classroom and approaches to working with students.

However, according to Engeström (1998) this "simple" mediational triangle ignores the "hidden curriculum", the factors in education in schools that influence fundamentally what is possible for teachers and their students, and ultimately for didacticians in a developmental project such as LCM. Engeström (1998, 1999) extended the simple triangle to the more complex version (see Figure 2).

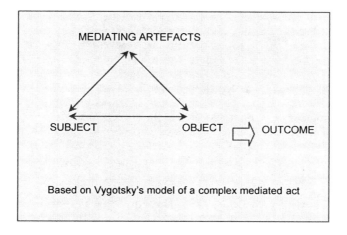

Figure 1. The simple mediational triangle.

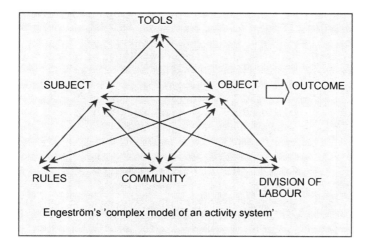

Figure 2. Engeström's mediational triangle including the hidden curriculum.

The progression from subject to object can be achieved in mediation through any of the paths indicated. Rules include the curriculum and its assessment, the ways in which school and educational systems operate, the societal and political expectations of schools and teachers. Community includes the established communities discussed above, as well as the project community in LCM. Division of labour includes the roles of participants, teachers in their school system, didacticians within a university setting; new roles developing through the project.

Issues and tensions arise when elements of the hidden curriculum challenge the achievement of goals. I use the theory of mediated action within communities of inquiry and the hidden curriculum expressed in Engeström's triangle to present some of the outcomes of the LCM project (in the rest of this section) and lead to more general observations concerning development in communities of inquiry (in the final section of this chapter).

Didacticians' Roles

A tension with which didacticians have grappled since the beginning of the project concerns a didactician's role in working with teachers, either in a workshop or in a school environment. To what extent were we to offer our own thinking, viewpoint or expertise? In one early meeting, considering our role in a workshop small group, the term "coordinator" was used and rejected. Someone equated it with being "the boss". The words "facilitator" was preferred (Cestari, Daland, Eriksen, & Jaworski, 2006). It was clear that the didactician in a group had some responsibility to ensure the smooth working of the group according to the declared task. This might mean ensuring that all participants were included in dialogue and activity. It might mean helping to keep the group focused. It might mean taking initiative to suggest roles for participants. It was agreed that it should not mean explaining the mathematics, or giving the solution of a problem. However, to what extent should a didactician participate in the mathematics? To what extent should he or she present a personal point of view in discussion? We had no clear answers to such questions. It remained for us to work according to broadly agreed principles and respond to particular circumstances. Activity was mediated through workshops tasks, experience from our activity in other communities, responses from the community of teachers present and so on. Mediation through subsequent sharing of experience with the didactician team enabled our awareness to grow and strengthened our ability to act knowledgeably according to agreed principles. For example, after one workshop, a didactician praised the actions of one colleague in enabling discussion in a small group. A further meeting was planned to watch a video recording of this group and to synthesise from the praised actions. From such interactivity over time, we learned both to live with uncertainty and to recognize the nature of growth in being a didactician in such a project. Despite saying these things so simply, this was not always a comfortable process.

The Locus of Power and Control

This issue of the didactician's role in activity with teachers adumbrates a fundamental issue that underpinned much of the LCM project – that of where the power and responsibility in the project was located, and its implications.

Undeniably, the project originated with the didacticians; they were responsible to the research council, owned both conceptualization and operationalisation to a high degree, and controlled funding. Schools had volunteered to be in the project and signed a contract with the university regarding their participation (Jaworski, 2005). Teachers participated with willingness and enthusiasm, and there was also much evidence of enjoyment. Teachers were also critical of what they experienced, and expressed points of view that were not always in accord with didacticians' concepts of events.

For example, although workshop activity in small groups which crossed school levels was presented by didacticians as valuable for understanding students' experience beyond one's own level, teachers preferred overwhelmingly to work with colleagues at the same school level, and said so! After the very early months, small groups were usually same-level (and sometimes same-school) groups. Some teachers were critical of mathematical problems that were not clearly related to a topic in their own curriculum. They indicated that demands of curriculum and available time meant there was no possibility for them to use such problems, even though the problems were interesting and often fun to engage with. One teacher expressed this point of view after having chosen himself to engage with a 'fun' problem in a workshop. The implication was that in his lessons there was no time for 'fun'. Didacticians responded to such comments by designing mathematical tasks which could be seen as clearly curriculum-related, but nevertheless might be fun to engage with. Teachers responded that such tasks could be seen as valuable, but were much more time consuming than the text book tasks they used. However, the teachers expressing this point of view in one school invited didacticians to engage with them in designing more open tasks that could engage students conceptually. This resulted in a set of lessons, according to the teachers, quite different from those they held normally. They reported that students had seemed to have a better understanding of the mathematical concepts than earlier groups. Nevertheless, they were clear that they could not afford generally the amount of time demanded by these tasks (Fuglestad et al., 2006; Hundeland et al., 2007).

We see here clear examples of critical alignment by both didacticians and teachers – a complex set of actions and reactions in and to project activity closely related to school activity. On the one hand, activity was led by design of tasks and group organization designed by didacticians. On the other, teachers' responses and perspectives led to reconceptualization and redesign; for example, groups became mainly same-level groups; tasks were increasingly curriculum-related. Teachers spoke from their own experiences and perspectives rooted in their normal activity in school communities and from the demands of the rules of schooling, for example the pressure of needing to "cover" the national curriculum. Rules and communities mediating the thinking and actions of teachers impinged on the project and mediated the design of tasks and workshop groupings. In order to achieve project goals didacticians needed to recognize and respond to teachers' concerns. Teachers surprised didacticians nevertheless by engaging in activity in ways that showed workshop goals being achieved in classrooms. Thus, control shifted between didacticians and teachers in interesting ways showing a complex division of labour in the project.

Mutual Adaptation and Learning

The first year of activity with schools constituted Phase 1 of the project.[9] Before the start of the second year (Phase 2), didacticians responded to teachers' comments on workshops by holding a consultative meeting. Teachers were invited to express frankly their views on workshops and to make suggestions for workshops in the coming phase of activity. Many indicated that finding time in school for the kinds of planning meetings they needed to design activity for classrooms was extremely difficult. School structures militated against such meetings and time was limited. They would like the opportunity to plan together with colleagues from other schools at the same level, to produce classroom tasks and to report on the classroom activity on a future occasion. These suggestions were so strongly supported across school levels, that Phase 2 of the project became structured accordingly. The Norwegian phrase "planlegge et opplegg" (devise the lesson plan) became a watchword for Phase 2. Here didacticians could be seen clearly to take on board teachers' perspectives and to build these into ongoing activity in workshops. Increasingly in Phase 2, input from teachers relating to activity in classrooms became a central feature of plenary sessions. Curriculum topics were used explicitly as a focus for mathematical activity. Same-level groups predominated. Feedback from a focus group interview with each school team at the end of Phase 2 indicated that teachers had appreciated didacticians' accommodation to their perspectives in a range of factors and showed corresponding activity in classrooms. Invitations from teachers to didacticians to videorecord innovative activity in classrooms resulted in a bank of videodata charting development in classrooms. We might see, in retrospect the meeting between Phases 1 and 2 as a watershed in project activity. Engeström's (1999) theory of expansive learning might be seen to capture this watershed.

Expansive Learning

The outcome of tensions, such as those expressed above, in the LCM project was that activity went on. We did not see a breakdown. Trust, good will and positive intentions led to realization (both recognition and making-real) of ways of working that enabled some achievement of some goals (on both sides) to some extent. In this process, there was some event or initiative which acted as a force to resolve tensions – expressed by Engeström (1999) as *"expansive learning"*. For example, during the first phase we had seen a build up of tension as teachers engaged with activity, provided clear evidence of valuing the project and their participation, yet

---

[9] The LCM project was funded for four years. During this time, there were three Phases of activity, each of one school year, in which didacticians and teachers worked together as described here.

at the same time increasingly expressed a wish for modified forms of action (such as the nature of small groups or the kinds of mathematical tasks). The meeting between the phases allowed overt expression of desire for alternative action and clear suggestions for the form such action might take.

Expansive learning is rooted in the activity theory concepts expressed above – notably goal directed mediated action, based in Vygotsky (1978) and Leont'ev (1979). Engeström (1999, p. 382), following Leont'ev (1979), expresses it as a dialectic of "ascending from the abstract to the concrete" and adds (pp. 382–383):

> A method of grasping the essence of an object by tracing and reproducing theoretically the logic of its development, of its historical formation through the emergence and resolution of inner contradictions. [...] The initial simple idea is transformed into a complex object, a new form of practice. [...] The expansive cycle begins with individual subjects questioning the accepted practice, and it gradually expands into a collective movement or institution.

Through complex interactions traceable to all three elements of the hidden curriculum, participants in the project are able to recognize and isolate the *inner contradictions* expressed by Engeström (1999). In the case above, the concerns about groups and about tasks in workshops, through the between-phases meeting, led to the emergence of the new idea of *planlegge et opplegg* through which planning in homogenous groups in a workshop with didacticians' support could lead to teachers having suitable activity for their classrooms leading to development for students' learning of mathematics. What started as internal rumblings within activity resulted in an external development explicit for all to engage with. Such analysis enables us to trace our activity, noting its historical development and becoming clearer about the issues, tensions or contradictions inherent in the developmental process.

As a further example, I refer to an event with took place in Phase 3 of the project. This phase was introduced (by didacticians) as focusing on declaring and achieving school goals for development of mathematics learning and teaching within a school. Activity in Phase 3 proceeded along familiar lines with engagement in workshops and associated work in schools and with associated issues and tensions acknowledged but not resolved. The focus on school goals was elusive and progression towards school goals not achieved. Then one didactician suggested a task that was to have important consequences for the goals of Phase 3. The task was connected to a series of three workshops focusing on *algebra*. It involved teachers in undertaking some focused observation of some of their own students related to work on algebra. Teachers were asked to bring to the next workshop some input from their observations. The workshop was organized to develop a "red thread" through observations at different levels of students' algebraic understanding across the range of school levels. In order to visualize teachers' judgement on the quality of students' algebraic thinking, teachers were asked to pin their written observations to a line which was strung across the workshop's main room. The coffee break allowed all to view the line and think about its contents. The quality of teachers' perceptions expressed in the final plenary discussion and comments received from several teachers after the workshop indicated that this had been an important experience for teachers: most significant had been their insights into the thinking and understanding of their own students and recognition of the task as a research event with serious learning outcomes for themselves. The task had provided the opportunity for expansion and for a breakthrough in activity.

Teachers' participation and comments in and from this activity suggested to didacticians that certain goals had been achieved. Teachers had engaged overtly in a research task, conducting activity in their schools, findings the time to do so, recognizing their learning, and valuing their insights into students' perceptions/thinking/understandings of algebra. This signified for didacticians strong developmental outcomes from their own activity and participation – with evidence of both teachers' learning and didacticians' associated learning. For example, teachers suddenly came to see, through their study of students' thinking and activity in algebra, how they could explore in their school environment ways to develop teaching and learning; didacticians saw the nature of a task that could lead to teachers' effective recognition of the nature of school goals for students' development and learning in mathematics.

Seeing the enterprise in terms of an activity system made it possible to pick out elements in the complexity and trace developmental patterns for participants in the project (see Goodchild & Jaworski, 2005; Jaworski & Goodchild, 2006). In this process, tensions became evident as catalysts providing opportunity for learning. We see the nature of community as central to this provision of opportunity. During the three years, the members of the project community came to know each other as colleagues, appreciating good intentions, trusting good will, recognizing differences, respecting alternative points of view and becoming aware of developing thinking and associated possibility for action. This is not to claim hugely visible changes to the everyday practices in which established communities were rooted, but rather to recognize a relationship between developmental aims and the realities of normal working life. For example, the structure in a school could not change to suit the aims of the project; nor should the project fail because these aims could not be met. So, in what ways might we accommodate to achieve the aims? Through such recognition also, the aims become more understandable and perhaps more open to flexibility in their achievement – that is we were able to relate the aims to real settings and work out alternative approaches compatible with the aims.

A MORE GENERAL PERSPECTIVE

This chapter has interwoven complex aspects of theory and a specific developmental research project to illuminate notions of the development of mathematics learning and teaching through developmental research in inquiry communities involving teachers and didacticians.[10]

In this final section of the chapter my purpose is to pull out to a more general viewpoint on communities of inquiry and the associated theoretical perspectives. Key areas of theory have been

- Communities of practice with notions of belonging through engagement, imagination and alignment (Wenger, 1998) shifting to critical alignment through inquiry (Jaworski, 2006);

- Mediated activity between people involving individuals acting with mediational means (Vygotsky, 1978; Wertsch, 1991);

- The motivated nature of activity involving goal-directed action (Leont'ev, 1979);

- Engeström's expanded mediational triangle and the concept of expansive learning (Engeström, 1998, 1999).

The concept of *community* is clearly central in all of these and needs no further comment. The place of *inquiry* perhaps needs further elucidation. Inquiry brings the critical element to community of practice through which participants can inquire into existing practices with possibility to modify and improve. Inquiry can be seen as a mediational tool in social settings enabling development of knowing between people and hence of participative individuals. Inquiry as in the design/inquiry cycle promotes goal-directed action leading to developmental outcomes. Inquiry ways of being allow the possibility of contradictions emerging as powerful motivators for expansion within an activity system.

The *inquiry community* starts with intentions to use inquiry as a tool for learning and development. Through engagement with an inquiry cycle in the design of tasks and opportunity for participation, a community grows into inquiry ways of being which encourage mediation of complexity within the hidden curriculum of systems and structures that constrain development. As compared to established communities of practice, in which norms of practice nurture undesirable states, the inquiry community is emergent. It does not avoid issues, tensions and contradictions, but deals with them as part of emergent recognition and understanding leading to possibilities for expansive learning. Inquiry ways of being accept the unfinished nature of learning and development. There is not an end point.

---

[10] For those interested in knowing more about the LCM project, the website http://fag.hia.no/lcm/ contains a list of relevant publications and the book (Jaworski, Fuglestad, Bjuland, Breiteig, Goodchild, & Grevholm, 2007) charts the project as a whole.

EPILOGUE

LCM ended in December 2007. However, in 2006, an extension to LCM was already started in the form of a new project, TBM, *Teaching Better Mathematics*, funded again by the RCN. This new project involves a consortium including five centres in different parts of Norway linking didacticians with schools and rooted in a philosophy of inquiry communities. At Agder University, TBM is linked to LBM (*Learning Better Mathematics*), a parallel project owned by schools. LBM and TBM work in concert with a managing committee including school leaders and didacticians. Schools pay for the work of one didactician based at the university with a responsibility for liaising between the two projects and supporting teachers' participation. Both schools and didacticians contribute to conceptualization, planning and engagement in project activity in workshops and classrooms.

The consortium has come about through didacticians in institutions in the five regions recognizing shared goals rooted in developing inquiry communities between didacticians and teachers in their own region. Each regional group has their own specific project with its own clear focus and goals, but all share the same theoretical basis. The research council has seen value in such collaboration in supporting the project. Its invitation to the Agder community to offer a dedicated day conference in Oslo in October 2007 was a further indication of its support. We see this as very positive encouragement from an important part of the establishment to continue this developmental approach.

ACKNOWLEDGEMENTS

I should like to thank most sincerely Gertraud Benke, Simon Goodchild, and Konrad Krainer for their kind but critical and extremely helpful comments on an early draft of this chapter.

REFERENCES

Bassey, M. (1995). *Creating education through research.* Edinburgh, UK: British Educational Research Association.

Borgersen, H. E. (1994). Open ended problem solving in geometry. *Nordic Studies in Mathematics Education, NOMAD, 2*(2), 6–35.

Brown, S., & McIntyre, D. (1993). *Making sense of teaching.* Buckingham, UK: Open University Press.

Brousseau, G. (1984). The crucial role of the didactical contract in the analysis and construction of situations in teaching and learning mathematics. In H. G. Steiner, N. Balachef, J. Mason, H. Steinbring, L. P. Steffe, T. J. Cooney, & B. Christiansen (Eds.), *Theory of mathematics education (TME)* (pp. 110–119). Bielefeld, Germany: Universität Bielefeld, IDM.

Cestari, M. L., Daland, E., Eriksen, S., & Jaworski, B. (2006). Working in a developmental research paradigm: The role of didactician/researcher working with teachers to promote inquiry practices in developing mathematics learning and teaching. In M. Bosch (Ed.), *Proceedings of the 4th Congress of the European Society for Research in Mathematics Education (2005)* (pp. 1348–1357). Sant Feliu de Guíxols, Spain: Universitat Ramon Llull.

Cochran Smith, M., & Lytle, S. L. (1999). Relationships of knowledge and practice: Teacher learning in communities. *Review of Research in Education, 24,* 249–305.

Daland, E. (2007). School teams in mathematics, what are they good for? In B. Jaworski, A. B. Fuglestad, R. Bjuland, T. Breiteig, S. Goodchild, & B. Grevholm (Eds.), *Learning communities in mathematics* (pp. 161–174). Bergen, Norway: Caspar.

Engeström, Y. (1998). Reorganising the motivational sphere of classroom culture. In F. Seeger, J. Voigt, & U. Wascgescio (Eds.), *The culture of the mathematics classroom* (pp. 76–103). Cambridge, UK: Cambridge University Press.

Engeström, Y. (1999). Activity theory and individual and social transformation. In Y. Engeström, R. Miettinen, & R.-L. Punamäki (Eds.), *Perspectives on activity theory* (pp. 19–38). Cambridge, UK: Cambridge University Press.

Eriksen, S. (2007). Mathematical tasks and community building – "Early days" in the project. In B. Jaworski, A. B. Fuglestad, R. Bjuland, T. Breiteig, S. Goodchild, & B. Grevholm (Eds.), *Learning communities in mathematics* (pp. 175–188). Bergen, Norway: Caspar.

Fuglestad, A. B., Goodchild, S., & Jaworski, B. (2006). Utvikling av inquiry fellesskap for å forbedre undervisning og læring i matematikk: Didaktikere og lærere arbeider sammen [Development of inquiry communities to improve teaching and learning in mathematics]. In M. B. Postholm (Ed.), *Forsk med! Lærere og forskere i læringsarbeid undervisningsutvikling* [Research with us! Teachers and researchers in co-learning development of teaching] (pp. 34–73). Oslo, Norway: N W Damm & Søn.

Goodchild, S. (2007). Inside the outside: Seeking evidence of didacticians' learning by expansion. In B. Jaworski, A. B. Fuglestad, R. Bjuland, T. Breiteig, S. Goodchild, & B. Grevholm, (Eds.), *Learning communities in mathematics* (pp. 189–204). Bergen, Norway: Caspar.

Goodchild, S., & Jaworski, B. (2005). Identifying contradictions in a teaching and learning development project. In H. L. Chick & J. L. Vincent (Eds.), *Proceedings of the 29th Conference of the International Group for the Psychology of Mathematics Education* (Vol. 3, pp. 41–47). Melbourne, Australia: University of Melbourne.

Gravemeijer, K. (1994). Educational development and developmental research in mathematics education. *Journal for Research in Mathematics Education, 25*, 443–471.

Grønmo, L. S., Bergem, O. K., Kjærnsli, M., Lie, S., & Turmo, A. (2004). *Hva i all verden har skedd i realfagene?* [What in all the world has happened in natural sciences?]. Oslo, Norway: Universitetet i Olso.

Holland, D., Lachicotte, W. Jr., Skinner, D., & Cain, C. (1998). *Identity and agency in cultural worlds.* Cambridge, Ma: Harvard University Press.

Hundeland, P. S., Erfjord, I., Grevholm, B., & Breiteig, T. (2007). Teachers and researchers inquiring into mathematics teaching and learning: The case of linear functions. In C. Bergsten, B. Grevholm, H. S. Måsøval, & F. Rønning (Eds.), *Relating practice and research in mathematics education. Proceedings of Norma05, 4th Nordic Conference on Mathematics Education* (pp. 299–310). Trondheim, Norway: Tapir Akademisk Forlag.

Jaworski, B. (1999). Mathematics teacher education research and development: The involvement of teachers. *Journal of Mathematics Teacher Education, 2,* 117–119.

Jaworski, B. (2004a). Grappling with complexity: Co-learning in inquiry communities in mathematics teaching development. In M. J. Høines & A. B. Fuglestad (Eds.), *Proceedings of the 28th Conference of the International Group for the Psychology of Mathematics Education* (Vol. 1, pp. 17–32). Bergen, Norway: Bergen University College.

Jaworski, B. (2004b). Insiders and outsiders in mathematics teaching development: The design and study of classroom activity. In O. Macnamara & R. Barwell (Eds.), *Research in mathematics education: Papers of the British Society for Research into Learning Mathematics* (Vol. 6, pp. 3–22). London: BSRLM.

Jaworski, B. (2005). Learning communities in mathematics: Creating an inquiry community between teachers and didacticians. In R. Barwell & A. Noyes (Eds.), *Research in mathematics education: Papers of the British Society for Research into Learning Mathematics* (Vol. 7, pp. 101–119). London: BSRLM.

Jaworski, B. (2006). Theory and practice in mathematics teaching development: Critical inquiry as a mode of learning in teaching. *Journal of Mathematics Teacher Education, 9,* 187–211.

Jaworski, B., & Goodchild, S. (2006). Inquiry community in an activity theory frame. In J. Novotná, H. Moraová, M. Krátká, & N. Stelíková (Eds.), *Proceedings of the 30th Conference of the International Group for the Psychology of Mathematics Education* (Vol. 3, pp. 353–360). Prague, Czech Republic: Charles University.

Jaworski, B., Fuglestad, A. B., Bjuland, R., Breiteig, T., Goodchild, S., & Grevholm, B. (Eds.). (2007). *Learning communities in mathematics.* Bergen, Norway: Caspar.

Kelly, A. E. (2003). Research as design. *Educational Researcher, 32*(1), 3–4.

Kjærnsli, M., Lie, S., Olsen, R. V., & Turmo, A. (2004). *Rett spor eller ville veier? Norske elevers prestasjoner i matematikk, naturfag og lesing i PISA 2003* [Right track or out in the wilderness? Norwegian pupils' achievements in mathematics, science and reading in Pisa 2003]. Oslo, Norway: Universitetsforlaget.

Lave, J., & Wenger, E. (1991.). *Situated learning: Legitimate peripheral participation.* Cambridge, UK: Cambridge University Press.

Leont'ev, A. N. (1979). The problem of activity in psychology. In J. V. Wertsch (Ed.), *The concept of activity in Soviet psychology* (pp. 37–71). New York: M. E. Sharpe.

Mullis, I. V. S., Martin, M. O., Gonzalez, E. J., & Chrostowski, S. J. (2004). *TIMSS 2003 international mathematics report: Findings from IEA's Trends in International Mathematics and science study at the fourth and eighth grades.* Boston MA: TIMSS & PIRLS International Study Center, Boston College.

Mullis, I. V. S., Martin, M. O., Beaton, A., Gonzalez, E., Kelly, D., & Smith, D. (Eds.). (1998). *Mathematics and science achievement in the final year of secondary school: IEA's Third International Mathematics and Science Study (TIMSS).* Chestnut Hill, MA: Boston College.

Nardi, B. (1996). Studying context: A comparison of activity theory, situated action models and distributed cognition. In B. Nardi (Ed.), *Context and consciousness: Activity theory and human computer interaction* (pp. 69–102). Cambridge, MA: MIT Press.

Rogoff, B., Matusov, E., & White, C. (1996). Models of teaching and learning: Participation in a community of learners. In D. R. Olson & N. Torrance (Eds.), *The handbook of education and human development* (pp. 388–414). Oxford, UK: Blackwell.

Vygotsky, L. (1978). *Mind in society.* Cambridge, MA: Harvard University Press.

Wagner, J. (1997). The unavoidable intervention of educational research: A framework for reconsidering research-practitioner cooperation. *Educational Researcher, 26*(7), 13–22.

Wells, G. (1999). *Dialogic inquiry: Toward a sociocultural practice and theory of education.* Cambridge, UK: Cambridge University Press.

Wenger, E. (1998). *Communities of practice: Learning, meaning and identity.* Cambridge, UK: Cambridge University Press.

Wertsch, J. V. (1991). *Voices of the mind.* Cambridge, MA: Harvard University Press.

Wood, T., & Berry, B. (2003). Editorial: What does "Design Research" offer mathematics teacher education? *Journal of Mathematics Teacher Education, 6,* 195–199.

Barbara Jaworski
Mathematics Education Centre
Loughborough University
UK

NANETTE SEAGO

14. MATHEMATICS TEACHING PROFESSION

Recommendations for the professionalization of teaching were made over two decades ago. One of the most difficult problems facing the professionalization of mathematics teachers has been the definition and description of the specialized knowledge needed by teachers. Mathematical knowledge for teaching has been given recent attention as a specialized knowledge needed for teaching by focusing attention on the considerable mathematical demands that are placed on classroom teachers. This chapter will show how professional development opportunities that use records of classroom practice such as student work, classroom videotapes, or lesson plans, can support the learning of mathematical knowledge for teaching and provide the opportunity to further develop the mathematics teaching profession by increasing teachers' authority as reliable source of professional knowledge.

INTRODUCTION

Professionalization commonly refers to the process in which an occupation engages in the improvement of the conditions or standards of their work, and is based on the assumption that professions have distinctive characteristics that distinguish them from other occupations. Professionalization involves the extent to which members of that occupation has autonomy over the content of their work and the degree to which society places value on this work.

Recommendations for the professionalization of teaching were made over two decades ago (Carnegie Task Force, 1986; Holmes Group, 1986). These groups used existing professions such as law and medicine to suggest graduate level specialized education for teachers. In addition, they proposed that a board of professionals be created to manage the testing and licensing of teaching candidates. They sparked a groundswell of support to strengthen teaching as a profession – in which teachers were perceived as professionals who made important decisions in a complex setting. This movement was intended to upgrade the quality of teaching and public education, increase public confidence in teachers, raise the status of teachers and support their efforts to develop professionally (National Board of Professional Teaching Standards, 1988).

Two decades have passed since the recommendations were made and during that time technological advances have changed the world in dramatic ways. Of all the occupations that are labelled as professions, it is teaching that is responsible for creating the human skills and capacity that will enable individuals to survive and succeed in today's information society. The kind of professionalism needed is a more up-to-date version of the one recommended in the 1980s. Hargreaves (2003)

K. Krainer and T. Wood (eds.), Participants in Mathematics Teacher Education, 331–352.

reminds us in his book, *Teaching in the Knowledge Society*, "as catalysts of successful knowledge societies, teachers must be able to build a special kind of professionalism". He argued that this professionalism is not based in old paradigms in which teachers had the autonomy to teach in ways that are most familiar to them. Instead, Hargreaves (2003, p. 24) points to a new professionalism for the information age that requires teachers as professionals to:

> Promote deep cognitive learning; learn to teach in ways they were not taught; commit to continuous professional learning; work and learn in collegial teams; treat parents as partners in learning; develop and draw on collective intelligence; build a capacity for change and risk; and foster trust in processes.

Yet in the midst of a rapidly changing information society, many people still cling to basic premises of a pre-professional age – that anyone who knows a subject matter fairly well can teach it to secondary students and anyone who loves children can teach primary school. Still others believe that people are born teachers or that teaching is something you learn individually by trial and error, within the confines of your own classroom. In a world that changes so quickly, it is impossible for any one teacher to obtain enough knowledge alone to improve him or herself. *New professionalism* requires teachers to engage in continual, collaborative professional learning communities. Indeed, over the past two decades, teachers in many countries have become more expert at and experienced in working with their colleagues, yet more work is needed to truly professionalize mathematics teaching.

In this chapter, I will first discuss the issue of the professionalization of mathematics teaching – what it means and why it is important to the further development of the mathematics teaching profession. Second, I will talk about how professional development that holds certain design principles can provide opportunities for teachers to develop as professionals. Then I will use an example to illustrate the enactment of these design principles, and describe how they provided teachers the opportunity to learn and professional expertise, judgement and trust. Finally, I will summarize the issues, challenges and possibilities of the further development of mathematics teaching in the information age.

PROFESSIONALIZATION AND MATHEMATICS TEACHING

With an assumption that professionalization was a necessary condition for teachers to successfully implement the NCTM Standards (NCTM, 1989), the push for professionalism continued when the National Council of Mathematics Teachers published the *Professional Standards for Teaching Mathematics* (NCTM, 1991). These standards assumed that the type of instruction they promoted required professionalism – a high degree of autonomy, individual responsibility and authority. This perspective acknowledges "the teacher as a part of a learning community that continually fosters growth in knowledge, stature, and responsibility" (NCTM, 1991, p. 6). To give guidance to the development of such professionalism in mathematics teaching, the *Professional Standards for Teaching Mathematics* consisted of separate sections of specific standards: (1) Standards for teaching mathematics, (2) Standards for the evaluation of the teaching of mathematics, (3) Standards for the professional development of teachers of mathematics, (4) Standards for the support and development of mathematics teachers and teaching. These teaching standards were intended as a set of principles accompanied by illustrations or indicators to give direction and guidance for moving toward excellence in teaching mathematics.

One year after the publishing of the *Professional Standards for Teaching Mathematics*, Noddings (1992) pointed out that a culture that downplays the complexity involved in teaching works against the professionalization of teaching. If one holds a pre-professional view that once you are qualified to teach, you know the basics of teaching forever; that once you gain managerial control over your students, teaching is easy; then the quest for the professionalization of teaching does not make sense. However, if one believes teaching is a complex practice involving specific skills and knowledge that require ongoing, collaborative professional learning, it makes sense that professionalization should be coveted and pursued. Noddings (1992, p. 202) argued the latter and suggested that one of the biggest challenges facing the professionalization of mathematics teachers in particular is the definition and description of the specialized body of knowledge needed by teachers. She states:

> Knowledge of mathematics cannot be sufficient to describe the professional knowledge of teachers. What does a mathematics *teacher* know that someone with similar mathematical preparation does not? What specialized knowledge does the teacher have?

Over the past two decades, a number of studies have attempted to define the nature and elements of knowledge specific to mathematics teaching. Most of this research has used teachers' practice as the site for investigating this specialized knowledge. These studies make the claim that the knowledge required for teaching is rooted in the mathematical demands of teaching itself and that this differs from the knowledge that a teacher gains from formal education (Ball & Bass, 2003).

Lee Shulman's pioneering notion of "pedagogical content knowledge" began to address the kind of specialized knowledge that Noddings referred to by labeling and describing a type of knowledge specific to teaching that teachers need to employ within their practice (Shulman, 1986, 1987, 1989). Shulman distinguished three categories of teacher content knowledge: subject matter knowledge, pedagogical content knowledge and curricular knowledge. Although these categories are not specific to mathematics teaching, many mathematics education researchers have used this classification as a framework for their work. In particular, the notion of pedagogical content knowledge (PCK) as "bundled" mathematical, pedagogical, and cognitive/developmental knowledge, Shulman argued could help teachers anticipate and address typical issues of students' learning mathematics. His groundbreaking work opened educators' eyes to the possibility that teaching requires specialized professional knowledge – a view he continues to work toward today. Noddings (1992, p. 198) suggested that PCK was more of a "political rallying cry than a label for an actual body of knowledge as it appears in actual practitioners".

Building upon Shulman's work but with more of a focus on describing the specialized mathematical knowledge needed for teaching, Deborah Ball and colleagues have spent two decades analysing videotapes and other records of practice to extrapolate the nature and type of mathematical demands that arise in teaching (e.g., Ball & Cohen, 1999; Ball & Bass, 2003). Their basic research questions focused on the actual body of knowledge practitioners' use: what mathematical knowledge (including skills, practices, dispositions, etc.) is entailed by the work of teaching mathematics? And, where and how is such mathematical knowledge used in teaching mathematics? These questions have led them to label the term "*mathematical knowledge for teaching*" (MKT). This category is used to capture the relationship between mathematics content knowledge and teaching. They have further refined their definition by distinguishing two elements: common knowledge of mathematics that any well educated adult should have and specialized mathematical knowledge that only teachers need to know (Ball, Hill, & Bass, 2005).

Claiming that MKT differs from Shulman's PCK, Ball and Bass posit an "unbundled", complementary mathematical knowledge that teachers must call upon as needed in the course of classroom practice to effectively engage students in learning. As opposed to Shulman's PCK that draws upon knowledge and pedagogy in teaching, the conception of MKT by Ball and Bass (2000, pp. 88-89, italics in original) draws upon *mathematics* as used in teaching. As they explain the difference:

> Pedagogical content knowledge provides a certain anticipatory resource for teachers, it sometimes falls short in the dynamic interplay of content with pedagogy in teachers' real-time problem solving. [...]. [A]s they meet novel situations in teaching, teachers must bring to bear considerations of content, students, learning, and pedagogy. They must reason, and often cannot simply reach into a repertoire of strategies and answers. [...]. It is what it takes *mathematically* to manage these routine and nonroutine problems that has preoccupied our interest. [...]. It is to this kind of *pedagogically useful mathematical* understanding that we attend to in our work.

They also argue that the kind of pedagogically useful mathematical knowledge and understanding differs in a number of ways from the mathematical knowledge and understanding required in other disciplines that use mathematics such as research mathematicians, engineers and scientists. Although the refined mathematical knowledge of mathematicians is an elegant and well-structured domain, the mathematical knowledge teachers are called upon to use is very different. The mathematical knowledge held and expressed by students in classrooms is often incomplete and difficult to understand (Ball, Hill, & Bass, 2005). Teachers are in the unique position of using professional judgement to scrutinize, interpret, and extend this knowledge. In addition, they must explain, listen, and examine students' work. They must use professional expertise to choose careful examples, useful models, and accurate representations. They must be fluent and fluid with mathematical language, symbols and notation. In short, they must use a kind of specialized professional knowledge that they have not had a chance to learn in formal mathematics or education courses. These practices and specialized knowledge distinguish the mathematics teaching profession from mathematicians and everyday people.

Ball and colleagues' analysis of teaching has shown that pedagogy is highly mathematical work and they propose that mathematics teaching can be thought of as a type of mathematical problem solving. Among the tasks of teaching that require this kind of specialized knowledge include "decompressing" (unpacking) mathematical ideas, analysing the mathematical reasoning within student thinking, choosing representations to effectively convey mathematical ideas, and negotiating mathematically productive discussions. The Ball and Bass mathematical knowledge for teaching definition and description helps to address the challenges facing the professionalization of teaching that Noddings talked about. Since professionalization assumes the possession and organization of a *specialized* knowledge, describing and labelling mathematical knowledge for teaching helps to further develop the mathematics profession.

PROFESSIONALIZATION THROUGH PROFESSIONAL DEVELOPMENT

It is generally assumed that professionalization involves *professional development*. Professional development refers to the process in which a practitioner acquires and improves the specialized knowledge and skill required for effective professional practice. However, not all of professional development is created equal – there exists great variance in teachers' opportunities to learn. On the one hand, professional development that creates opportunities for strong professional learning communities in which discourse and inquiry among teachers are about real problems of practice and that provides opportunities for teachers to learn necessary specialized knowledge, supports the process of professionalization (NCTM, 1991; Hargreaves, 2003). On the other hand, professional development that focuses on fixing teachers inadequacies, driving teachers to teach to the test, addressing only issues of technique, or tying them to scripted curriculum, results in devaluing the act of teaching and learning and prevents long-term development of competence and confidence in the teaching force (Darling-Hammond, 1985; Hargreaves, 2003).

Although cultural diversity exists across various international professional development programmes with differing national characteristics, there are some *common themes* among the approaches for improving teachers' mathematical knowledge for teaching. The increasing awareness of the importance of practice-based materials in the development of teachers' specialized knowledge has led to programmes that use representations of teacher material (lessons, classroom episodes, teacher questions, student work and observations) as sources of knowledge about content and students (Carpenter & Fennema, 1989; Markovits & Even, 1994; Even, Tirosh, & Markovits, 1996; Schifter et al., 1999a; Driscoll et al.,

2001; Franke, Carpenter, Levi, & Fennema, 2001). These programmes have used students' ways of mathematical thinking as a primary vehicle for professional learning opportunities.

In their chapter in the *Handbook of Research on the Psychology of Mathematics Education*, Llinares and Krainer (2006) noted differing goals for professional development aimed at improving teachers' MKT: (1) raising teachers' awareness of mathematical process and content, and (2) raising teachers' awareness of students' mathematical thinking. They noted an international shift in reported studies – from a focus on improving teachers' knowledge of the process of doing mathematics (Murray, Olivier, & Human, 1995) to using mathematical tasks in professional development to solve challenging problems (Zaslavsky, Chapman, & Leikin, 2003). Internationally, much of the research conducted brings to the fore the importance of analysis and reflection on teaching practice (observing other teachers' lessons or analysing their own teaching) as critical learning processes for teachers (Cobb, 1994; Goffree & Oonk, 2001; Sullivan & Mousley, 1998).

Recent research projects in the US suggest that professional development projects which utilize records of practice, such as classroom videotapes, lesson plans, classroom cases, and student thinking, can be effective tools in efforts to increase teachers' opportunity to learn mathematical knowledge for teaching (Hill & Ball, 2004; Borko et al., 2005; Seago & Goldsmith, 2006). By bringing the authentic work of teaching into the professional development setting, these tools enable teachers to scrutinize and unpack the mathematics in classroom activities, examine instructional strategies and student learning, and discuss ideas for improvement (e.g., Ball & Cohen, 1999). These types of opportunities can result in the further development of teaching because they place value on the act of teaching and learning and are designed to increase teachers' mathematical knowledge for teaching. They honour teachers' practice as a site for study and analysis, recognizing the complex and intellectual nature of the teaching profession.

PROFESSIONAL DEVELOPMENT DESIGN PRINCIPLES

Three *primary principles* seem to emerge from designing for and using records of practice (e.g., written and video cases, student work, lessons, vignettes) in professional development aimed at improving teachers' mathematical knowledge for teaching and professional expertise. These principles can help to provide criteria for the further development of the mathematics teaching profession by supporting an analytic stance toward records of practice; a stance which can help teachers deepen their understanding of the mathematics students' grapple with, the ways that students think about important mathematical ideas, and the tasks of teaching involved in furthering student learning. In short, these principles have the potential to support professional development that aims to increase teachers' authority as reliable source of professional knowledge.

Principle One: Design and/or Use Records of Practice to Support Teachers in the Investigation of Student Thinking and Understanding Embedded Within the Records

This principle points to the importance of using records of practice to provide opportunities for teachers to develop an increasing ability and/or disposition towards:
- Expressing curiosity and professional judgment about the thinking behind the records of practice
- Grounding interpretations of thinking in evidence and data from the records of practice
- Generating plausible alternative interpretations of thinking, and supporting these with evidence
- Seeing strengths (not just weaknesses) in the thinking and understanding captured in records of practice
- Making connections to previously studied records to compare/contrast the thinking under study

Principle Two: Design and/or Use Records of Practice to Investigate the Mathematical Content Specific to Teaching

This principle points to the importance of using records of practice to support teachers in developing specialized professional content expertise:
- The mathematical ideas that underlie the work represented in the record of practice
- The connections between the mathematical ideas represented in the record of practice and the related mathematical ideas
- Insights into the various representations of mathematical ideas represented in records of practice
- Norms of mathematical argument that include respectful and sometimes spirited disagreement and debate grounded in mathematical logic
- The propensity to compare/contrast mathematical arguments and solution methods represented in the records of practice

Principle Three: Design for and Use Records of Practice to Investigate One's Own Mathematical Teaching Practice

This principle points to the importance of using records of practice to increase teachers' individual responsibility and professional autonomy by providing opportunities for teachers to develop an ability and/or disposition towards:
- Using the professional learning community discourse to connect with issues of one's own teaching practice

- Taking individual responsibility in one's own communication and interaction with students
- Making professional judgments about the relationship between one's own learning goals and student interactions with the curriculum
- Gaining the professional expertise to see the strengths (not just weaknesses) in the thinking and understanding of one's own students
- Improving professional skills to listen carefully to students' ideas and reasoning

Explicating design principles, such as these, can be useful in both creating new professional development materials and in helping teacher educators to effectively select and use records of practice in professional development settings to promote learning mathematical knowledge for teaching and professional expertise. The notion that professional expertise involves the development of particular ways of organizing and attending to the environment runs through a variety of different disciplines, from archaeology to chess to teaching (deGroot, 1965; Goodwin, 1994; Mason, 2002; Nussbaum, 1990). Principles such as these can support the participants in teacher education to move closer to becoming a profession by creating opportunities for them to not only gain in a specialized professional knowledge, but to become actively involved in an intellectually serious discourse community that challenge, argue, disagree and use evidence.

AN EXAMPLE OF PRINCIPLED PROFESSIONAL DEVELOPMENT

Various professional development materials are beginning to emerge that aim to support teachers in gaining professional expertise in mathematical knowledge for teaching by following the design principles discussed previously. In this chapter I will use one set of professional development materials, Learning and Teaching Linear Functions: VideoCases for Mathematics Professional Development (LTLF) (Seago, Mumme, & Branca, 2004), as a case to illustrate how a professional development that makes use of the design principles can support the learning of MKT and develop as professionals. I will first describe the materials and their design, and then move to explain how they create opportunities for mathematics teachers to learn MKT and develop as professionals. I will then return to address issues of the further development of the profession more generally.

The Professional Development Materials

Learning and Teaching Linear Functions: VideoCases for Mathematics Professional Development (LTLF) (Seago et al., 2004) is a video-based mathematics professional development curriculum, designed to deepen teachers' mathematical knowledge for teaching through developing their understanding of the distinctions and linkages among various representations of linearity and to enrich teachers' ability to teach linear relationships. Each session is considered a "video case" with the video episode as its centrepiece followed by four activities that reflect the design principles stated above:

1. Teachers engage in the exploration of the same mathematical tasks as those portrayed in the videos. (Principle 2)
2. Teachers view, analyse, and discuss video episodes. (Principle 1)
3. Teachers compare and contrast issues raised in the videos across cases. (Principle 2)
4. Teachers engage in activities that bridge the gap between the learning that takes place within the session and their own practice. (Principle 3)

These materials have been designed to provide teachers the opportunity to gain professional expertise, judgment and trust within an on-going collegial learning community by developing their analytic skills for examining classroom interactions, increasing their propensity to back up their claims with evidence, learning to hone in on the mathematical issues that arise within the complexities of practice, and gaining mathematical knowledge for teaching.

Specifically, teachers have opportunities to:

- *Decompose complex and seemingly simple mathematical ideas.* This involves interpreting and analysing student thinking that emerge from within the video-cases. Over the course of their work, teachers examine and follow the logic of the students in the video, compare representations, and unpack mathematical ideas in ways that makes the basic underlying concepts visible (Ball & Bass, 2000; Ma, 1999).

- *Examine, compare and connect various mathematical representations.* Teachers compare and relate various representations (lines, algebraic formulas, tables, graphs, geometric models, etc.). Over the course of their work, teachers reflect on such things as: What are effective representations of slope? y intercept? Linear growth? How does one accurately represent discrete and continuous functions? Why is a line a representation of a linear function?

- *Examine and interpret student thinking.* Teachers follow the incomplete (and sometimes meandering) mathematical logic of students within the videos. Teachers are called upon to use specialized professional skill as they scrutinize, interpret, analyse and detect the evolving mathematics of their students – both individually and collectively.

- *Extract relevant data from "messy" authentic classroom interactions – to hone in on particular aspects of teaching.* The process of identifying and extracting key information from classroom video parallels the professional skill demanded in teaching. Moment-by-moment teachers are required to recognize and consider real data while immersed in the act of teaching within cluttered and distracting environments. Engaging teachers in this process with video provides a mediated experience paralleling what is demanded of them in real time analysis in their classroom and allows them the opportunity to gain in professional judgement.

- *Develop new norms of professional interaction as well as to redefine the nature of what they interact about.* The discussions around the videos are designed to produce productive disagreements, arguments and counter-arguments, as well as opportunities for posing, encouraging and exploring alternative perspectives and multiple possibilities. Teachers' support and dispute assertions or conjectures with specific evidence from the video as well as size up a situation from moment to moment.

- *Develop a concrete and precise language of practice.* Most professions such as medicine and law have specific and specialized language and terms of their practice. The language that is used to talk about teaching is often overly general and lacking in precision. Even where language exists, the language used may mean different things to different people. Elements of practice in the videos are pointed to, identified and named in order to engage in collective discussion in which participants learn what people mean by the words they use when discussing practice.

- *Attend to critical features of mathematics teaching and students' mathematical thinking/learning.* In part, this involves asking teachers to suspend the tendency to evaluate the surface features of the work captured in the video (e.g., "Angel's work is incorrect"; "the teacher shouldn't have asked James to come to the board if James said he didn't want to"). Instead, teachers learn to consider the student and teacher thinking behind the activity the video captures. In part, this shift of attention involves teachers learning to attend to different aspects of the classroom (and the curriculum) then they may traditionally considered (e.g., what Angel did understand, what the teacher knew about James's work and why he might have wanted James to come to the board).

HOW DOES EXPERIENCING THESE MATERIALS CREATE OPPORTUNITIES TO LEARN MKT AND GAIN AS PROFESSIONALS?

In professional development settings, learning takes place at both the individual and collective levels. Llinares and Krainer (2006) remind us that educational research is increasingly emphasizing the social and organizational aspects of teacher learning. Hargreaves suggested that the "new professional" will require teachers to work and learn in collegial teams (Hargreaves, 2003). Several studies assessed various aspects of individual and collective teacher learning from the use of these particular materials. The learning the teachers displayed involved gains in professional judgment and specialized content knowledge expertise. For example, Hill and Collopy (2002) found that teachers improved in their ability to algebraically represent problems involving geometric patterns, connect their algebraic representation to the geometric pattern, and compare and link alternative representations of the same linear function. They also were better able to identify potential student misunderstandings that involved using a recursive method for predicting the next term in a sequence. Heck found that in terms of exhibiting mathematical knowledge pertinent to the teaching of mathematics, the LTLF participants in their study were statistically more likely than control group teachers to increase in their ability/propensity to connect their work on the mathematics tasks back to the pictorial representations in which the task originated (Heck,

2003). In addition, Heck found that teachers learned to be more analytic about student thinking: performance on post-programme written assessments indicated that participants' analyses of video and written student work were more grounded in evidence, more focused on the mathematics captured in the records, and more attentive to the mathematical potential of students' ideas (instead of just the correctness of the work) than those of a comparison group. Goldsmith and colleagues' analysis of the LTLF professional development discourse indicated participants' analysis of mathematical thinking became more sustained, extensive, and nuanced over time, and they developed more differentiated, representation-rich, and flexible approaches to mathematics (Goldsmith, Seago, Driscoll, Nikula, & Blasi, 2006; Seago & Goldsmith, 2006).

The LTLF teachers in each of the studies mentioned above were part of a professional learning community and gained as professionals in several important ways. First, they gained specific mathematical knowledge that is unique to the profession of mathematics teaching. They gained in *professional knowledge*. Secondly, they gained as professionals in their ability to use data and evidence to make informed analysis about mathematics teaching practice. They gained in *professional judgement*. Thirdly, they gained in their ability to see with critical eyes the subtle nuances of their specific profession (mathematics teaching) that outsiders cannot see. They gained in *professional expertise*. And finally, they gained *professional trust* in their colleagues by actively committing to shared work, openness, and collective learning. In order to make progress as professionals and have an impact in the complex world of schools, teachers must learn to trust and value colleagues that are different from them as well as those that are the same (Hargreaves, 2003).

In order to gain more insights into how the learning of MKT created opportunities for the teachers to further develop as professionals, I will describe one group of teachers' collective professional learning. Additionally, I will give details of the learning of two of the teachers from that group to illustrate how teachers from the same experience can learn different things and thus gain as professionals in differing ways – an important point in thinking about professional autonomy.

The Professional Development Context

The professional development took place during the 2002-2003 academic years in an urban, US school district. Six middle school and three secondary school teachers participated in eight 3-hour sessions after school. Each session began with situating the day's work in relation to the previous session and discussing teachers' thoughts and observations about their between-seminar assignment. This was followed by the group's exploration and discussion of the mathematics problem used by the teacher in the video case. This work includes: solving the problem for themselves and forecasting alternative solutions, comparing different solutions, and anticipating students' misconceptions. The mathematical work was designed to prepare teachers for a focused examination of the mathematics as it unfolds within the classroom video clip – to increase their awareness of alternative possibilities.

In the first and the last session (sessions 1 and 8), teachers viewed and discussed a video segment of ninth grade (14 year old) students presenting solutions to the Growing Dots problem (see Figure 1). Prior to viewing the video, the teachers worked on the problem themselves, sharing and discussing their own solution strategies. The video segment captures the beginning of the whole group discussion that follows individual work of the problem in which two students, Danielle and James, share their solutions for the number of dots at t = 100 minutes. Danielle uses a closed solution to describe the growth.

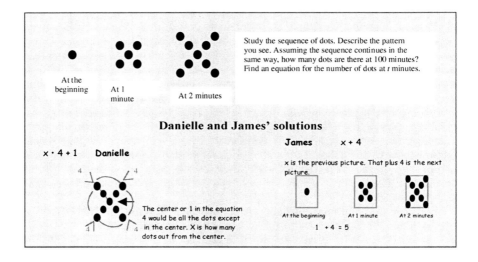

Figure 1. Growing Dots problem and student solutions.

In the video segment, Danielle explains her solution: "I got the equation x times 4 plus 1. The plus 1 being the center [...] x being the dots around it, or 100, and 4 being all the dots except the center." She illustrates her solution (at the teacher's request) on the board (see Figure 1). When she is done the teacher asks, "Can I get somebody who maybe sees this a little bit differently?" James then describes a recursive solution:

> I wasn't worried about this [dot] in the center. I didn't really think of that as 1. [...]. [The problem] says like 'the sequence' or whatever. Well, this [first stage] started at 1 and over here [the second stage] is 5, and 9 over here. I just took. [...] they added four every time. See like four, four, four. And that's why I got x plus 4 for the equation.

In both sessions 1 and 8, the teachers were encouraged to discuss the important mathematical moments within this video segment. They first talked amongst themselves in small groups prior to coming together as a whole group to discuss their interpretations and analysis.

Session 1. This conversation opened with a comment about James's inattention to the proper use of variables, and quickly moved away from discussion of James's work to a general observation about "what kids generally do". Bruce observed,

> I just think that [an issue is] identifying the variable again. I just think it's one of the common mistakes that the students don't read what the question says. When they get to looking at a problem, sometimes the directions go out the window and they're just looking to see what it's doing and not answering the question.

Walter expressed puzzlement at James's solution, and several teachers interpreted James's description of x ("the number that I was adding it to in the previous picture") as simply an idiosyncratic oversight on his part. The teachers had difficulty connecting James's approach with their own ways of thinking about the closed solution, $4x + 1$.

> Janice: So his variable is not consistent throughout. The variable changes from the beginning to minute 1 to minute 2. It's not a constant variable. It changes [. . .].

> Walter: It's kind of curious. How did he get the 400 if he didn't know the one before? Cause he needed [...] to know the one before to add 4.

No one responded to Walter's question. Instead, there was a brief discussion about James's decision to ignore the (unchanging) centre dot, in which Bruce suggested that the teacher had missed an opportunity to work on vocabulary: "it seems to me [this] would be a good [...] place for him to bring up this term constant". Walter still seemed puzzled by James's work and again raised the issue of how James got his answer.

> Walter (consulting transcript): At 19:10 [transcript time code] James tries to explain where he got x plus 4. [...]. Kirk is trying to get him to explain what is x and he never really did.

> Tom: Cause that would have been one hundred four [...].

> Annie: But he got 400. I can't figure out how he got 400 with his formula [...].

> Janice: The only thing I can think of, yeah, is that he, he drew the picture.

Tom: I think he had the picture in his mind. He could see that it was growing and so [...].

Annie (interrupts): But his formula didn't match his answer.

Tom: Right. And we're obviously going to get that in every class. Kids are going to see it differently.

Annie: And that's like what we were saying about how a kid will pick up a formula and he'll never check it.

The teachers were quite engaged in the conversation, identifying James's focus on the growing part of the pattern as mathematically interesting. They did not dismiss his work as wrong (in fact, they specifically noted later in the conversation that he was not actually incorrect), but the teachers were not sure of his reasoning and did not pursue the question about how his notation and his numerical answer were connected. They seemed genuinely puzzled by his mathematical reasoning and did not recognize the recursive thinking employed by James.

The teachers did not talk about Danielle's method until probed by the facilitator. While they noted that her notation would have been confusing to understand without hearing her explanation, they were not particularly inclined to examine it for insights into the details of her thinking or as a contrast or connection to James's ideas.

Janice: I thought she [Danielle] did a great job with that.

Tom: She had, she has an A on it.

Annie: At first I didn't know what she was talking about, about 4, and she drew a little "4" on the end? [...]. Like, 1, 2, 3, 4. That was the only thing I didn't understand. [...]. I mean, I knew what she was trying to do, I just didn't. [...].

Janice: Right. If I had walked in off the street and looked at what she had drawn, not having been there for her explanation, I would never have been able to figure out how she got her answer. Because I would have thought that would have been 4 times four. {Laura: four, four, and four, yeah.} Not one times four.

The teachers began their work together with a tendency to judge the correctness of the work captured in the video episode, rather than to examine the nature of the students' thinking. In addition, they were not inclined to probe "correct" solutions even when the student logic might be faulty. It was as if they filled in the student's logic from their own perspective of the problem – assuming a correct solution corresponded to conceptual understanding. They didn't work and learn as a collegial team or draw upon the collective intelligence of the group. They didn't display a professional trust in each other. Instead, they analysed practice from an individualized perspective drawn from their own familiar teaching experiences.

Session 8. When the group revisited the video five months later, teachers collectively gained in mathematical knowledge for teaching and collective professional expertise. The teachers were generally more engaged in the analysis of James's response and far less puzzled by his solution. Absent were general student comments such as "James didn't answer the question that the Dots problem asked" from session 1, which focused on inattention to the assignment as the source of students' errors, or suggesting opportunity for promoting vocabulary learning. Instead, the group was engaged in collectively making sense of James's thinking in its own right. They displayed more professional trust in each other's analysis. This second conversation was more mathematically coherent as well, in that the ideas the teachers raised were more tightly interconnected and built on each other more than in the earlier discussion. More importantly, the teachers spent time trying to unpack James's strategy, focusing more on what he understood than on what was problematic about his solution. This showed a gain in a kind of professional expertise – interpreting the mathematical logic of a student's reasoning and the ability to unpack and examine an idea with collective eyes. For example, the conversation begins with what James did understand, rather than with what he had failed to do.

Laura: He [James] is describing it. [...]. Look at the beginning, you know, as x, plus $4 - [...]$ that's a pattern. You look at minute 1, that's x, plus 4, and he got to minute two. So he's not all that wrong. Now, he, he's not thinking broadly enough, but [...].

Trevor: He'd gotten so deep into the table that he forgot the part that starts the table going [...] if you just looked at lines 2, 3, and 4, you'll see a change taking place for sure, but that doesn't give you your initial conditions because you're seeing the changes taking place as you march down the table [...].

Walter: He thought that if he counted the center one, you would be counting something that had not been added; and his interpretation was, "how many had been added? What's the pattern?" [...]. What's the pattern. Yeah – he answered, "what is the pattern?" [...].

Sally: He was looking at what was generated off the centre.

Trevor: He was looking at the growth.

The discussion also reflected the group's willingness to consider James's solution from the student's mathematical perspective, rather than to assume that he was either being careless or that he simply fell short of being able to produce the expected, closed notational form. And in trying to understand James's ideas, the group was able to see the potential for building on his ideas to help James develop a deeper understanding of the linear relationships represented in the problem.

Sally: [James was] just seeing pieces of it […].

Walter: Yeah. {several others: uh huh} He was looking here, said "plus 4" […].

Janice: He was looking at each step as an independent […] as something independent of the previous.

Trevor: He was looking at the step process and not seeing the entirety […].

Janice: As soon as James got from point A to point B, he forgot about all about point A. And now point A became point B […] and he moved on […].

The session 8 conversation about Growing Dots was more extensive, complex, and elaborated than one five months earlier. The teachers' collective professional expertise improved. There was more detail in their observations about James's treatment of the pattern of growth and more speculation about his reasoning for not counting the centre dot. Teachers talked about what both Danielle and James "saw" in the problem, and recognize the potential for James to gain even deeper understanding. Several of the teachers related James' solution to recursive thinking. While the group as a whole gained mathematical knowledge for teaching and professional expertise skills, individual teachers within the group gained in differing ways. An individual professional is a person who has control over their own classroom environment and who exhibits self-monitoring, upgrading and reviewing of his or her own personal professional knowledge. To illustrate this phenomenon, the stories of Trevor and Laura follow.

Trevor and Laura. Trevor had an undergraduate university degree in mathematics and taught high school. He wrote that he had signed up for the professional development in hopes of "finding alternative approaches to teaching algebraic thinking and computational skills". He was in pursuit of upgrading his professional knowledge. Over the course of the eight sessions, Trevor showed specific improvement in solving problems that required him to employ conceptual understanding of y-intercept (as evidenced by his pre-post gains on an MKT measure), and to interpret linear growth in terms of geometric representations (as evidenced by his analysis of classroom video segments). This marked a gain in specialized professional content knowledge. Trevor also gained in professional trust. He participated very little in the first discussion about James and Danielle's solutions; he reflected at one point in the discussion about his own teaching – that he [Trevor] often looses students when he shifts gears while giving an explanation for a solution. Later, Trevor talked about moving students to the conventional, generalized form for linear relationships: "Just change problems and then do their own induction to come up with a general purpose formula." During the eighth session however, Trevor was a more active participant in the collective discussion of the two students' thinking, commenting about James' solution.

> He'd gotten so deep into the table that he forgot the part that starts the table going. […] if you just looked at lines 2, 3, and 4, you'll see a change taking place for sure, but that doesn't give you your initial conditions because you're seeing the changes taking place as you march down the table.

After some discussion by the group about how to build on James' idea and help him to see the initial starting point, Trevor suggests "b + mx" as an alternative order to the conventional y = mx + b as a way to algebraically represent James' focus on the "starting with the first dot, you add four each time". This subtle but important distinction suggests that Trevor had learned to appreciate a conceptual difference that placing the "b" first might represent symbolically. This marks an important MKT learning – he has unpacked the parts of a linear equation – since "b" is the starting point, it is placed first as opposed to the conventional placement at the end of the equation as an add on (+ b). Trevor gained in his professional judgement and expertise.

Laura had a general education degree and taught sixth grade. She signed up for the professional development "in order to learn new teaching skills in hopes of becoming a better teacher". She was in pursuit of upgrading her professional knowledge. Her self-review led her to enter into the professional development for pedagogical learning, yet she gained specialized professional knowledge for teaching specifically around choosing representations to effectively convey mathematical ideas. Overall, Laura increased her professional expertise in her use of mathematical representations in solving the problems – she shifted from employing only visual methods for solving problems to using tables, geometric models, arithmetic expressions and some algebraic notation (as evidenced by his pre-post gains on an MKT measure). Though she showed signs of struggles with algebraic notation, she demonstrated an increase in willingness to solve the problems. Initially Laura commented mostly with general and non-mathematical statements. For example, when asked specifically about what she noticed about two students' thinking in a video segment, Laura's pre-programme response was:

> It was simple and to the point. You can tell they worked together on the problem and discussed it. They seemed confident in their abilities.

In the post programme analysis, she wrote:

> They did not just solve the problem, they checked to make sure that it worked. They are looking at the "arms".

Laura shifted from initially noticing management and social issues in the video episode to a more mathematical focus – from how many students in the class were on task to noticing that the students were looking at the "arms" of the figure. In addition, she improved in her ability to analyse student thinking more accurately and specifically – on one analysis of student work she went from focusing on neatness to noticing recursive thinking. On another student's work, she initially commented on the amount of written explanation, but in the post analysis she noticed mathematical inconsistencies. This shift marks a gain in MKT for Laura that is different from the learning to unpack that Trevor learned.

In session 1, Laura spoke very little during the discussion of James and Danielle. She appeared to be still grappling with the mathematics of the problem as she bent over her paper, working on the problem as others discussed the video. In session 8, she participated in the collective discussion, focusing on James potential reasoning:

> He [James] is describing it. […]. Look at the beginning, you know, as x, plus 4 – […] that's a pattern. You look at minute 1, that's x, plus 4, and he got to minute two. So he's not all that wrong. Now, he, he's not thinking broadly enough, but […].

Laura was working to interpret how James was thinking and what his x meant. She was able to trace James' description and representation to the visual representation of the problem. She gained as a professional in several ways. First, she gained in her ability to contribute within a professional learning community because she increased her specialized content knowledge. In addition, she gained professional trust in her colleagues as she gained confidence in her own specialized knowledge. Finally, she gained in professional autonomy by increasing her mathematical independence, confidence and decision-making.

THE PROFESSIONALIZATION OF THE TEACHING PROFESSION

The experience allowed participants to see more than they might ordinarily see in a real time observation, to attend to classroom interactions with new tools for analysing mathematics teaching and learning previously not available to them. For example, participating teachers projected the possible mathematical thinking of the teacher and students and pushed the investigation of the mathematics from several different perspectives. Seeing more is a kind of growing as an expert and expertise is an important component of professionalism. The expert-novice research backs up the fact that expert teachers possess more pedagogical knowledge, content knowledge, and pedagogical content knowledge than novices (Borko & Shavelson, 1990). Gaining more specialized knowledge results in increased professional expertise.

By using design principles that pair the exploration of teachers' own mathematical solutions to problems with study of cases of students' work with the same problems, teachers strengthen the mathematical understanding needed to interpret student work (Borko, 2004; Kazemi & Franke, 2003; Seago & Goldsmith, 2006). In part, this involves gaining the professional expertise to go beyond a simple assessment of whether or not a student's work is correct to following (or speculating about) the mathematical ideas behind student's work. For example, how does the student's solution provide clues about how the student seems to understand certain mathematical ideas? Are there mathematical inconsistencies in the work? How do the representations the student uses provide clues to his or her understanding? As teachers consider these kinds of questions, in their work, they gain in professional judgement and expertise. They develop specialized professional knowledge that is a more detailed and articulated ("unpacked", or "decompressed") understanding of the mathematical ideas under consideration, and can make connections to related ideas (Ball, Hill, & Bass, 2005; Ferrini-Mundy, Floden, McCrory, Burrill, & Sandow, 2004).

The group of teachers gained professional expertise in mathematical knowledge for teaching, while individuals within the group learned and used differing types of professional knowledge. This highlights the importance of recognizing that participants in teacher education can use knowledge collectively and differ individually. Professionalization does not mean that everyone draws upon the same knowledge at the same time, in the same way. In fact, if they did this it would *not* be professional. Professionals are not robots, they make educated judgements within complex situations. An essential characteristic of professionals is autonomy and self-control regarding the development and application of the specialized knowledge that they are expert. Specialized professional knowledge cannot be reduced to rules or prescriptions for practice. Using professional judgement requires teachers to draw upon differing types of knowledge. Professionalization does not mean that teachers follow uniform practice, it means that they exercise a responsible professional judgement, which is far more demanding (Darling-Hammond, 1985).

In order to gain practice and skill in the technical decision-making that is the role of teachers, more opportunities for discourse and inquiry among teachers about practice are needed. Darling-Hammond (1985, p. 214) wrote about the making of a profession:

> Teachers need opportunities to analyse practice, to observe and be observed by their colleagues, to collectively diagnose school problems and invent new approaches, to share teaching ideas, to develop programs and curricula, to assess the progress of their school and students, and to learn from each other.

As members of a teaching profession, teachers should be involved as participants in continuing teacher education. Through teacher education activities, teachers can not only contribute to their own further development, but also to the further development of the whole profession. It should be an obligation of teachers to participate in the type of professional development that is designed to increase teachers' specialized professional knowledge and expertise.

It has been almost two decades since the National Council of Teachers of Mathematics (NCTM) developed a set of principles for teaching mathematics that was intended to support the kind of instruction needed to implement the NCTM standards (NCTM, 1991). In advocating professionalism for teachers (high degree of individual responsibility, authority, and autonomy), they gave general guidance for the development of professionalism in mathematics. For professionalization to be realized, more specific professional standards of practice are needed in order to guide the technical decision-making that is the role of teachers. If we are to improve students' opportunities to learn, we need to improve teachers' opportunities to gain in specialized knowledge, experience principled professional development, and participate in a collective professionalization process.

The timing may be better now than in the past. Teaching for today's society is technically more complex and wide-ranging than teaching has ever been. Knowledge about effective teaching is continually growing and expanding. Today's teachers need to be committed to and continually engaged in pursuing, upgrading, self-monitoring and reviewing their own professional learning in both face-to-face and virtual learning environments (Hargreaves, 2003). As the world has become more globalized economically, the opportunities for professional learning communities that cross international boundaries have increased. Perhaps we can use this opportunity to work together as teacher educators to further the development of the mathematics teaching profession.

REFERENCES

Ball, D. L., & Bass, H. (2000). Interweaving content and pedagogy in teaching and learning to teach: Knowing and using mathematics. In J. Boaler (Ed.), *Multiple perspectives on the teaching and learning of mathematics* (pp. 83–104). Westport, CT: Ablex.

Ball, D. L., & Bass, H. (2003). Toward a practice-based theory of mathematical knowledge for teaching. In B. Davis & E. Simmt (Eds.), *Proceedings of the 2001 Annual Meeting of the Canadian Mathematics Education Study Group* (Vol. 1, pp. 3–14). Edmonton, CN: CMESG/GCEDM.

Ball, D. L., Hill, H., & Bass, H. (2005). Knowing mathematics for teaching: Who knows mathematics well enough to teach third grade, and how can we decide? *American Educator*, Fall, 2005, 1–10.

Ball, D. L., & Cohen, D. K. (1999). Developing practice, developing practitioners: Toward a practice-based theory of professional education. In L. Darling-Hammond & G. Sykes (Eds.), *Teaching as the learning profession: Handbook of policy and practice* (pp. 3–32). San Francisco: Jossey-Bass.

Borko, H. (2004). Professional development and teacher learning: Mapping the terrain. *Educational Researcher, 33*(8), 3–15.

Borko, H., Frykholm, J., Pittman, M., Eiteljorg, E., Nelson, M., Jacobs, J., Clark, K. K., & Schneider, C. (2005). Preparing teachers to foster algebraic thinking. *Zentralblatt für Didaktik der Mathematik: International Reviews on Mathematical Education, 37*(1), 43–52.

Borko H., & Shavelson, R. J. (1990). Teachers' decision making. In B. Jones & L. Idols (Eds.), *Dimensions of thinking and cognitive instruction* (pp. 311–346). Hillsdale, NJ: Lawrence Erlbaum.

Carnegie Task Force on Teaching as a Profession (1986). *A nation prepared.* New York: Carnegie Forum on Education and the Economy.

Carpenter, T. P., & Fennema, E. (1989). Building on the knowledge of students and teachers. In G. Vergnaud, J. Rogalski, & M. Artigue (Eds.), *Proceedings of the 13th Psychology of Mathematics Education Conference* (Vol. 1, pp. 34–45). Paris: Bicentenaire de la révolution française.

Cobb, P. (1994). Where is the mind? Constructivist and sociocultural perspectives on mathematical development. *Educational Researcher, 23*(7), 13–20.

Darling-Hammond, L. (1985). Valuing teachers: The making of a profession. *Teachers College Record. 87*(2), 205–218.

de Groot, A. (1965). *Thought and choice in chess.* The Hague, the Netherlands: Mouton.

Driscoll, M., Zawojewski, J., Humez, A., Nikula, J., Goldsmith, L., & Hammerman, J. (2001). *The fostering algebraic thinking toolkit: A guide for staff development.* Portsmouth, NH: Heinemann.

Even, R., Tirosh, D., & Markovits, Z. (1996). Teachers subject matter knowledge and pedagogical content knowledge: Research and development. In L. Puig & A. Gutierrez (Eds.), *Proceedings of the 20th Conference of the International Group for the Psychology of Mathematics Education* (Vol. 1, pp. 119–134). Valencia, Spain: University of Valencia.

Ferrini-Mundy, J., Floden, R., McCrory, R., Burrill, G., & Sandow, D. (2004). *A conceptual framework for knowledge for teaching school algebra.* Unpublished manuscript. East Lansing, MI: Michigan State University.

Franke, M. L., Carpenter, T. P., Levi, L., & Fennema, E. (2001). Capturing teachers' generative change: A follow-up study of professional development in mathematics. *American Educational Research Journal, 38,* 653–689.

Goffree, F., & Oonk, W. (2001). Digitizing real teaching practice for teacher education programmes: The MILE approach. In F.-L. Lin & T. Cooney (Eds.), *Making sense of mathematics teacher education* (pp. 111–146). Dordrecht, the Netherlands: Kluwer.

Goldsmith, L. T., Seago, N., Driscoll, M. J., Nikula, J., & Blasi, Z. (2006, April). *Turning to the Evidence: Examining the impact of two practice-based professional development programs.* Symposium paper presented at the Annual Meeting of the American Educational Research Association. San Francisco, CA.

Goodwin, C. (1994). Professional vision. *American Anthropologist, 96,* 606–633.

Hargreaves, A. (2003). *Teaching in the knowledge society: Education in the age of insecurity.* New York: Teachers College Press.

Heck, D. J. (2003, April). *Measuring teacher knowledge in mathematics professional development using embedded assessments.* Paper presented at the Annual Meeting of the American Educational Research Association, Chicago, IL.

Hill, H. C., & Ball, D. L. (2004). Learning mathematics for teaching: Results from California's Mathematics Professional Development Institutes. *Journal for Research in Mathematics Education, 35,* 330–351.

Hill, H., C, & Collopy, R. (2002). *What might teachers learn: An evaluation of the potential opportunities to learn in Videocase.* An evaluation report to VCMPD. Ann Arbor, MI: University of Michigan.

Holmes Group (1896). *Tomorrow's teachers.* East Lansing, MI: Author.

Kazemi, E., & Franke, M. (2003). *Using student work to support professional development in elementary mathematics.* Center for Study of Teaching and Policy: University of Washington.

Llinares, S., & Krainer, K. (2006). Mathematics (student) teachers and teacher educators as learners. In A. Gutiérrez & P. Boero (Eds.), *Handbook of research on the psychology of mathematics education* (pp. 429–459). Rotterdam, the Netherlands: Sense Publishers.

Ma, L. (1999). *Knowing and teaching elementary school mathematics.* Mahwah, NJ: Lawrence Erlbaum Associates.

Mason, J. (2002). *Researching your own practice: The discipline of noticing.* London: Routledge Falmer.

Markovits, Z., & Even, R. (1994). Teaching situations: Elementary teachers' pedagogical content. In J. P. Ponte & J. F. Matos (Eds.), *Proceedings of the 18th PME International Conference* (Vol. 3, pp. 225–232). Lisbon, Portugal: University of Lisbon.

Murray, H., Olivier, A., & Human, P. (1995). Teachers' mathematical experiences as links to children's needs. In L. Meira & D. Carraher (Eds.), *Proceedings of the 19th PME International Conference* (Vol. 3, pp. 312–319). Recife, Brazil: Universidade Federal de Pernambuco.

National Board for Professional Teaching Standards (1988). *Institutional mission.* Washington, DC: Author.

NCTM – National Council of Teachers of Mathematics (1989). *Curriculum and Evaluation Standards for School Mathematics.* Reston, VA: Author.

NCTM – National Council of Teachers of Mathematics (1991). *Professional Standards for Teaching Mathematics.* Reston, VA: Author.

Noddings, N. (1992). Professionalization and mathematics teaching. In D. Grouws (Ed.), *Handbook of research on mathematics teaching and learning* (pp. 197–208). Reston, VA: National Council of Teachers of Mathematics.

Nussbaum, M. C. (1990). *The discernment of perception: An Aristotelian conception of private and public rationality. Love's knowledge: Essays on philosophy and literature.* Oxford, UK: Oxford University Press.

Schifter, D., Bastable, V., Russell, S. J., Lester, J. B., Davenport, L. R., Yaffee, L., & Cohen, S. (1999a). *Building a system of tens: Facilitator guide.* Parsippany, NJ: Dale Seymour.

Seago, N., & Goldsmith, L. T. (2006). Learning mathematics for teaching. In J. Novotná, H. Moraová, M. Krátká, & N. Stehliková (Eds.), *Proceedings of the 30th Conference of the International Group for the Psychology of Mathematics Education* (Vol. 5, pp 73–80). Prague, Czech Republic: Charles University.

Seago, N., Mumme, J., & Branca, N. (2004). *Learning and teaching linear functions.* Portsmouth, NH: Heinemann.

Shulman, L. S. (1986). Those who understand: Knowledge growth in teaching. *Educational Researcher, 15*(2), 4-14.

Shulman, L. S. (1987). Knowledge and teaching: Foundations of the new reform. *Harvard Educational Review, 56,* 1–22.

Shulman, L. S. (1989). The pedagogy of a discipline is the highest stage of learning. *The Holmes Group Forum, 3*(3), 4-5.

Sullivan, P., & Mousley, J. (1998). Conceptualising mathematics teaching: The role of autonomy in stimulating teacher reflection. In A. Olivier & K. Newstead (Eds.), *Proceedings of the 22nd Conference of the International Group for the Psychology of Mathematics Education* (Vol. 4, pp. 105–112). University of Stellenbosch, South Africa: University of Stellenbosch.

Zaslavsky, O., Chapman, O., & Leikin, R. (2003). Professional development in mathematics education: Trends and tasks. In A. J. Bishop, M. A. Clements, C. Keitel, J. Kilpatrick, & F. K. S. Leung (Eds.), *Second international handbook of mathematics education* (Vol. 2, pp. 877–915). Dordrecht, the Netherlands: Kluwer.

Nanette Seago
WestEd (US nonprofit research, development, and service agency)
Mathematics, Science, & Technology Program
USA

SECTION 6

CRITICAL RESPONDANTS

GILAH C. LEDER

15. PATHWAYS IN MATHEMATICS TEACHER EDUCATION: INDIVIDUAL TEACHERS AND BEYOND

Pathways for supporting high quality delivery of mathematics instruction and promoting optimum environments for the learning of mathematics are the themes that permeate the chapters in this volume. The contributions are diverse: in terms of their theoretical perspectives; the scope and focus of the programs discussed; the specific groups selected for particular scrutiny; and the geographical locations in which practical interventions have taken place. The many different players who, jointly, bear the responsibility for the optimum delivery of mathematics education are given clear prominence. The emphasis in the different chapters is variously on prospective and practising teachers – working alone or in groups, face-to-face or in a virtual environment; on administrators at both local and much broader levels; on teacher educators and researchers. At times, the focus is on the recipients of teacher education programmes; at others, on those charged with the planning and delivery of such programmes. Much, it appears, seems already to have been learnt from past endeavours. Yet collectively, the authors propose multiple avenues for further exploration – some more practical and realistically attainable than others.

INTRODUCTION

In many countries, the quality of teacher education, for both prospective and practising teachers, continues to be closely scrutinized, within and beyond teacher education circles. In their comparison of teacher quality and national achievement in 46 countries, Akiba, Le Tendre, and Scibner (2007, p. 371) state:

> Education policy makers around the world have paid attention to teacher quality as a major vehicle to improve student learning [...]. Attracting competent candidates for the teaching profession, retaining highly qualified teachers by providing incentives, and ensuring students' access to high-quality teaching have been major focuses of educational reforms in many countries.

Mathematics education has featured prominently in those initiatives. The rationale for focusing on mathematics is often blunt and pragmatic. For example, The US Department of Education (2006, p. iii, emphasis added) stresses:

> In order to strengthen our nation's competitiveness in the global market place [...] we must be certain that teacher proficiency in *mathematics, science, technology*, and foreign languages is sufficient to enable America's students to achieve at grade level and above in these subjects.

K. Krainer and T. Wood (eds.), Participants in Mathematics Teacher Education, 355–368.

Reference to Australian data reveals the intensity and regularity with which teacher education has been examined, at least in that country. The persistent preoccupation of its State and Federal governments with teacher education can be inferred readily from the data in Table 1. At least 102 inquiries on various aspects of teacher education, it can be seen, were published between 1979 and 2006.

Table 1. Reports on Teacher Education published in Australia 1991-2006

YEAR	N (Reports)	YEAR	N (Reports)
1979	6	1993	2
1980	7	1994	4
1981	2	1995	2
1982	1	1996	2
1983	-	1997	5
1984	2	1998	3
1985	5	1999	1
1986	4	2000	2
1987	3	2001	3
1988	4	2002	6
1989	2	2003	11
1990	5	2004	6
1991	5	2005	4
1992	4	2006	1
TOTAL	**50**	**TOTAL**	**52**

(Source: House of Representatives Standing Committee on Education and Vocational Training, 2007, pp. 169–179)

The quality of mathematics teachers and teaching has featured prominently among the concerns addressed in many of these publications. To quote from a recent Australian report (Senate Standing Committee on Employment, Workplace Relations and Education, 2007, p. 58):

The committee received more evidence in relation to the quality of mathematics teaching than on any other aspect of the curriculum. Many of the submissions and much of the testimony was critical to the point of being pessimistic about the likelihood of improved standards, as well as being fearful of a further decline in standards and performance.

But what have these inquiries achieved? To quote from yet another report (House of Representatives Standing Committee on Education and Vocational Training, 2007, pp. 1–2, emphasis added):

Many inquiries in the last 25 years have examined teacher education. To some extent this simply reflects the need for teacher education to keep pace with the changes in schooling and in society. However, many of the issues reappear in inquiry after inquiry suggesting that recommendations have not been taken up or have not been implemented *or were simply not the right answer to problems identified.*

The same Committee cited a number of reasons for the perceived persistence of problems with teacher education. At least one of these is of particular relevance for the contents of this volume with its focus on the scrutiny and exploration of different pathways in mathematics teacher education (House of Representatives Standing committee on Education and Vocational Training, 2007, p. 2):

A failure of policies involving teacher education to reflect that teacher education does not finish at graduation from an initial teacher education course but continues through induction into the profession as a beginning teacher through to established, advanced and leadership stages.

The international perspectives, provided in this volume on ways and means of involving and challenging diverse groups and individuals in mathematics education to examine, diversify, and update their practices as new resources and research findings become available, are thus particularly timely. What, collectively, can we learn from the past, and from initiatives trialled and proved successful elsewhere or within our own country, in order to achieve better practices for the benefit of teachers and the students in their mathematics classes? What theoretical advances and practical benefits do the new pathways promise?

The contributions are clustered under different, but inevitably overlapping, headings. This approach highlights the many different players who, jointly, bear the responsibility for the optimum delivery of mathematics education. The emphasis in the different chapters is variously on prospective and practising teachers – working alone or in groups, face-to-face or in a virtual environment; on administrators at both local and much broader levels; on teacher educators and researchers. At times, and most frequently, the focus is on the recipients of the teacher education courses and programmes; at others, on those charged with the planning and delivery of such programmes.

INDIVIDUAL MATHEMATICS TEACHERS AS LEARNERS

In the first of the chapters in this section, *Hélia Oliveira* and *Markku S. Hannula* focus on the development of *individual prospective teachers*, and in particular: on their beliefs about mathematics learning and on the mathematical knowledge they gain as they prepare for their professional lives as teachers; on the acquisition of their pedagogical skills; and on their willingness to see themselves as life long learners whose craft as teachers can be honed perpetually.

The apparently large body of research focusing on prospective teachers – often carried out by teacher educators or higher degree research students – has yielded fewer insights on individual teachers' growth than the authors expected: in part, these authors argue, because these studies "often do not target the individual with great depth". It appears that prospective teachers' beliefs about the mathematics they themselves have learnt, the mathematics they will be required to teach, and their intended strategies for doing so, may or may not be affected by the mathematics they do during their initial teacher education, by the aids to which they are exposed as part of this learning, by their experiences of observing how students tackle mathematical problems, and by the opportunities they have for constructive reflection on what they have experienced and observed.

Learning from practice, for example, from fieldwork and the practicum experience, is critical for the development of instructional and classroom management skills. Much has been written in the mathematics research literature about the challenge of enabling prospective mathematics teachers to deviate, where current wisdom deems this to be appropriate, from the instructional practices they themselves experienced in the mathematics classroom. From Oliveira and Hannula's review it seems that much is still to be learnt about which strategies and settings are particularly productive for promoting and sustaining the mathematical and pedagogical growth of individual prospective teachers, and of their identity as a teacher. That longitudinal studies may offer a rich source of information seems confirmed by the more detailed description, in the final section of the chapter, of four secondary mathematics teachers whose professional identity development was followed during, and for three years beyond, their period of teacher education. The relevance, however, of situation specific findings for teachers in very different settings is still unclear.

In their chapter, *Marie-Jeanne Perrin-Glorian, Lucie DeBlois,* and *Aline Robert* turn the spotlight onto *individual practising teachers,* and in particular on the catalysts and obstacles that are thought to promote or prevent changes in their classroom practices. Several carefully selected case studies, which pragmatically illustrate at least some of the factors which prevented or facilitated change in the teachers observed, are used to support the authors' contention that more than "new curricula or new standards" are needed to achieve a change in teachers' practices. Instead, they conclude, some form of – direct or possibly subtle and indirect – intervention is invariably required. A discursive review of literature is used to reinforce this claim. Along the way, the authors cover many different areas: the strengths and weaknesses of the *theoretical models* used to conceptualize teachers' practices, knowledge and beliefs, the observed or predicted interactions between these, and the different methodologies employed to interrogate the data gathered. Yet some questions remain unanswered. Whatever lenses are used, aspects of tracing teacher development remain elusive. In the words of the authors: "the review of the literature shows how difficult it is to organize the variety of results and develop some conceptualisation". Inescapably, there is a direct link between the scope, design, and length of a research study and the insights gained into the intricate pathways enabling the professional growth of teachers. Somehow, it seems, *the whole is more than the sum of its parts* when it comes to understanding and predicting how individual teachers craft and hone their teaching skills. Future research, Perrin-Glorian and her co-authors suggest optimistically, should "study teaching in its context", should try to understand how "a deeper transformation of practice" rather than isolated, limited, and transient changes can be achieved, and should focus on the full scope of teachers' work inside and beyond the classroom.

TEAMS OF MATHEMATICS TEACHERS AS LEARNERS

The challenges faced by mathematics teacher educators as they aim to prepare prospective mathematics teachers in their care for the tasks in the classroom are highlighted by *Roza Leikin* through a *multifaceted review* of literature. Her initial, general, review – of teacher education initiatives focusing on *prospective teachers' work in teams* – is clustered under four headings: the choice of mathematical activities in the classroom, including work beyond the teacher's comfort zone; the adoption of new teaching approaches that incorporate new technologies when appropriate; balancing different yet interweaving aspects of teachers' knowledge and beliefs; and the hurdles faced by novice teachers as they stride along the path of induction into the teaching profession. This overview serves as a context for a more focused examination of 30 research papers dealing with the education of prospective mathematics teachers and published between 1998 and 2007 in high impact mathematics education research journals. Six specific themes are traced: the type of knowledge explored – subject matter knowledge or pedagogical content knowledge; the type of participant – prospective elementary or secondary teachers; the number of participants – for example, case study, small or larger group; the setting of the study – and in particular, mathematics course, didactic course, or teaching practicum; the research tools used – including, interviews, questionnaires, artefacts; and the core issues of the research – for example, learning of specific mathematical content, pedagogical issues, learning in and from the practicum. The overall findings are initially clustered under various headings, readily gleaned from the chapter itself, and then discussed further under the same four headings which were used in the initial, first level review of the literature. Clearly, despite the diversity of research settings, of the methods of inquiry, of the participants, and of the main questions explored, there is already an extensive and robust set of core of findings that can be used by mathematics educators to devise productive and constructive courses and activities for prospective teachers. To these, Leikin adds a multitude of questions – answers to which, she suggests, would further "support MTEs [mathematics teacher educators] in their complex tasks of preparing their students for teaching careers at all levels". Individual readers will themselves need to judge the worth and relevance of these questions and the likely practical benefits of any answers obtained.

Professional development for teachers, it is already clear from the earlier chapters, can be delivered in many different ways. In her contribution, *Susan Nickerson* concentrates particularly on programmes where *teams of practising teachers* work together in groups "mostly selected by management, with predetermined goals which [...] create rather tight and formal connections within the team". Thus the author reports on programmes whose agenda and scope have been externally determined, for example, "to support practising teachers in reorganizing their instructional practice to become more learner-centred and

359

conceptually focused". The scale, approach, and outcomes of a range of programmes often aimed at improving children's mathematical achievement and set in diverse geographic locations, are described. Some involved primary school teachers; in others the participants were secondary mathematics teachers. In a number of programmes, features of the teachers' own teaching were examined. In others, the focus was more explicitly on helping teams of teachers understand and improve students' mathematical thinking and development. In yet other programmes, exemplar practices were examined and critiqued. Outside experts were often involved.

A description of two case studies concludes the chapter. The first involved upper-elementary teachers from different schools in a large urban school district in the United States; the second focused on a large-scale school based programme in New Zealand. Given the markedly different groupings and settings, the participants' experiences and the programmes' outcomes defy easy generalizations. Instead, these two examples "highlight the interdependence of institutional context, relevant management, and teachers themselves as learners".

Many different programmes, published over the past decade and located on every continent, are referenced and described in the chapter. The impression left by this body of research is both uplifting and depressing. On the one hand, it is clear that well organized and strongly supported group-delivered professional development is, at best, of great benefit to the teachers themselves and to their students. But how sustainable are these benefits? What happens when the extra support – personal and/or financial – is withdrawn from these programmes? Why do so many programmes still focus on introducing more student centred instructional practices into the classroom? Has there been a tendency for researchers and mathematics educators to minimize or ignore the sought-for changes in practice, to highlight instead organizational and instructional strategies they consider outmoded, and thus emphasize perceived negative aspects of the profession? Is this a testament to the tenacity of the traditional, teacher centred classroom, an indication that the wide spread pre-occupation with constructivist, student-centred teaching has, at best, had only a limited impact on practice? Or is this confirmation that the impact of many programmes is short term rather than sustained – an issue taken up in more detail in a subsequent chapter in this volume.

COMMUNITIES AND NETWORKS OF MATHEMATICS TEACHERS AS LEARNERS

The impetus for *prospective teachers* to participate in a *face-to-face learning community*, and the benefits to be derived from this participation, are identified and described by *Fou-Lai Lin* and *João Pedro da Ponte*. Their chapter contains examples of such learning communities in two different locations: Taiwan and Portugal. These countries share the problem of a declining population and – related to that – a decreasing need for teachers, as well as an increased attention on teacher preparation pathways. They differ, however, in the level of demand from students wishing to enter teacher education programmes.

A variety of examples is provided: self initiated and institutionally promoted groups; groups consisting of prospective elementary teachers or of prospective secondary school teachers; groups of different sizes; and homogeneous or heterogeneous groups organized around a regular course, a research project, or a teaching activity. Invariably group members meet face-to-face, unlike the virtual communities described in other chapters in the volume.

Although versions of such groups are often found in teaching education courses elsewhere, what distinguishes the examples described in the chapter is that the groups are largely self-selected and driven by a common need. Group members typically share common aims and purposes, and negotiate their own goals and tasks. These factors combine to enable the groups to develop into *face-to-face learning communities*.

The different group compositions were often pragmatic and contextually driven. Their intended – and often achieved – outcomes were as varied as the purposes that fuelled the establishment of the group. But, as in other learning settings, a willingness if not a keen desire to learn from others in their group was an aim shared by all participants in the programmes that proved successful, whether those programmes were formally or informally constituted.

The notion of *face-to-face learning communities* and *networks* is further explored by *Stephen Lerman* and *Stefan Zehetmeier*. The scope, organization, distinguishing features, and – where applicable – the *sustainability* of several school based and broader face-to-face programmes mounted to enhance the quality of teaching and hence student learning are discussed early in the chapter. Given the authors' emphasis on *practising* rather than *prospective* teachers, the activities discussed vary substantially from those listed in the previous chapter. Included in the list of programmes is the Innovations in Mathematics, Science and Technology Teaching [IMST] project, also discussed in the chapters by Pegg and Krainer and by Benke, Hošpesová, and Tichá in this volume. Such overlap reinforces both the commonality between some face-to-face programmes and action research, and the difficulties of uniquely clustering programmes under specified headings.

The changes achieved through professional development programmes, and their sustainability, operationalized as "the lasting continuation of achieved benefits and effects of a project or initiative beyond the termination of a professional development project or effort", are fore grounded through and in the authors' selection of programmes discussed in the second half of the chapter. Constructive ways of classifying impact are discussed and constituent elements seemingly critical for achieving (sustained) change are identified. Community building and networking are core factors. Providing time out of class for meetings and involving academics to supplement the expertise within the group, for example, to add a stronger research dimension to the network's activities, have also been found to be facilitative if not critical. The authors' final, cautionary, note is worth highlighting:

Whether dissemination of the outcomes and experiences of one network can or will be taken up by another network or by individual teachers remains an unresolved question. If it is the case that teachers' change and growth [...]

GILAH C. LEDER

only takes place when teachers engage in these activities themselves and not through reading the work of others, we may need [...] systematic national initiatives to foster learning communities in every school as part of its work.

Teacher education programmes increasingly utilize and rely on new communication tools facilitated by advances in technology. Opportunities for *prospective teachers to work in virtual communities* are part of this evolutionary process. How these designs and tools can, or should, be used in teacher education, and in particular in the education of prospective mathematics teachers, is an important question tackled in various ways by *Salvador Llinares* and *Federica Olivero*. The reader is taken on a multi-tiered journey in this chapter. The over riding theoretical framework – sociocultural perspectives – is articulated effectively and serves as an important and consistent filter through which the different bodies of research are reviewed and analysed. Areas covered, theoretically and with practical examples, include factors critical for the formation of constructive and productive communities of practice; methods conducive to "knowledge building" and "meaning making"; and the tools that seemingly promote these processes. How, and what, online interaction stimulated and promoted knowledge building among a group of prospective elementary teachers is described through a detailed account of a recent (2007) activity. Different tools and ways of utilizing, or trialling, on line learning environments are further elaborated through reference to studies conducted by teacher educators in preparatory teacher courses in a variety of countries. The examples discussed include creating and sustaining virtual communities; constructing meaning through online interactions; and writing and reading blogs and video papers. Throughout, the emphasis is on both the creation of a shared community and what members of that community can learn. In their reporting of the application of the different information and communicating tools to mathematics education, the authors manage to convey a realistic balance between successes and insights already achieved and the challenges still ahead.

How technology tools can mediate the ways in which practising mathematics teachers collaborate and construct knowledge in *virtual communities*, is illustrated further by *Marcelo Borba* and *George Gadanidis*. This is done first in general terms and then quite specifically by sharing the findings from different practical exercises initially spawned by local needs and conditions and subsequently modified in response to feedback from participants.

The opening paragraphs serve as both an introduction and justification for the focus of the paper – online programmes developed and delivered in Brazil and in Canada. The two sections of the chapter are well merged and allow the reader to follow the strengthening of the emerging knowledge base. The logical flow of the "story" is enhanced by the occasional cross referencing between the various activities conducted in the different settings. Throughout the chapter, theoretical justifications and implications are loosely interwoven with the descriptions and outcomes of the activities depicted.

362

The successive sets of experiments described in the Brazilian setting included online courses involving sustained chat sessions, ones in which video conferencing supplemented other synchronous and asynchronous means of communication, and ones in which the introduction of newly devised special tools facilitated the exploration of mathematical concepts and problems. "In the examples presented", the authors write, "we emphasized how mathematics gains different characteristics, and teachers collaborate in different ways, depending on the interface used". In the Canadian case, too, pragmatic considerations, improved technology, and (often informal) feedback ensured an evolving rather than static mode of delivery. Collectively, the data sets highlight the many pathways opened through on line learning and the benefits and challenges faced by instructors and students alike. The combined picture that emerges from the separate and linked Brazilian and Canadian experiences is richer than would have been provided by focusing on one of these sets only. Once again, *the whole is more than the sum of its parts.*

SCHOOLS, REGIONS, AND NATIONS AS MATHEMATICS LEARNERS

"How teachers' participation in multiple and potentially overlapping communities of practice shapes and re-shapes their identities and constitutive skills and knowledge as teachers of mathematics" is explored by *Elham Kazemi* primarily through an expansive review of the literature on *school development* initiatives aimed at improving mathematics teaching. In contrast to the earlier chapters in this volume, Kazemi focuses not only on (groups of) individuals, but also on the organizational aspects of professional development. The body of research set at the classroom level and work concerned with organizational and policy implementation were found to be fertile sources by the author. Covered in some detail is mathematics education research dealing with means for improving instructional practice within the classroom, facets of the structure of organizations, and factors promoting or inhibiting policy implementation. Inevitably there is some overlap with views already articulated in previous chapters. Here, however, particular emphasis is placed on ways of activating school leaders, dealing with micropolitical issues among teachers (evocatively described by the author as navigating fault lines), developing and sustaining focus, and engaging parents as intellectual resources – a powerful asset all too often ignored, as Kazemi notes. How members of the school community actually interact with one another, and in particular "the multi-directional influence between participation in joint inquiry and the individuality of classroom practice" are scrutinized in some detail. Studying productive interactions between individual and contextual factors has yielded a rich body of work and has produced many different and often positive outcomes. Yet, Kazemi concludes, there is more to be achieved by introducing further refinements when planning research projects on the delivery and designs for school development.

Within the various chapters in this volume, and in the broader mathematics education research literature, reference is frequently made to programmes and initiatives which have been successful in a particular setting. How such success might be reproduced in a wider context, in particular at *school and district level*, is a challenge explored by *Paul Cobb* and *Thomas Smith*. As in the chapter by Kazemi, organizational development and general conditions for supporting schools, are the focus of attention. The authors' quest to design "for improvement in mathematics teaching and learning at scale" is contextualized within the US, a country with a decentralized education system and a long history of local control of schooling. It is an undoubtedly a daunting task given the relative stability of classroom teaching and learning processes. Longitudinal data gathered over four years are to be used to test and continuously refine hypotheses "developed about school and district support structures that might enhance the effectiveness of mathematics professional development". In the first instance, inclusion of key elements expected to be linked to – specified – district wide outcomes are discussed and justified by the authors. At the risk of over-simplifying the chapter's rich contents, the flavour of the model proposed is sketched here through two examples. Strong teacher networks (categorized as a primary support structure), coupled with allocated time for collaboration and access to expertise (subsumed under the heading of facilitating support structures), are hypothesized to promote social support for the development of ambitious instructional practices. Also to be traced are the effects on the equity in students' learning opportunities of de-tracking instructional programmes and the category system used for classifying students. The multiple ways the data will be gathered, analysed, reported to the stake holders, and fed back into the model are also outlined. Subsequent reports of the progress and outcomes of this study should attract widespread attention.

Descriptions of four large-scale, *national reform initiatives* aimed at achieving teacher change through rich, carefully targeted and contextualized professional development programs, and – it is anticipated – thus improve student learning outcomes in mathematics (and science), are presented by *John Pegg* and *Konrad Krainer*. As the authors note, these initiatives all exemplify "efforts to improve teaching and learning at scale". The first such project discussed, the IMST project, was developed in Austria; the second, in Ohio in the US; the next in (rural) Australia; and the last in South Korea. Important drivers for these geographically diverse, large scale, and expensive, government funded projects, were, in Austria, Australia, and South Korea, poor results on large-scale international surveys such as TIMSS and PISA and, in Ohio, Australia and South Korea, poor district or regional results in state or national surveys. In three of the cases discussed, a university located centre was given primary responsibility for the coordination and planning of the large scale initiatives. Invariably, help was sought from other relevant groups, care was taken to involve local stake holders as appropriate, and much emphasis was placed on collaborative work.

Cohesion in the reporting of these quite different programs is achieved through clustering important information under common headings. From these: impulse for the initiative; goals and intervention strategy; implementation and communication; evaluation and impact; and challenges and further steps, the foci and broad objectives of the programs can also be inferred. Detailed descriptions of the four projects highlight the enormous diversity in the professional development approaches adopted, in the settings in which the teachers worked, and in the resources to which they would normally have access. The careful evaluations embedded in the programs, devised to accommodate local objectives and conditions, but all aimed at improving teachers' professional learning, revealed that many positive results have been achieved. How many of these outcomes will be sustained, rather than transient, may become evident in due course. The continuing funding promised in at least some of the cases discussed may be an important influencing factor.

TEACHERS AND TEACHER EDUCATORS AS KEY PLAYERS IN THE FURTHER DEVELOPMENT OF THE MATHEMATICS TEACHING PROFESSION

Action research is widely recognized as a useful and viable approach to exploring educational decisions at the local level. Its use in professional development for teachers is discussed by *Gertraud Benke, Alena Hošpesov,* and *Marie Tichá,* first in general terms and then via two case studies located respectively in Austria and in the Czech Republic.

In the first part of the chapter, key features of action research in education are described: the focus is on problem solving at a local level; practitioners (teachers) are involved to varying degrees; thoughtful reflection is an important part of the process; some aspect of classroom practice is often problematized; changes in practice are, it is argued, more likely to lead to changes in beliefs than the reverse; groups rather than individuals have been involved in the more recent action research projects; and a distinction between first and second order action research should be made, for example, between those facilitating the project (often researchers) and those critically engaged in the research (often teachers). However, the authors' focus is not so much on the use of action research as a means of "providing new insights into teaching and learning" but rather "as a way to foster professional development" and their review of relevant research is slanted accordingly. Four areas are highlighted in this review: the choice of topic and the impetus for the research; authorship and reporting of the project; the mathematical content; and the need for comprehensive and accurate reporting of the results.

Though not stated explicitly, glimpses of these aspects permeate the reporting of the two action research projects discussed in the latter part of the chapter. Their very different nature (as well as those of projects discussed in other chapters of this volume, e.g., by Lerman & Zehetmeier), is testimony to the diversity of work subsumed under the action research umbrella. In the Austrian study (IMST, aspects of which are discussed in other chapters in the volume), teachers nominated their own project, had strong ownership of the scope and direction of the project, and had access to expert help when this was sought. In contrast, the parameters for the Czech action research study were shaped by the needs of a larger international project. Predictably, differences in the conceptualization, organization, and duration of the two projects are reflected in the outcomes reported. Reflected, too, are the quite different professional development opportunities fostered and enabled by the two quite distinct projects. The authors' conclusion that "the strong and theoretically well supported tenet to work with problems located at the chosen sites precludes any easy systematic evaluation of the overall impact of action research and the differential contribution of specific implementations" bears further scrutiny. What realistically counts as global answers when such diverse, contextually driven projects are examined?

How co-learning inquiry communities in mathematics teaching development might be built and sustained can be gleaned from the account given by *Barbara Jaworski* of experiences fuelled by the *Learning Communities in Mathematics* [LCM] project set in Norway. Various theoretical constructs – supported by references to relevant literature – underpin the work discussed. These include: practice and knowledge acquisition in a sociocultural setting; co-learning inquiry; inquiry community; and activity theory as an analytical tool. As implied by the co-learning perspective, all participants – both didacticians and teachers, were viewed as researchers. Specific goals could be negotiated and different activities trialled as participants worked towards their common goal of developing "better learning environments for students in mathematics at the levels of schooling with which we were associated". The scope of the work done and the processes followed are illustrated not only through reference to, and excerpts from, specific examples but also subjected to the theoretical lenses which guided the overall work.

Conflicting roles and responsibilities within and beyond the LCM projects inevitably shaped and modified aspects of the projects:

> As compared to established communities of practice in which norms of practice nurture undesirable states, the inquiry community is emergent. It does not avoid issues, tensions and contradictions, but deals with them as part of emergent recognition and understanding leading to possibilities for expansive learning.

Jaworski offers a comprehensive and rich account of the – at times tortuous and challenging – journeys travelled as diverse members of the mathematics education community sought to improve their own practice in their work setting.

In the final chapter in this section, *Nanette Seago* covers three main areas relevant to furthering the development of the *mathematics teaching profession*: the professionalization of mathematics teaching; features of programmes likely to promote the development of teachers as professionals, which comprises the bulk of the chapter; and the "challenges and opportunities for the development of mathematics teaching in the information age". Three main principles found useful by the author and in other programs for designing practice-based professional development programmes are enumerated and a specific development programme designed to promote mathematical knowledge for teaching is described at some length. Principles underpinning this program included: decomposing complex and seemingly simple mathematical ideas; exploring mathematical representations; examining and interpreting student thinking; extracting relevant data from classroom interactions captured on videotapes; negotiating forms of professional interaction; developing a shared language of practice; and examining their practice for critical features likely to facilitate or impede students' mathematical thinking and learning.

FINAL WORDS

The choice of headings under which the contents of this volume have been organized highlight effectively the complexity of the different constituents, layers, and approaches subsumed under the label of teacher education. The roles, responsibilities, and options of individual teachers are the focus of the early chapters. By focussing alternately on prospective and practising teachers both the different needs of individuals within these broad groups and the cyclic and cumulative nature of professional development are emphasized. The inevitable interactions and collaborations of the prospective and practising teachers, as part of the practicum or field work experiences, for example, are an implicit testimony to the many formal and informal learning opportunities available to individuals at different stages of their careers. But teachers do not learn or function in isolation. By moving, as is done in the second part of the volume, the focus somewhat away from the individual to different groups of which that individual can be a member, additional challenges, responsibilities, and enriching possibilities for learning from practice – from one's own and from that of group members – emerge. But groups can be formed in many different ways and for many different purposes – as is given prominence in the next section in the volume, with its emphasis on learning in communities or networks. Again the emphasis is variously on prospective and practising teachers so that adequate consideration can be given to the different needs, opportunities, and context within which the different groups function. New opportunities enabled by new technology, and the accompanying challenges faced by both the participants in those programmes and those who devise and deliver them, stand out in this section. That the specific contexts in which programmes evolve inevitably shape and modify those that prove successful serves as a useful caution that care and attention are needed if courses are to be "transplanted" successfully. This theme is explored in more detail and from different perspectives in the volume's two final sections. The first of these has a strong theoretical focus; the second contains descriptions of projects heavily dependent for their success on the cooperative and collaborative efforts of teachers and teacher educators. Collectively, the writers in this volume have woven a rich and complex tapestry of those who participate in, and contribute to, mathematics teacher education.

Given the different theoretical stances, terminology, and perspectives adopted by the writers of different chapters it is not surprising that the same research article may well have stimulated subtly different interpretations or findings considered worth reporting. The tension between recognizing that results obtained in a particular study may be heavily influenced by the nature of the participants and their specific contexts and the wish to generalize such findings to a broader setting is not easily resolved. Indeed, it should be asked, (when) is it reasonable and profitable to expect such a generalization? Whether, and when, short term gains made by participants in professional development programmes linger more permanently all too often remains unknown or even unquestioned. Accessibility to technology, undreamt of even a few decades ago, is opening new pathways for professional development with their own – often yet not fully realized – fresh strengths and challenges. As implied by the multitude of inquiries into teacher education highlighted in the beginning of this chapter, the education of prospective and practising teachers is of great importance to a nation concerned with the development of its youth, mathematically and more broadly. For a profession to maintain high standards and warrant universal respect it must be prepared to monitor and realistically assess its practices, adapt to new challenges, and productively embrace new resources. The chapters in this volume contribute variously to this ongoing process.

REFERENCES

Akiba, M., LeTendre, G. K., & Scribner, J. P. (2007). Teacher quality, opportunity gap, and national achievement in 46 countries. *Educational Researcher, 36*, 369–387.

House of Representatives Standing Committee on Education and Vocational Training (2007, February). *Top of the class*. Report on the inquiry into teacher education. Canberra, Australia: Commonwealth of Australia.

Senate Standing Committee on Employment, Workplace Relations and Education (2007, September). *Quality of school education*. Canberra, Australia: Commonwealth of Australia.

US Department of Education (2006). *The secretary's fifth annual report on teacher quality: A highly qualified teacher in every classroom*. Washington, DC: US Department of Education.

Gilah Leder
Institute for Advanced Study
La Trobe University – Bundoora, and
Faculty of Education
Monash University – Clayton
Australia

HEINZ STEINBRING

16. INDIVIDUALS, TEAMS AND NETWORKS: FUNDAMENTAL CONSTRAINTS OF PROFESSIONAL COMMUNICATION PROCESSES OF TEACHERS AND SCIENTISTS ABOUT TEACHING AND LEARNING MATHEMATICS

The chapter offers a theoretical perspective on fundamental problems in the context of researching on "Individuals, Teams, Communities and Networks" in mathematics teacher education – especially it elaborates on central questions of how communication functions between different individuals and communities coming from the wide range of mathematics education research (theory) and everyday mathematics teaching (practice). The chapter endeavours to refer to central points raised in the chapters of this third volume "Participants in Mathematics Teacher Education: Individuals, Teams, Communities and Networks" of the International Handbook on Mathematics Teacher Education.

INTRODUCTION

This third volume of the *International Handbook of Mathematics Teacher Education* focuses on the various kinds of participants and relevant environments of mathematics teacher education. In particular, the following three perspectives are taken and distinguished:

- the individual teacher (as learner);
- the teams of cooperating teachers (e.g., from the same school); and
- the networks of cooperating teachers from different schools and school districts.

These perspectives and the analyses of mathematics teachers' co-operations and activities are carried out by mathematic-didactical researchers, who closely cooperate with mathematics teachers within these different working contexts. Thus the circle of the interacting and cooperating persons expands from mathematics teachers to researchers (see e.g., Jaworski, this volume). This leads to the consequence that scientific research not only has to take note of the problems and challenges of the institutional and interactive conditions of the mathematics teachers' professional practice, but also the relation to scientific theory within mathematic-didactical research.

Furthermore, it must be noticed that the analyses of mathematics teacher education has to take into account two more essential particularities:

K. Krainer and T. Wood (eds.), Participants in Mathematics Teacher Education, 369–382.

- the subject of every interaction and co-operation between the participating teachers and researchers, namely (school) mathematics; and
- the teaching and learning process of mathematical knowledge, which teachers and students participate in.

From this, the following extended perspectives on the topic, *Participants in Mathematics Teacher Education: Individuals, Teams, Communities and Networks*, treated in this volume arise:

- the theory-practice-problem in didactics of mathematics as a fundamental condition beyond the present institutional borders; and
- the (mathematical) interaction processes between the participating persons (students, teachers, researchers) as communicative processes of reciprocal stimulation and animation.

By means of these perspectives, new, important aspects come into play, which have to be regarded particularly as fundamental conditions within this field of research and which cannot simply be abrogated. Therefore, they require a sensible attention in order that no illusions develop about the general borders and possibilities of realizing developments, changes and improvements in mathematics teacher education, which also cannot be implemented by didactics of mathematics exclusively. In particular, this concerns the concrete influence capabilities of didactical research onto teaching practice and the sustainability of processes of change within teaching practice in the frame of co-operations and networks. Cobb and Smith (this volume) see this question as a fundamental problem: "The central problem that we address in this chapter is how mathematics education research can generate knowledge that can contribute to the ongoing improvement of mathematics teaching and learning at scale."

THE THEORY-PRACTICE-PROBLEM WITHIN DIDACTICS OF MATHEMATICS – A FEATURE OF ESSENTIAL DIFFERENCES OF PROFESSIONAL ORGANISATION IN MATHEMATICS TEACHER EDUCATION

For more than two decades, the theory-practice problem and its modifications have been intensively analysed and studied by means of exemplary cases in didactics of mathematics (Bazzini, 1994; Even & Ball, 2003; Seeger & Steinbring, 1992; Verstappen, 1988; see also Jaworski, this volume). Didactics of mathematics stand in the area of conflict between scientific research and constructive development work. This is linked to the general standard that – by means of didactical research and development – support, positive influences and changes for teaching, learning and educational processes within school and university can be produced.

In view of this complementary task of research and constructive development, didactics of mathematics is faced with the following fundamental question concerning the theory-practice-problem: "Which is the special nature of the relationship between theory and practice?" A long lasting, traditional view, according to which respective knowledge and contents are being thoroughly researched and elaborated in mathematic-didactical theory in order to be then given to school practice, has been emphatically criticised and displaced by other conceptions. As a fundamental idea, it is assumed that (school) practice as well as (mathematic-didactical) science have to be seen as two relatively autonomous institutions and fields of work, between which there are no direct possibilities of influence or change (for more about this see Bartolini-Bussi & Bazzini, 2003; Krainer, 2003; Scherer & Steinbring, 2006; Steinbring, 1994, 1998). Each of these two fields is subject to its own expectations and goals, as well as system-internal requirements and norms, which cannot be directly abrogated from the outside in order to influence the other field immediately and purposefully.

The relative separation and respective autonomy of (mathematic-didactical) theory and (school) practice cannot mean that no reciprocal actions between the two fields exist. In the relation between theory and practice, the respective other field can rather be seen as a necessary environment, in which irritations and stimulations appear, which indirectly animate one's own field in order to bring about changes, alternative ways of proceeding and further developments. It is important to take into account that such changes in (school) practice – but also in mathematic-didactical theory – ultimately emerge from the inside and "out of themselves" and need to establish themselves. For this, irritations and stimulations from the outside are helpful and necessary, yet they are no deterministic steering tools. Benke, Hošpesová, and Tichá (this volume) express this important orientation by the following quote: "Helus (2001, p. 37) emphasizes: 'A successful effort to change the school is only possible if the teacher becomes its leading agent.'". Furthermore, a particular difficulty and challenge consists in keeping these autonomous institutional development processes going and to give them sustainability (see Cobb & Smith; Lerman & Zehetmeier, this volume).

The fundamental problem of the difficult reciprocal action between different institutional contexts – particularly on the border between theory and practice – is, among others, the subject of consideration in many chapters of this volume – expressed partly implicitly and partly explicitly (see e.g., Cobb & Smith; Benke, Hošpesová, & Tichá; and Lerman & Zehetmeier). An important possibility of relating theory and practice within teacher education in a fruitful way in spite of fundamental differences is summed up by Oliveira and Hannula (this volume) in their chapter:

> The recognition of the importance of theory and practice integration led many programs to develop frameworks for promoting learning in context. [...]. However, from the point of view of both researchers and prospective teachers, there are still many problems to solve in order to guarantee that the teaching practice is an opportunity for learning to occur. Sometimes, the perspectives of the prospective teacher are that what they have learned at the university is not suitable for the reality, the school placement is not adequate, and they need to conform to the practices of the tutor, among others.

MATHEMATICS AS THE SUBJECT OF INTERACTIVE TEACHING AND LEARNING PROCESSES – THE ESSENTIAL COMPONENTS OF MATHEMATICS TEACHERS' ACTIVITIES

The profession of teaching mathematics is characterised by two essential features: By the social activities of teaching – and the students' learning – and by the taught subject, mathematics. At first sight, this appears to be an obvious matter of course, but by means of the following modified point of view the particularity and importance of these two features becomes clear. In the education of future teachers and for the everyday practice of teaching mathematics, one cannot simply assume that mathematical knowledge is a more or less *finished matter*, which is available to the teacher. Teaching itself also is not a mere *routine task of transferring* the knowledge, which the teacher has methodically prepared, to the students.

In scientific mathematic-didactical discussion, such one-sided and simple positions about *teaching* and *subject matter* are no longer held. The fundamental problems connected to the processes of *teaching mathematics* can be describes as a relative contradiction between two poles:

- The *activity of teaching* is subject to a general tension between immediate involvedness and critical dissociation of the teacher (Krainer, 2001; Scherer & Steinbring, 2006; Seeger, 1998; Seeger & Steinbring, 1992). Within the current teaching events, the teacher is directly involved in the interaction with the students and cannot simultaneously play the role of a distanced observer of the events. The development and change of the activity of teaching requires a critical consideration, and thus a distance, out of which one's own activity can be reassessed (Krainer, 2003).

- As academic knowledge, *mathematics* and thus ultimately also school mathematics, is a consistent, correct and finished asset of knowledge. In this function, the finished mathematical knowledge is a necessary component of professional teacher knowledge (Shulman, 1986). However, school mathematics, as finished given knowledge, is not the *actual subject of teaching* in an unchanged way. Mathematical knowledge only emerges and develops in an effectively new and independent way, within the instructional interaction with the students. Thus, finished, elaborated mathematics is not an independent input of the teacher into the teaching process, which could then become an acquired output by means of students' elaboration processes.

In scientific didactical discussion, these essential poles of teaching activity, *immediate involvedness* and *critical distance,* and of mathematical knowledge, *finished product* and *interactive process,* (Freudenthal, 1973) are described and analysed under different perspectives and with different concepts.

In the discussion about the theory-practice-problem within didactics of mathematics the role of the teacher in the frame of his or her teaching activity is described as the one of a moderator, or facilitator, initiator or supporter of the student's learning processes (as e.g. Lerman & Zehetmeier's chapter; Seeger & Steinbring, 1992; Steinbring, 1994; Verstappen, 1988). Scientific works about teacher education and advanced training point out the *particularities of professional teacher knowledge* and of the activity of teaching in contrast to other professions, for example, the great complexity and variety of the participating knowledge components of the teacher profession (chapters in this volume; AG Mathematiklehrerausbildung, 1981; Bromme, 1994; Otte, 1979; Shulman, 1986; Steinbring, 1998) and also the necessary sensitive reflection of teaching and learning processes (Krainer, 1996; Krainer & Posch, 1996).

The tension in which the subject of teaching – the mathematical knowledge – is located is essentially expressed by Freudenthal's designation of mathematics as product and process (Freudenthal, 1973, p. 114): "Every mathematician knows at least unconsciously that besides ready-made mathematics there exists mathematics as an activity. But this fact is almost never stressed, and non-mathematicians are not at all aware of it." Freudenthal (1973, p. 118) also highlights:

The opposite of ready-made mathematics is mathematics in statu nascendi. [...] the pupil himself should re-invent mathematics. [...]. The learning process has to include phases of directed invention, that is, of invention not in the objective but in the subjective sense, seen from the perspective of the student.

This important procedural character of mathematical knowledge is elaborated, for example, by means of a description of the *development* of knowledge oriented on the history of mathematics, in contrast with a *static interpretation* of finished mathematics. Wittmann (1995, p. 358) makes a distinction between the highly specialised scientific discipline mathematics, and context-oriented MATHEMATICS, which is in many ways relevant to everyday life and which he writes in capital letters:

[One] [...] must conceive of, "mathematics" as a broad societal phenomenon whose diversity of uses and modes of expression is only a part reflected by specialized mathematics as typically found in university departments of mathematics. I suggest a use of capital letters to describe MATHEMATICS as mathematical work in the broadest sense; this includes mathematics developed and used in science, engineering, economics, computer science, statistics, industry, commerce, craft, art, daily life, and so forth according to the customs and requirements specific to these contexts.

In mathematic-didactical research and development studies of the last years, a more and more differentiated view of these two essential components of the profession of mathematics teaching, namely *teaching* and *mathematics*, has been elaborated, which tries to give consideration to the difficult and comprehensive challenge of education and practice of mathematics teachers.

Many chapters in this third volume increasingly examine conditions and measures, which can centrally support and enable a realisation of these challenges inherent to the development of mathematics teachers' professional activities. For example, the chapter by Oliveira and Hannula explicitly emphasises mathematics and teaching as central components and formulates as an essential guideline: "There are two different types of learning activities for those who learn to become mathematics teachers. Firstly, they need to learn mathematics, and secondly, they need to learn how to teach it". The chapter by Perrin-Glorian, DeBlois, and Robert extensively and critically discusses all essential knowledge components of professional mathematics teacher knowledge. Here in this chapter, particularly research studies are presented, in which the relation of the particular school mathematical knowledge to the other professional knowledge components (e.g., PCK and others) within teacher education are examined.

Also, there are efforts not to think only about mathematical knowledge in school and about teaching problems quasi "in general" any longer, but to make one's own teaching activity and the interactive constitution of mathematical knowledge which can be observed there the central topic of a common reflection – for example in co-operation with and between teacher students, or among teacher colleagues and also in conversation with scientists. This point of view is also addressed in many contributions of this volume (e.g., the two case studies about co-operation between and with mathematics teachers in the chapter by Borba & Gadanidis).

A NEW POINT OF VIEW: TEACHING ACTIVITY INSTEAD OF TEACHER – ACTION AND REFLECTION

Requirements and considerations about the improvement of the quality of mathematics teaching come from different societal areas, for example, from pedagogical research, from mathematic-didactical research and from mathematics teacher education at universities and not least increasingly also from teaching practice. In the face of the results of TIMSS and PISA, the discussion in science and among educational policy makers about effective improvement measures becomes more and more concrete. In this context, challenges appear which demand a common reflection of one's own teaching activity. In the wake of the bad results of TIMSS and currently of PISA – for example, in Germany – the main responsible researcher of PISA 2000 makes the following demand (Jürgen Baumert in Die Zeit, 2001, p. 47):

> Teachers, who teach the same subject, have […] to visit each other during lessons. A surgeon, after all, is being watched while he operates. When there are new techniques, the colleagues follow his cuts on the monitor. […]. Why should a teacher not […] have his lessons taped and discuss the recording with his colleagues?

This new and increasingly advanced demand of making the activity of teaching – connected to the students' learning activities – the subject of a common reflection and thorough analysis in the co-operation of teachers, can also be found in almost all chapters of this volume, sometimes by means of short allusions and quotes or side notes (e.g., Kazemi; Jaworski; Benke, Hošpesová, & Tichá in their case studies), but also in a more extensive and explicit way such as in the chapter by Seago. For her, the use of video documents in order to improve the teaching profession is a central concern. A well-planned and systematic analysis of mathematical teaching and learning processes the videographing and the subsequent common observation and practical analysis of short video scenes is an indispensable help. Seago in her chapter sums this up:

> Recent research projects have suggested that that professional development projects that utilize records of practice, such as classroom video, lesson plans, classroom cases, and student thinking, are effective tools in efforts to increase teachers' opportunity to learn mathematics knowledge for teaching.

And later:

> Video is seen as an exciting innovation with great potential. [...]. There have been significant efforts to use video-taped records of practice as concrete activities that allow for teachers to discuss observations and hypotheses in an evidenced and reasoned way.

Even if the epistemological character of mathematical knowledge is seen much more differentiated, and if the interactive processes of teaching and learning mathematics are not regarded as a transition of knowledge from the teacher to his students, yet it remains an important future research problem to find out, in what particular way *mathematics* and *interactions* are connected and affect each other in a reciprocal way (see Steinbring, 2005). The specific connection between the interaction processes (teaching, learning, communicating about mathematics) and the mathematical knowledge is a demanding research problem. One can receive the impression that, in some chapters of this volume, the learning subject of mathematics could be replaced by physics or biology, thus that the analysed research questions about "Individuals, Teams and Networks" might just as well have been applied to Teacher Education in other subject matter areas.

In terms of the considerations above, one has to bear in mind that mathematics can and may not enter teaching activity unchanged and smoothly as a finished, elaborated matter, but that the subject of mathematics becomes an effective factor, which is complementary to the activity of teaching and learning. The teaching activity does not merely determine the role of the mathematical knowledge, and vice versa, the mathematical knowledge co-determines the kind of teaching and learning.

A perspective on the improvement of mathematics teaching, which rudimentarily pays attention to the importance of both of the two essential components, *mathematics* and *teaching*, has been elaborated, for example, in the book, *The Teaching Gap,* by Stigler and Hiebert (1999). In this book they discuss the special nature of mathematical knowledge as a cause for different teaching patterns (p. 89). Whether mathematics is regarded rather as a product or as a process − to follow Freudenthal − is essential for the style of the respective teaching activity and for the students' learning. An important aspect in Stigler's and Hiebert's considerations consists in the designation of teaching as a cultural activity. This means that teaching activity cannot be perceived or even studied as merely a collection of different, elaborated and well-defined techniques; just like other cultural activities, teaching cannot be acquired by means of fixed rules and regulations, but this activity is obtained in a great part by means of participating, witnessing and practicing within the social context of teaching with colleagues. Furthermore, Stigler and Hiebert (p. 75) emphasise that teaching represents a system:

> Teaching is a system. It is not a loose mixture of individual features thrown together by the teacher. [...]. This is a very different way of thinking about teaching. It means that individual features make sense only in terms of how they relate with others that surround them. It means that most individual features, by themselves, are not good or bad. Their value depends on how they connect with others and fit into the lesson.

Against the background of these considerations, Stigler and Hiebert then establish one of their central principles for the improvement of mathematics teaching: a reorientation from the attention of the question what makes a so-called "good teacher" towards the conscious perception and common reflection of everyday teaching activities. This principle is marked with the slogan "Focus on Teaching, Not Teachers". On the one hand, this principle presents the essential professional tool in order to improve everyday mathematics teaching, and on the other hand, it is understood to help build and sustain the "collective memory" of the teaching profession, otherwise, successful teaching events disappear from the teachers' professional body of knowledge with the retirement of good and committed teachers, who worked individually and isolated. These demands to construct a collective memory, however, can of course only be realised by cooperating teams of teachers and by broad networks.

CONDITIONS OF COMMUNICATION PROCESSES – BASIS OF COMMON REFLECTIONS OF TEACHERS AND SCIENTISTS ABOUT QUESTIONS OF MATHEMATICS TEACHER EDUCATION

Mathematic-didactical research about problems and changes in the education of mathematics teachers deals with processes of communication and interaction about mathematical knowledge in different social and institutional contexts. The students communicate with each other about mathematical contents in learning processes. The teacher communicates with the students during lessons. A group of teachers communicate with each other during lesson preparation or during the reflection on mathematics teaching. And in the frame of co-operations between mathematical teaching practice and mathematic-didactical research, there also is communication between teachers and participating scientists (see Figure 1).

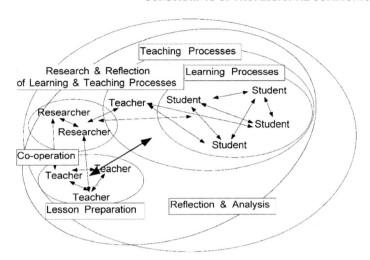

Figure 1. The complexity of reflection and communication activities in mathematics teacher education within the educational system.

In different social settings and co-operations between and across different institutional borders, there are many different activities involved. Students interacting in learning processes; the teacher interacts with students in teaching activities. The teacher prepares and reworks mathematical lessons, be it that the teacher performs these activities alone or together with colleagues. Teachers on their own as well as with researchers reflect and analyse teaching and learning activities (using e.g., video episodes as described in Seago's chapter).

Within this complex arrangement, the two following observations are important: (1) There is communication *with each other*, but also communication *about* processes of communication and interaction; (2) common reflection and communication always affect one's individual perception and the individual perception affects the communication.

These two essential characteristics of communicative processes shall be elaborated briefly in the frame of communication theory according to the sociologist Luhmann (1996). He characterises "communication" as the constitutive concept of sociology: "[…] if communication is to be accomplished, a […] closed […] autopoietic system must become active, namely a social system, which reproduces communication by means of communication and does nothing else but this" (p. 279).

The concept of the "autopoietic system" has been introduced by Maturana and Varela (see e.g., 1987). It designates systems which autonomously exist and develop by means of their self-reference. They consist of components, which are produced permanently within the system in order to sustain the system. Not only biological activities are examined with this concept, but it is also applied to social and psychic processes.

What are the difference and the reciprocal relation between social and psychic system? The psychic system is based on *consciousness* and the social system is based on *communication*. "A social system cannot think; a psychic system cannot communicate. Causally seen, there still are immense, highly complex interdependencies" (Luhmann, 1997, p. 28). How can these interdependencies be understood? Baraldi, Corsi, and Esposito (1997, p. 86) state:

> Communication systems and psychic systems (or consciousness) form two clearly separated autopoietic areas; [...]. These two kinds of systems, however, are connected with each other in a particularly close relation and reciprocally form a "portion of necessary environment": Without the participation of consciousness systems there is no communication, and without the participation in communication there is no development of consciousness.

Thus it is clearly stated that, as a basic principle, one has to assume a separation between communication and consciousness, and to distinguish between social and individual. At the same time, however, it is pointed out that both systems – communication and consciousness – represent a necessary environment for the other system, that they animate and stimulate the other system and thus can bring about changes within the other system. Thus, it is not about the question whether the individual or the social is the basis for the other one. Rather, a particular interrelation between social and individual is expressed, in which both positions are necessary in a complementary way, in spite of the concurrent separation.

The participating persons are involved in the communication and interaction, which take place. They continuously carry out communicative operations in the communication system. But only by means of a distanced observation, is it possible to reflect the respective current communication system. "Observation is able to identify objects and can [...] distinguish the inner processes of a system from what does not belong to it, can discover causal relations between inside and outside, can ascribe a goal to the system" (Baraldi et al., 1997, p. 125). On the one hand, within the communication system itself, communicative operations take place, which ultimately cannot be observed by means of inner operations of the system. And on the other hand, the observation of a communication system leads itself to a new communicative system. Baraldi et al. (1997, pp. 154-155) highlight:

> Reflection is understood as a specific form of the self-observation of a system. [...]. Reflection leads [...] to the state of a system being compared with other possible states and to the question about any advantages and disadvantages being asked – and that it can be tried to change the system accordingly in the best direction.

Common reflection thus represents a new communicative system itself (see Figure 1).

In their actively discovering, social learning and understanding processes, the students are integrated in the necessary interrelation between one's own consciousness and common communication. This communication, however, is not analysed itself as an object in a further, external observation. This is different for the teachers. An essential part of the mathematics teacher's profession consists of mathematical communication and interaction processes, in which a teacher often participates with him- or herself. During the common systematic reflection in a group of teachers about their own teaching processes with students thus emerges a further communication system, which again has to deal with the necessary interrelation between one's own consciousness and common communication. This communication now has communication processes as its subject and it is supposed to animate a professional consciousness.

The two fundamental conditions for every communication process, that one (1) has to distinguish individual consciousness and social interaction as a basic principle, and that (2) communication processes can only be compared and changed by means of further communication processes with the help of an external observation, need to be respected on all levels; these fundamental conditions also must exist in mathematical interaction processes and in cooperative work between mathematics teachers and scientists.

The participants in communication processes taking place during lessons often unconsciously assume that the system borders between the social and the psychic, between interaction and communication, and can be directly negotiated; for example, that one could immediately intervene in the students' consciousness by means of communication operations (as it is shown by the two familiar interactive funnel patterns, see e.g., Bauersfeld, 1978; Krummheuer & Voigt, 1991, p. 18; Wood, 1994, p. 153; 1998). Insofar, it is important to pay attention to the present separation, which exists as a matter of principle in the complex events of teaching, learning and understanding, taking place in the interrelation of consciousness and communication.

Two initially clearly separated, but then complementary aspects of teaching, learning and understanding in mathematical interaction processes, have been discussed with the designation "Conscious Reflection". In this, already, a complexity is inherent, which is effective for the whole teaching process and the relation between didactical science and school practice. These processes between students and teachers, as well as then in interaction with scientists, are never linear, strictly goal-oriented communication processes with a direct transfer of mathematical knowledge to learners. Communication in the interrelation with consciousness is always an evolutionary process of reciprocal stimulation between relatively autonomous communication partners.

For this, teachers require systematic preparations and supports in their everyday teaching practice. Furthermore, such co-operations with everyday teaching practice also are invaluable chances for didactical science to learn from practice and to carry out didactical research projects about important questions in the context of "mathematical interaction processes". The mathematic-didactical research subject "mathematical interaction processes" represents a challenge, which is relevant for research as well as for education, at university as well as in mathematics teaching. It is essential that in this complex theory-practice-relationship, no hierarchic dependences are effective, according to which for example theory alleges or could allege to practice how it should behave. With their respective assignments of tasks and institutional contexts, theory and practice have to be regarded as relatively independent systems, which do not directly influence each other, but which can stimulate and animate each other in a positive way by means of common co-operations.

The didactical research subject "mathematical interaction processes" (within and beyond different institutional system borders) can be considered as an interface research problem. At different interfaces – from human to human, from teacher to learning students, from teachers to other teachers (in their different professional roles), from teachers to researchers, and so forth – it is about the analysis how the participating persons (in their respective professional role) can communicate about mathematical knowledge, understanding and meanings in reciprocal interactions in such a way that they can make and further develop their own interpretations of the knowledge, as the knowledge itself and its allegedly objective meaning cannot be directly communicated from one person to another.

REFERENCES

Arbeitsgruppe Mathematiklehrerausbildung (1981). *Perspektiven für die Ausbildung des Mathematiklehrers* [*Perspectives of mathematics teacher education*]. Köln, Germany: Aulis-Verlag.

Baraldi, C., Corsi, G., & Esposito, E. (1997). GLU. *Glossar zu Niklas Luhmanns Theorie sozialer Systeme* [*Glossary to Niklas Luhmann"s theory of social systems*]. Frankfurt am Main, Germany: Suhrkamp.

Bartolini-Bussi, M. G., & Bazzini, L. (2003). Research, practice and theory in didactics of mathematics: towards dialogue between different fields. *Educational Studies in Mathematics, 54*, 203–223.

Bauersfeld, H. (1978). Kommunikationsmuster im Mathematikunterricht – Eine Analyse am Beispiel der Handlungsverengung durch Antworterwartung [*Patterns of communication in mathematics teaching. An analysis with the example of narrowed fields of activity by expected outcomes*]. In H. Bauersfeld (Ed.), *Fallstudien und Analysen zum Mathematikunterricht* [*Case studies and analyses on mathematics teaching*] (pp. 158–170). Hannover, Germany: Schroedel.

Bazzini, L. (Ed.). (1994). *Theory and practice in mathematics education. Proceedings of the Fifth International Conference on Systematic Cooperation between Theory and Practice in Mathematics Education in Grado*. Padua, Italy: ISDAF.

Bromme, R. (1994). Beyond subject matter: A psychological topology of teachers' professional knowledge. In R. Biehler, R. W. Scholz, R. Sträßer, & B. Winkelman (Eds.), *Didactics of mathematics as a scientific discipline* (pp. 73–88). Dordrecht, the Netherlands: Kluwer Academic Publishers.

Even, R., & Ball, D. L. (Eds.). (2003). Connecting research, practise and theory in the development and study of mathematics education, *Special Issue of Educational Studies in Mathematics, 54*, 2–3.

Freudenthal, H. (1973). *Mathematics as an educational task*. Dordrecht, the Netherlands: D. Reidel.

Krainer, K. (1996). Probleme und Perspektiven der Lehrerfortbildung [Problems and perspectives of continuous teacher education]. In G. Kadunz, H. Kautschitsch, G. Ossimitz, & E. Schneider (Eds.), *Trends und Perspektiven, Beiträge zum 7. internationalen Symposium zur "Didaktik der Mathematik"*, in Klagenfurt vom 26.–30.9.1994 (pp. 205–230). Vienna: Hölder-Pichler-Tempsky.

Krainer, K. (2001). Teachers' growth is more than the growth of individual teachers: The case of Gisela. In F.-L. Lin & T. Cooney (Eds.), *Making sense of mathematics teacher education* (pp. 271–293). Dordrecht, the Netherlands: Kluwer Academic Publishers.

Krainer, K. (2003). "Selbstständig arbeiten – aber auch gemeinsam und kritisch prüfend!" Aktion, Reflexion, Autonomie und Vernetzung als Qualitätsdimensionen von Unterricht und Lehrerbildung ["Working independently – but also jointly and critically examining!" Action, reflection, autonomy; and networking as quality dimensions of teaching and teacher education]. In H.-W. (Ed.), *Beiträge zum Mathematikunterricht* (pp. 25–32). Hildesheim, Germany: Franzbecker.

Krainer, K., & Posch, P. (Eds.). (1996). *Lehrerfortbildung zwischen Prozessen und Produkten.* Hochschullehrgänge "Pädagogik und Fachdidaktik für Lehrerinnen" (PFL): Konzepte, Erfahrungen und Reflexionen [Continuing teacher education between processes and products. Universitary courses "Pedagogy and subject-specific didactics for teachers" (PFL): Conceptions, experiences and reflections]. Bad Heilbrunn, Germany: Klinkhardt.

Krummheuer, G., & Voigt, J. (1991). Interaktionsanalysen von Mathematikunterricht – Ein Überblick über Bielefelder Arbeiten [Interaction analysis of mathematics teaching – A survey of Bielefeld works]. In H. Maier & J. Voigt (Eds.), *Interpretative Unterrichtsforschung [Interpretative lesson research]* (pp. 13–32). Köln, Germany: Aulis.

Luhmann, N. (1996). Takt und Zensur im Erziehungssystem [Cycle and mark in the educational system]. In N. Luhmann & K.-E. Schorr (Eds.), *Zwischen System und Umwelt. Fragen an die Pädagogik [Between system and environment. Questions for pedagogy]* (pp. 279–294). Frankfurt am Main, Germany: Suhrkamp.

Luhmann, N. (1997). *Die Gesellschaft der Gesellschaft [Society's society].* Frankfurt am Main, Germany: Suhrkamp.

Maturana, H. R., & Varela, F. J. (1987). *Der Baum der Erkenntnis. Die biologischen Grundlagen des menschlichen Erkennens [The tree of knowledge. The biological roots of human understanding].* Bern, Switzerland: Scherz.

Otte, M. (1979). The education and professional life of mathematics teachers. In UNESCO (Ed.), *New trends of mathematics teaching* (Vol. 4, pp. 107–133). Paris: UNESCO.

Scherer, P., & Steinbring, H. (2006). Noticing children's learning processes – Teachers jointly reflect on their own classroom interaction for improving mathematics teaching. *Journal of Mathematics Teacher Education, 9*, 157–185.

Seeger, F. (1998). Discourse and beyond: On the ethnography of classroom discourse. In H. Steinbring, M. G. Bartolini-Bussi, & A. Sierpinska (Eds.), *Language and communication in the mathematics classroom* (pp. 85–101). Reston, VA: National Council of Teachers of Mathematics.

Seeger, F., & Steinbring, H. (Eds.). (1992). *The dialogue between theory and practice in mathematics education: Overcoming the broadcast metaphor. Proceedings of the Fourth Conference on Systematic Cooperation between Theory and Practice in Mathematics Education (SCTP).* Brakel. (IDM Materialien und Studien 38). Bielefeld, Germany: IDM, Universität Bielefeld.

Shulman, L. S. (1986). Those who understand: Knowledge growth in teaching. *Educational Researcher, 15*(2), 4–14.

Steinbring, H. (1994). Dialogue between theory and practice in mathematics education. In. R. Biehler, R. W. Scholz, R. Sträßer, & B. Winkelmann (Eds.), *Didactics of mathematics as a scientific discipline* (pp. 89–102). Dordrecht, the Netherlands: Kluwer Academic Publishers.

Steinbring, H. (1998). Elements of epistemological knowledge for mathematics teachers. *Journal of Mathematics Teacher Education, 1*, 157–189.

Steinbring, H. (2005). *The construction of new mathematical knowledge in classroom interaction – An epistemological perspective.* Mathematics Education Library, Vol. 38. Berlin, Germany: Springer.

Stigler, J. W., & Hiebert, J. (1999). *The teaching gap.* New York: The Free Press.

Verstappen, P. F. L. (Ed.). (1988). *Report of the second conference on systematic cooperation between theory and practice in mathematics education.* Enschede, the Netherlands: SLO.

Wittmann, E. C. (1995). Mathematics education as a „design science". *Educational Studies in Mathematics, 29*, 355–374.

Wood, T. (1994). Patterns of interaction and the culture of mathematics classrooms. In S. Lerman (Ed.), *Cultural perspectives on the mathematics classroom* (pp. 149–168). Dordrecht, the Netherlands: Kluwer Academic Publishers.

Wood, T. (1998). Alternative patterns of communication in mathematics classes: Funneling or focusing? In H. Steinbring, M. G. B. Bussi, & A. Sierpinska (Eds.), *Language and communication in the mathematics classroom* (pp. 167–178). Reston, VA: National Council of Teachers of Mathematics.

Heinz Steinbring
Fachbereich Mathematik
Universität Duisburg-Essen, Campus Essen
Germany